## Praise for *The Economics of E...*

"In today's public policy conversations, the word 'equity' is all the rage. But all too often 'equity' serves as little more than a buzzword to cover highly ideological claims. Goldy Brown and Christos Makridis's book is quite different. By taking steady and unswerving aim at the research evidence on costs and benefits, they bring a level of concrete sensibility to a conversation that's sorely needed by policy makers." —**Max Eden, research fellow, American Enterprise Institute (AEI)**

"America's schools face unprecedented challenges as a result of the pandemic and the decline in trust in schools and educators. This timely book provides a sober, research-based look at the evidence on what works in education and provides solid guidance on the work that is needed in the years ahead." —**Raymond Domanico, senior fellow and director of education policy, Manhattan Institute**

"Promoting educational freedom is a necessary ingredient to ensure the rising generation has an opportunity to live the American Dream. The contributors of this book make a solid case for improving K-12 education, most notably through the need for widespread school choice." —**Ian Rowe, senior fellow, American Enterprise Institute**

"The struggle in education has always been how to provide a quality education that is both equitable and efficient. *The Economics of Equity in K-12 Education* provides a first look at the key topics relative to this issue." —**Craig A. Schilling, EdD, professor and program chair, Concordia University Chicago**

"This volume will help education stakeholders and policy makers navigate promising, evidence-based policy options." —**Sofoklis Goulas, senior research associate, CREDO, Stanford University**

"A review of the measurable impacts of current, post-pandemic issues as they relate to financing K-12 education, this book covers a broad range of issues and endeavors to quantify the impact of each from a perspective that considers equity and financial success. *The Economics of Equity in K-12 Education* has the potential to significantly inform practice in the public school sector." —**Tammy T. White, assistant professor and director, Master's Program in Educational Leadership, Winthrop University**

"This book rips the cover off the idea that just providing more money is what is needed—asserting that the money needs to be strategically targeted or those on the margins will continue to remain there. Going beyond surface fixes for various issues in providing equitable education, *The Economics of Equity in K-12 Education* examines needed changes in policies affecting education and the very structure of education itself to maximize impact. If the playing field is ever going to be leveled and equitable education achieved, this is where educational policy makers must start." —**Elizabeth Timmerman Lugg, JD, PhD, Illinois State University**

# The Economics of Equity in K-12 Education

## Connecting Financial Investments with Effective Programming

Edited by

Goldy Brown III
*Whitworth University*

and

Christos A. Makridis
*Arizona State University*

ROWMAN & LITTLEFIELD
*Lanham • Boulder • New York • London*

Associate Acquisitions Editor: Courtney Packard
Assistant Acquisitions Editor: Sarah Rinehart
Sales and Marketing Inquiries: textbooks@rowman.com

Credits and acknowledgments for material borrowed from other sources, and reproduced with permission, appear on the appropriate pages within the text.

Published by Rowman & Littlefield
An imprint of The Rowman & Littlefield Publishing Group, Inc.
4501 Forbes Boulevard, Suite 200, Lanham, Maryland 20706
www.rowman.com

86-90 Paul Street, London EC2A 4NE

British Library Cataloguing in Publication Information Available

**Library of Congress Cataloging-in-Publication Data**
Names: Brown, Goldy, 1977– editor. | Makridis, Christos A., 1991– editor.
Title: The economics of equity in K-12 education : connecting financial investments with effective programming / Edited by Goldy Brown III, Whitworth University and Christos A. Makridis, Arizona State University.
Description: Lanham : Rowman & Littlefield, [2023] | Includes bibliographical references and index.
Identifiers: LCCN 2022029092 (print) | LCCN 2022029093 (ebook) | ISBN 9781538168981 (cloth) | ISBN 9781538168998 (paperback) | ISBN 9781538169001 (epub)
Subjects: LCSH: Educational equalization—Economic aspects—United States. | Education—United States—Finance. | School improvement programs—United States. | Children with social disabilities—Education—United States. | Educational change—United States.
Classification: LCC LC213 .E35 2023 (print) | LCC LC213 (ebook) | DDC 379.2/60973—dc23/eng/20220707
LC record available at https://lccn.loc.gov/2022029092
LC ebook record available at https://lccn.loc.gov/2022029093

# Brief Contents

List of Tables and Figures     xiii

Introduction     1
*Christos Makridis and Goldy Brown III*

## PART I: EDUCATIONAL PROGRAMS THAT HAVE PRODUCED POSITIVE RESULTS

1   The Economic Value of Parent and Community Involvement     13
*Albert A. Cheng and Robert Maranto*

2   The Educational Equalizer: Funding Students Instead of Systems     37
*Corey DeAngelis*

3   Quality and Intentionality: Making After-School Programs More Effective     55
*Goldy Brown III*

4   Career, Technical, and Higher-Education Opportunities for Traditionally Underserved Students     69
*Walter G. Ecton*

5   Turning Hurdles Into Launch Pads: Improving Equity and Efficiency Through Increased High School Graduations in the United States     97
*Aidan Vining and David Weimer*

## PART II: CHANGES NEEDED AT THE STATE AND LOCAL LEVEL TO MAKE POSITIVE RESULTS MORE WIDESPREAD

6 Getting Past the Current Trade-Off Between Privacy and Equity in Educational Technology      123
*Ryan Baker*

7 Identifying, Establishing, and Distributing the Economic Value of the Classroom Teacher      139
*Christopher D. Brooks and Matthew G. Springer*

8 Ensuring All Children Succeed with Social-Emotional Learning      177
*Nicole A. Elbertson, Mark A. Brackett, Tangular A. Irby, and Krista L. Smith*

9 Only Systemic Change Will Do      195
*F. Mike Miles*

References      215

Index      257

About the Editors and Contributors      267

# Contents

List of Tables and Figures     xiii

Introduction     1
    *Christos Makridis and Goldy Brown III*

    This Book's Objective     2
    Table I.1. Educational Funding Since 1960     2
    Figure I.1. The Relationship Between Education, Equity, and Economics     3
    Early Childhood Education     3
    Table I.2. Program Recommendations     5
    Summary of State and Local Policy Recommendations     6

**PART I: EDUCATIONAL PROGRAMS THAT HAVE PRODUCED POSITIVE RESULTS**

1    **The Economic Value of Parent and Community Involvement**     13
    *Albert A. Cheng and Robert Maranto*

    Changing Family Structure, Schools, and Society     13
    School and Family Inputs     16
      The Education Production Function     16
      The Coleman Report     17
      Waning Attention to Family Inputs     18
      Waxing Attention to School Finance     19
    Family Inputs and Children's Outcomes     20
      Sociology Research and Evidence     20
      Evidence From the Understanding America Study     22
    Figure 1.1. Educational Attainment and Employment Status
      by Childhood Family Structure     23

Figure 1.2. Household Income by Childhood Family Structure     23
Figure 1.3. Positive and Negative Affect by Childhood Family Structure     24
    Educational Research on Parent Involvement and Community
       Engagement     25
Evaluations of Family Support Interventions     26
Implications for Policy and Practice and Future Research     27

**2 The Educational Equalizer: Funding Students Instead of Systems**     37
*Corey DeAngelis*

COVID Revealed a Massive Power Imbalance in Education     37
Politicization of Public School COVID-19 Responses     39
Incentives in the Governance of Public and Private Schools     41
Empowering Families and Improving Outcomes     41
Understanding the Incentives Behind Funding Students, Not Systems     43
Table 2.1. The Effect of Private-School Choice on Math and Reading
    Test Scores     46
Implementable State Policy Recommendations     47
K-12 Education's New Special Interest     47

**3 Quality and Intentionality: Making After-School Programs More Effective**     55
*Goldy Brown III*

Taxonomy of Government-Funded After-School Interventions     55
Academic Improvement     56
Social-Emotional Learning     56
Exposure, Recreation, and STEM     57
Improving After-School Programs: Quality and Intentionality     58
Implementation Questions and Recommendations     58
    Recommendations for Programming     58
Table 3.1. After-School Programs     59
    Personnel and Attendance     59
    Funding     60
Potential Cost-Effective Analysis     61
Table 3.2. Cost-Effective Analyses for After-School Program     62
    Preventing Negative Behavior     62
Further Research Regarding After-School Programming     63

**4 Career, Technical, and Higher-Education Opportunities for
Traditionally Underserved Students**     69
*Walter G. Ecton*

Background and Evidence on CTE Outcomes     70
Vocational Education in the International Context     73
Examining CTE in Today's Context     74

Data 74
Descriptive Findings 76
Figure 4.1. Distribution of Student CTE Credit Accumulation 77
Figure 4.2. Average CTE Credits per Student by Career Cluster 78
Table 4.1. CTE Credits Taken by Student and School Characteristics 79
Methods 80
Table 4.2. OLS Regression Results: Predictors of Selection as CTE
  Concentrator and Select Outcomes of Interest 81
Table 4.3. Balance Check: Comparing CTE Concentrators with
  Matched Comparison Groups 82
Results and Discussion 85
Table 4.4. Propensity Score Results: CTE Concentrators Compared
  to Matched Students 85
Table 4.5. OLS Regression Results: Effect of CTE Concentration 86
Recommendations for Policy and Practice 88
Define Intended Outcomes for Specific CTE Programs 88
Build Partnerships to Strengthen CTE Programs 89
Only Offer High-Quality, Relevant CTE Programs 90
Ensure Access to CTE for the Students Who Stand to Benefit Most 90
Focus on Equitable Participation in CTE 91

5  **Turning Hurdles Into Launch Pads: Improving Equity and Efficiency
Through Increased High School Graduations in the United States** 97
*Aidan Vining and David Weimer*

Available Evidence on Ethnicity/Race (Minority) and Income Differences 98
Table 5.1. Public School Adjusted Cohort Graduation Rate by Ethnic
  Group for the 2012 Through 2018 School Years (percent) 99
Why Does It Matter? The Social Value of High School Completion 100
High School Graduation Shadow Prices for the United States 101
Estimation Steps 101
Estimation Issues 102
Table 5.2. Steps in Estimating Disadvantaged High School Graduation
  Shadow Price 103
Shadow Price Estimates 105
Benefits and Discount Rates 105
Table 5.3. US High School Graduation Estimates: Alternative
  Discount Rates and Specifications, Point Estimates,
  and Monte Carlo Means (and Standard Deviations)
  in 1,000s of 2021 Dollars 106
Benefits Including Externalities 107
Applicability of the Estimates to Minority and Economically
  Disadvantaged Students 107
Increasing Minority and Disadvantaged Student Graduation 109

CBA and CEA Evidence                                              110
Promising Interventions That Have Not (Yet) Been Shown to
    Offer Positive Net Benefits                                  112
Conclusions and Policy Implications                               114

## PART II: CHANGES NEEDED AT THE STATE AND LOCAL LEVEL TO MAKE POSITIVE RESULTS MORE WIDESPREAD

6   **Getting Past the Current Trade-Off Between Privacy and Equity
    in Educational Technology**                                  **123**
    *Ryan Baker*

    The Promise of Artificially Intelligent Educational Technology   124
    The Risk of Algorithmic Bias                                     126
    The Push Toward Prioritizing Privacy                             127
    Alternative Ways to Protect Privacy While Improving Algorithmic
        Effectiveness                                            129
    Recommendations for State Educational Agencies and School Districts   130
        Provide Demographic Data to Vendors for the Purpose of Checking
            for Algorithmic Bias                                  131
        Incentivize Vendors to Conduct Algorithmic Bias Audits,
            or Conduct Them Directly                              131
        Rather Than Asking Vendors to Delete Data, Ask Them to Secure It   131
        Encourage Vendors to Adopt Data Infrastructures That Enable
            Privacy-Protecting Analyses                           131
    Conclusions                                                      132

7   **Identifying, Establishing, and Distributing the Economic Value of the
    Classroom Teacher**                                          **139**
    *Christopher D. Brooks and Matthew G. Springer*

    Quantifying the Economic Value of Teachers                       140
    Table 7.1. Dimension and Examples of Teacher Production          140
    Maximizing Teacher Value: Policy Reforms to Compensation,
        Recruitment, Evaluation, and Retention                   146
        The Problem: Teacher Compensation Policies Fail to Recognize
            the Value of Teachers                                 146
    Table 7.2. Step-and-Lane Salary Schedule in Carroll County
        Public Schools, MD (in US dollars)                       148
        Potential Policies for Improvement: Teacher Performance Incentives   149
    Challenges in Evaluating and Retaining the Most Effective and
        Valuable Teachers                                        152
        The Problem: Teacher Evaluation Systems Neither Adequately
            Differentiate Teachers by Ability Nor Emphasize the
            Economic Value of Teachers                            152

The Solution: Evaluation Systems That Emphasize Robust Measures
  of Value Added                                                         155
The Problem: Teacher Retention Is Low, Especially for Highly
  Effective Teachers, and School Leaders Have Limited Capacity
  for Removing Ineffective Teachers                                      156
Potential Policies for Improvement: Tenure Reforms, Principal
  Accountability, and Increased Incentives                               158
Equity: How Can We Get the Most-Effective Teachers to Work
  with the Least-Advantaged Students?                                    160
Conclusion and Recommendations                                          163
  Compensation                                                          164
  Evaluation                                                            165
  Retention                                                             165
  Distribution                                                          166

8  **Ensuring All Children Succeed with Social-Emotional Learning**      177
*Nicole A. Elbertson, Mark A. Brackett, Tangular A. Irby, and Krista L. Smith*

RULER as a Case Study                                                   179
Best Practices in Equitable Implementation of SEL                      181
  Commit to Making Equitable SEL a Priority                             182
  Hire and Maintain a Diverse Staff to Instruct and Model SEL           182
  Get to Know Students to Ensure That Lessons and Examples Are
    Relevant and Meaningful                                            183
  Acknowledge Ethnocentrism and Bias in SEL Programs and
    Practices and Correct for Them                                     184
  Ensure That SEL Is Not Misused to Control Marginalized Groups         185
  Choose Words Carefully                                                185
  Ensure Accessibility of All Tools, Strategies, and Content            186
  Consider Using SEL as a Means to Transform Inequitable Settings
    and Systems                                                        187
  Partner with Parents, Caregivers, and the Community                   187
  Be Curious and Open to Feedback                                       188
  Use SEL for Prevention as Well as Intervention                        188
  Monitor All SEL Efforts Over Time and Strive for Continuous
    Improvement                                                        189
Conclusion and Policy Implications                                     189

9  **Only Systemic Change Will Do**                                      195
*F. Mike Miles*

Ignoring System Principles                                             196
A Different System                                                     197
Key Obstacles to Systemic Change                                       198
  The Navarré Point                                                    198
  Other Obstacles                                                      199

How to Change the System                                              200
Eight Principles of a New Education System                            202
   Learning Happens Everywhere and Anytime            202
   Learning Is Personalized, and Students Own Their Learning   202
   Parents Have Access to an Expanded Number of Choices of
     Schools and Programs                     202
   The System Offers a New Employee Value Proposition, and
     Compensation Is Tied to What the System Values Most   202
   Learning Increasingly Is Focused on How to Think and How
     to Learn                                 202
   The School, Community, and Family Provide Students With a
     Set of Required Experiences, Not Just Specific Courses   203
   Community Groups Are Tapped to Educate Students in Many
     Non-Core Subjects                        203
   Governing Entities Check and Balance One Another and
     Encourage Innovation                     203
At the Operational Level                                              205
   A Focus on Outcomes                                  205
   Alignment Throughout the Organization                205
   Accountability                                       205
   Support                                              206
   Monitoring Progress                                  206
   Budget Priorities                                    206
   Compensation and Incentives                          206
   Capacity                                             206
   Leadership Density                                   206
   System Principles                                    206
   Vision for the Future                                207
   The Pace of Change                                   207
   Adaptability                                         207
   A Model for Systemic Reform                          207
The Pace of Change                                                   207
Reimagined Schools?                                                  208
Table 9.1. Nascent Level                                             209
Table 9.2. Progressing Level                                         210
Table 9.3. Proficient Level                                          211
Table 9.4. Advanced Level                                            213

References                                                           215

Index                                                                257

About the Editors and Contributors                                   267

# Tables and Figures

Table I.1. Educational Funding Since 1960     2

Figure I.1. The Relationship Between Education, Equity, and Economics     3

Table I.2. Program Recommendations     5

Figure 1.1. Educational Attainment and Employment Status by
Childhood Family Structure     23

Figure 1.2. Household Income by Childhood Family Structure     23

Figure 1.3. Positive and Negative Affect by Childhood Family Structure     24

Table 2.1. The Effect of Private-School Choice on Math and Reading
Test Scores     46

Table 3.1. After-School Programs     59

Table 3.2. Cost-Effective Analyses for After-School Program     62

Figure 4.1. Distribution of Student CTE Credit Accumulation     77

Figure 4.2. Average CTE Credits per Student by Career Cluster     78

Table 4.1. CTE Credits Taken by Student and School Characteristics     79

Table 4.2. OLS Regression Results: Predictors of Selection as
CTE Concentrator and Select Outcomes of Interest     81

Table 4.3. Balance Check: Comparing CTE Concentrators with
Matched Comparison Groups     82

Table 4.4. Propensity Score Results: CTE Concentrators Compared
to Matched Students     85

Table 4.5. OLS Regression Results: Effect of CTE Concentration     86

Table 5.1. Public School Adjusted Cohort Graduation Rate by Ethnic
Group for the 2012 Through 2018 School Years (percent)     99

Table 5.2. Steps in Estimating Disadvantaged High School Graduation
Shadow Price     103

Table 5.3. US High School Graduation Estimates: Alternative Discount
   Rates and Specifications, Point Estimates, and Monte Carlo Means
   (and Standard Deviations) in 1,000s of 2021 Dollars ... 106
Table 7.1. Dimension and Examples of Teacher Production ... 140
Table 7.2. Step-and-Lane Salary Schedule in Carroll County
   Public Schools, MD (in US dollars) ... 148
Table 9.1. Nascent Level ... 209
Table 9.2. Progressing Level ... 210
Table 9.3. Proficient Level ... 211
Table 9.4. Advanced Level ... 213

# Introduction

*Christos Makridis and Goldy Brown III*

The United States ranks 25th on the list of 38 OECD (Organisation for Economic Co-operation and Development) countries in its overall poverty gap—that is, the difference in the proportion between people in and out of poverty—and it ranks 26th in its poverty gap for children (OECD, 2021). And yet, real gross domestic product per capita has grown by 24.5% between 1990 and 2019.

How can the economy appear to grow so rapidly but simultaneously struggle to achieve a standard of living that at least surpasses the poverty level for many Americans? We believe that a major reason resides with the system for K-12 education and the degree to which children cultivate human capital. Absent adequate human capital investments in childhood, individuals eventually enter the workforce unprepared. Already, we are seeing substantial manifestations of these forces: labor shortages (Burning Glass, 2018), which have amplified since 2020 (Mitchell, Zmora, Finlay, Jutkowitz, & Gaugler, 2021), and growing polarization in the income and employment distribution (Autor & Dorn, 2013). The simultaneity of these patterns highlights a fundamental tension and vulnerability in the US education system and the necessity to deliver learning at scale in the evolving economy.

Many of the conversations about education have been about equity, which is generally framed in terms of fairness—that is, "making sure each child receives what they need to develop to their full academic and social potential" (Unterhalter, 2009). For example, unambiguous causal evidence links lower parental investments, which often arise from a single-parent household, with worse student outcomes and childhood development. If we only focus on student outcomes without examining the underlying factors behind them, we might misattribute the driving sources of student outcomes that lead to bad policy, rather than underlying sources of the human capital investments that influence the child's economic outlook.

Especially since 2020 with the onset of COVID-19, now is an important time to commit to the transmission of human capital with clear goals, beginning with the recognition that education is fundamentally about empowering individuals to achieve their full potential. If we impact short-run outcomes without changing the underlying process, then we risk undermining our very objectives and, at best, only attain them for a brief period. The disagreements that we are seeing play out on a national and local level are particularly noteworthy given the surge in federal spending allocated toward educational programs.

These increases in spending on education programs, however, will be made in vain absent a change. Moreover, the urgency to deliver better outcomes for learners comes at a time of deep technological change as automation and artificial intelligence continue to expand and impact the labor market (Brynjolfsson & McAfee, 2014; Acemoglu & Restrepo, 2018). Whether increased funding will improve—or perhaps even stifle—student outcomes depends crucially on how it will be used.

## THIS BOOK'S OBJECTIVE

The contribution of this book is to not only take stock of what we know about pre-K-12 education in the scientific literature, but also make recommendations about educational programming that should be invested in that has shown potential to mitigate the opportunity gap and increase human capital. Especially, following the COVID-19 pandemic, the decline in access to education may mean that America's future workforce will be devastated by the declining number of children in our pre-K-12 system, a phenomenon predicted to begin showing its effects in 2025, with a lower number of high school graduates going into postsecondary education and the workforce due to a reduced birthrate during the great recession, and dismal student achievement outcomes on the 2022 National Assessment for Education Progress (NCES, 2022) which hit a 30-year low in Reading and Math achievement for American students. Simply increasing funding will have little impact in driving improved outcomes if the funds are not used wisely; indeed, expenditures per student have roughly tripled since 1960 (see table I.1).

Unfortunately, increased funding efforts, though necessary to meet new educational mandates and the rising population in America, have fallen short in delivering the hypothesized results. Though strong cases are being made for more funding, we cannot assume that the benefits of increased funding will pass directly to students

**Table I.1.   Educational Funding Since 1960**

| Year | 1960 | 1980 | 2000 | 2016 |
|------|------|------|------|------|
| Pupil-Teacher Ratio | 25.8 | 18.7 | 16.4 | 16.0 |
| Per-Pupil Expenditure | $2,959 | $6,675 | $10,131 | $12,339 |

Data on expenditures per pupil are adjusted for inflation using the Consumer Price Index.

*Source*: US Department of Education (2019).

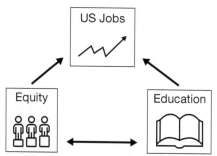

**Figure I.1. The Relationship Between Education, Equity, and Economics**

and compensate for their losses without a renewed focus and understanding of the strategic initiatives that confer results to learners. Increases should be made to programs that are effective while decreasing or defunding ineffective programs. We refocus the conversation at local, state, and federal levels on human capital, reporting on educational programming that has produced positive results that warrant further investment and providing practical, local recommendations to scale them.

## EARLY CHILDHOOD INTERVENTION

The empirical evidence is perhaps the most unambiguous in the case of early childhood education intervention. Some of the most critical years of childhood development are between birth and age five, influencing the child's long-run outcomes (Cunha & Heckman, 2007; Cunha, Heckman, & Schennach, 2010). However, differences in the quality and quantity of investment among children in early childhood mean that they enter school and eventually the labor market in substantially different positions. That has spurred a flurry of public policy initiatives to rectify the developmental gap.

However, these attempts have been, at best, modestly effective. Scholars have found that one of the major reasons behind policy ineffectiveness is the presence of dynamic complementarities: knowledge, skills, and abilities developed at one stage increase the productivity of investments received at later stages. In other words, these first five years correlate to whether a child will be ready for their first years of school, which tend to be very important regarding their economic outlook. From birth to five will have an impact on a child's performance in kindergarten through grade three. That, in turn, will impact their performance in grades four through 12, which will impact performance postsecondary and career-wise. The longer the delay in interventions, the weaker the results will be.

Early childhood interventions are the first needed steps to potentially help overcome barriers such as poverty and negative childhood experiences that can limit a person's economic outlook (Betts & Thai, 2022). Some of these barriers include but are not limited to being born to a mother with lower education who is more likely to smoke or drink alcohol while pregnant, both of which can impair brain development (Härkönen, Lindberg, Karlsson, Karlsson, & Scheinin, 2018); or the "vocabulary gap," reflecting the fact that affluent children are more likely to be exposed to more vocabulary during the first years of life than low-income students (Gilkerson et al., 2017), which is important to overall language acquisition. The language gap translates into a child's primary educational experience. If a child does not transition from learning to read to reading to learn by fourth grade, the chances that she will ever be a reader at grade level are significantly reduced. The third-grade reading assessment has been correlated with whether a child is more likely to be incarcerated, graduate high school, and other individual economic factors.

Often these quantitative studies do not provide concrete and practical guidance about the specific steps to ensure adequate development in early childhood. We view the Social Genome Model 2.0 (developed through a partnership with the Brookings Institution, Urban Institute, and Child Trends) as a particularly useful conceptual and quantitative tool to think about the life cycle of a child's development. The model is structured around key life stages, which span from circumstances at birth to adulthood at age 30. At each life stage, key developmental outcomes are considered for a child's success, including (Werner et al., 2021):

- Circumstances at Birth: Born at a normal birth weight to a nonpoor, married mother at least 18 years old.
- Prekindergarten (age 5): Acceptable reading and math scores, behavior, interpersonal skills, parent-child relationships, and health.
- Early Elementary School (age 8): Acceptable reading and math scores, behavior, self-control, parent-child relationship, and health.
- Middle Childhood (age 11): Acceptable reading and math scores, behavior, self-control, peer relationship, and health.
- Early Adolescence (age 14): Acceptable ASVAB score, behavior, mental health, and health.
- Adolescence (age 19): High school graduate with a GPA of at least 2.0; acceptable behavior, mental health, and health.
- Transition to Adulthood (age 24): Family income at least 200% of FPL or 100% of FPL if a student; acceptable mental health and health.
- Adulthood (age 30): Family income at least 200% of FPL or 100 % of FPL if a student; acceptable mental health and health.

In table I.2, we use the Social Genome Model 2.0's conceptual framework and standards of success at each life stage to offer practical program recommendations for state and local policy makers.

This book has identified other programming being funded that has the potential to produce economic benefits as well. Though findings are not as widespread as early childhood, the programming mentioned in part I of the book has shown to be successful on a small scale. Recommendations are being made to scale these programs' success and for further inquiry that will be necessary to find solutions to reduce programming ineffectiveness.

**Table I.2. Program Recommendations**

| Social Genome Model 2.0 Life Stage | Program Recommendations |
|---|---|
| | Circumstances at birth<br>Effective parental support and involvement programming |
| Prekindergarten | Early childhood program expansion<br>Rigorous curriculum taught by effective educators<br>Social-emotional learning curriculum for early childhood students |
| Early elementary school | Early childhood program expansion<br>Rigorous curriculum taught by effective educators<br>Social-emotional learning curriculum for early childhood students |
| Middle childhood | Rigorous curriculum taught by effective educators<br>High school graduation programs<br>Effective after-school programs<br>Social-emotional learning programs<br>School choice options<br>Effective parental involvement<br>Career and technical education exposure |
| Early adolescence | Rigorous curriculum taught by effective educators<br>High school graduation programs<br>Effective after-school programs<br>Social-emotional learning programs<br>School choice options<br>Effective parental involvement<br>Career and technical education exposure |
| Adolescence | High school graduation programs<br>Career and technical education programs<br>Two- or four-year colleges |
| Transition to adulthood | High school graduation programs<br>Career and technical education programs<br>Two- or four-year colleges |
| Adulthood | High school graduation programs<br>Career and technical education programs<br>Two- or four-year colleges |

Finally, this book is not making curriculum recommendations. Every state has standards and has identified curricula that should be used to help students reach learning objectives. Standards are created with stakeholders and identify the necessary skills children need to learn to become successful adults. In addition, teacher evaluation systems are more sophisticated now than ever; most have been aligned to standards and student growth.

# SUMMARY OF STATE AND
# LOCAL POLICY RECOMMENDATIONS

Parental and Community Involvement: This chapter explores the role of parental and community involvement in childhood development with special attention to family structure and interventions that have been successful.

- Family instability can result not only from a single-parent household where children do not have access to investments from both parents but also from having "too many" caregivers. Parents need to consider the potential unintended effects of child care or other caregivers on childhood development.
- One way to decrease caregiver instability is by implementing "looping"—that is, allowing the same teacher to instruct children across multiple grades.
- Educators should connect with their students' families to understand the broader context that the student operates within outside of the classroom.
- Establishing a common set of operating procedures (e.g., thresholds for disciplinary action), and even language, is important for all parties.
- Simply increasing funding for educational programs has proven ineffective at best and sometimes counterproductive given the incentives that exist. Funding needs to be carefully targeted and linked to the attainment of specific outcomes.

Funding Students Instead of Systems: This chapter explores how COVID-19 school closures exposed a power imbalance between public schools and families, increasing support for and implementation of school choice policies. The chapter discusses the logic of funding K-12 students directly and empowering families to choose the education providers that best meet their children's needs.

- Families would benefit from an "education savings account program" where the child's state-level taxpayer-funded education dollars would follow him to a family-directed education savings account, rather than to the school district. Families can use that money to send children to the school of their choosing.
- Implement private school vouchers, but these programs generally only allow the funding to cover private school tuition and fees.
- Implement education savings accounts and scholarships funded via tax credits.

Quality and Intentionality: This chapter analyzes the role of quality (e.g., adequate personnel and resources) and intentionality (e.g., measurable outcome for participants) in after-school programs. Rather than providing a set of direct recommendations, the chapter produces a series of questions as a sort of "checklist" for decision makers.

- What are the shortcomings of the youth in our community, school district, or schools that negatively impact their life chances? These outcomes could include but are not limited to illiteracy, low math scores, high teenage pregnancy rates, high juvenile crime rates, high levels of drug and alcohol abuse, poor school attendance, negative school behavior, lack of exposure, and low graduation rates.

- What resources (funding, facilities, technology, community partnerships, and personnel) do we have to create a quality and intentional after-school program?
- Considering our resources, what quality and intentional after-school program(s) can we put together to address an identified shortcoming?
- Once implemented, how will we measure our program's effectiveness?

Career, Technical, and Higher-Education Opportunities for traditionally underserved students: This chapter examines the evidence and potential value of CTE programs at the high school and college level, considers the extent to which access to high-quality CTE programs is equitable, and discusses recommendations for expanding opportunities to students most likely to benefit from CTE.

- The outcomes associated with specific CTE programs must be clearly identified and tracked to ensure a quality experience for the learners.
- CTE programs function best when there are meaningful partnerships with local businesses and other stakeholders.
- High-quality CTE programs are those with high enrollment, quality instruction, and job placement in high-demand areas at the local, state, and national level.
- Access to CTE programs for students who stand to benefit the most should be prioritized. These include students who are not college bound and/or are from low-income families whose economic outlook could be dramatically improved if they acquire skills through quality CTE programs.
- CTE programs should have equitable participation. When the demographic composition of a CTE program does not match its state demographics, those involved should study the factors that might obstruct broader participation.

Turning Hurdles into Launch Pads: The chapter reports on interventions that have targeted various categories of disadvantaged students and that have passed a CBA or CEA threshold. Consideration of the evidence on other interventions that appear to improve disadvantaged student high school performance in various ways but have not (yet) been demonstrated to increase graduation rates or evaluated from a CBA (or close to it) perspective is discussed as well. This presents the following programs:

- The five most cost-effective interventions are Talent Search, JOBSTART, New Chance, National Guard Youth Challenge (NGYC), and Job Corps.
- Other programs that have shown potential in mitigating these high school graduation gaps are early childhood programs in high-poverty areas, 9th-grade intervention programming, peer and adult counseling programs, students of color having more teachers of color, and smaller schools (often charter schools).
- Though there was no known intervention, home environment plays a big factor in whether a student graduates from high school.

Educational Technology and Equity: This chapter explores the promise of artificially intelligent educational technology and the evidence about whether such systems are improving outcomes for learners. Special attention is paid to the potential for algorithmic bias and how it reduces effectiveness for the students who need support most.

- Provide demographic data to vendors for the purpose of checking for algorithmic bias. If the technology is working as anticipated, then the improvements in student outcomes should be borne out in the corresponding demographic data.
- Incentivize vendors to conduct algorithmic bias audits whereby neutral third parties test whether the algorithms are generating systematically different errors across different types of learners (e.g., race and socioeconomic status).
- Rather than asking vendors to delete data, schools secure it so that the data can be used to conduct audits and ensure that learners are benefiting proportionately.
- Encourage vendors to adopt data infrastructures that enable analyses to protect privacy that would enable quantitative evaluations of algorithmic applications on student outcomes without any release of personal identifiable information. If adverse effects are identified, then they should be rectified to ensure that every student is at least better off than without the use of AI.

Classroom Teachers: This chapter explores the best estimates presently available for measuring the value of effective teaching. It then highlights how legislation fails to recognize the value of teachers, a fact reflected in teacher compensation, evaluation, and retention policies. And finally, the chapter considers how teachers, as a highly valuable resource for students, are often inequitably distributed between and within schools, and the implications of this distribution for educational opportunity and social justice. It makes the following recommendations:

- The differences in compensation between teachers and comparably educated individuals should be reduced to attract higher-quality employees.
- Teacher compensation and tenure should more explicitly reward more effective teachers based on their demonstrated and consistent impact on student outcomes.
- States should revisit efforts to incorporate test score value added as a primary component of teacher evaluation for teachers for whom multiple years of testing data are available, because that is one metric of student outcomes.
- Probationary status should last longer than three years or should be extendable when teaching effectiveness has not been demonstrated to an adequate degree.
- Teachers should be returned to probation if they are repeatedly ineffective.
- School districts should deliberate on the distribution of quality teachers across and within schools to ensure adequate outcomes at a geographic level.
- One incentive mechanism for attracting talented teachers is to pay teachers to move districts and condition some of future compensation on performance.
- Districts should also be mindful of the pay premium that is required to motivate talented teachers to work in areas that are higher need.

Social and Emotional Learning: This chapter guides the development and implementation of SEL, with a case study of the evolution of one SEL approach, RULER, as a template for future applications. This chapter recommends that local school districts do the following:

- Skills cultivated through proper applications of SEL curricula are relevant for not only interventions but also preventive and longer-term investments.
- SEL interventions must have clear metrics linked to student learning and achievement that are monitored continuously with adjustments when needed.
- Involve parents and caregivers in the development and application of SEL curricula and ensure that learners have opportunities to put the lessons learned into practice within the broader community.
- All SEL tools, strategies, and content should be made accessible, but not at the expense of quality in the curricula.

Expanding Effective Systemic School Changes: This chapter studies meaningful reforms of school quality. One fundamental failure of public education over the past several decades has been our inability to change or make significant improvements to the education *system*. It recommends the following systemic changes and provides a framework for school districts to measure the effectiveness of these changes:

- School districts should adhere to a principle of accountability for outcomes versus accountability for process or compliance requirements.
- Compensation of employees in a school district should be tied to what the system values most versus years of experience.
- School districts should prioritize the provision of resources to student academic needs versus providing relatively equal per-pupil funding.
- Unsatisfactory and ineffective teachers should be removed rather than retained to avoid conflict; such teachers are already harming children's development.
- School district principles should ensure that learning should be increasingly focused on how to think and how to learn (versus "what" to think and learn).
- School district organizations should ensure that learning can and does happen everywhere and anytime.
- School governance should be designed with three arms (branches) that check and balance one another.

## REFERENCES

Acemoglu, D., & Restrepo, P. (2018). The race between man and machine: Implications of technology for growth, factor shares, and employment. *American Economic Review, 108*(6), 1488–1542.

Autor, D. H., & Dorn, D. (2013). The growth of low-skill service jobs and the polarization of the US labor market. *American Economic Review, 103*(5), 1553–1597.

Brynjolfsson, E., & McAfee, A. (2014). *The second machine age: Work, progress, and prosperity in a time of brilliant technologies.* Norton.

Burning Glass Technologies. (2018). Different skills, different gaps: Measuring and closing the skills gap. https://www.economicmodeling.com/2018/03/14/skills-gap-different-skills-different-gaps/

Cunha, F., & Heckman, J. (2007). The technology of skill formation. *American Economic Review, 97*(2), 31–47.

Cunha, F., Heckman, J., & Schennach, S. (May 2010). Estimating the technology of noncognitive skill formation. *Econometrica, 78*(3), 883–931. http://www.econometricsociety.org/

Gilkerson, J., Richards, J. A., Warren, S. F., Montgomery, J. K., Greenwood, C. R., Kimbrough Oller, D., Hansen, H. L., & Paul, T. D. (2017). Mapping the early language environment using all-day recordings and automated analysis. *American Journal of Speech-Language Pathology, 26*(2), 248–265. https://doi.org/10.1\044/2016\_AJSLP-15-0169

Härkönen, J., Lindberg, M., Karlsson, L., Karlsson, H., & Scheinin, N. M. (2018). Education is the strongest socio-economic predictor of smoking in pregnancy. *Addiction, 113*(6), 1117–1126. https://doi.org/10.1111/add.14158

Mitchell, L. L., Zmora, R., Finlay, J. M., Jutkowitz, E., & Gaugler, J. E. (2021). Do big five personality traits moderate the effects of stressful life events on health trajectories? Evidence from the health and retirement study. *Journals ofGerontology, Series B, 76*(1), 44–55. https://doi.org/10.1093/geronb/gbaa075

National Center for Education Statistics (NCES). (2022). "NCES Database." NCES. nces.ed.gov/nationsreportcard

Organisation for Economic Co-Operation and Development (OECD). (2021). "OECD-Stat Database." Paris: OECD. https://stats.oecd.org/. Google Scholar.

Unterhalter, E. (2009). What is equity in education? Reflections from the capability approach. *Studies in Philosophy and Education, 28*, 415–424. https://doi.org/10.1007/s11217-009-9125-7

Werner, K., Blagg, K., Acs, G., Martin, S., McClay, A., Moore, K. A., Pina, G., & Sacks, V. (2021). *Social genome model 2.0 technical documentation and user guide*. Urban Institute.

# Part I

## EDUCATIONAL PROGRAMS THAT HAVE PRODUCED POSITIVE RESULTS

# 1

# The Economic Value of Parent and Community Involvement

*Albert A. Cheng and Robert Maranto*

## CHANGING FAMILY STRUCTURE, SCHOOLS, AND SOCIETY

> *There are entire neighborhoods where young people, they don't see an example of somebody succeeding . . . and for a lot of young boys and young men, in particular, they don't see an example of fathers or grandfathers, uncles, who are in a position to support families and be held up and respected. . . . There's no more important ingredient for success—nothing that would be more important for us reducing violence—than strong, stable families, which means we should do more to promote marriage and encourage fatherhood.*
>
> —Barack Obama, quoted in *USA Today* (2013)

> *In Ohio, I had grown especially skillful at navigating various father figures.*
>
> —J. D. Vance, in *Hillbilly Elegy*

Arguably, save for increased wealth and longer life spans (Deaton, 2013), the most dramatic social changes in the West generally and US society particularly have involved family change. By the early 20th century in the United States, nuclear families largely had replaced traditional extended families. In the past half century, long-term nuclear families have increasingly yielded to single-parent and blended-family models of varying duration. Only about half of American children live with the same two parents through childhood (Zill, 2015). Before the mid-20th century, family fluidity usually resulted from the death or destitution of one or both parents. Today, it usually reflects adult decisions to leave marriages or long-term relationships, or to procreate without having formed them in the first place (Murray, 2012; Edin & Kefalas, 2005; Therborn, 2004; Haskins & Sawhill, 2016). These individual-level decisions have had profound influences on communities, which in turn, as President Obama put it in the quote above, reinforce individual perceptions of limited options, affecting whole communities (Chetty, Hendren, Jones, & Porter, 2020; Murray, 2012; Wilcox, 2018).

These trends carry important implications for schools. Specifically, weaker relationships in formal social institutions such as families and houses of worship (Campbell, Layman, & Green, 2021) and, in turn, in informal communities have increased the importance of strong relationships in other formal social institutions such as schools. As families become less stable, schools are increasingly called upon to take on roles that families previously filled. Over the past half century, schools in America and the West generally have increased staff-to-student ratios, in part to offer more intensive mentoring, emotional, and behavioral support as well as to provide for health and physical needs (Maranto, van Raemdonck, & Vasile, 2016).

US public schools feed and counsel students who in earlier times would receive material and emotional support from nuclear or extended family members. During the COVID-19 pandemic, the local public schools near where we live and where one of us has a child have taken enormous efforts to publicize and provide for the feeding of children by the school system: parents could drive to a car line, while masked, to retrieve a school-prepared meal. The same district ended finals and most homework, seeing academic needs as less pressing than physical needs, which parents in our affluent town might not provide. Yet as an extensive literature indicates, meeting physical needs goes only so far; indeed, as Mayer (1997) documents empirically, since the 1960s, government assistance has provided adequate support for the physical needs of the poor to such an extent that material wants no longer constitute substantial measurable barriers to upward mobility.

In high-poverty communities, where formal institutions have weakened the most, traditional public schools generally have had limited success in preparing students for college and their careers (Payne, 2008; Duncan & Murnane, 2011). Empirical studies likewise demonstrate that family structure is critical for the well-being of children. Controlling for a wide range of variables, children who grow up with both biological parents are less likely to drop out of high school and more likely to complete college, which, in turn, translates into higher wages in the labor market (Amato, 2010; Mayer, 1997; Mohanty & Ullah, 2012; Sweeney, 2011; Wilcox & Stokes, 2015). Children from lower socioeconomic backgrounds are more likely to grow up without an intact family; scholars have argued that such differences in family structure have a significant impact on socioeconomic inequalities (Amato, 2010; Matysiak, Styrc, & Vignoli, 2014; McLanahan, 2004; McLanahan & Jacobsen, 2015). Nonetheless, family structure remains important for children from higher socioeconomic backgrounds. Some studies, for example, find that the negative outcomes of divorce are more pronounced for children from higher socioeconomic backgrounds (Bernardi & Radl, 2014).

Since the development of attachment theory more than a half century ago, psychologists have provided theoretical and empirical bases for expecting that long-term stability among primary caregivers, particularly in childhood but extending into adolescence, fosters personal security, agency, and resiliency, better preparing young people to succeed both in school and later, in workplaces, which are relatively impersonal institutions, with obvious economic implications (Ainsworth & Bowlby, 1965). Of importance, from the very beginning, attachment theory–related findings were scientifically validated both in Western and non-Western societies (Ainsworth, 1967). They are also supported by philosophical and religious traditions, Western and non-Western, dating back millennia (Haidt, 2006) and by modern evolutionary psychology (Haidt, 2012). In short, the notion that family structure *might not* matter is a relatively recent one, arguably reflecting large blind spots in the social sciences and perhaps reflecting the isolation of (particularly postmodern) academia from society (Lukianoff & Haidt, 2018; Campbell & Manning, 2018; Pluckrose & Lindsay, 2020).

Economists have long theorized that family structure mediates educational attainment and labor market outcomes through the capacity for parents to invest in their children. Resources of money and time are typically greater in two-parent homes than in single-parent homes, providing children in the former with greater access than in the latter to investments by their parents. Two-parent homes can, therefore, allocate more time and financial resources to building up their children's human capital, whether it be in the form of literacy and numeracy skills or social and emotional well-being. Some economic research even indicates that time and affection, resources scarcer in single-parent homes, have more impact than money, in accord with attachment theory (Becker, 1981; Mayer, 1997). Regardless of the precise causal mechanisms, families play an essential role in the upbringing of their children.

In this chapter, we discuss the economic value of family involvement. The remainder of the chapter is divided into four sections:

1. We begin by discussing the role of the family and its place in the economics of education, namely, in the study of the education production function. In this discussion, we pay particular attention to the seminal work of Gary Becker and James Coleman.
2. The second section summarizes the empirical literature that explicitly estimates correlations between student outcomes and family inputs, particularly family structure. As will become apparent, the economics of education as a field has paid relatively little attention to the role of family inputs in human capital production.
3. In the third section, we return to the economics literature to summarize the strongest evidence of parent and community-involvement interventions. We describe a variety of programs that have been subjected to empirical evaluations.
4. Based on the research about family and community involvement we have summarized up to this point, we conclude in the final section with directions for future research and implications for policy and educational practice.

# SCHOOL AND FAMILY INPUTS

## The Education Production Function

Ever since Gary Becker's (1964) groundbreaking book *Human Capital: A Theoretical and Empirical Analysis with Special Reference to Education*, economists of education have scrutinized the development of skills, knowledge, health, and values—all of which contribute to an individual's economic and psychic well-being. Education plays a central role in the production of human capital, as Becker's title suggests. Becker demonstrated, for example, that incomes and the labor productivity of college-educated adults are higher than adults with only a high school education. The finding that more years of formal education, on-the-job training, and other opportunities to increase the stock of human capital raise an individual's earnings and labor productivity continue to be reproduced in data today (Autor, 2014).

Although economists studying the production of human capital have primarily focused on education, they have also recognized the role of other inputs, particularly the family. In the third edition of *Human Capital*, Becker (1994, p. 21) writes, "No discussion of human capital can omit the influence of families on the knowledge, skills, values, and habits of their children." Becker (1981) further described the dynamics of the ways parents invest in their children in *A Treatise on the Family*, where he viewed households as firms deciding how to allocate time, money, and other resources toward a variety of ends, including child care. Parents invest in their children's education by enrolling them in formal schools and other extracurricular enrichment programs. They spend resources to provide additional schooling such as postsecondary education, to live in a particular neighborhood to attend a school in its catchment area, to pay private-school tuition, or to purchase additional learning materials and services such as books and tutors. Parents also spend time to provide their own instruction to develop their children's numeracy, literacy, and other cognitive skills. Aside from cognitive skills, parents pass on—explicitly or tacitly—the values they espouse to their children. The transmission of these values shapes children in consequential ways. For example, the educational aspirations of parents and the value they place on hard work, independence, and thrift are major predictors of their children's future educational attainment and employment decisions (Cheng, Henderson, Peterson, & West, 2021; Mendez & Zamarro, 2018).

Other economists have explored the significance of the timing of parents' investments in their children. Cunha and Heckman (2007), for instance, argue that investments at younger ages are more effective at improving human capital. Earlier investments build a base of skills that are then used to acquire additional skills later on, a feature referred to as *dynamic complementarity*. According to this theory, family environments and parental investments in children are not only crucial factors in the formation of human capital but are more critical in their children's earlier years (Francesconi & Heckman, 2016).

These theories about human capital development have been modeled in the education production function, which can be stated in a basic form:

$$Y = f(x_1, x_2, \ldots x_n).$$ (1)

In the model, a student's human capital, Y, is expressed as a function $f$ of inputs $x_1, \ldots x_n$ such as years of schooling, school resources, parent's educational attainment, or the student's existing stock of human capital. The magnitude of each input has been the subject of a large economic literature.

## The Coleman Report

Emerging from this research is long-standing debate about the relative magnitude of the influence of families and schools on the production of human capital. In other words, do family inputs play a more central role than school inputs in the formation of their children's human capital? Or do school inputs play a larger role? These debates came to a head in 1966 when the US Office of Education released another groundbreaking work, a 737-page report titled *Equality of Educational Opportunity*. This report is more commonly known as the "Coleman Report" after its lead author and Johns Hopkins sociologist, James Coleman. At the time, the US Civil Rights Act of 1964 required the commissioner of education to study inequalities in educational opportunity. Indeed, this report is the first instance of documenting empirically the achievement gap between Black and White students. More significantly, however, the report examined the relative influence of families and schools on student learning. Consistent with the conventional wisdom at the time, Coleman expected that the data—which included almost 600,000 students, more than 44,000 teachers, and nearly 4,000 schools—would demonstrate that school inputs such as teacher characteristics, per-pupil spending, and class size were the most significant contributors to student learning. Coleman and his colleagues, however, found that a student's family background played the most central role. Specifically, variables such as parental education, family size, family structure, parent's educational aspirations for their kids, and items in the home explained most of the variation in student learning.

The Coleman Report was quietly released on the weekend before the Fourth of July, but it eventually gained attention, becoming one of the most significant empirical studies on education ever conducted. It catalyzed decades of research dedicated to understanding the factors that contribute to student learning and, more generally, human capital formation. Even so, uncertainty around whether schools or families play a more important role in human capital formation endures today. The Coleman Report did not settle the debate, especially because of its methodological limitations.

Coleman first demonstrated the strong correlation between family background variables and student learning. He then demonstrated that the inclusion of variables for school inputs alongside variables for family inputs did not explain much additional variation in student learning. However, family background and school inputs themselves are correlated. Families with higher levels of parental education and more resources also tend to select schools that are more effective at teaching. Without the benefits of an experimental design or another source of exogenous variation, Coleman could not separate the influence of family from school.

Interestingly, in the years since the Coleman Report and the Moynihan Report (1965) on changing family structure in Black communities, interest in family structure among social scientists has generally waned, even though the impacts of family structure have been highlighted by politicians such as Barack Obama and Bill Clinton, who themselves lacked extensive contact with biological fathers (Pearlstein, 2011; Obama, 1995). Generally, despite initial support from Martin Luther King and other civil rights leaders, dominant liberal opinion in elite news media and in universities (particularly in the policy sciences) often treated serious discussions about the rise of single-parent homes as inherently racist because single-parent homes now dominate in African American communities, and accordingly as blaming the victim for structural racism (e.g., Geary, 2015). This occurred even though individuals from White and non-White ethnic backgrounds generally have agreed on the desirability of two-parent homes as a model, as well as on a wide range of other issues (Kaufmann, 2019; Pearlstein, 2011).

**Waning Attention to Family Inputs**

An important 2011 collection of papers described by some as a successor to the Coleman Report (Duncan & Murnane, 2011) limited discussions of family structure impacts to just one of the book's 24 substantive chapters. Nonetheless, this single chapter (Sweeney, 2011) offered an extensive summary of largely overlooked research, reporting, among other things, that adolescents living with a single mother display levels of school engagement just under half a standard deviation lower than those living with two married biological parents. Not surprisingly, 90% of youth living with two biological parents in eighth grade graduate from high school compared to 69% who live with a never married solo mother and 75% living with a divorced solo mother.

Demographers estimate that up to 41% of the economic inequality created between 1976 and 2000 was the result of changed family structure. Yet as Maranto and Crouch (2014, p. A13) point out in their summary of the literature, in the early 2010s both the American Political Science Association and the American Education Research Association dedicated their annual meetings to inequality without featuring a single paper or presentation (from among several thousand) on the impacts of family structure. The authors complain:

> In the past four years, our two academic professional organizations—the American Political Science Association and the American Educational Research Association—have each dedicated annual meetings to inequality, with numerous papers and speeches denouncing free markets, the decline of unions, and "neoliberalism" generally as exacerbat-

ing economic inequality. Yet our searches of the groups' conference websites fail to turn up a single paper or panel addressing the effects of family change on inequality.

The authors consider this scientific malpractice, akin to a medical conference on cancer ignoring the impacts of smoking. Similarly, treatments of such matters as school discipline (e.g., works within Winn & Winn, 2021) virtually never address the discipline difficulties faced by children, particularly boys, from single-parent homes or with instability of primary caregivers. The topic is essentially verboten.

## Waxing Attention to School Finance

Despite the Coleman Report's conclusions as well as Becker's work on the economics of the family, attention to family background characteristics in the economics of education waned over the next several decades. Research on school inputs, on the other hand, waxed among economists.

For instance, a few years after the release of the Coleman Report, the California Supreme Court made a landmark ruling regarding school finance in *Serrano v. Priest*. This ruling propelled a litany of school finance litigation, despite the Coleman Report's conclusions about school finance. A commensurate increase in research around the question of the effects of school spending rose alongside these lawsuits. Economists and educational researchers alike turned to studying this question empirically, and the debate about the impacts of spending increases on student learning persists today (Hedges, Laine, & Greenwald, 1994; Hanushek, 1994; Jackson, 2020). Parenthetically, some social scientists make considerable sums testifying as expert witnesses in school finance cases.

About a decade after the advent of school finance litigation in 1985, Tennessee began Project STAR, a statewide initiative in which students were randomly assigned to classes with different student-to-teacher ratios. Project STAR together with the state of California's subsequent adoption of a class-size reduction policy in the 1990s elevated student-to-teacher ratios as key school input for economists to study.

Then, 25 years after Project STAR, teacher-quality research gained salience in the economics of education. Much of this work has focused on developing teacher value-added scores and other measures of teacher effectiveness to provide estimates of the magnitude of a teacher's contribution to student learning, net of student family background variables (Chetty, Friedman, & Rockoff, 2014a). Using teacher value-added measures, researchers have found that teacher quality has a large impact on student learning and longer-run outcomes such as income, educational attainment, and likelihood of teenage birth (Chetty, Friedman, & Rockoff, 2014b; Hanushek & Rivkin, 2010).

With such long-standing attention to teacher quality, class size, and school finance, most economists of education continue to focus on the connection between school inputs and student outcomes. Few economists, however, have continued to explore the role of family background. Empirical studies from the economics of education do not ignore family characteristics altogether, but they are rarely the central focus. If anything, econometric models typically include a small set of family background variables such as race or ethnic background, household income, and parent's educational attainment. Sometimes they include a lagged measure of student achievement to serve as a proxy for the cumulative investment that a family has thus far made in the student. Moreover, whenever measures of family inputs are included in models, they are rarely the primary variable of interest. In sum, compared to the measures considered in the Coleman Report, measures of family background are minimally modeled in most research of the education production function.

## FAMILY INPUTS AND CHILDREN'S OUTCOMES

### Sociology Research and Evidence

Although largely absent from the economics of education literature, sociologists have undertaken efforts to research the relationship between family inputs and student outcomes. Coleman, as a sociologist, once again played a significant role in shaping the field. In particular, in a well-known 1988 *American Journal of Sociology* study, he developed the concept of social capital. Social capital refers to an individual's network of personal relationships and the social norms that govern them. Coleman argued that human capital and social capital often complement each other. For instance, children may have access to their parents' human capital, but if their parents are not part of their lives, then their parents' stock of human capital becomes irrelevant. Echoing the conclusions he drew from the Coleman Report, he noted in the study that the "physical presence of adults in the family" and "attention given by the adults to the child" play a vital role in the child's educational outcomes (p. S111). Coleman specifically raised the issue of family structure using data from *High School and Beyond*, a nationally representative sample of 10th and 12th graders in the 1980s to demonstrate empirically the increased high school dropout rates of students from single-parent families compared to those of students from two-parent families.

Sociologists have since been prolific at considering the influence of family structure on children's life trajectories. Though this scholarship has not examined the issue from an education production function framework, the insights are critical to understanding the role of family inputs on the lives of children. Demographers have dubbed the period beginning in the 1960s when fertility and marriage rates declined while divorce rates and the prevalence of nonmarital births increased the Second Demographic Transition (McLanahan, 2004). Many sociologists have studied these shifts, documenting a bifurcation in the childhood experiences of individuals who grew up in intact families—that is, families in which the child's biological mother and father were married to each other since his or her birth—and children who did not grow up in intact families.

An extensive literature documents the diverging life trajectories of children who grow up in intact families compared to those who do not. For example, perhaps corroborating Becker's theories about the advantage of dual incomes in two-parent homes, children who grow up in intact families are less likely to be in poverty (Lopoo & DeLeire, 2014; McLanahan, 2004; McLanahan & Jacobsen, 2015). The income advantage along with the larger capacity to invest time in their children potentially contributes to differences in performance at school. Some evidence suggests that children from single-parent homes are more often tardy to or absent from school (Dronkers, Veerman, & Pong, 2017; Wallerstein, Lewis, & Rosenthal, 2013). Scores on standardized achievement tests and school grades are higher for students who grow up in intact families (Cavanagh, Schiller, & Riegle-Crumb, 2006; De Lange, Dronkers, & Wolbers, 2014; Dronkers et al., 2017; Pong, 1998).

In addition, children from intact families are less likely to experience low self-esteem, depression, weaker emotional bonds with their parents, child abuse, and externalizing behavioral problems compared to other children (Amato, 2005, 2010; Amato & Keith, 1991; Astone & McLanahan, 1991; Cavanagh & Huston, 2006; Jarvis, Otero, Poff, Dufur, & Pribesh, 2021; McLanahan, Tach, & Schneider, 2013; Sedlak et al., 2010; Turney & Goodsell, 2018). These differences, together with the extensive research documenting strong positive correlations between social and emotional health and educational success, suggest that the relationship between family structure and educational outcomes might be partly mediated by the child's social and emotional health (Almlund, Duckworth, Heckman, & Kautz, 2011; Corcoran, Cheung, Kim, & Xie, 2018).

Lower achievement as measured by school grades and standardized test scores eventually leads to lower levels of educational attainment. Indeed, numerous studies find that children who grow up in intact families are more likely to complete high school, attend college, and graduate from college (Amato, 2010; Bernardi & Boertien, 2017; Doherty, Willoughby, & Wilde, 2015; McLanahan et al., 2013). Data from the National Longitudinal Study of Adolescent Health, for instance, suggest that among children with college-educated mothers, those who grew up with a single parent or with a stepparent are 40% to 60% less likely to graduate from college compared to those who grew up with both of their biological parents (Wilcox & Stokes, 2015).

Though the already cited research from attachment theory suggests otherwise, we must acknowledge that some research indicates that links between family structure and educational attainment may be heterogeneous. Kearney and Levine (2017) find evidence that the divergence in educational attainment between children from intact families and those from non-intact families is smallest for the lowest- and highest-income families. To explain this U-shaped curve, they theorize that benefits of growing up in an intact family are not great enough to matter for the poorest of families, who lack many other resources, and the wealthiest of families, who have access to many other compensating resources.

Given the important link between education and labor-market outcomes (Autor, 2014; Becker, 1964) and the lower educational attainment levels of individuals who did not grow up in intact families, it would not be unreasonable to hypothesize links between family structure and outcomes such as employment and adult earnings.

Indeed, studies relying on longitudinal data demonstrate that adults who grew up in intact families are more likely to be employed, work more hours per week, and have higher incomes compared to adults who did not grow up in intact families (Bloome, 2017; Lerman, Price, & Wilcox, 2017; Lopoo & DeLeire, 2014; Mohanty & Ullah, 2012). Meanwhile, studies have documented the higher propensities of children who do not grow up in intact families to engage in criminal behavior and to be arrested (TenEyck, Knox, & El Sayed, 2021; Harper & McLanahan, 2004).

### Evidence From the Understanding America Study

To illustrate the magnitudes of the differences in outcomes by family structure, we analyzed data from the Understanding America Study (UAS). Administered by the Center for Economic and Social Research at the University of Southern California, the UAS is a nationally representative internet panel of US adults. Using our analytic sample of more than 5,000 adults who responded to the UAS in 2016, we compared respondents who grew up with both biological parents to those who did not along a series of outcome variables: educational attainment, employment status, household income, and positive and negative affect.

Specifically, we first computed the percentage of respondents who grew up in an intact family with a bachelor's degree and the corresponding percentage of respondents who did not grow up in an intact family. We then computed the percentage of respondents in both groups who are currently employed. Next, we divided the sample into household income quartiles. We computed percentage of respondents who grew up in an intact family and the percentage of respondents who did not grow up in an intact family that belonged to each quartile.

Finally, we used a short version of a psychometric scale developed by the Center for Epidemiological Studies that measures depression (Lewinsohn, Seeley, Roberts, & Allen, 1997). Respondents were asked to think about the feelings they experienced in the past week and then to indicate whether they felt the particular way described in each item. For instance, some items asked if the respondent felt happy or enjoyed life while others asked if the respondent felt lonely, sad, or could not get going. We split the seven items into two subscales designed to measure positive and negative affect, respectively, and scaled the scores to have mean equal to zero and standard deviation equal to one. Cronbach's alpha scores for the two subscales was sufficiently high to verify the internal consistency of the subscales ($\alpha = 0.81$ for positive affect and $\alpha = 0.77$ for negative affect). A confirmatory factor analysis procedure demonstrated that all seven items loaded properly onto the two subscales as intended. In our analysis, we compare the standardized measures of positive and negative affect for respondents who grew up in an intact family and respondents who did not.

Figure 1.1 shows the differences in educational attainment and employment by family structure. Whereas more than one-third of respondents who grew up in an intact family earned at least a bachelor's degree, only one-fifth of respondents who did not grow up in an intact family did the same. Employment rates between the two

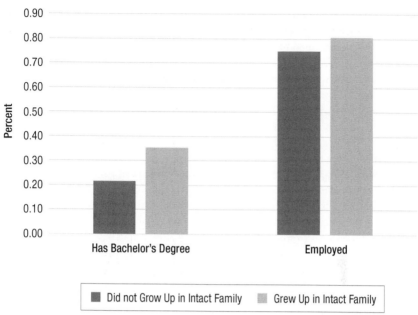

**Figure 1.1.** Educational Attainment and Employment Status by Childhood Family Structure

groups of respondents are less pronounced. About 80% of respondents who grew up with both of their biological parents are employed, a rate 5 percentage points higher than respondents who did not grow up with both of their biological parents.

Figure 1.2 displays the percentage of respondents in each of the four household income quartiles by childhood family structure. Generally, respondents who grew

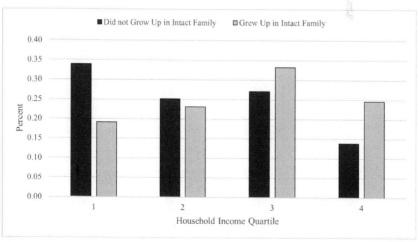

**Figure 1.2.** Household Income by Childhood Family Structure

up in an intact family have higher household incomes as adults. One quarter of these respondents are in the highest household income quartile compared to less than 15% of respondents who did not grow up in an intact family. One-third of respondents who did not grow up in an intact family belong to the lowest household income quartile compared to just under one-fifth of respondents who grew up in an intact family.

Finally, figure 1.3 displays measures of positive and negative affect. Even moving away from labor-market outcomes to consider measures of subjective well-being, we find an advantage for respondents who grew up with both of their biological parents. Positive affect scores for these families are higher than the scores for families who did not grow up with both of their biological parents. The opposite is true for negative affect scores. Growing up with both biological parents is associated with a lower incidence of negative affect as measured by the Center for Epidemiological Studies' depression scale.

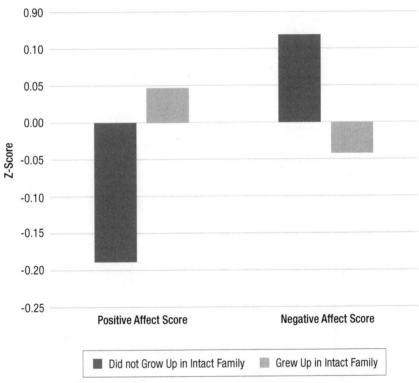

**Figure 1.3.   Positive and Negative Affect by Childhood Family Structure**

## Educational Research on Parent Involvement and Community Engagement

Research in education and school leadership has likewise recognized the important role families play in their children's success in school, though the literature is not as extensive as that in the sociological literature. In particular, educational researchers, teachers, and school leaders have encouraged parental involvement in their child's life at school through a variety of policies and practices. These policies and practices include regular communication about their child's progress, providing educators with professional training about working with families, providing parents with opportunities to make decisions about school policies, including parents with their child's homework or other learning activities, and hosting a variety of community events (Becker & Epstein, 1982; Kessler-Sklar & Baker, 2000). Though not primarily based on randomized-control trials that allow for strong causal inference, educational research consistently finds positive correlations between parent involvement practices and outcomes such as student achievement, student social-emotional development, and positive school climates (Castro et al., 2015; Jeynes, 2007; Kim, Mok, & Seidel, 2020; Park, Stone, & Holloway, 2017; Smith, Sheridan, Kim, Park, & Beretvas, 2020; Tan, Lyu, & Peng, 2020).

Theoretically, increasing parental involvement and community engagement in schools increases the level of social capital in a school community, and indeed there is some evidence for this (Murray, Domina, Petts, Renzulli, & Boylan, 2020; Wilcox, 2018). The social connectedness within a school community, in turn, enables parents to support their children more effectively. Prior research has proposed that these social connections help parents not only access support systems and information from other parents but also enforce community norms and behavioral expectations—all of which are conducive to helping children succeed in school (Carbonaro, 1998; Putnam, 2015).

Other research suggests that intergenerational closure, or the extent to which children, their friends, their parents, and their friends' parents personally know each other, is positively correlated with academic success (Coleman, 1988; Geven & van de Werfhorst, 2020; Rodriguez-Menes & Donato, 2015), though some studies fail to find such correlations (Gamoran, Miller, Fiel, & Valentine, 2011; Geven & van de Werfhorst, 2020; Morgan & Todd, 2009). Further, some research has found that the share of single-parent families within a school is negatively correlated with individual student achievement, and that the relationship is due to relatively lower levels of social capital in schools with higher shares of single-parent families (De Lange, Dronkers, & Wolbers, 2014; Dronkers et al., 2017).

More generally, in their study of intergenerational economic mobility, Chetty, Hendren, Jones, and Porter (2020) find that aside from a lower prevalence of racial bias among White individuals, a higher prevalence of two-parent homes among Blacks has the highest association with smaller Black-White income gaps. As Wilcox (2018) points out, much research understates the impacts of family structure on racial income, achievement, and arrest gaps because it fails to consider neighborhood effects: where single parent homes are dominant, disadvantages in all these areas are magnified, likely in part due to a loss of male role models, as noted by President Obama's quote at the start of this chapter. This fits with a long line of sociological research, and indeed with the entire Chicago School of Sociology regarding how communities and institutions affect the individuals therein (e.g., Wilson, 1987).

Taken together, the sociological, education, and economics literatures suggest that family inputs play a key, independent role alongside school inputs such as finances, teacher quality, and class sizes in children's human capital development and life outcomes. Yet what is the promise of programmatic interventions to increase the support that children receive from their families? In the next section, we review evidence on such interventions.

## EVALUATIONS OF FAMILY SUPPORT INTERVENTIONS

Some research examines family support interventions. A systematic review of 16 clinical trials of programs promoting parent involvement in adolescent depression interventions finds some evidence of success for certain programs, contingent on the nature of the involvement (Dardas, van de Water, & Simmons, 2018). Evaluations based on self-reported surveys found the 32-hour Supporting Father Involvement training program for low-income fathers to substantially reduce couple conflict and reported misbehavior among toddlers and preschool children. Of course, self-reports are not always reliable, and in any event longer-term impacts are uncertain (Pruett, Cowan, Cowan, Gillette, & Pruett, 2019). The same could be said regarding evaluations of the 20-hour TYRO Dads responsible fatherhood training program designed to improve father-child relationships among primarily low-income, nonresidential, and unmarried fathers. A randomized-control evaluation of the program found short-run increases in fathers' satisfaction with parenting and increased time with their children immediately after the program (Kim & Jang, 2018).

A Campbell Collaborate summary reports that although parental support improves school success, school and community-based programs to increase that support have mixed, though generally positive results. They admit that one possible drawback is the inconsistent nature of such programs and their highly varied implementation by schools. Even if such interventions succeed, we may have difficulty identifying why, which particular interventions caused success, and how to replicate them (Nye, Turner, & Schwartz, 2006). Indeed, more recent evaluations of programs designed to offer parenting strategies seem to show little success when taken to scale (Hill et al., 2021). Similarly, an evaluation of a community-based mentoring program for troubled British elementary school students across multiple sites found no impacts (Axford et al., 2021).

On the other hand, programs with very specific goals, such as increasing the number of minutes that parents read to their children through nudges via text messages, seem to have at least short-term impacts (Doss, Fahle, Loeb, & York, 2019). Longer-term impacts have yet to be studied empirically, though concerns and evidence of fade-out have been documented in similar nudge experiments (Bailey, Duncan, Cunha, Foorman, & Yeager, 2020). Additional concerns lie here, because nearly half of parents, disproportionately more disadvantaged parents, turn off nudge technologies; thus, even if they bring academic improvements, they may widen achievement gaps (Bergman, 2019).

One likely possibility is that such interventions may depend on the culture and capacity of the schools or other providers doing the interventions, variables difficult for distant researchers and policy makers to grasp. We suspect that for reasons noted for decades (Lindblom & Cohen, 1979), single interventions are unlikely to have much success, especially because they do not change the underlying habits in a family. Rather, broad school cultures that reinforce particular values on a daily basis and working with parents, including single parents, to reinforce those values, may have considerable success.

Enormous quantitative and qualitative evidence indicates that certain charter schools built around parent and community involvement to reinforce academic values, such as the (recently changed) "Work Hard; Be Nice" slogan at the Knowledge Is Power Program (KIPP) schools, have strong positive effects on student outcomes (Cheng, Hitt, Kisida, & Mills, 2017; Maranto & Shuls, 2011; Maranto & Ritter, 2014; Thernstrom & Thernstrom, 2003). Notably, in charter schools founded by Turkish immigrants to the United States, educators refer to the *triad* of the parent, student, and school, with the understanding that if all work together, the child is guaranteed success. These schools have notable records of success but are severely understudied (Maranto, Franklin, & Camuz, 2014; Maranto, Shakeel, & Rhinesmith, 2018).

## IMPLICATIONS FOR POLICY AND PRACTICE AND FUTURE RESEARCH

To return to a previous theme, attachment theory, we suggest that the more caretaker instability a child endures, the less able that child is to thrive and the more that state interventions are both needed and apt to fail. Further, to repeat Wilson (1987), Coleman (1988), and Wilcox (2018), impacts of family instability are magnified in whole communities where family instability is the norm, and thus children lack role models for stable relationships in childhood and adolescence and upward mobility later. This may explain why, regarding human capital, Asian and Hispanic immigrants, who generally have relatively stable extended family structures and often live in co-ethnic communities where these are the norms, generally have somewhat faster increases in academic achievement than do White and Black students (Shakeel & Peterson, 2021), which is nearly certain to translate into later income gains (Thernstrom & Thernstrom, 2003). Notably, certain African immigrant groups have steeply successful trajectories similar to those of Hispanic and Asian immigrants, likely owing to similar family structures (Hamilton, 2019). Historically, Sowell (1978) documents similar trends among Caribbean immigrants, likely for similar reasons.

We started this chapter with a quote from *Hillbilly Elegy* author J. D. Vance regarding the difficulties, particularly for boys, of negotiating multiple parents with different values, rules, and expectations. If state interventions for achievement and equity are to succeed, we must acknowledge that different levels of resources and commitment may be required for different populations, designated more by levels of stability rather than by income or race, which are more traditional measures of disadvantage.

Quite simply, the more caregivers a child or adolescent has, the more disadvantage he may suffer, reflecting that family instability may disrupt the formation of human capital no matter the income level; though, of course, these disruptions are more likely in low-income communities, no matter their ethnicity (Mayer, 1997; Murray, 2012). In most states, schools already collect caregiver information annually; hence, one could distribute additional funds to schools serving large percentages of children with single caregivers or instability among multiple caregivers. Quite possibly, additional resources could be targeted to schools serving large numbers of relatively unstable families. Notably, any such aid should be targeted to the individual school, because school districts tend to redistribute aid intended for the low-income to wealthier communities, where teachers prefer to teach, and hence, have more senior (and more extensive) staffs, as well as additional funds that parents raise (Roza, 2010).

Yet the continued debate on school finance literature suggests that merely increasing school funding is unlikely to have the sort of impact needed to diminish inequities driven by family instability (Hedges, Laine, & Greenwald, 1994; Hanushek, 1994; Jackson, 2020). Policy makers would also do well to heed particular case studies about broad-based increases in school funding without attention to the incentive structures that currently constrain schools. In *Missouri v. Jenkins* a federal judge *tripled* education spending in the late 1980s and early 1990s to improve education quality and thus integration in Kansas City public schools, as advised by leading education experts. Unfortunately, education experts proved wrong, and the schools remained low performing and segregated, suggesting the limited impacts of additional resources in improving educational equity (Dunn, 2008). Political theorists point to long-standing observations about the interests of budget-maximizing bureaucrats and bureaucratic standard operating procedures that undermine the use of additional resources that productively improve student outcomes (Downs, 1967; Niskanen, 1968). If schools continue to do the same things in the same ways, improvements are unlikely.

Further, if additional funding makes organizations more bureaucratic and complex, with a single child divided multiple ways across numbers of school-level caregivers, this will not help develop the stable bonds likely to foster human and later economic development. Indeed, Maranto and McShane (2012) argue that this tendency explains why large increases in funding have failed to improve schooling, because those increases have expanded specialized staff who may work at cross purposes at worst, and at best not know the whole child. Similarly, a considerable literature including Hess (2017) and Payne (2008) suggests that constant reform in school districts disrupts relationships between educators, in turn making it more difficult for those educators to either hold on to their idealism or better serve students.

As noted in the prior section, a common characteristic of schools that succeed in family unstable communities is high levels of school stability to build and sustain stable schooling relationships with young people who may have unstable home lives. Considerable evidence shows that, particularly for the most disadvantaged students, small schools may foster such relationships, later success in both school attainment and achievement, and later life outcomes (Bloom, Unterman, Zhu, & Reardon, 2020). One possibility is that smaller schools find it easier to cultivate higher levels of social capital that bond people together, in turn impacting students' noncognitive skills. Yet policy innovations exist, generally tied to broader school culture, that can foster success even for students with unstable home lives.

First, some quantitative evidence and enormous qualitative evidence show that looping, having the same teachers for multiple grades in elementary school (Maranto, 2015) or for multiple years and multiple classes in secondary schools (Ouchi, 2009) can increase both achievement and equity, by forging personal relationships between students and teachers, rather than allowing each party to give up on relationships and wait for something better the following year. Indeed, Ouchi notes that elite (and some nonelite) private schools have always operated in this way and finds that school districts in the United States and Canada that have restructured to reduce total student load in order to build faculty-student relationships have had considerable success.

Second, qualitative evidence indicates that reaching out to families through home visits can at least apprise educators of what is going on in the home, increasing the odds that they can work to overcome family instability through more knowledge of students' unique circumstances. This has been found in charter schools (Maranto & Shuls, 2011) and district schools (Middleton & Petitt, 2013).

Third, and related, having a common culture and common language of discipline within a school can ease transitions of students who now often must learn a new language and new set of rules in each classroom, a process particularly difficult for boys (Maranto, Franklin, & Camuz, 2014; Maranto & Shuls, 2011).

In short, where caregiver instability renders attachment and development difficult, schools can help fill the gaps. We need a robust research agenda, focusing on successful schools, to better understand how these innovations work in practice and how through either more school choice to create more institutions, or by reforming existing institutions, we can strengthen human attachments in schools, to compensate at least partly for less stable attachments in the household (Mayer, 1997; Murray, 2012).

# REFERENCES

Ainsworth, M. (1967). *Infancy in Uganda*. Baltimore: Johns Hopkins.

Ainsworth, M., & Bowlby, J. (1965). *Childcare and the growth of love*. London: Penguin.

Akerlof, G. A., Yellen, J. L., & Katz, M. L. (1996). An analysis of out-of-wedlock childbearing in the United States. *Quarterly Journal of Economics, 111*(2), 277–317. https://doi.org/10.2307/2946680

Almlund, M., Duckworth, A. L., Heckman, J. J., Kautz, T. D. (2011). Personality psychology and economics. In E. Hanushek, S. Machin, & L. Woessmann (Eds.), *Handbook of the economics of education* (Vol. 4, pp. 1–181). Amsterdam: Elsevier.

Amato, P. R. (2005). The impact of family formation change on the cognitive, social, and emotional well-being of the next generation. *Future of Children, 15*(2), 75–96.

Amato, P. R. (2010). Research on divorce: Continuing trends and new developments. *Journal of Marriage and Family, 72*(3), 650–666.

Amato, P. R., & Keith, B. (1991). Consequences of parental divorce for children's well-being: A meta-analysis. *Psychological Bulletin, 10*, 26–46.

Astone, N. M., & McLanahan, S. S. (1991). Family structure, parental practices, and high school completion. *American Sociological Review, 56*, 309–320.

Autor, D. H. (2014). Skills, education, and the rise of earnings inequality among the "other 99 percent." *Science, 344*(6186), 843–851.

Axford, N., Bjornstad, G., Matthews, J., Whybra, L., Berry, V., Ukoumunne, O. C., Hobbs, T., Wrigley, Z., Brook, L., Taylor, R., Eames, T., Kallitsoglou, A., Blower, S., & Warner, G. (2021). The effectiveness of a community-based mentoring program for children aged 5–11 years: Results from a randomized controlled trial. *Prevention Science, 22*(1), 100–112.

Bailey, D. H., Duncan, G. J., Cunha, F., Foorman, B. R., & Yeager, D. S. (2020). Persistence and fade-out of educational-intervention effects: Mechanisms and potential solutions. *Psychological Science in the Public Interest, 21*(2), 55–97.

Becker, G. S. (1964). *Human capital: A theoretical and empirical analysis with special reference to education*. Chicago: University of Chicago Press.

Becker, G. S. (1981). *A treatise on the family*. Cambridge, MA: Harvard University Press.

Becker, G. S. (1994). *Human capital: A theoretical and empirical analysis with special reference to education* (3rd edition). Chicago: University of Chicago Press.

Becker, H. J., & Epstein, J. L. (1982). Parent involvement: A survey of teacher practices. *Elementary School Journal, 83*(2), 85–102.

Bergman, P. (2019). Nudging technology use: Descriptive and experimental evidence from school information systems. *Education Finance and Policy, 15*(4), 623–647.

Bernardi, F., & Boertien, D. (2017). Non-intact families and diverging educational destinies: A decomposition analysis for Germany, Italy, the United Kingdom and the United States. *Social Science Research, 63*, 181–191.

Bernardi, F., & Radl, J. (2014). The long-term consequences of parental divorce for children's educational attainment. *Demographic Research, 30*(61), 1653–1680.

Bloom, H. S., Unterman, R., Zhu, P., & Reardon, S. F. (2020). Lessons from New York City's small schools of choice about high school features that promote graduation for disadvantaged students. *Journal of Policy Analysis and Management, 39*(3), 740–771. https://doi.org/10.1002/pam.22192

Bloome, D. (2017). Childhood family structure and intergenerational income mobility in the United States. *Demography, 54*(2), 541–569.

Campbell, B., & Manning, J. (2018). *The rise of victimhood culture: Microaggressions, safe spaces, and the new culture wars.* New York: Palgrave/Macmillan.

Campbell, D. E., Layman, G. C., & Green, J. C. (2021). *Secular surge: A new fault line in American politics.* New York: Cambridge University Press.

Carbonaro, W. J. (1998). A little help from my friend's parents: Intergenerational closure and educational outcomes. *Sociology of Education, 71,* 295–313.

Castro, M., Expósito-Casas, E., López-Martín, E., Lizasoain, L., Navarro-Asencio, E., & Gaviria, J. (2015). Parental involvement on student academic achievement: A meta-analysis. *Educational Research Review, 14*(1), 33–46.

Cavanagh, S. E., & Huston, A. C. (2006). Family instability and children's early problem behavior. *Social Forces, 85,* 575–605.

Cavanagh, S. E., Schiller, K. S., & Riegle-Crumb, C. (2006). Marital transitions, parenting, and schooling: Exploring the link between family-structure history and adolescents' academic status. *Sociology of Education, 79*(4), 329–354.

Cheng, A., Henderson, M. B., Peterson, P. E., & West, M. R. (2021). Cost-benefit information closes aspiration gaps—if parents think their child is ready for college. *Education Economics, 29*(3), 233–251.

Cheng, A., Hitt, C., Kisida, B., & Mills, J. N. (2017). "No excuses" charter schools: A meta-analysis of the experimental evidence on student achievement. *Journal of School Choice, 11*(2), 209–238.

Chetty, R., Friedman, J. N., & Rockoff, J. E. (2014a). Measuring the impacts of teachers I: Evaluating bias in teacher value-added estimates. *American Economic Review, 104*(9), 2593–2632. https://www.aeaweb.org/articles?id=10.1257/aer.104.9.2593

Chetty, R., Friedman, J. N., & Rockoff, J. E. (2014b). Measuring the impacts of teachers II: Teacher value-added and student outcomes in adulthood. *American Economic Review, 104*(9), 2633–2679. https://doi.org/10.1257/aer.104.9.2633

Chetty, R., Hendren, N., Jones, M. R., & Porter, S. R. (2020). Race and economic opportunity in the United States: An intergenerational perspective. *Quarterly Journal of Economics 135*(2), 711–783.

Coleman, J. S. (1988). Supplement: Organizations and institutions: Sociological and economic approaches to the analysis of social structure: Social capital in the creation of human capital. *American Journal of Sociology, 94,* 95–120. https://www.jstor.org/stable/i329085

Corcoran, R. P., Cheung, A. C. K., Kim, E., & Xie, C. (2018). Effective universal school-based social and emotional learning programs for improving academic achievement: A systematic review and meta-analysis of 50 years of research. *Educational Research Review, 25,* 56–72.

Cortes, K. E., Fricke, H., Loeb, S., Song, D. S., & York, B. N. (2021). Too little or too much? Actionable advice in an early-childhood text messaging experiment. *Education Finance and Policy, 16*(2), 209–232. https://doi.org/10.1162/edfp_a_00304

Cunha, F., & Heckman, J. (2007). The technology of skill formation. *American Economic Review, 97*(2), 31–47.

Dardas, L. A., van de Water, B., & Simmons, L. A. (2018). Parental involvement in adolescent depression interventions: A systematic review of randomized clinical trials. *International Journal of Mental Health Nursing, 27*(2), 555–570.

Deaton, A. (2013). *The great escape: Health, wealth, and the origins of inequality.* Princeton University Press.

De Lange, M., Dronkers, J., & Wolbers, M. H. J. (2014). Single-parent family forms and children's educational performance in a comparative perspective: Effects of school's share of single-parent families. *School Effectiveness and School Improvement, 25*(3), 329–350. https://doi.org/10.1080/09243453.2013.809773

Doherty, W. J., Willoughby, B. J., & Wilde, J. L. (2015). Is the gender gap in college enrollment influenced by nonmarital birth rates and father absence? *Family Relations, 65*(2), 263–274.

Doss, C., Fahle, E. M., Loeb, S., & York, B. N. (2019). More than just a nudge supporting kindergarten parents with differentiated and personalized text messages. *Journal of Human Resources, 54*(3), 567–603.

Downs, A. (1967). *Inside bureaucracy*. Boston: Little, Brown.

Dronkers, J., Veerman, G. M., & Pong, S. (2017). Mechanisms behind the negative influence of single parenthood on school performance: Lower teaching and learning conditions? *Journal of Divorce & Remarriage, 58*(7), 471–486.

Duncan, G. J., & Murnane, R. (Eds.). (2011). *Whither opportunity? Rising inequality, schools, and children's life chances*. New York: Russell Sage Foundation.

Dunn, J. D. (2008). *Complex justice: The case of* Missouri v. Jenkins. Chapel Hill: University of North Carolina Press.

Edin, K., & Kefalas, M. (2005). Unmarried with children. *Contexts, 4*(2), 16–22. https://doi.org/10.1525/ctx.2005.4.2.16

Francesconi, M., & Heckman, J. J. (2016). Child development and parental investment: Introduction. *The Economic Journal, 126*(596), F1–F27.

Gamoran, A., Miller, H. K., Fiel, J. E., & Valentine, J. L. (2011). Social capital and student achievement: An intervention-based test of theory. *Sociology of Education, 94*(4), 294–315.

Geary, Daniel. (2015). *Beyond civil rights: The Moynihan report and its legacy*. Philadelphia: University of Pennsylvania Press.

Geven, S., & van de Werfhorst, H. G. (2020). The role of intergenerational networks in students' school performance in two differentiated educational systems: A comparison of between- and within-individual estimates. *Sociology of Education, 93*(1), 40–64.

Gillborn, D., Warmington, P., & Demack, S. (2017). QuantCrit: Education, policy, "Big Data" and principles for a critical race theory of statistics. *Race Ethnicity and Education, 21*(2), 158–179.

Haidt, J. (2006). *The happiness hypothesis: Finding modern truth in ancient wisdom*. New York: Basic.

Haidt, J. (2012). *The righteous mind: Why good people are divided by politics and religion*. New York: Pantheon.

Hamilton, T. G. (2019). *Immigration and the remaking of Black America*. New York: Russell Sage Foundation.

Hanushek, E. A. (1994). Money might matter somewhere: A response to Hedges, Laine, and Greenwald. *Educational Researcher, 23*(4), 5–8.

Hanushek, E. A., & Rivkin, S. G. (2010). Generalizations about using value-added measures of teacher quality. *American Economic Review, 100*(2), 267–271. http://www.aeaweb.org/articles.php?doi=10.1257/aer.100.2.267

Harper, C. C., & McLanahan, S. S. (2004). Father absence and youth incarceration. *Journal of Research on Adolescence, 14*(3), 369–397. https://doi.org/10.1111/j.1532-7795.2004.00079.x

Haskins, R., & Sawhill, I. V. (2016). The decline of the American family: Can anything be done to stop the damage? *Annals of the American Academy of Political and Social Science, 667*(1), 8–34. https://doi.org/10.1177/0002716216663129

Hedges, L. V., Laine, R. D., & Greenwald, R. (1994). An exchange: Part I: Does money matter? A meta-analysis of studies of the effects of differential school inputs on student outcomes. *Educational Researcher, 23*(3), 5–14. https://www.jstor.org/stable/1177220?refreqid=excelsior%3A57baa9f3941e8c2060acb35245097637&seq=1#metadata_info_tab_contents

Hess, F. M. (2017). *Letters to a young education reformer.* Cambridge, MA: Harvard Education Press.

Hill, Z., Spiegel, M., Gennetian, L., Hamer, K., Brotman, L., & Dawson-McClure, S. (2021). Behavioral economics and parent participation in an evidence-based parenting program at scale. *Prevention Science, 22*, 891–902.

Jackson, C. K. (2020). Does school spending matter? The new literature on an old question. In L. Tach, R. Dunifon, & D. L. Miller (Eds.), *Confronting inequality: How policies and practices shape children's opportunities* (pp. 165–186). American Psychological Association. https://doi.org/10.1037/0000187-008

Jarvis, J. A., Otero, C., Poff, J. M., Dufur, M. J., & Pribesh, S. L. (2021). Family structure and child behavior in the United Kingdom. *Journal of Child and Family Studies.* https://doi.org/10.1007/s10826-021-02159-z

Jeynes, W. H. (2007). The relationship between parental involvement and urban secondary school student academic achievement: A meta-analysis. *Urban Education, 42*(1), 82–110.

Kaufmann, E. (2019, March 18). Americans are divided by their views on race, not race itself. *New York Times.* https://www.nytimes.com/2019/03/18/opinion/race-america-trump.html

Kearney, M. S., & Levine, P. B. (2017). *The economics of non-marital childbearing and the "marriage premium for children"* (Working Paper No. 23230). National Bureau of Economic Research.

Kessler-Sklar, S. L., & Baker, A. J. L. (2000). School district parent involvement policies and programs. *Elementary School Journal, 101*(1), 100–118.

Kim, Y-I., & Jang, S. J. (2018). Final evaluation report: A randomized controlled trial of the effectiveness of a responsible fatherhood program: The case of TYRO dads. *Faculty Publications—Department of World Languages, Sociology & Cultural Studies, 53.*

Kim, Y., Mok, S. Y., & Seidel, T. (2020). Parental influences on immigrant students' achievement-related motivation and achievement: A meta-analysis. *Educational Research Review, 30*(100327), 1–19.

Lerman, R. I., Price, J., & Wilcox, W. B. (2017). Family structure and economic success across the life course. *Marriage & Family Review, 53*(8), 744–758.

Lewinsohn, P. M., Seeley, J. R., Roberts, R. E., & Allen, N. B. (1997). Center for Epidemiological Studies-Depression Scale (CES-D) as a screening instrument for depression among community-residing older adults. *Psychology and Aging, 12*(2), 277–287.

Lindblom, C. E., & Cohen, D. K. (1979). *Usable knowledge: Social science and social problem solving.* New Haven, CT: Yale University Press.

Lopoo, L. M., & DeLeire, T. (2014). Family structure and the economic wellbeing of children in youth and adulthood. *Social Science Research, 43*(C), 30–44. https://pubmed.ncbi.nlm.nih.gov/24267751/

Lukianoff, G., & Haidt, J. (2018). *The coddling of the American mind.* New York: Penguin.

Maranto, R. (2015). Did the teachers destroy the school? Public entrepreneurship as creation and adaptation. *Journal of School Leadership, 25*(1), 69–101.

Maranto, R., & Crouch, M. (2014, April 20). Ignoring an inequality culprit: Single-parent families. *Wall Street Journal.* http://online.wsj.com/news/articles/SB100014240527023036 03904579493612156024266

Maranto, R., Franklin, J., & Camuz, K. (2014). Immigrant advantage: What makes Dove Science Academy fly? In R. A. Fox & N. K. Buchanan (Eds.), *Proud to be different: Ethnocentric niche charter schools in America*, 103–124. Lanham, MD: Rowman & Littlefield Education.

Maranto, R., & McShane, M. Q. (2012). *President Obama and education reform: The personal and the political.* New York: Palgrave/Macmillan.

Maranto, R.,& Ritter, G. (2014). Why KIPP is not corporate: KIPP and social justice. *Journal of School Choice, 8*(2) (April–June), 237–257.

Maranto, R., Shakeel, M. D., and Rhinesmith, E. 2018. Immigrant educational entrepreneurs: Measuring the performance of Turkish-founded charter schools. In C. L. Glenn (Ed.), *Muslim educators in American communities* (pp. 207–220). Charlotte, NC: IAP.

Maranto, R., & Shuls, J. V. (2011). Lessons from KIPP Delta. *Phi Delta Kappan, 93*, 52–56.

Maranto, R., van Raemdonck, D. C., & Vasile, A. (2016). The educational-industrial complex in comparative perspective. *International Journal of Educational Reform, 25*(3), 236–248.

Maranto, R., & Wai, J. (2020). Why intelligence is missing from American education policy and practice, and what can be done about it. *Journal of Intelligence, 8*(1). https://www.mdpi .com/2079-3200/8/1/2/htm

Matysiak, A., Styrc, M., & Vignoli, D. (2014). The educational gradient in marital disruption: A meta-analysis of European research findings. *Population Studies, 68*(2), 197–215.

Mayer, S. E. (1997). *What money can't buy: Family income and children's life chances.* Cambridge, MA: Harvard University Press.

McLanahan, S. (2004). Diverging destinies: How children are faring under the second demographic transition. *Demography, 41*(4), 607–627.

McLanahan, S., & Jacobsen, W. (2015). Diverging destinies revisited. In P. R. Amato, A. Booth, S. M. McHale, & J. Van Hook (Eds.), *Families in an era of increasing inequality: Diverging destinies* (pp. 3–23). New York: Springer.

McLanahan, S., Tach, L., & Schneider, D. (2013). The causal effects of father absence. *Annual Review of Sociology, 39*(1), 399–427.

Mendez, I., & Zamarro, G. (2018). The intergenerational transmission of noncognitive skills and their effect on education and employment outcomes. *Journal of Population Economics, 31*(2), 521–560.

Middleton, K. E., & Petitt, E. A. (2013). *Who cares? Improving public schools through relationships and customer service.* Tucson, AZ: Wheatmark.

Mohanty, M. S., & Ullah, A. (2012). Why does growing up in an intact family during childhood lead to higher earnings during adulthood in the United States? *American Journal of Economics and Sociology, 71*(3), 662–695.

Morgan, S. L., & Todd, J. J. (2009). Intergenerational closure and academic achievement in high school: A new evaluation of Coleman's Conjecture. *Sociology of Education, 82*(3), 267–286.

Moynihan, D. P. (1965). *The Negro family: The case for national action.* Washington, DC: Office of Policy Planning and Research, US Department of Labor.

Murray, B., Domina, T., Petts, A., Renzulli, L., & Boylan, R. (2020). "We're in this together": Bridging and bonding social capital in elementary school PTOs. *American Educational Research Journal, 57*(5), 2210–2244.

Murray, C. A. (2012). *Coming apart: The state of White America, 1960–2010.* New York: Crown.

Niskanen, W. A. (1968). Nonmarket decision making: The peculiar economics of bureaucracy. *American Economic Review, 58*(2), 293–305. JSTOR 1831817

Nye, C., Turner, H., & Schwartz, J. (2006). Approaches to parent involvement for improving the academic performance of elementary school age children. *Campbell Systematic Reviews, 2*(1): 1–49. https://doi.org/10.4073/csr.2006.4

Obama, B. (1995). *Dreams from my father: A story of race and inheritance.* New York: Touchstone.

Oreopoulos, P., & Petronijevic, U. (2019). *The remarkable unresponsiveness of college students to nudging and what we can learn from it* (Working Paper No. 26059). National Bureau of Economic Research.

Ouchi, W. G. (2009). *The secret of TSL: The revolutionary discovery that raises school performance.* New York: Simon & Schuster.

Park, S., Stone, S. I., & Holloway, S. D. (2017). School-based parental involvement as a predictor of achievement and school learning environment: An elementary school-level analysis. *Children and Youth Services Review, 82,* 195–206.

Payne, C. M. (2008). *So much reform, so little change.* Cambridge, MA: Harvard Education Press.

Pearlstein, M. (2011). *From family to collapse to America's decline.* Lanham, MD: Rowman & Littlefield.

Pluckrose, H., & Lindsay, J. (2020). *Cynical theories: How activist scholarship made everything about race, gender, and identity—and why this harms everybody.* Durham, NC: Pitchstone.

Pruett, M. K., Cowan, P. A., Cowan, C. P., Gillette, P., & Pruett, K. D. (2019). Supporting father involvement: An intervention with community and child welfare–referred couples. *Family Relations, 68*(1), 51–67.

Putnam, R. D. (2015). *Our kids: The American dream in crisis.* New York: Simon & Schuster.

Redstone, I., & Villasenor, J. (2020). *Unassailable ideas: How unwritten rules and social media shape discourse in American higher education.* New York: Oxford University Press.

Rodriguez-Menes, J., & Donato, L. (2015). Social capital, social cohesion, and cognitive attainment. In Yaojun Li (Ed.), *The handbook of research methods and applications in social capital* (pp. 324–343). England: Edward Elgar.

Roza, M. (2010). *Educational economics: Where do school funds go?* Washington, DC: Urban Institute.

Sedlak, A. J., Mettenburg, J., Basena, M., Petta, I., McPherson, K., Greene, A., & Li, S. (2010). *Fourth national incidence study of child abuse and neglect (NIS–4): Report to Congress.* Washington, DC: US Department of Health and Human Services, Administration for Children and Families.

Shakeel, M. D., & Peterson, P. E. (2021). *A half century of progress in U.S. student achievement: Agency and Flynn effects; ethnic and SES differences.* Cambridge, MA: Program on Education Policy and Governance, Harvard University.

Smith, T. E., Sheridan, S. M., Kim, E. M., Park, S., & Beretvas, S. N. (2020). The effects of family-school partnership interventions on academic and social-emotional functioning: A meta-analysis exploring what works for whom. *Educational Psychology Review, 32*(2), 511–544.

Sowell, T. (1978). Three Black histories. In T. Sowell (Ed.), *American ethnic groups.* Washington, DC: Urban Institute.

Sweeney, M. M. (2011). Family-structure instability and adolescent educational outcomes: A focus on families with stepfathers. In G. J. Duncan & R. J. Murnane (Eds.), *Whither opportunity? Rising inequality, schools, and children's life chances* (pp. 229–254). New York: Russell Sage Foundation.

Tan, C. Y., Lyu, M., & Peng, B. (2020). Academic benefits from parental involvement are stratified by parental socioeconomic status: A meta-analysis. *Parenting: Science and Practice, 20*(4), 241–287.

TenEyck, M. F., Knox, K. N., & El Sayed, S. A. (2021). Absent father timing and its impact on adolescent and adult criminal behavior. *American Journal of Criminal Justice.*

Therborn, G. (2004). *Between sex and power: Family in the world 1900–2000*. London: Routledge.

Thernstrom, A., & Thernstrom, S. (2003). *No excuses: Closing the racial gap in learning*. New York: Simon & Schuster.

Turney, K., & Goodsell, R. (2018). Parental incarceration and children's wellbeing. *Future of Children, 28*(1), 147–164.

USA Today. (2013). "Obama speaks on importance of fatherhood," February 17, 2013. https://www.usatoday.com/story/theoval/2013/02/17/obama-chicago-fatherhood-econ omy-gun-control/1925727/

Vance, J. D. (2016). *Hillbilly elegy*. New York: HarperCollins.

Wallerstein, J., Lewis, J., & Rosenthal, S. P. (2013). Mothers and their children after divorce: Report from a 25-year longitudinal study. *Psychoanalytic Psychology, 30*(2), 167–184.

Wilcox, W. B. (2018, March 22). For black boys, family structure still matters. *Institute for Family Studies* (blog). https://ifstudies.org/blog/for-black-boys-family-structure-still-matters

Wilcox, W. B., & Stokes, C. E. (2015). The family foundation: What do class and family structure have to do with the transition to adulthood? In P. R. Amato, A. Booth, S. M. McHale, and J. Van Hook (Eds.), *Families in an era of increasing inequality: Diverging destinies* (pp. 147–157). Cham: Springer International.

Williams, J. C. (2017). *White working class: Overcoming class cluelessness in America*. Cambridge, MA: Harvard Business Review.

Wilson, W. J. (1987). *The truly disadvantaged: The inner city, the underclass, and public policy*. Chicago: University of Chicago Press.

Winn, M. T., & Winn, L. T. (2021). *Restorative justice in education: Transforming teaching and learning through the disciplines*. Cambridge, MA: Harvard Education Press.

Zill, N. (2015, February 3). More than 60% of U.S. kids live with two biological parents. *Institute for Family Studies* (blog). https://ifstudies.org/blog/more-than-60-of-u-s-kids-live -with-two-biological-parents

# 2

---

# The Educational Equalizer: Funding Students Instead of Systems

*Corey DeAngelis*

## COVID REVEALED A MASSIVE POWER IMBALANCE IN EDUCATION

The public school system experienced profound difficulties over the past two years with the rise of school closures beginning in March 2020. However, these difficulties are not new. Rather, the COVID-19 pandemic has revealed the fragility of the public school system and K-12 education in America: a massive, long-existing power imbalance between the teachers-union-controlled public-school monopoly and individual families. Even though public schools were closed, imposing high costs on working parents and families (Christakis, Van Cleve, & Zimmerman, 2020; Hawrilenko, Kroshus, Tandon, & Christakis, 2021; Makridis, Piano, & DeAngelis, 2022), they continued to receive funding. In fact, if anything, school districts that went remote have higher revenues per student than their non-remote counterparts (DeAngelis & Makridis, 2022). Cumulatively, these patterns raise fundamental questions about the governance of public schools.

Private schools were fighting to reopen in person from the beginning of the pandemic. Pandey (2021) reported data indicating that only 5% of private schools went virtual in the fall of 2020, whereas 62% of public schools did the same. Henderson, Peterson, and West (2021) conducted a nationally representative survey of American parents with children in K-12 education in November and December 2020 and found that 60% of children in private schools received full-time in-person instruction, whereas only 24% of children in district-run public schools had access to fully in-person instruction. Data from San Diego County, last updated June 15, 2021, indicated that about 66% of private schools provided fully in-person instruction, whereas only 17% of public schools were doing the same.[1] Private schools filed legal cases to push for the right to provide in-person instruction in states such as California,[2] Kentucky,[3] Michigan,[4] Ohio,[5] and Wisconsin.[6] In Sacramento, California, a Catholic private school even rebranded itself as a day care by retraining its employees as child-care workers to get around a closure rule that arbitrarily applied to schools but not day cares.[7]

Public school teachers' unions, however, were fighting for the opposite by moving the reopening goalposts every step of the way. As expected, many influential teachers' unions pushed for more resources, vaccination requirements, and mitigation measures as prerequisites for reopening schools in person. But some of those unions also pushed for unscientific metrics to close schools for in-person instruction. Freedom of Information Act requests uncovered emails revealing that the nation's largest teachers' unions—the American Federation of Teachers and the National Education Association—influenced the Centers for Disease Control and Prevention (CDC) school reopening[8] and masking guidance.[9] The Chicago Teachers Union consistently called for an arbitrary 3% citywide positivity threshold[10] for opening and closing all Chicago Public Schools even though available data consistently demonstrated that community-wide COVID transmission was generally higher than transmission within schools—and that school reopenings were not major contributors to overall community transmission or hospitalizations (Christakis, Van Cleve, & Zimmerman,

1. School Reopening Dashboard. San Diego County Office of Education. Retrieved from https://covid-19.sdcoe.net/Reopening-Plan/School-Reopening-Dashboard#full-time-definition
2. California's school closure rules violated private school families' rights, appeals court rules. *Los Angeles Times*. Retrieved from https://www.latimes.com/california/story/2021-07-23/appeal-court-rules-in-favor-of-private-school-families
3. *Danville Christian Academy, Inc., et al v. Andy Beshear, Governor of Kentucky*. Supreme Court of the United States. Retrieved from https://www.supremecourt.gov/opinions/20pdf/20a96_e29g.pdf
4. Justice Department backs Michigan private schools in virus challenge. *U.S. News & World Report*. Retrieved from https://www.usnews.com/news/best-states/michigan/articles/2020-12-11/justice-department-backs-private-schoolsin-virus-challenge
5. Monclova Christian Academy; St. John's Jesuit High School & Academy; Emmanuel Christian School; Citizens for Community Values dba Ohio Christian Education Network v. Toledo-Lucas County Health Department. United States Court of Appeals for the Sixth Circuit. Retrieved from https://www.opn.ca6.uscourts.gov/opinions.pdf/20a0392p06.pdf
6. WI Supreme Court rules order to close Dane Co. schools was illegal. WKOW. Retrieved from https://www.wkow.com/news/politics/wi-supreme-court-rules-order-to-close-dane-co-schools-was-illegal/article_d20da8e9-8f37-56ef-9579-cd247d7ce382.html
7. Sacramento County must stop Capital Christian School's coronavirus "day care" stunt. *Sacramento Bee*. Retrieved from https://www.sacbee.com/opinion/editorials/article245037380.html
8. CDC Still Getting Interference. This Time From Teachers. Bloomberg Opinion. Retrieved from https://www.bloomberg.com/opinion/articles/2021-05-04/cdc-emails-with-teachers-union-show-politics-still-trump-science
9. CDC tightened masking guidelines after threats from teachers' union, emails show. Fox News. Retrieved from https://www.foxnews.com/politics/cdc-tightened-masking-guidelines-after-threats-from-teachers-union
10. Among the Chicago Teachers Union's demands: no to 'simultaneous instruction.' Chalkbeat Chicago. Retrieved from https://chicago.chalkbeat.org/2020/12/10/22168797/among-the-chicago-teachers-unions-demands-no-to-simultaneous-instruction

2020; Harris, Ziedan, & Hassig, 2021; Honein, Barrios, & Brooks, 2021; Oster, 2020; Oster, Jack, Halloran, Schoof, & McLeod, 2021; UNICEF, 2020).

Honein et al. (2021) concluded that "the preponderance of available evidence from the fall school semester has been reassuring insofar as the type of rapid spread that was frequently observed in congregate living facilities or high-density worksites has not been reported in education settings in schools" and that "there has been little evidence that schools have contributed meaningfully to increased community transmission." UNICEF (2020) reported that "data from 191 counties collected from February to September 2020 show no consistent association between school reopening status and COVID-19 infection rates." Zimmerman et al. (2021) examined data from 11 school districts in North Carolina and found that "no instances of child-to-adult transmission of SARS-CoV-2 were reported within schools."

Teachers' unions also gave away the game by lumping unrelated political demands in their school reopening plans. The Los Angeles teachers' union, for example, called for a wealth tax, Medicare for All, and a ban on their competitors—public charter schools—in their report on safely reopening schools.[11] On at least two occasions, at least a dozen major teachers' unions joined with the Democratic Socialists of America[12] at "National Day of Resistance" rallies to "Demand Safe Schools." The list of demands included more federal funding, police-free schools, rent cancellation, and a ban on new public charter schools. The public-school monopoly sought to protect itself from the get-go. Just as school closures started in March 2020, unions in states such as Pennsylvania[13] and Oregon lobbied to make it illegal for families to switch their children to virtual public charter schools. In March 2020, for example, the *Wall Street Journal* editorial board reported[14] that about 1,600 students were blocked from transferring to Oregon Connections Academy in just a few days because the teachers "unions were alarmed by this mass exodus from the public schools."

## POLITICIZATION OF PUBLIC SCHOOL COVID-19 RESPONSES

The teachers' unions regularly engaged in over-the-top rhetoric in their calls to keep schools closed for in-person instruction. The Chicago Teachers Union, for example, in December 2020 posted a now-deleted tweet claiming that "the push

---

11. The Same Storm, but Different Boats: The Safe and Equitable Conditions for Starting LAUSD in 2020-21. United Teachers Los Angeles. Retrieved from https://www.utla.net/sites/default/files/samestorm diffboats_final.pdf

12. Teachers' unions make the case for school choice. National Review. Retrieved from https://www.nationalreview.com/2021/02/teachers-unions-make-the-case-for-school-choice/

13. Pa. must fund students, not school districts. *Philadelphia Inquirer*. Retrieved from https://www.inquirer.com/opinion/commentary/philadelphia-virtual-learning-school-choice-coronavirus-pandemic-20200902.html

14. Oregon's Coronavirus Education Lockdown. *Wall Street Journal*. Retrieved from https://www.wsj.com/articles/oregons-coronavirus-education-lockdown-11585697080

to reopen schools is rooted in sexism, racism and misogyny."[15] The same union also threatened to strike and even posted an interpretative dance video to protest reopening schools in person. Washington, DC, public school employees lined up fake body bags outside of the school system's offices in July 2020 to protest a partial in-person reopening. New York City teachers took to the streets in fall 2020 to "demand safe schools" with props such as a fake coffin and guillotine. The Florida Education Association filed a lawsuit against Governor Ron DeSantis to prevent school reopenings in summer 2020, and the Miami-Dade teachers union organized a caravan including a hearse to protest reopening schools in fall 2020. An Arizona teachers' union encouraged its members to send fake obituaries and epitaphs to Governor Doug Ducey to protest reopening schools in fall 2020. The hypocrisy from politicians and union officials seemed endless. A Chicago Teachers Union board member, for example, was caught vacationing in Puerto Rico while fighting against going back to work in person. The president of the Berkeley teachers' union was caught sending his child to in-person preschool while opposing his members returning to work in person.

The differing responses to the pandemic by school sector does not mean that people in the private sector are necessarily more competent or well-intentioned. Instead, the main difference is one of incentives. One of these sectors received children's education dollars regardless of whether they opened their doors for business. Private schools fought to reopen not because of more altruistic motivations or greater levels of competence, but because their leaders understood that their customers could vote with their feet if the benefits of the services rendered did not justify the costs of tuition and fees. In fact, Hartney and Finger (2021) examined nationwide data and found that public school districts in counties with more Catholic private schools were more likely to reopen in person, suggesting competitive pressures had something to do with school reopening decisions. Scafidi, Tutterow, and Kavanagh (2021) conducted a multistate survey and found that private schools were more likely to experience enrollment increases in areas with a higher proportion of public-school districts that were closed for in-person instruction, suggesting that families, indeed, provided competitive pressures by voting with their feet. Dee, Huffaker, Phillips, and Sagara (2021) found that public schools that kept their doors closed for in-person instruction experienced a 42% larger loss in enrollment that those that offered in-person learning. Flanders (2021) similarly found that public school districts in Wisconsin that implemented virtual instruction in 2020 experienced the largest enrollment declines. Musaddiq, Stange, Bacher-Hicks, and Goodman (2021) also found that Michigan private schools in areas with a higher proportion of closed public school districts experienced greater enrollment increases.

---

15. Editorial: CTU and embarrassing conduct. When will teachers rise up? *Chicago Tribune*. Retrieved from https://www.chicagotribune.com/opinion/editorials/ct-editorial-ctu-covid19-misogyny-tweet-cps-20201214-ir27n2x425gixofp64ptqemtby-story.html

## INCENTIVES IN THE GOVERNANCE
## OF PUBLIC AND PRIVATE SCHOOLS

It's not just that the public-school employees understood that they could keep their benefits the same in terms of job security and pay without providing full-time in-person services. The incentive structure was more problematic than that. Teachers' unions could leverage the state of disorder and hold children's educations hostage to lobby for more taxpayer resources. And that strategy apparently worked. Congress has allocated about $190 billion in COVID "relief" to K-12 education since March 2020—and most of the funding was not contingent upon reopening schools in person. In fact, Missouri senator Roy Blunt introduced an amendment to the American Rescue Plan that would have made this federal relief funding conditional upon reopening schools in person if all teachers were vaccinated, but the amendment failed with a 50-50 vote strictly along party lines. In general, underperforming private schools shut down. Underperforming district schools get more money. Again, this is not a problem with the employees within the public school system. It is a problem with the perverse set of incentives that is baked into the system itself.

At least six studies have found that public school districts in areas with stronger teachers' unions were substantially less likely to reopen in person in 2020 (DeAngelis & Makridis, 2021; Flanders, 2020; Grossman, Reckhow, Strunk, & Turner, 2021; Harris, Ziedan, & Hassig, 2021; Hartney & Finger, 2021; Marianno, Hemphill, & Loures-Elias, 2022). DeAngelis and Makridis (2021), for example, analyzed data on school reopening decisions for more than 800 public school districts provided by Education Week and for more than 10,000 public school districts provided by MCH Strategic Data.

The study found that school districts in states without right-to-work laws were about 11 percentage points less likely to fully reopen in person, a 44% reduction relative to the sample mean. In addition, the study found that a 10% rise in union workers at the county level and a 10% increase in union power—as measured by Fordham Institute's state ranking of teachers' union strength—were both associated with around a 1 percentage point decline in the probability of public schools reopening in person. In addition, some studies found that school reopening decisions were related to political partisanship but generally unrelated to COVID risk as measured by cases and deaths per capita (DeAngelis & Makridis, 2021; Flanders, 2020; Hartney & Finger, 2021; Valant, 2020) and per-student funding (DeAngelis & Makridis, 2022). The main takeaway is that the school reopening debate was more about politics and power than safety concerns and the needs of millions of families.

## EMPOWERING FAMILIES AND IMPROVING OUTCOMES

The traditional district-run public school system holds substantial monopoly power because of residential assignment and compulsory funding through property taxes

(DeAngelis & Holmes Erickson, 2018; Friedman, 1955). If a family is unhappy with the education services their residentially assigned public school provided, they generally only have a few costly or ineffective options. That family could (1) move to a residence that is assigned to a better district-run school, (2) pay out of pocket for private school tuition and fees in addition to paying for the unused public school through property taxes, (3) pay the financial and opportunity costs associated with homeschooling, or (4) advocate for change at the local school board meeting and vote for school board leaders who will push for the policies the family prefers.

Because each of these options is ineffective or costly, especially for the least advantaged in society, residentially assigned public schools can fail to meet the needs of many families without facing real bottom-up accountability through the threat of exit. These assignments are tantamount to forcing people to move houses or eat at a restaurant—and pay the rent and bill though not receiving the services. Those high transaction costs associated with voting with your feet would provide the residentially assigned option little incentive to cater to your needs.

The only way to truly hold schools accountable is to fund students directly and empower families to choose the education provider that best meets their children's needs. Funding students directly would give public schools incentives to cater to the needs of families, not the other way around. In fact, 25 of 27 studies on the topic (e.g., Chakrabarti, 2008; Egalite & Mills, 2021; Figlio, Hart, & Karbownik, 2021; Rouse, Hannaway, Goldhaber, & Figlio, 2013) find statistically significant positive effects of private school choice competition on student outcomes in public schools (EdChoice, 2021). Egalite (2013) similarly found that 20 of the 21 existing studies on the topic at the time showed positive effects of private school choice competition on public school student outcomes. The most comprehensive meta-analysis of the evidence similarly found "small positive effects of competition on student achievement" overall (Jabbar et al., 2019). Figlio et al. (2021), for example, found that scaling up Florida's private school choice program had positive effects on public school students' test scores, attendance, and behavior.

The majority of the 17 random assignment studies on the topic (e.g., Barnard, Frangakis, Hill, & Rubin, 2003; Cowen, 2008; Greene, 2001; Greene, Peterson, & Du, 1999; Howell, Wolf, Campbell, & Peterson, 2002; Rouse, 1998; Wolf et al., 2013) find that winning a lottery to attend a private school using a school choice program leads to higher math or reading test scores overall and for subgroups of students (EdChoice, 2021). The latest, most comprehensive peer-review meta-analysis on the subject finds, in addition, that funding students directly generally improved test scores. Shakeel, Anderson, and Wolf (2021) estimated that winning a lottery to access a private school in the United States increased math and reading achievement by 4.3% to 4.7% of a standard deviation, respectively. Betts and Tang (2019) performed a comprehensive systematic review and meta-analysis of 38 rigorous studies and found that, overall, access to public charter schools increased reading achievement by 2% of a standard deviation and increased math achievement by 3.3% of a standard deviation.

The non-test-score outcomes are generally more favorable than the results for test scores, perhaps because school quality is multidimensional, and parents also care about other factors such as school safety, curriculum, transparency, mission, and values (Bedrick & Burke, 2018; Catt & Rhinesmith, 2017; Holmes Erickson, 2017; Kelly & Scafidi, 2013). For example, 28 of 30 studies on the subject find that funding students directly is associated with higher levels of satisfaction (EdChoice, 2021). Rhinesmith (2017) reviewed this evidence and similarly concluded that each of the 19 studies found positive effects of funding students directly on satisfaction. Schwalbach and DeAngelis (2020) found 11 rigorous studies linking access to private schooling to reports of school safety, and each found positive results. Each of the six peer-reviewed studies on the topic find that public and private school choice is associated with reductions in criminal activity (DeAngelis & Wolf, 2019, 2020; Deming, 2011; Dills & Hernández-Julián, 2011; Dobbie & Fryer, 2015; McEachin Lauen, Fuller, & Perera, 2020).

Multiple reviews of the evidence have also found that funding students directly is generally associated with improvements in civic outcomes such as tolerance of others, political participation, and civic knowledge (DeAngelis, 2017; EdChoice, 2021; Wolf, 2007). When possible, future research should examine the link between funding students directly and other nonacademic outcomes that are largely unexplored such as employment, earnings, happiness, family structure, and mental health (e.g., DeAngelis & Dills, 2021).

## UNDERSTANDING THE INCENTIVES BEHIND FUNDING STUDENTS, NOT SYSTEMS

Taxpayers already fund students directly when it comes to initiatives such as Pell Grants and the GI Bill for higher education. The money goes to students who can choose to spend the funding at the higher education provider of their choosing. The students can choose to take their taxpayer-funded Pell Grant dollars to the nearby community college if they want, but they can also choose to use it at a public or private (religious or nonreligious) university. The same goes for many taxpayer-funded pre-K initiatives such as the federal Head Start program, as well as other industries, including food stamps, Medicaid, and Section 8 housing vouchers. Most people would find it absurd to force low-income families to spend their taxpayer-funded food stamp dollars at a residentially assigned government-run grocery store. Instead, families can spend those dollars at the grocery provider of their choosing, whether it be Walmart, Safeway, Trader Joe's, or just about any other grocery store that meets their needs. With each of these initiatives, the funding follows the decision of student or the family. We should apply the same logic to K-12 education and fund students instead of systems.

And yet, many of the people who support funding individuals as opposed to institutions in all these other domains are only opposed when it comes to the in-between years of K-12 education. This raises an important question: why would anyone support funding people instead of buildings for everything else except K-12 education? The only way to bridge that apparent logical inconsistency is to understand the difference in power dynamics. Choice is the norm in higher education, pre-K, and just about every other industry, but choice threatens an entrenched special interest—the teachers' unions—when it comes to the in-between years of K-12 education. This entrenched special interest fights as hard as possible against any change to the status quo that might threaten their monopoly on taxpayer funding for K-12 education.

The teachers' union seeks to protect itself at the expense of families year after year—and their main argument against allowing the funding to follow the child reveals their desire to limit access to their competition. Opponents of funding students directly repeat the argument that it would "defund public schools." But the money doesn't belong to the public schools in the first place (DeAngelis & McCluskey, 2020). Education funding is meant for educating children—not for propping up and protecting a particular institution. School choice doesn't defund public schools. If anything, public schools in the current system defund families. School choice initiatives simply return the funding to the rightful owners—or at least the intended beneficiaries.

No one would argue that allowing families to choose their grocery store "defunds" Walmart. That's because we all understand that a family's grocery dollars, including their food stamp dollars, do not belong to Walmart, Safeway, or any other grocery provider. Pell grants similarly do not "defund" community colleges just because students have the choice to take the funding to a private university. Medicaid similarly does not "defund" government-run hospitals just because people can choose to take the money to private hospitals.

The establishment's primary argument against funding students directly also raises an important question: why would giving families a choice "defund" public schools? Defenders of the public-school monopoly can only respond to that question in one of two ways, both of which only further tarnish their position. The obvious response is that public schools will only lose funding if families voluntarily choose to take their children's taxpayer-funded education dollars elsewhere. With this response, the status quo is essentially admitting that they are well aware of the fact that many families are not happy with the services provided in their public schools. In other words, school choice does not "defund" public schools—if anything, public schools defund themselves when they fail to meet the needs of families year after year. That they understand families would flee when given the opportunity to choose another educational option is an argument for school choice, not against it. The children of low-income families should not be trapped in government-run schools for 13 years without exit options just to protect those institutions. Even in the case of the expansion of right-to-work laws, which led to a decline in union density, well-being among union workers increased, in part because unions were forced to become more competitive and deliver greater value to their members (Makridis, 2020).

The second response that the status quo can offer to my rhetorical question is that they believe low-income families would only choose alternative options because they were tricked into doing so—that these families do not have the capacity to understand that the alternatives are inferior to their child's residentially assigned public school. This is the paternalistic argument against choice—and opponents of educational freedom often do not say the quiet part out loud because of how elitist it sounds. The other problem with this view is that parents generally know and care more about their children's education needs than bureaucrats sitting in offices hundreds of miles away. Parents, in general, have more on-the-ground knowledge about their children's needs—and they have stronger incentives to get decisions right about their education—than just about anyone else.

The argument that funding students directly "defunds" public schools is further weakened by the fact that public schools are only partially funded based on enrollment counts[16]—and because these programs are generally funded at a fraction of what would have been spent per student in the public schools. It is true that public schools lose some funding when they lose students to their competition. However, because public schools only lose a fraction of the funding associated with educating students after they leave their institution, they benefit financially on a per-student basis. Data from the US Census Bureau (2019) indicate that public schools spent more than $15,000 per student in 2019. Imagine that a public school loses half of that funding—or $7,500—when a family chooses to send a child to a private school. Mathematically, the public school must end up with higher levels of funding for each student who remains in their institution. Imagine if Walmart were able to keep half of your grocery bill in perpetuity, even after you started shopping at Trader Joe's. That would be a great deal for Walmart. Public schools are getting a great deal as well because they are able to keep thousands of dollars for students they no longer educate.

The public-school closures during the pandemic highlighted inequities existing in the current system. More-advantaged families were more likely to have access to in-person public schools and to have the resources necessary to have their children access an in-person education with private schools, "pandemic pods," and "microschools." Agostinelli, Doepke, Sorrenti, and Zilibotti (2020), for example, found that "school closures have a large and persistent effect on educational outcomes that is highly unequal" and that "high school students from poor neighborhoods suffer a learning loss of 0.4 standard deviations, whereas children from rich neighborhoods remain unscathed." Hawrilenko et al. (2021) similarly found that "attending school remotely during the COVID-19 pandemic was associated with disproportionate mental health consequences for older and Black and Hispanic children as well as children from families with lower income." Just as school closures disproportionately harmed the least-advantaged families, fighting against funding students directly

---

16. Student-based allocation. Edunomics Lab at Georgetown University. Retrieved from https://edunomicslab.org/our-research/student-based-allocations/

disproportionately prevents low-income families from accessing educational options. The most-advantaged families already have "school choice." These families are at least more likely to have the resources to afford private alternatives. Funding students directly allows more families to access educational options. In this sense, school choice is an equalizer. At the same time, funding students directly gives public schools stronger incentives to cater to the needs of students, leading to improvements across the board (EdChoice, 2021; Egalite, 2013; Jabbar et al., 2019). As shown in table 2.1, 25 of 27 studies on the topic find that private school choice competition improves outcomes in public schools.

**Table 2.1. The Effect of Private-School Choice on Math and Reading Test Scores**

| Study | Location | Result |
|---|---|---|
| Greene & Forster (2002) | Milwaukee, WI | + |
| Hoxby (2002) | Milwaukee, WI | + |
| Carnoy et al. (2007) | Milwaukee, WI | + |
| Chakrabarti (2008) | Milwaukee, WI | + |
| Greene & Marsh (2009) | Milwaukee, WI | + |
| Mader (2010) | Milwaukee, WI | + |
| Greene & Winters (2007) | Washington, DC | + |
| Gray, Merrifield, & Adzima (2016) | San Antonio, TX | + |
| Greene & Forster (2002) | San Antonio, TX | + |
| Egalite & Catt (2020) | Indiana | + |
| Egalite & Mills (2021) | Louisiana | + |
| Forster (2008) | Ohio | + |
| Carr (2011) | Ohio | + |
| Figlio & Karbownik (2016) | Ohio | + |
| Hammons (2002) | Maine | + |
| Hammons (2002) | Vermont | + |
| Greene (2001) | Florida | + |
| Figlio & Rouse (2006) | Florida | + |
| West & Peterson (2006) | Florida | + |
| Forster (2008) | Florida | + |
| Winters & Greene (2011) | Florida | + |
| Chakrabarti (2013) | Florida | + |
| Rouse et al. (2013) | Florida | + |
| Figlio & Hart (2014) | Florida | + |
| Figlio et al. (2021) | Florida | + |
| Bowen & Trivitt (2014) | Florida | − |
| Greene & Winters (2004) | Florida | Null |

*Notes:* A "+" means that the study found any positive effects of private-school choice on outcomes in public schools. A "−" means that the study found any negative effects of private-school choice on outcomes in public schools. "Null" means that the study did not find statistically significant effects of private-school choice on outcomes in public schools. These studies can be found at https://www.edchoice.org/wp-content/uploads/2021/04/2021-123s-SlideShare_FINAL.pdf

## IMPLEMENTABLE STATE POLICY RECOMMENDATIONS

Policy makers can empower families by allowing their children's taxpayer-funded education dollars to go to education providers of their choosing. The gold-standard solution is an "education savings account program." The child's state-level taxpayer-funded education dollars would follow him to a family-directed education savings account.[17] The funding could be used to cover any approved education expenses including private school tuition and fees, tutoring, instructional materials, online courses, and special needs educational therapies. The full amount of funding could also follow the child to his assigned public school if his parents choose that default option. This solution is the purest form of funding students instead of systems, and it allows families to customize the education that best meets the needs of their children.

Policy makers could also implement private school vouchers, but these programs generally only allow the funding to cover private school tuition and fees.[18] Policy makers could, in addition, implement education savings accounts and scholarships funded via tax credits.[19] Individuals and organizations would receive a tax credit for donating funding to scholarship granting organizations. Eligible families would then be able to apply for the funding from the scholarship granting organization to cover private school tuition or other approved K-12 education expenses.

## K-12 EDUCATION'S NEW SPECIAL INTEREST

Teachers' unions overplayed their hand, showed their true colors, and awakened a sleeping giant: parents who want more of a say in their children's education. The latest RealClear Opinion Research polling found that support for funding students directly surged by 8 percentage points among registered voters nationwide—from 64% support in April 2020 to 72% support in February 2022.[20] This support for school choice notably jumped 9 percentage points among Democrats. Another national survey conducted in 2021 by Morning Consult similarly found that 78% of American adults overall—and 84% of school parents—support education savings account programs that allow families to take their children's taxpayer-funded education dollars to the education providers of their choosing.[21] It appears that families

---

17. Education Savings Accounts (ESAs). EdChoice. Retrieved from https://www.edchoice.org/school-choice/types-of-school-choice/education-savings-account/

18. School Vouchers. EdChoice. Retrieved from https://www.edchoice.org/school-choice/types-of-school-choice/what-are-school-vouchers-2/

19. Tax-Credit Education Savings Accounts (ESAs). EdChoice. Retrieved from https://www.edchoice.org/what-is-a-tax-credit-education-savings-account/

20. New Poll: Overwhelming Support for School Choice. American Federation for Children. Retrieved from https://www.federationforchildren.org/new-poll-72-support-for-school-choice/

21. The Top 10 Findings from EdChoice's 2021 Schooling in America Survey. EdChoice. Retrieved from https://www.edchoice.org/engage/the-top-10-findings-from-edchoices-2021-schooling-in-america-survey/

are finally figuring out there isn't any good reason to fund systems when we can fund students directly instead.

This past year, 2021, has also been named the "Year of School Choice" because of the historic legislative victories at the state level. Nineteen states enacted or expanded programs to fund students instead of systems in 2021, and the number of states with education savings accounts—the gold standard of funding K-12 students directly—doubled from 5 to 10 states in the same year.[22] The victories in many states were also substantial in size and scope. West Virginia, for example, did not have any public charter schools or private school choice programs in 2020. However, in 2021, West Virginia passed the most expansive education savings account program in the nation, allowing nearly all families—regardless of income—to take their children's state education dollars to the education providers of their choosing. Bedrick and Tarnowski (2021) estimated that these state-level expansions in 2021 will increase the number of additional eligible students by about 4.4 million—and that the maximum allowable participation in these programs will grow by about 1.6 million students.

Families voted with their feet for public charter schools and homeschooling. Veney and Jacobs (2021) examined data from 41 states and the District of Columbia and found that enrollment in district-run schools dropped by about 1.5 million students, a 3.3% drop, from school years 2019–20 to 2020–21. On the other hand, the data revealed that enrollment in public charter schools increased by about 240,000 students, a 7.1% increase, in the same locations over the same period. Similarly, the US Census Bureau's (2021) nationwide American Pulse Survey found that homeschooling more than doubled over the pandemic period with the proportion of households reporting homeschooling at least one child increasing from 5.4% in 2019–20 to 11.1% in 2020–21. Further, the expansion of homeschooling was in large part a causal result of the expansion of remote schooling (Makridis, Piano, & DeAngelis, 2022).

Many families felt powerless when it came to their children's education in 2020. Parents are now paying attention—and they will push to make sure they don't feel powerless like they did in 2020 ever again. Parents are voicing their opinions at local school board meetings in an attempt to hold the system democratically accountable. But in an apparent attempt to avoid democratic accountability, the National School Boards Association (NSBA)—after coordinating with the White House—sent a letter to the US Department of Justice on September 29, 2021, comparing some parents to domestic terrorists.[23] This supposed plan backfired, however, and only further emboldened parents to hold their children's schools accountable. In less than three months after that letter was sent, 18 state-level school boards associations decided to discontinue NSBA membership, participation, and/

---

22. School choice victories. American Federation for Children. Retrieved from https://www.federation forchildren.org/school-choice-victories/

23. NSBA coordinated with White House, DOJ before sending notorious "domestic terrorists" letter: emails. Fox News. Retrieved from https://www.foxnews.com/politics/nsba-coordinated-with-white -house-doj-before-sending-notorious-domestic-terrorists-letter-emails

or dues payments, leading to a loss of an estimated 42% of NSBA dues payments coming from state school boards associations.

Parental rights also became a top issue in the 2021 Virginia gubernatorial election, especially after Democrat Terry McAuliffe said, "I don't think parents should be telling schools what they should teach" during his final debate with Republican Glenn Youngkin. In a state that went 10 percentage points to Joe Biden in 2020, Youngkin beat Terry McAuliffe by 2 percentage points just a year later. A *Washington Post* exit poll found that 24% of voters said education was their top issue, making it the second most important issue in the race, and that Youngkin led McAuliffe by 6 percentage points with those voters.[24] Teachers' unions have been the most influential special interest group in K-12 education for a long time—but it appears that the jig is up. Parents are the new special interest in town—and they aren't going away any time soon.

## REFERENCES

Agostinelli, F., Doepke, M., Sorrenti, G., & Zilibotti, F. (2020). *When the great equalizer shuts down: Schools, peers, and parents in pandemic times* (Working Paper No. 28264). National Bureau of Economic Research.

Barnard, J., Frangakis, C. E., Hill, J. L., & Rubin, D. B. (2003). Principal stratification approach to broken randomized experiments: A case study of school choice vouchers in New York City. *Journal of the American Statistical Association, 98*(462), 299–323.

Bedrick, J., & Burke, L. (2018). *Surveying Florida scholarship families: Experiences and satisfaction with Florida's tax-credit scholarship program.* EdChoice. https://www.edchoice.org/wp -content/uploads/2018/10/2018-10-Surveying-Florida-Scholarship-Families-byJason-Bed rick-and-Lindsey-Burke.pdf

Bedrick, J., & Tarnowski, E. (2021, August 19). *How big was the year of educational choice?* Education Next. https://www.educationnext.org/how-big-was-the-year-of-educational -choice/

Betts, J. R., & Tang, Y. E. (2019). The effects of charter schools on student achievement. In M. Berends, R. J. Waddington, & J. Schoenig (Eds.), *School choice at the crossroads: Research perspectives* (pp. 67–89). New York: Routledge.

Bowen, D. H., & Trivitt, J. R. (2014). Stigma without sanctions: The (lack of) impact of private school vouchers on student achievement. *Education Policy Analysis Archives, 22*(87), 1–22.

Carnoy, M., Adamson, F., Chudgar, A., Luschei, T. F., and Witte, J. F. (2007). Vouchers and Public School Performance: A Case Study of the Milwaukee Parental Choice Program. Retrieved from Economic Policy Institute website: https://www.epi.org/publication /book_vouchers

Carr, M. (2011). The Impact of Ohio's EdChoice on Traditional Public School Performance. *Cato Journal, 31*(2), 257–284.

---

24. Exit poll results from the 2021 election for Virginia governor. *Washington Post.* Retrieved from https://www.washingtonpost.com/elections/interactive/2021/exit-polls-virginia-governor/

Catt, A. D., & Rhinesmith, E. (2017). *Why Indiana parents choose: A cross-sector survey of parents' views in a robust school choice environment.* EdChoice. https://files.eric.ed.gov/fulltext/ED579213.pdf

Chakrabarti, R. (2008). Can increasing private school participation and monetary loss in a voucher program affect public school performance? Evidence from Milwaukee. *Journal of Public Economics, 92*(5–6), 1371–1393.

Chakrabarti, R. (2013). Vouchers, public school response, and the role of incentives: Evidence from Florida. *EconomicIinquiry, 51*(1), 500–526.

Christakis, D. A., Van Cleve, W., & Zimmerman, F. J. (2020). Estimation of US children's educational attainment and years of life lost associated with primary school closures during the coronavirus disease 2019 pandemic. *JAMA Network Open, 3*(11), e2028786–e2028786. doi:10.1001/jamanetworkopen.2020.28786

Cowen, J. M. (2008). School choice as a latent variable: Estimating the "complier average causal effect" of vouchers in Charlotte. *Policy Studies Journal, 36*(2), 301–315.

DeAngelis, C. A. (2017). Do self-interested schooling selections improve society? A review of the evidence. *Journal of School Choice, 11*(4), 546–558.

DeAngelis, C. A., & Dills, A. K. (2021). The effects of school choice on mental health. *School Effectiveness and School Improvement, 32*(2), 326–344.

DeAngelis, C. A., & Holmes Erickson, H. (2018). What leads to successful school choice programs? A review of the theories and evidence. *Cato Journal, 38*(1), 247–263.

DeAngelis, C. A., & Makridis, C. (2021). Are school reopening decisions related to union influence? *Social Science Quarterly, 102*(5), 2266–2284.

DeAngelis, C., & Makridis, C. (2022). Are school reopening decisions related to funding? Evidence from over 12,000 districts during the COVID-19 pandemic. *Journal of School Choice, 16*(3), 454–476.

DeAngelis, C. A., & McCluskey, N. P. (Eds.). (2020). *School choice myths: Setting the record straight on education freedom.* Cato Institute.

DeAngelis, C. A., & Wolf, P. J. (2019). Private school choice and crime: Evidence from Milwaukee. *Social Science Quarterly, 100*(6), 2302–2315.

DeAngelis, C. A., & Wolf, P. J. (2020). Private school choice and character: More evidence from Milwaukee. *Journal of Private Enterprise, 35*(3), 13–48.

Dee, T., Huffaker, E., Phillips, C., & Sagara, E. (2021). *The revealed preferences for school reopening: Evidence from public-school disenrollment* (Working Paper No. 29156). National Bureau of Economic Research.

Deming, D. J. (2011). Better schools, less crime? *Quarterly Journal of Economics, 126*(4), 2063–2115.

Dills, A. K., & Hernández-Julián, R. (2011). More choice, less crime. *Education Finance and Policy, 6*(2), 246–266.

Dobbie, W., & Fryer, R. G., Jr. (2015). The medium-term impacts of high-achieving charter schools. *Journal of Political Economy, 123*(5), 985–1037.

EdChoice (2021, April 14). *The 123s of school choice: What the research says about private school choice programs in America* [PowerPoint slides]. SlideShare. https://www.edchoice.org/wp-content/uploads/2021/04/2021-123s-SlideShare_FINAL.pdf

Egalite, A. J., & Catt, A. D. (2020). Competitive Effects of the Indiana Choice Scholarship Program on Traditional Public School Achievement and Graduation Rates. Working Paper 2020-3. EdChoice.

Egalite, A. J., Kisida, B., & Winters, M. A. (2015). Representation in the classroom: The effect of own-race teacher assignment on student achievement. *Economics of Education Review, 45*(1), 44–52.

Egalite, A. J., & Mills, J. N. (2021). Competitive impacts of means-tested vouchers on public school performance: Evidence from Louisiana. *Education Finance and Policy, 16*(1), 66–91.

Figlio, D., & Hart, C. (2014). Competitive effects of means-tested school vouchers. *American Economic Journal: Applied Economics, 6*(1), 133–156.

Figlio, D. N., Hart, C., & Karbownik, K. (2021). *Effects of scaling up private school choice programs on public school students* Working Paper No. 9056, CESifo, retrieved from: https://www.cesifo.org/en/publikationen/2021/working-paper/effects-scaling-private-school-choice-programs-public-school

Figlio, D., & Karbownik, K. (2016). Evaluation of Ohio's EdChoice Scholarship Program: Selection, Competition, and Performance Effects. Thomas B. Fordham Institute.

Figlio, D. N., & Rouse, C. E. (2006). Do accountability and voucher threats improve low-performing schools? *Journal of Public Economics, 90*(1-2), 239–255.

Flanders, W. (2020). *Politics in the pandemic: The role of unions in school reopening decisions.* Wisconsin Institute for Law & Liberty. https://will-law.org/wp-content/uploads/2020/12/reopening-brief.pdf

Flanders, W. (2021). Opting out: Enrollment trends in response to continued public school shutdowns. *Journal of School Choice, 15*(3), 331–43.

Forster, G. (2008). Promising Start: An Empirical Analysis of How EdChoice Vouchers Affect Ohio Public Schools. School Choice Issues in the State. Friedman Foundation for Educational Choice.

Forster, G. (2008). Lost Opportunity: An Empirical Analysis of How Vouchers Affected Florida Public Schools. School Choice Issues in the State. Retrieved from: http://www.edchoice.org/wp-content/uploads/2015/09/Lost-Opportunity-How-Vouchers-Affected-Florida-Public-Schools.pdf

Friedman, M. (1955). The role of government in education. Collected Works of Milton Friedman Project records. Hoover Institution Archives, Stanford, CA.

Gray, N. L., Merrifield, J. D., & Adzima, K. A. (2016). A private universal voucher program's effects on traditional public schools. *Journal of Economics and Finance, 40*(2), 319–344.

Greene, J. P. (2001). An Evaluation of the Florida A-Plus Accountability and School Choice Program. Retrieved from Manhattan Institute website: http://www.manhattan-institute.org/pdf/cr_aplus.pdf

Greene, J. P. (2001). Vouchers in Charlotte. *Education Next, 1*(2), 55–60. https://www.educationnext.org/vouchersincharlotte/

Greene, J. P., & Forster, G. (2002). Rising to the Challenge: The Effect of School Choice on Public Schools in Milwaukee and San Antonio. Civic Bulletin.

Greene, J. P., & Marsh, R. H. (2009). The Effect of Milwaukee's Parental Choice Program on Student Achievement in Milwaukee Public Schools. SCDP Comprehensive Longitudinal Evaluation of the Milwaukee Parental Choice Program. Report# 11. School Choice Demonstration Project.

Greene, J. P., Peterson, P. E., & Du, J. (1999). Effectiveness of school choice: The Milwaukee experiment. *Education and Urban Society, 31*(2), 190–213.

Greene, J. P., & Winters, M. A. (2004). Competition passes the test: still more evidence from Florida that public schools improve when threatened with the loss of students and money. *Education Next, 4*(3), 66–72.

Greene, J. P., & Winters, M. A. (2007). An Evaluation of the Effect of DC's Voucher Program on Public School Achievement and Racial Integration After One Year. *Journal of Catholic Education, 11*(1), pp. 83–101. http://dx.doi.org/10.15365/joce.1101072013

Grossman, M., Reckhow, S., Strunk, K., & Turner, M. (2021). *All states close but red districts reopen: The politics of in-person schooling during the COVID-19 pandemic* (EdWorkingPaper No. 21-355). Annenberg Institute at Brown University. https://www.edworkingpapers.com/sites/default/files/ai21-355.pdf

Hammons, C. (2002). The Effects of Town Tuitioning in Vermont and Maine. School Choice Issues in Depth. Retrieved from: https://www.edchoice.org/wp-content/uploads/2019/03/The-Effects-of-Town-Tuitioning-in-Vermont-and-Maine.pdf

Harris, D., Ziedan, E., & Hassig, S. (2021). *The effects of school reopenings on COVID-19 hospitalizations*. National Center on Education Access and Choice. https://www.reachcentered.org/uploads/technicalreport/The-Effects-of-School-Reopenings-onCOVID-19-Hospitalizations-REACH-January-2021.pdf

Hartney, M. T., & Finger, L. K. (2021). Politics, markets, and pandemics: Public education's response to COVID-19. *Perspectives on Politics, 20*(2), 457–473. doi:https://doi.org/10.1017/S1537592721000955

Hawrilenko, M., Kroshus, E., Tandon, P., & Christakis, D. (2021). The association between school closures and child mental health during COVID-19. *JAMA Network Open, 4*(9), e2124092.

Henderson, M. B., Peterson, P. E., & West, M. R. (2021). Pandemic parent survey finds perverse pattern: Students are more likely to be attending school in person where Covid is spreading more rapidly: Majority of students receiving fully remote instruction; private-school students more likely to be in person full time. *Education Next, 21*(2), 34–48.

Holmes Erickson, H. (2017). How do parents choose schools, and what schools do they choose? A literature review of private school choice programs in the United States. *Journal of School Choice, 11*(4), 491–506.

Honein, M. A., Barrios, L. C., & Brooks, J. T. (2021, January 26). Data and policy to guide opening schools safely to limit the spread of SARS-CoV-2 infection. *JAMA Network.* https://jamanetwork.com/journals/jama/fullarticle/2775875

Howell, W. G., Wolf, P. J., Campbell, D. E., & Peterson, P. E. (2002). School vouchers and academic performance: Results from three randomized field trials. *Journal of Policy Analysis and Management, 21*(2), 191–217.

Hoxby, C. M. (2002). How School Choice Affects the Achievement of Public School Students. In Paul T. Hill (Ed.), *Choice with Equity* (pp. 141–78). Retrieved from https://books.google.com/books?id=IeUk3myQu-oC&lpg=PP1&pg=PA141

Jabbar, H., Fong, C. J., Germain, E., Li, D., Sanchez, J., Sun, W. L., & Devall, M. (2019). The competitive effects of school choice on student achievement: A systematic review. *Educational Policy, 36*(2), 247–281. https://doi.org/10.1177/0895904819874756

Kelly, J. P., & Scafidi, B. (2013). More than scores: An analysis of why and how parents choose private schools. Indianapolis, IN: Friedman Foundation for Educational Choice (EdChoice). https://www.edchoice.org/wp-content/uploads/2015/07/More-Than-Scores.pdf

Mader, N. S. (2010). School Choice, Competition, and Academic Quality: Essays on the Milwaukee Parental Choice Program (Doctoral dissertation). ProQuest.

Makridis, C. A. (2020). Do right-to-work laws work? Evidence on individuals' well-being and economic sentiment. *Journal of Law and Economics, 62*(4), 713–745. https://www.journals.uchicago.edu/doi/10.1086/707081

Makridis, C., Piano, C., & DeAngelis, C. (2022). *The effects of school closures on homeschooling and mental health: Evidence from the COVID-19 pandemic.* Available at SSRN 4001953.

Marianno, B. D., Hemphill, A., & Loures-Elias, A. S. (2022). Power in a pandemic: Teachers' unions and their responses to school reopening. *AERA Open, 8.* https://journals.sagepub .com/doi/10.1177/23328584221074337

McEachin, A., Lauen, D. L., Fuller, S. C., & Perera, R. M. (2020, June). Social returns to private choice? Effects of charter schools on behavioral outcomes, arrests, and civic partici-pation. *Economics of Education Review, 76,* 101983.

Musaddiq, T., Stange, K. M., Bacher-Hicks, A., & Goodman, J. (2021). The pandemic's effect on demand for public schools, homeschooling, and private schools (Working Paper No. 29262). National Bureau of Economic Research.

Oster, E. (2020). Schools are not spreading covid-19. This new data makes the case. *Wash-ington Post.* https://www.washingtonpost.com/opinions/2020/11/20/covid-19-schoolsdata -reopening-safety/

Oster, E., Jack, R., Halloran, C., Schoof, J., & McLeod, D. (2021). *COVID-19 mitigation practices and COVID-19 rates in schools: Report on data from Florida, New York and Mas-sachusetts.* medRxiv. doi: https://doi.org/10.1101/2021.05.19.21257467

Pandey, E. (2021, January 2). Private schools pull students away from public schools. *Axios.* https://www.axios.com/2021/01/02/private-schools-coronavirus-public-schools

Rhinesmith, E. (2017). A review of the research on parent satisfaction in private school choice programs. *Journal of School Choice, 11*(4), 585–603.

Rouse, C. E. (1998). Private school vouchers and student achievement: An evaluation of the Milwaukee Parental Choice Program. *Quarterly Journal of Economics, 113*(2), 553–602.

Rouse, C. E., Hannaway, J., Goldhaber, D., & Figlio, D. (2013). Feeling the Florida heat? How low-performing schools respond to voucher and accountability pressure. *American Economic Journal: Economic Policy, 5*(2), 251–281.

Scafidi, B., Tutterow, R., & Kavanagh, D. (2021). This time really is different: The effect of CO-VID-19 on independent K-12 school enrollments. *Journal of School Choice, 15*(3), 305–330.

Schwalbach, J., & DeAngelis, C. A. (2020). School sector and school safety: A review of the evidence. *Educational Review, 74*(4), 882–898.

Shakeel, M. D., Anderson, K. P., & Wolf, P. J. (2021). The participant effects of private school vouchers around the globe: A meta-analytic and systematic review. *School Effectiveness and School Improvement, 32*(4), 509–542. https://www.tandfonline.com/doi/abs/10.1080/0924 3453.2021.1906283

UNICEF. (2020, November). *Averting a lost COVID generation.* https://www.unicef.org /reports/averting-lost-generation-covid19-world-childrens-day-2020-brief

US Census Bureau. (2019). *2019 public elementary-secondary education finance data.* https:// www.census.gov/data/tables/2019/econ/school-finances/secondary-education-finance.html

US Census Bureau. (2021, March 22). *Homeschooling on the rise during COVID-19 pandemic.* https://www.census.gov/library/stories/2021/03/homeschooling-on-the-rise-during-covid -19-pandemic.html

Valant, J. (2020, July 29). School reopening plans linked to politics rather than public health. *Brown Center Chalkboard* (blog). https://www.brookings.edu/blog/brown-centerchalk board/2020/07/29/school-reopening-plans-linked-to-politics-rather-than-public-health/

Veney, D., & Jacobs, D. (2021). Voting with their feet: A state-level analysis of public charter school and district public school enrollment trends. https://www.publiccharters.org/our -work/publications/voting-their-feet-state-level-analysis-public-charter-school-and-district

West, M. R., & Peterson, P. E. (2006). The efficacy of choice threats within school account-ability systems: Results from legislatively induced experiments. *Economic Journal, 116*(510), C46–C62.

Winters, M. A., & Greene, J. P. (2011). Public school response to special education vouchers: The impact of Florida's McKay Scholarship Program on disability diagnosis and student achievement in public schools. *Educational Evaluation and Policy Analysis, 33*(2), 138–158.

Wolf, P. J. (2007). Civics exam: Schools of choice boost civic values. *Education Next, 7*(3), 66–72.

Wolf, P. J., Kisida, B., Gutmann, B., Puma, M., Eissa, N., & Rizzo, L. (2013). School vouch-ers and student outcomes: Experimental evidence from Washington, DC. *Journal of Policy Analysis and Management, 32*(2), 246–270.

Zimmerman, K. O., Akinboyo, I. C., Brookhart, M. A., Boutzoukas, A. E., McGann, K. A., Smith, M. J., Panayotti, G. M., Armstrong, S. C., Bristow, H., Parker, D., Zadrozny, S., Weber, D. J., & Benjamin, D. K., Jr.; ABC Science Collaborative. (2021). Incidence and secondary transmission of SARS-CoV-2 infections in schools. *Pediatrics, 147*(4).

# 3

# Quality and Intentionality: Making After-School Programs More Effective

*Goldy Brown III*

After-school programming in the United States has been an ongoing investment at the federal level for the past three decades. Created by the 1994 Improving America's Schools Act, 21st Century Community Learning Centers (CCLC) is the most widespread after-school program. In 1998, Congress approved $40 million for the program, with a steady annual increase in funding ever since. Like many educational programs designed to mitigate educational performance gaps, after-school programs have produced mixed results on a district-by-district level.

This chapter has four sections: a taxonomy of after-school interventions, improving after-school program effectiveness, potential cost-effectiveness, and future research recommendations.

## TAXONOMY OF GOVERNMENT-FUNDED AFTER-SCHOOL INTERVENTIONS

The most immediate purpose of after-school programs is to serve as a structured place to go after school for the significant number of children who are unsupervised between 3:00 and 6:00 p.m. (Afterschool Alliance, 2016; US Bureau of Labor Statistics, 2021; Kane, 2004; McCombs, Whitaker, & Yoo, 2017; National Institute of Out-of-School-Time, 2021). After-school programs emerged in response to community pressure to use school buildings following the end of the school day (Dynarski et al., 2003), then evolved into more-focused programming due to the accountability movement beginning in 2001, with programming focused on improving schools' academic scores (Dynarski et al., 2004; Lauer et al., 2004). After-school programs also sought to provide a structured environment in an effort to lower crime, as contemporary studies emphasized that juvenile crime peaked between 3:00 p.m. and 6:00 p.m. (Weisman

& Gottfredson, 2001). Further, after-school programs tried to lower student engagement in high-risk sexual behavior and substance abuse (Biglan et al., 1990; Dishion, Patterson, Stoolmiller, & Skinner, 1991). Unfortunately, results-oriented studies have not found wide-scale value in these programs from a research standpoint. Lester, Chow, & Melton (2020), Neild, Wilson, & McClanahan (2019), Kremer, Maynard, Polanin, Vaughn, & Sarteschi (2015), and Durlak (2010) conducted respective meta-analyses and reviews of after-school programs, and Granger, Durlak, Yohalem, & Reisner (2007) found that programming that produces positive results is implemented with "quality." Further, Roth, Malone, and Brooks-Gunn (2010) identified four traits of a quality after-school program:

1. meets regularly throughout the school year,
2. is supervised by adult leaders,
3. offers a variety of activities (e.g., tutoring, group activities, and recreation), and
4. is structured around group activities.

Other research goes beyond quality, maintaining that after-school programming must be intentional to be effective (Birmingham, Pechman, Russell, & Mielke, 2005; Jordan, Parker, Donnelly, & Rudo, 2009; Chase & Valorose, 2010). In other words, programs should identify their purpose (improve academics, reduce teenage pregnancy, juvenile delinquency, etc.) and assess whether they are meeting it. Quality programs listed in Lester et al. (2020), Neild et al. (2019), Kremer et al. (2015), and Durlak (2010) meta-analyses found that the majority of after-school programs provide interventions in the following categories: academic improvement, social-emotional learning, and exposure to include STEM and recreation.

## ACADEMIC IMPROVEMENT

National assessments do not evidence any national gains in student achievement that can be correlated to after-school programming, nor have any strong empirical findings been reported positively on a national level (Zief, Lauver, & Maynard, 2006). Studies have shown a few individual local successes with regard to academic results, most notably in math (Carbone, 2010; Chittum, Jones, Akalin, & Schram, 2017; Delucchi, 2010; Dreyer, 2011; Fink, 2011; Franklin, 2017; Girod, Martineau, & Yong, 2004; Hu et al., 2012; Jarratt, 2014; Jones, 2014; Luce, 2018; Vandell, Reisner, & Pierce, 2007). Programs that have had success in increasing academics maintain the attendance of targeted students and have highly capable instructors and a strong, routinely evaluated academic program.

## SOCIAL-EMOTIONAL LEARNING

Hurd and Deutsch (2017) recommended that after-school programs could be a great place to implement SEL programs because of fewer distractions than during the regular school day, such as curriculum and policy demands. Other research emphasizes that programs focusing on social-emotional learning in after-school programs have the best chance of producing positive results in comparison to programs that focus on other activities (Durlak, 2010; Minney, Garcia, Altobelli, Perez-Brena, & Blunk, 2019; Wallace & Palmer, 2018). Specifically, Durlak, Weissberg, & Pachan (2015) found that after-school programs that focus on delivering quality social-emotional learning can lead to better results in academic areas. They can also present another positive adult relationship for students who would otherwise be in an unstructured environment. Positive adult interactions during this time can increase academic skills and social-emotional aspects of youth development (Grossman & Bulle, 2006; Jones & Deutsch, 2011).

## EXPOSURE, RECREATION, AND STEM

After-school programming can—and is—exposing many students to educational opportunities they would otherwise not have. This type of programming has the potential to increase interest in school for many students who might not otherwise be exposed to academic opportunities. Hidi and Renninger (2006) defined interest as a motivational variable with demonstrated influence on attention, goals, and level of training. When children are exposed to things that are interesting, they have higher intrinsic motivation and concentration (Larson & Kleiber, 1993).

Many states have attempted to address this concern by implementing different types of programs. After-school network in Ohio, Georgia, Connecticut, Washington, Minnesota, and New York developed global learning initiatives funded through many different resources. Students in these programs benefit from curriculum on racial equity issues, social skills, college and career readiness, and global workforce initiatives, to name a few. These programs were developed at the state level and are being implemented by districts that partner with this statewide organization in selected states.

In addition, national organizations have picked up such programming, including the YMCA, Boys and Girls Clubs, and 4-H (Sparr, Frazier, Morrison, Miller, & Bartko, et al., 2020). These programs provide field trips to museums, sporting events, theater, and recreational activities such as golf, tennis, hiking, and yoga. However, no specific findings report on the effectiveness of these programs other than their potential to make up for the estimated educational opportunity time deficit between affluent and low-income students.

According to Noonan (2017) employment changes in STEM will see an 8.9% increase over the next decade; the median wage in 2021 is $89,780. Non-STEM occupations will see a 6.4.% increase. The American economy will see a huge need in this area, thus presenting a golden opportunity for low-income students who acquire skills in this area to become affluent adults. Research on individual case studies has shown some examples of quality programs that can increase student interest and skills in STEM-based careers (Boyer, 2010; Carbone, 2010; Carr, 2015; Delucchi, 2010; Dreyer, 2011; Franklin, 2017; Girod et al., 2004; Grolnick, Farkas, Sohmer, Michaels, & Valsiner, 2007; Krishnamurthi, Ballard, & Noam, 2014; Kennedy & Smolinsky, 2016).

# IMPROVING AFTER-SCHOOL PROGRAMS: QUALITY AND INTENTIONALITY

Reviewed research, previously mentioned, asserts that positive academic, social, and behavior development are possible in after-school programs implemented with quality and intentionality. The variety of focus, quality level, and intentionality of after-school programs may have led some policy makers to have misguided and unrealistic expectations about outcomes. Specifically, academic improvement has not been produced on a large scale (Lauer et al., 2006; Neild et al., 2019). Sparr et al. (2020) recommended after-school program focuses that could meet the needs of low-income students more effectively in closing the skills gap other than focusing on academic outcomes.

## IMPLEMENTATION QUESTIONS AND RECOMMENDATIONS

Below is a sample sequence of questions decision makers may use to decide how to implement after-school programming:

1. What are the deficiencies of the youth in our community, school district, or schools (illiteracy, low math scores, high teenage pregnancy rates, high juvenile crime rates, high levels of drug and alcohol abuse, poor school attendance, negative school behavior, lack of exposure, low graduation rates, etc.)?
2. What resources (funding, facilities, technology, community partnerships, and personnel) do we have to create a quality and intentional after-school program?
3. Considering our resources, what quality and intentional after-school program(s) can we put together to address the identified deficiencies?
4. Once implemented, how will we measure our programs' effectiveness?

### Recommendations for Programming

Based on reviewed research, the following is a list of programming with the potential to be effective if implemented with quality and intentionality at each grade level. Though a more efficient process may be necessary, it is important to identify the direction of future programming.

Though the listed implementation questions can lead to an intentionally targeted program, it does not guarantee program quality. The most significant challenges with regard to program quality are consistent, qualified, and trained personnel to implement programs that will meet the desired outcomes and foster student attendance regularly in order to participate in the program and facilitate the outcomes.

Table 3.1.  After-School Programs

| Age | Potential After-School Program Recommendations |
|---|---|
| **Early Childhood: Pre-K-3** | Literacy intervention pending qualified staff<br>Math intervention pending qualified staff<br>Social-emotional learning programs<br>Recreational programs<br>Exposure: field trips, and so forth<br>Anti–substance abuse programs<br>Introduction to STEM |
| **Middle Childhood: Grades 4–6** | Literacy intervention pending qualified staff<br>Math intervention pending qualified staff<br>Social-emotional learning programs<br>Exposure: field trips, and so forth<br>Introduction to STEM<br>Recreation/competitive sports/arts<br>Anti–substance abuse programs |
| **Adolescence: Grade 7–8** | Homework clubs<br>Math intervention pending qualified staff<br>Social-emotional learning programs<br>Exposure: field trips, and so forth<br>Introduction to STEM/coding clubs/and so forth<br>Career and technical education exposure<br>Recreation and the arts<br>Anti–teenage pregnancy clubs: CAS-Carrera<br>Anti–substance abuse programs |
| **High School** | Homework clubs leading to graduation<br>Math intervention pending qualified staff<br>Social-emotional learning programs<br>Exposure: field trips, and so forth<br>STEM exposure/coding clubs/and so forth<br>Career and technical education exposure<br>Recreation and the arts<br>Social clubs: common interest, cultural, political, and so forth<br>Anti–teenage pregnancy clubs: CAS-Carrera<br>Community service clubs<br>Anti–substance abuse programs |

## Personnel and Attendance

After-school programming personnel tend to be poorly paid, which leads to high turnover. In addition, staff has little training or does not have the qualifications to produce many of the desired outcomes. The reality is that without quality personnel, no program will reach its intended outcome. Many programs have desired outcomes (increase reading and math achievement scores, better school behavior and attendance) but do not have the revenue to hire the necessary staff to produce the desired outcomes. Programs should have realistic expectations and generate those expectations based on the personnel they can afford to hire. Personnel should have training opportunities on how to produce the desired outcomes of the programs in which they work.

Attendance is also a key indicator of program effectiveness (Kremer et al., 2015). Although attendance alone will not produce desired outcomes, all other after-school programming recommendations are irrelevant if the program does not have consistent attendance. The challenge is finding outcome-based programming that will also have positive attendance. According to Grolnick, W., et al. (2007), it is more challenging to maintain attendance for children ages 13 through 18 in after-school programs. Such students have more autonomy as individuals, and these programs are not a requirement for classes or grade promotion. Having highly trained and consistent staff makes for a better programming experience. Notably, better attendance is found in low-income communities with consistent and high-quality programming personnel. Most important for personnel to maintain attendance is building relationships with students (St. Clair & Stone, 2016).

To be sure, after-school programming alone will not bring about necessary changes if no other quality programming exists throughout the school day or in the community. After-school programming only has the potential to enhance programming, which is why intentionality is critical to implementation. If the program is not looking to address high school graduation, behavior, teenage pregnancy, substance abuse, and the like, or other needs in the local community, then efforts to maintain funding may be hindered going forward, as policy makers routinely debate funding this initiative based on the limited success it has shown from a data standpoint.

## Funding

More than 25 states in the United States fund after-school programs that contribute nationwide to more than $1.5 billion in funding. Revenue varies based on the state, and allocation decisions are determined differently as well. At the time this chapter is being written, the Biden administration is proposing an increase of more than $100 million to this initiative and an unprecedented expansion of other programs that support out-of-school time activities such as the Child Care and Development Block Grant, Title 1, Title IV part A, and Every Student Succeeds Act. In addition, this funding addresses student support, academic enrichment grants, and work-study programs at the federal level.

ESSA (2015) was designed to give more flexibility to state and local school decision makers to determine the best approach in offering educational programming for their students, including before-school, after-school, and summer learning programs. Title I (ESSA, 2015a) is a component of ESSA and provides funding to school districts and schools serving a high percentage of children from low-income families. This grant is a formula-based award. Monies go to school districts and target students from low-income families who are failing or at risk of failing. Schools with more than 40% of students considered low-income can receive money for after-school programs.

Title IV, Part B (ESSA, 2015b) authorizes 21st Century Community Learning Centers as an after-school program. This program provides grants to states for after-school and summer programs. State education departments require potential recipients to apply for the grant and show how they plan to meet the priorities of school-day academic alignment, enrichment activities, and family engagement.

After-school funding can be provided through the Child Care and Development Block Grant (CCDBG). The CCDBG program distributes formula-based grants to states to provide and improve child-care services (First Five Years Fund, 2022). The Biden administration is proposing a $1.5 billion increase for FY2022.

Students in local communities have different needs. In urban, suburban, small town, rural, and tribal school districts, after-school programming should have the flexibility to look different, enhance programming, and meet local needs. Local communities must have the flexibility to put money toward their specific needs.

## POTENTIAL COST-EFFECTIVE ANALYSIS

Efforts to provide concrete and cost-effective after-school programming have presented significant challenges. Too many types of programs and funding streams exist to gauge the economic effect of after-school programs. After-school programs provide students with social-emotional learning skills, can potentially prevent negative behaviors (crime, high-risk sexual activity, substance abuse), and assist in the provision of academic skills that lead to graduation and job preparation, all of which have economic benefits. Acquired skills, academic milestones such as graduation, and the avoidance of consequential negative behaviors can improve an individual's economic life chances. They can also save taxpayer money on corrections, welfare, and substance abuse recovery programming.

Levin and McEwan (2003) developed a cost-effectiveness model for implementing education programs. After-school programs based on reviewed research could potentially provide cost effectiveness in four areas: reduce juvenile delinquency, reduce teenage pregnancy, increase graduation rates, and provide child care, in addition to increasing academic achievement in reading and math, and improving the social-emotional skills of students. After-school programs also have the potential to reduce juvenile delinquency (Apsler, 2009; Gottfredson, Cross, Wilson, Connell, & Rorie, 2010; Gottfredson, Cross, & Soulé, 2007; Gottfredson, Gottfredson, & Weisman, 2001).

US taxpayers spent more than $9 billion in 2010 on health care, foster care, and incarceration costs of children of teen parents while also losing tax revenue due to the lower levels of education and income of teen mothers. Vidourek and King (2019) found that short- and long-term negative outcomes of teen pregnancy serve as a primary motivator for preventing teen pregnancy. They also report after-school programming as a key deterrent to high-risk sexual activity.

**Table 3.2. Cost-Effective Analyses for After-School Program**

| Program Objective | Measure of Effectiveness |
| --- | --- |
| Reduce Juvenile Delinquency | Local Juvenile Delinquency Rates |
| Reduce Teenage Pregnancy | Local Teenage Pregnancy Rates |
| Increase Graduation Rates | Local High School Graduation Rates |
| Provide Child Care to Parents | State and Local Employment Rates |
| Reading and Math Programming | Reading and Math Assessments |
| Social-Emotional Skills Programming | Attendance and Behavior Reports |

Evidence from a US Department of Justice Report in 2000 suggested that children who are unsupervised after school are more likely to use alcohol, drugs, and tobacco. Cycles of poverty continue when youth fall into the penal system, teenage pregnancy, and substance abuse. For children to maximize their economic potential as adults, it is important not only to invest in programming that can help them acquire the necessary skills but also keep them from consequential outcomes stemming from poor choices. Grannis and Sawhill (2013) asserted that to maximize their economic future, children in pre-K-12 must avoid the penal system and teenage pregnancy.

After-school programs and participation in them have increased over the past decades due to more women joining the workforce. According to reports, the gap between children being released from school and their parents getting off work can be 20 to 25 hours per week (US Department of Justice, 2000). Lacking supervision during this time can have innumerable negative consequences for individual families financially and for the American economy more generally. According to one state report on child care (US Department of Commerce, 2019), a state's businesses lose billions of dollars when child care breakdowns require people to miss work; in addition, many state's employees have to change work annually due solely to child-care issues.

**Preventing Negative Behavior**

With regard to juvenile delinquency, after-school programming may have helped in reducing offenders over the past three decades. According to the Office of Juvenile Justice and Delinquency Prevention Organization, the crime rate in 1996 for children between the ages of 10 and 17 was 6,493.7 per every 100,000. In 2018, that number fell significantly, to 2,083 per every 100,000. Of the crimes committed, 28% took place between the hours of 3:00 and 7:00 p.m. More than half of the juvenile crimes take place between 3:00 and 10:00 p.m. The research does not correlate specific program focuses (academic, recreational, behavior, etc.) to decreasing juvenile delinquency, but some studies have found that participation in any of these programs may have contributed to its decline (Gotfreddson et al., 2007; Snyder & Sickmund, 1999). Regarding juvenile delinquency, according to the Justice Policy Institute (2020), the average number of incarcerated children under the age of 18 on any given day in the United States is 60,000. In 2020, the average annual cost to incarcerate a juvenile delinquent, which varies by state, was $588 per day, or $214,620 per year.

Over the past three decades, teenage pregnancy and abortions have decreased significantly. In 2019, Pew Research reported that, in 1991, teenage girls between the ages of 15 and 19 reported pregnancies of 61.8 per 1,000. This number declined to 17.4 per 1,000 in 2018. The same report showed a similar rate drop for abortions among teenage girls between those ages, from 40 per 1,000 to 10.6 to 1,000. Teenage pregnancy significantly reduces the economic life chances of children (Grannis & Sawhill, 2013).

Though limited quality research shows a correlation between after-school programming and these statistics, we can hypothesize that students in a structured environment will fare better than those in an unstructured environment from 3:00 p.m. until 6:00 p.m. Since the 1990s, after-school programs have become more widespread. We thus also hypothesize that they have contributed in some way to the declining delinquency rates, especially during the hours of 3:00 p.m. and 6:00 p.m., and may be one of many other factors and programming that have served to lower teenage pregnancy rates. This claim does not intend to assert that these programs alone have led to declines in juvenile delinquency and teenage pregnancy; further inquiry is necessary to make that claim. However, juvenile delinquency and high-risk sexual activity among teens usually takes place during unstructured, unsupervised time.

No ranking order shows what programming appears to be the most effective. However, an after-school program's biggest potential impact economically and in improving a local community comes from identifying and meeting a deficiency among the community youth. The only common theme identified in effective after-school programs is a positive adult-student interaction. Most important, create an intentional program targeted at improving that deficiency and produce a *quality* program that provides the necessary structure and resources to make the targeted objective(s) realistic.

## FURTHER RESEARCH REGARDING AFTER-SCHOOL PROGRAMMING

The randomness of programming nationwide regarding after-school programs means that many areas remain for future research. A cost-based analysis of after-school programming is the biggest gap in the research from a policy standpoint, and the creation of a formula to use in a local community would be very beneficial. This researcher did not find any quality research that shows the specific return on investment to the American taxpayer, only estimates in many state reports. In addition, literature seems to be promoting a transition from more academic-focused programs to curriculum that is more social and emotional in nature, or at least targets other skills that can produce human capital (Sparr et al., 2020; Grolnick, W., et al., 2007). Studies on this type of programming's effectiveness must continue to make more concrete recommendations. In addition, substance abuse among teens in certain areas of the country is higher than others. Further inquiry as to the potential positive impact that after-school programming can yield in this area could be useful as well. Lester, Chow, & Melton (2020) have asserted that, for better results, researchers and practitioners must increase the rigor of study design across individual program evaluations.

# REFERENCES

Afterschool Alliance. (2016). *America after 3 pm special report: Afterschool in communities of concentrated poverty.* Washington, DC.

Apsler, R. (2009). After-school programs for adolescents: A review of evaluation research. *Adolescence, 44,* 1–19.

Biglan, A., Metzler, C. W., Wirt, R., Ary, D., Noell, J., Ochs, L., French, C., & Hood, D. (1990). Social and behavioral factors associated with high-risk sexual behaviors among adolescents. *Journal of Behavioral Medicine, 13*(3), 245–261.

Birmingham, J., Pechman, E. M., Russell, C. A., & Mielke, M. (2005). *Shared features of high-performing after-school programs: A follow-up to the TASC evaluation.* Policy Studies Associates.

Boyer, K. A. M. (2010). *Investigating differences among Asian American youth participating and not participating in grant-funded high school after-school programs* [Doctoral dissertation]. California State University. https://scholarworks.calstate.edu/downloads/ks65hd43b

Carbone, P. M. (2010). *The effects of an after-school tutoring program on the Pennsylvania System of School Assessment* (Publication No. 3399823) [Doctoral dissertation]. Youngstown State University, Youngstown, OH. ProQuest Dissertations.

Carr, E. M. (2015). *Afterschool program interventions that support the academic achievement, behavior, and engagement of at-risk student populations.* University of Houston-Clear Lake. http://proxy.library.vcuEdu/login?url=https://search.proquest.com/docview/305175724?accountid=14780

Chase, R., & Valorose, J. (2010). *Child care use in Minnesota: Report of the 2009 statewide household child care survey.* Wilder Research.

Chittum, J. R., Jones, B. D., Akalin, S., & Schram, Á. B. (2017). The effects of an afterschool STEM program on students' motivation and engagement. *International Journal of STEM Education, 4*(1), 1–16.

Delucchi, G. R. (2010). *An evaluation of an after-school program for low-income elementary and middle school students.* Fordham University. http://proxi.library.vcu.edu/login?accountid=14780

Dishion, T. J., Patterson, G. R., Stoolmiller, M., & Skinner, M. L. (1991). Family, school, and behavioral antecedents to early adolescent involvement with antisocial peers. *Developmental Psychology, 27*(1), 172–180.

Dreyer, K. J. (2011). *An examination of academic outcomes for students who attend a school based afterschool program.* University of Pittsburgh. http://proxy.library.vcu.edu/login?url=https://search.proquest.com/docview/746583937?accountid=14780

Durlak, Joseph A. (Ed.). (2015). *Handbook of social and emotional learning: Research and practice.* Guilford Publications.

Durlak, J. A., Weissberg, R. P., & Pachan, M. (2010). A meta-analysis of after-school programs that seek to promote personal and social skills in children and adolescents. *American Journal of Community Psychology, 45*(3–4), 294–309.

Dynarski, M., James-Burdumy, S., Moore, M., Rosenberg, L., Deke, J., & Mansfield, W. (2004). *When schools stay open late: The national evaluation of the 21st-Century Community Learning Centers program—New findings.* US Department of Education.

Dynarski, M., Moore, M., Mullens, J., Gleason, P., James-Burdumy, S., Rosenberg, L., Pistorino, C., Silva, T., Deke, J., Mansfield, W., Heaviside, S., & Levy, D. (2003). *When schools stay open late: The national evaluation of the 21st-Century Community Learning Centers program: First year findings.* US Department of Education. http://www.educationnewyork .com/files/firstyear.pdf

ESSA (Every Student Succeeds Act). I § 1001-1601. (2015a). https://www.everystudentsucceeds act.org/title-i-improving-basic-school-programs-operated-by-state-and-local-educational -agencies

ESSA (Every Student Succeeds Act). Title IV § 4201–4206. (2015b). https://www.everystudent succeedsact.org/title-iv-21st-century-schools

Fink, B. L. (2011). *The effect of a seventh grade after school leadership program on the developmental assets, academic achievement, and behavior of non-thriving students* (Publication No. 3465) [Doctoral dissertation]. University of Nebraska at Omaha. Digital Commons at University of Nebraska at Omaha. https://digitalcommons.unomaha.edu/cgi/viewcontent .cgi?article=4472&context=studentwork

First Five Years Fund. (2022). Child Care & Development Block Grant (CCDBG). https:// www.ffyf.org/issues/ccdbg/

Franklin, C. (2017). *Effects of the afterschool program on student achievement of students with disabilities in a rural Georgia middle school* (Publication No. 1500) [Doctoral dissertation]. Liberty University, Lynchburg, VA. Scholars Crossing: Institutional Repository of Liberty University. https://digitalcommons.liberty.edu/cgi/viewcontent.cgi?article=2556&context =doctoral

Girod, M., Martineau, J., & Yong, Z. (2004). After-school computer clubhouses and at-risk teens. *American Secondary Education, 32*(3), 63–76.

Gottfredson, D. C., Cross, A., & Soulé, D. A. (2007). Distinguishing characteristics of effective and ineffective after-school programs to prevent delinquency and victimization. *Criminology & Public Policy, 6*(2), 289–318.

Gottfredson, D. C., Cross, A. B., Wilson, D. M., Connell, N., & Rorie, M. (2010). *A randomized trial of the effects of an enhanced after-school program for middle-school students.* Final Report submitted to the US Department of Education Institute for Educational Sciences.

Gottfredson, D. C., Gottfredson, G. D., & Weisman, S. A. (2001). The timing of delinquent behavior and its implications for after-school programs. *Criminology & Public Policy,* 1, 61–86.

Granger, R. (2010). Understanding and improving effectiveness of after-school practice. *American Journal of Community Psychology, 45*(3–4), 441–446. https://pubmed.ncbi.nlm .nih.gov/20238158/

Granger, R. C., Durlak, J., Yohalem, N., & Reisner, E. (2007). *Improving after-school program quality* (Working paper). William T. Grant Foundation.

Grannis, K. S., & Sawhill, I. V. (2013). *Improving children's life chances: Estimates from the Social Genome Model.* Washington, DC: Brookings Institution.

Grolnick, W. S., Farkas, M. S., Sohmer, R., Michaels, S., & Valsiner, J. (2007). Facilitating motivation in adolescents: Effects of an after-school program. *Journal of Applied Developmental Psychology, 28*(4), 332–344.

Grossman, J. B., & Bulle, M. J. (2006). Review of what youth programs do to increase the connectedness of youth with adults. *Journal of Adolescent Health, 39*(6), 788–799.

Hidi, S., & Renninger, K. A. (2006). The four-phase model of interest development. *Educational Psychologist, 41*(2), 111–127.

Hu, X., Craig, S. D., Bargagliotti, A. E., Graesser, A. C., Okwumabua, T., Anderson, C., Cheney, K. R., & Sterbinsky, A. (2012). The effects of a traditional and technology-based after-school program on 6th grade student's mathematics skills. *Journal of Computers in Mathematics and Science Teaching, 31*(1), 17–38.

Hurd, N., & Deutsch, N., (2017). SEL-focused after-school programs. *Future of Children, 27*(1), 95–115.

Jarratt, K. (2014). *Mathematics achievement outcomes for middle school students attending school-based afterschool mathematics programs* [Doctoral dissertation]. Union University, Jackson, TN.

Jones, B. R. (2014). *An after-school program and its effect on the math and reading performance levels of the standardized testing and reporting (STAR) for identified at-risk students* [Doctoral dissertation]. Capella University, Minneapolis, MN.

Jones, J. N., & Deutsch, N. L. (2011). Relational strategies in after-school settings: How staff–youth relationships support positive development. *Youth & Society, 43*(4), 1381–1406. https://search.proquest.com/docview/1497967944/abstract/F46A90DBC46A47D6PQ/I

Jordan, C., Parker, J., Donnelly, D., & Rudo, Z. (Eds.). (2009). *Building and managing quality afterschool programs. A practitioner's guide.* Austin, TX: SEDL.

Justice Policy Institute. (2020). Sticker Shock 2014–2020: The Cost of Youth Incarceration.

Kane, T. (2004). *The impact of after-school programs: Interpreting the results of four recent evaluations* (Working paper). William T. Grant Foundation.

Kennedy, E., & Smolinsky, L. (2016). Math circles: A tool for promoting engagement among middle school minority males. *EURASIA Journal of Mathematics, Science and Technology Education, 12*(4), 717–732.

Kremer, K. P., Maynard, B. R., Polanin, J. R., Vaughn, M. G., & Sarteschi, C. M. (2015). Effects of after-school programs with at-risk youth on attendance and externalizing behaviors: A systematic review and meta-analysis. *Journal of Youth and Adolescence, 44*, 616–636. https://doi.org/10.1007/s10964-014-0226-4

Krishnamurthi, A., Ballard, M., & Noam, G. G. (2014). *Examining the impact of afterschool STEM programs.* Washington, DC: Afterschool Alliance.

Larson, R. W., & Kleiber, D. A. (1993). Structured leisure as a context for the development of attention during adolescence. *Loisir et Société/Society and Leisure, 16*(1), 77–98.

Lauer, P. A., Akiba, M., Wilkerson, S. B., Apthorp, H. S., Snow, D., & Martin-Glenn, M. (2004, January). The effectiveness of out-of-school-time strategies in assisting low-achieving students in reading and mathematics: A research synthesis. Denver, CO: Mid-continent Research for Education and Learning.

Lauer, P. A., Akiba, M., Wilkerson, S. B., Apthorp, H. S., Snow, D., & Martin-Glenn, M. L. (2006). Out-of-school-time programs: A meta-analysis of effects for at-risk students. *Review of Educational Research, 76*(2), 275–313.

Lester, A., Chow, J., & Melton, T. (2020). Quality is critical for meaningful synthesis of afterschool program effects: A systemic review and meta-analysis. *Journal of Youth and Adolescence, 49*, 369–382. https://doi.org/10.1007/s10964-019-01188-8

Levin, H. M., & McEwan, P. J. (2003). Cost-effectiveness analysis as an evaluation tool. In *International handbook of educational evaluation* (pp. 125–152). Berlin: Springer, Dordrecht.

Luce, F. C. (2018). *The effects of an after-school program on sixth-grade students' PARCC scores in a high-poverty urban location in New Jersey* [Doctoral dissertation]. Saint Peter's University, Jersey City, NJ. http://search.proquest.com/docview/2092265378/abstract/934CF09 625EA4E4FPQ/1

McCombs, J. S., Whitaker, A. A., & Yoo, P. Y. (2017). *The value of out-of-school time programs.* Santa Monica, CA: Rand Corporation.

Minney, D., Garcia, J., Altobelli, J., Perez-Brena, N. J., & Blunk, E. (2019). Social-emotional learning and evaluation in after-school care: A working model. *Journal of Youth Development, 14*(3). https://jyd.pitt.edu/ojs/jyd/article/view/19-14-03-PA-02

National Institute of Out-of-School-Time. NOIST.org

Neild, R., Wilson, S., & McClanahan, W. (2019). *Afterschool programs: Review of evidence under the Every Student Succeeds Act.* United States Department of Education.

Noonan, R. (2017). STEM Jobs: Update. Economics and Statistics Administration. US Department of Commerce, Washington, DC.

Philp, K. D., & Gill, M. G. (2020). Reframing after-school programs as developing youth interest, identity, and social capital. *Policy Insights from the Behavioral and Brain Sciences 7*(1), 19–26.

Roth, J. L., Malone, L. M., & Brooks-Gunn, J. (2010). Does amount of participation in afterschool programs relate to developmental outcomes? A review of literature. *American Journal of Community Psychology, 45*(3–4), 310–324.

Sparr, M., Frazier, S., Morrison, C., Miller, K., & Bartko, W. T. (2020). *Afterschool programs to improve social-emotional, behavioral, and physical health in middle childhood: A targeted review of the literature.* Washington, DC: Office of the Assistant Secretary for Planning and Evaluation & Office on Women's Health, Office of the Assistant Secretary for Health, U.S. Department of Health and Human Services.

St. Clair, L., & Stone, T. (2016). Who gets the better educators in afterschool? An analysis of teaching and learning interactions and student economic status. *School Community Journal, 26*(2), 71–81.

US Department of Commerce. (2019). https://www.commerce.gov/data-and-reports/reports

US Department of Education. Every Student Succeeds Act (ESSA). https://www.ed.gov /essa?src=rn

US Department of Justice. (2000). *Annual report to Congress.* National Institute of Justice. https://www.ojp.gov/pdffiles1/nij/189105.pdf

Vandell, D. L., Reisner, E. R., & Pierce, K. M. (2007, October). *Outcomes linked to high-quality afterschool programs: Longitudinal findings from the study of promising afterschool programs.* Policy Studies Associates, with Charles Stewart Mott Foundation.

Vidourek, R. A., & King, K. A. (2019). Socio cultural influences on teenage pregnancy and contemporary prevention measures.

Wallace, A., & Palmer, J. (2018, June). *Building social and emotional skills in afterschool programs: A literature review.* In National Conference of State Legislatures. https://www.ncsl .org/Portals/1/Documents/educ/Social_Emotional_32470.pdf

Weisman, S. A., & Gottfredson, D. C. (2001). Attrition from after school programs: Characteristics of students who drop out. *Prevention Science, 2*(3), 201–205.

Zief, S. G., Lauver, S., & Maynard, R. A. (2006). Impacts of after-school programs on student outcomes. *Campbell Systematic Reviews, 2*(1), 1–51.

# 4

# Career, Technical, and Higher-Education Opportunities for Traditionally Underserved Students

*Walter G. Ecton*

Career and Technical Education (CTE)—historically referred to as "vocational education"—has long played a prominent role in American high schools. When implemented properly, CTE can confer substantial benefits by helping students who struggle to find success in a college preparatory curriculum and those who plan to enter the workforce directly after high school by offering them the opportunity to receive crucial preparation and training for specific jobs.

Although the nation's high school curriculum has largely come into alignment with college preparatory requirements in recent decades (Rosenbaum, 2001; Mishkind, 2014), not all students go to college, and even fewer leave college with a credential. For students who do not enter and graduate college immediately after high school, CTE provides one potential avenue to ensure that students can be prepared for meaningful work in well-paying jobs. By offering a way for students to obtain marketable skills and experience through hands-on learning, prepare for certification and licensure exams, and build connections with potential future employers, CTE is an attractive option for many students. Moreover, the project-based learning and real-world relevance can appeal to those who may otherwise be relatively disengaged in high school.

Recent reports from the Department of Education suggest that between 85% and 92% of high school students earn credit from at least one Career and Technical Education (CTE)-designated course during their high school career (Levesque et al., 2008; Hudson, 2014). More than 98% of public high school districts offered CTE courses in the 2016–17 school year (Gray & Lewis, 2018). Even though CTE remains a common part of many high school students' educational experience, it is often misunderstood or based on outdated perceptions.

This chapter provides readers with a sense of the current status of high school CTE in the United States and provides researchers, policy makers, and practitioners with key questions and considerations to guide their work in ensuring that high-quality CTE is provided in a way that is equitable and leads to positive outcomes for all students.

The chapter begins with an overview of the evolving state of research on outcomes from CTE programs, with a focus on the shift in evidence in the 21st century as the emphasis of many CTE programs changed. The chapter then provides a brief discussion of CTE in the international context and what American CTE might learn from other countries' experiences. I then use a nationally representative survey to examine who currently takes CTE courses in the US context, finding that (in somewhat of a departure from studies in the 1970s and 1980s that found vocational education was especially targeted at Black students), taking CTE courses today is widespread, with CTE students disproportionately White, rural, and southern. Echoing other recent studies, I find that taking CTE courses is associated with an increase in high school graduation and a modest decrease in college enrollment. Finally, the chapter concludes with recommendations for policy and practice, along with opportunities for future research and questions for future consideration for all those interested in ensuring that high-quality CTE is equitable and accessible to all, especially those who could most benefit.


## BACKGROUND AND EVIDENCE ON CTE OUTCOMES

Much of the national perception of CTE is shaped by research from the 1970s and 1980s that painted vocational education as a tool for sorting or "tracking" students in ways that decreased social mobility and equity, particularly for low-income students, students of color, and students with disabilities (Bowles & Gintis, 1976; Tyack, 1974; Grubb & Lazerson, 1982). This two-tiered system of education often limited the opportunity of some students to attend college, which became increasingly important as more and more career paths demanded a college education. Moreover, given the historical context of racial integration of public schools, many scholars (Anderson, 1982; Oakes, 1983) found that vocational "tracks" were used to keep racial minorities separated from their White peers, exacerbating inequalities.

Largely because of this research, "vocational" education fell somewhat out of favor in the 1990s and early 2000s, replaced in many ways by the shift in focus toward a "college for all" framework for public secondary education (Rosenbaum, 2001; Grubb & Lazerson, 2005; Dougherty & Lombardi, 2016). During this time, the phrase "career and technical education" (CTE) gained prominence, signaling both a nominal and substantive shift. Over the past two decades, policy makers have increasingly embraced "college and career readiness" as the primary goal of high schools (Stone & Aliaga, 2005). Increasingly, policy makers have come to view the skills necessary for college readiness and career readiness to be closely aligned (Lucas, 1999; ACT, 2015; White House, 2011), rather than separate "college-preparatory" versus "vocational" tracks. For example, the most recent reauthorization of the

Perkins Act (the federal government's primary program supporting CTE) makes this shift particularly explicit, with new language that encourages funding for CTE programs that prepare students for college *and* career, rather than programs that only lead students directly into the workforce.

Since the shift from "vocational education" to "CTE" and a greater emphasis on applied STEM, a growing body of evidence has pointed to the potential for CTE to lead to positive outcome for students, particularly those who have been historically marginalized in education. In one of the first studies to use strong causal methodology, Kemple and Willner (2008) used a lottery process in which some students were randomly assigned to career academies. These students earned 11% more than noncareer academy students who had applied (with male students seeing an even-larger 17% increase in earnings). Hemelt, Lenard, and Paeplow (2019) also found positive returns to students who were admitted through a lottery to STEM-focused career academies, with an 8% increase in high school graduation rates and benefits largely accruing to men.

In addition to these lottery studies, a growing number of studies also use regression discontinuity designs to consider outcomes for students in CTE programs that had more applicants than spots available. Dougherty (2018), for example, found that students in vocational schools were 7%–10% more likely to graduate high school, more likely to earn a certificate in their career field, and more likely to pass state assessments, again with especially strong impacts for male students. Brunner et al. (2022) took a similar approach in Connecticut and found that CTE concentrators see a 31% increase in quarterly earnings without a significant difference in college attendance. Bonilla (2020) found that schools receiving more money to support CTE instruction saw reduced dropout rates, suggesting that financial investments (which can be spent on equipment and other important infrastructure) can improve the quality of CTE and lead to a meaningful difference for students.

Although these studies provide growing evidence that career and technical education can be effective, they leave questions about generalizability, given that they focus on highly sought-after programs with more applicants than spaces for students. It may be that these schools were highly sought after because of a strong sense of mission or buy-in among faculty and may not necessarily represent the quality of CTE nationwide, where CTE is offered in many ways other than just the whole-school CTE approach that is the basis for much of the causal evidence. Still, this research base offers compelling and growing evidence that done well, CTE can have positive effects.

Because of limitations to the generalizability of this research base, a sizable body of research from nationally representative data also provides important information about outcomes for CTE students. Many of these studies have focused specifically on CTE offered in a dual-enrollment context (primarily at community colleges), which is one common mode of CTE delivery in many regions. Cellini (2006), Stone and Aliaga (2005), and Yettick, Cline, and Young (2012) all report mixed findings on the effects of postsecondary enrollment from dual-enrollment CTE programs but find consistent evidence pointing to positive effects on high school completion. Indeed, one of the prime mechanisms through which CTE might benefit students is by making high school more engaging for students who were otherwise disengaged in traditional high school classrooms and by providing students with a strong feeling that their courses are relevant to their post–high school plans. For students who prefer hands-on, project-based approaches to their learning, CTE might provide an avenue that keeps some students in school to and through high school graduation.

A number of studies have also used nationally representative data to consider the effects of high school CTE in a more generalizable context. Although these studies are more subject to concerns of omitted variable bias, they find relatively similar evidence of positive returns to high school graduation and early career earnings as more causally identified research.

In addition, in estimates of returns to CTE, one key finding from these studies is that the type of CTE courses, when they are taking those courses, and which students participate seem to matter when considering outcomes. Kreisman and Stange (2020), for example, find that the benefits of CTE primarily go to those students who take upper-level CTE coursework, suggesting that in-depth concentration in a particular career pathway is especially important. Similarly, Gottfried and Plasman (2018) also found that CTE coursework taken later in high school can lead to a substantial increase in high school graduation.

Several studies have also considered the impact of CTE on specific populations, with especially promising returns for students with disabilities (Plasman & Gottfried, 2018; Theobald, Goldhaber, Gratz, & Holden, 2019) and for low-income students (Plasman, Gottfried, & Klasik, 2021; Dougherty, 2018; Kreisman & Stange, 2020), with evidence that higher levels of attendance and engagement in school may be important mechanisms through which CTE students see positive outcomes.

Although evidence is growing that CTE can yield positive benefits, Ecton and Dougherty (2021) argue that CTE should not be thought of as a single monolithic policy, finding substantially different outcomes for students in career clusters as wide-ranging as health care, IT, manufacturing, and construction. Instead, certain career clusters are more likely to lead to college (particularly when there is an aligned pathway at local community colleges, such as nursing), and others (e.g., construction or transportation) that are more likely to lead to direct employment after high school. Moreover, certain students see more positive returns than others; in particular, students not attending college see by far the largest earnings gains from CTE (along with a reduction in the likelihood of unemployment), suggesting that CTE may be an especially important safety net for students not attending college and those who might be at the greatest risk of economic instability in their young adulthood.

Finally, although this chapter focuses on CTE at the high school level, it is important to note that CTE also occurs at the secondary level, especially at community and technical colleges. Although some may mistakenly think of a "college versus CTE" dichotomy, that is far from the reality in today's context. Many high school CTE programs are explicitly designed to prepare students for related CTE programs in postsecondary institutions. Indeed, many jobs today require more training than just a high school diploma but less than a bachelor's degree, and many individuals currently in the workforce could fill needed job openings in areas with higher pay after pursuing additional training (Blair et al., 2020; Carnevale, Strohl, Ridley, & Gulish, 2018; Holzer & Baum, 2017). CTE programs at community and technical colleges provide one way for working adults to transition into higher-paying career paths. Although a thorough review of this literature is outside the scope of this chapter, Carruthers and Sanford (2018), Stevens, Kurlaender, and Grosz (2019), Carruthers and Jepsen (2021), and Sublett, Ecton, Klein, Atwell, and D'Amico (2021) provide useful overviews of key topics in postsecondary CTE.

## VOCATIONAL EDUCATION IN THE INTERNATIONAL CONTEXT

Although the body of evidence is growing in the United States, CTE (often still called vocational education internationally) has long played a prominent role around the globe, allowing us to gain certain insights by looking at vocational education in international settings. As Dougherty and Ecton (2021) document in a review of research on the returns to international vocational programs, vocational education in many countries often is separated explicitly from the academic education system, with many vocational programs often targeted explicitly for lower-income students, often those who have dropped out of traditional academic schools. Especially in developing economies, vocational education is often viewed as a poverty alleviation tool and a way to provide skills and training for young adults who otherwise were likely to be unemployed or employed outside the formal sector. In these developing economy contexts, evidence of positive economic returns to vocational education in countries is as widespread as India (Maitra & Mani, 2017), Uganda (Alfonsi et al., 2020), the Dominican Republic (Acevedo, Cruces, Gertler, & Martinez, 2020), and Colombia (Barrera-Osorio, Kugler, & Silliman, 2020). In these contexts, students not enrolled in vocational programs would often not be enrolled in education or training programs at all, leaving vocational programs as somewhat of a "safety valve" (Pugatch, 2014) for young adults at high risk for poverty and unemployment.

In many European countries, vocational education often takes the form of apprenticeships and distinct tracks for secondary school students. In this context, some longitudinal studies (Hanushek, Ruhose, & Woessmann, 2017; Hampf & Woessman, 2017) find that the short-term earnings' benefit diminishes over time, with vocational students earning less than their peers in general academic programs by mid-career. However, given the changing nature of many vocational programs in these countries (more STEM-based and service industry-based, less traditional trades-based), it is worth considering whether longitudinal studies of students who were in high school decades ago truly reflect the experiences of students engaging with vocational education today. Still, questions about long-term versus short-term payoffs are important and worthy of further attention.

Another finding in the research on vocational education in Europe is that in many cases, recent policies have increased exposure to academic coursework for vocational students, by either delaying the vocational tracking or adding more academic requirements. The outcomes of these policy shifts are not positive, with evidence from Croatia (Zilic, 2018), Norway (Bertrand, Mogstad, & Mountjoy, 2019), and Sweden (Hall, 2012) that these increased academic requirements led to increases in dropout rates, especially among men. These findings add evidence that vocational education may serve as an attractive alternative that keeps some students in school who otherwise would have left and provides some caution against efforts to force vocational students to take a curriculum that looks too similar to that from which some students might have been attempting to get away.

## EXAMINING CTE IN TODAY'S CONTEXT

To examine the landscape of high school CTE engagement in today's policy context in the United States, I next use a nationally representative survey of students who were high school freshmen in 2009 to study the effects of various levels of taking CTE courses. This analysis seeks to answer the following research questions:

1. Who engages with CTE courses under the era of college and career readiness, and what student and school characteristics predict taking CTE courses? Given long-standing concerns that CTE historically has been used to track students of certain backgrounds, do we continue to see students with certain demographic characteristics systematically taking more CTE courses?
2. Does CTE concentration affect student outcomes such as high school dropout, on-time high school graduation, and postsecondary enrollment?

### Data

This study uses data from the High School Longitudinal Study of 2009, a longitudinal survey administered by the US Department of Education's (2015) National Center for Education Statistics (NCES) that follows a nationally representative cohort of students who were in 9th grade (the start of their secondary education careers) in the fall of 2009. NCES used stratified random sampling procedure to identify 1,889 public and private high schools in the 50 states and the District of Columbia that included both ninth and 11th grade. Of these, 944 schools (approximately 50%) agreed to participate, and 25,206 ninth-grade students were chosen from those schools. Approximately 15% of selected students did not participate, and 548 students were deemed incapable of participating due to language barriers or severe disabilities, leaving 21,444 student participants in the base-year sample.

Due to attrition over four years between the initial survey and the third follow-up (which also collected student transcript data), this chapter only considers study participants observed in the third wave, for a final analytic sample of 16,303 students. Although survey attrition represents a potential threat to the representativeness of this sample, NCES develops probability robust frequency weights that allows the 16,303 students observed in the analytic sample to represent the full national population of students in the fall 2009 ninth-grade cohort. Applying these frequency weights, as applied throughout the paper, the sample is designed to represent 4,150,651 students nationally.

In the base year, students took a mathematics exam developed specifically for NCES by the American Institute for Research, together with a panel of university mathematics professors and K-12 educators. This 73-item exam provides a baseline measure of academic achievement and reasoning at the beginning of the high school experience, before high school factors such as curricular choices (and importantly, secondary CTE participation) could take effect.

Along with the ninth-grade mathematics exam, students also completed a survey asking a wide range of questions about their background, perceptions about themselves, academic goals, career aspirations, among other topics. For the purposes of this study, student characteristics considered include basic demographic information (including gender, race, and special education status)[1], how much education the ninth grader expects to obtain eventually, how sure the ninth grader is that he will graduate high school, whether he thinks he would be unable to get into college (even if he tried), and whether he thought his closest friends were planning to go to college. Using these student responses, together with the students' math exam scores, allows for a rich assessment of students' standing in regard to future educational plans at the beginning of his high school experience. In addition to information collected from students, NCES also surveyed parents in the fall of 2009, allowing for consideration of parents' levels of education and family income, which NCES condenses into a single composite measure of socioeconomic status (SES).

NCES also obtained school information from the Common Core of Data, Private School Survey, and from administrator surveys. In this study, school characteristics include whether a school was private or public, the school's total enrollment (in number of students), the level of urbanicity of the school's location, and geographic region. Also included are an indicator of whether an administrator responded that

---

1. I create a "special education" definition in which a student is considered to be a special education student if *any* of the following statements were true: In the ninth-grade parent survey, parents responded either that (1) their student was currently receiving Special Education Services, (2) a doctor or school had told them that their student had an intellectual disability, (3) a doctor or school has told them that their student had a learning disability, or it was in the student's high school transcript, (4) the student has earned credits in designated special education courses, or (5) the student has an Individual Education Plan (IEP). This allows for an inclusive categorization of students who may be labeled, to varying degrees, with a special education status. Given concerns around tracking and the tradition of reliance on vocational education for students with disabilities, an inclusive consideration of special education students is the most appropriate way to consider how special education students (loosely defined) are impacted by CTE.

the school offered "career clusters, pathways, or programs of study" to get a sense of each school's commitment to offering coherent CTE programming.

In addition to these characteristics collected about students at the beginning of their high school experience, HSLS collected data in the fall of 2013, after the modal student graduated from high school. The key variable of interest for this study is the number of CTE-designated credits a student earned during her high school experience, which is collected from transcripts provided by the high school. Credits were designated as CTE by NCES staff according to the School Courses for the Exchange of Data (SCED). Specifically, NCES staff identified the closest match to SCED uniform course code for all courses in students' transcripts. SCED designates as CTE those courses typically offered in the 16 Career and Technical Education Career Clusters. Generally, each one-semester course in a traditional academic schedule is a 0.5-credit course; each one-semester course in a standard block schedule is a one-credit course.

This chapter considers three outcomes:

1. First, whether a student ever dropped out of high school. In general, a student is classified as having "dropped out" if, at any point in her high school career, she stopped attending school for at least four weeks (not including exceptions, such as illness or if a family decided to homeschool).
2. Second, whether a student received a high school diploma, as indicated by his school transcript in the fall of 2013. Therefore, this indicator counts students who received a high school diploma "on-time" (four years after their ninth-grade year), as well as students who earn their diploma within a "grace period" of the summer after "on-time" completion. Notably, this indicator of having received a high school diploma does *not* include students still enrolled in high school in the fall of 2013, or students who earned a GED, certificate of attendance, or other high school equivalent.
3. Finally, whether a student was enrolled in postsecondary education in the fall after "on-time" high school graduation. Data were collected from both school transcripts and student surveys in the fall of 2013; if *either* the student survey *or* the student's transcript indicated that a student was enrolled in postsecondary education (full-time *or* part-time) in the fall of 2013, she was listed as being enrolled in college.

## Descriptive Findings

Before considering any potential effects of CTE, it is informative to consider who takes CTE courses in today's high schools. Given earlier research that low-income students, racial minorities, and students with disabilities may be tracked into CTE courses, it is particularly relevant to assess whether certain student groups are systematically taking more or fewer CTE courses in today's high schools. First, it is notable that taking CTE courses is widespread among the entire sample population, with the students taking an average of 2.899 CTE credits over the course of high school. This translates to an average of nearly six semesters of courses in CTE under a traditional academic schedule.

Although this mean is skewed by a relatively small number of students taking an especially large number of CTE courses, the median student still completes a sizable two CTE credits, or four semesters of CTE courses. Figure 4.1 shows the distribution of CTE credits for the overall sample, as well as select subpopulations of interest. Of note, figure 4.1 highlights that a larger number (though certainly not all) of students appear to take CTE courses in full-credit increments (either through a single block semester or two semesters under a traditional schedule), as a larger percentage of students completes whole numbers of credits, as opposed to half credits. Moreover, figure 4.1 highlights that many students (9.8%) take no CTE courses at all, whereas an additional 19.6% take only a half or single credit of CTE, often referred to as CTE "dabblers." However, figure 4.1 also illustrates that a substantial number of students engage with CTE courses in especially substantial amounts.

Figure 4.2 highlights the broad range of fields in which students take CTE, by illustrating the average number of courses in each of the NCES's 12 CTE fields. Computer science is most common, with students taking nearly a half credit (a typical one-semester course) on average, likely reflecting that introductory computing classes remain a common fixture in many schools' standard curriculum. Next most common are business and communications. Manufacturing, historically one of the first fields that comes to mind when thinking of vocational education, is the least

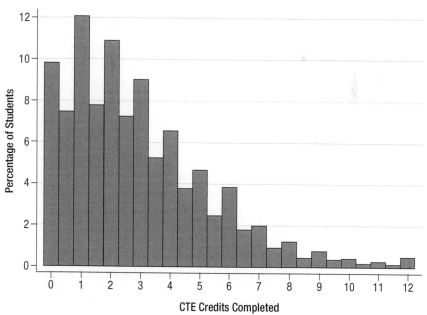

**Figure 4.1. Distribution of Student CTE Credit Accumulation**

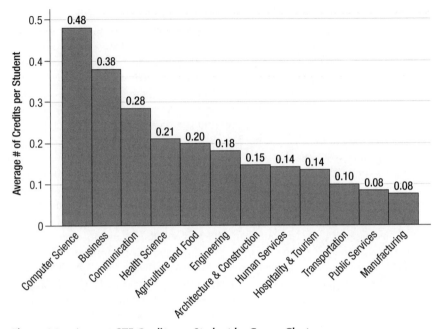

**Figure 4.2.   Average CTE Credits per Student by Career Cluster**

popular of all the career clusters. Given the shift to CTE as part of a college- and career-readiness agenda and the decline of manufacturing on the whole in America, this seems particularly notable.

Table 4.1 highlights key differences in taking CTE courses across different student types and school settings. A few findings are of particular interest. First, men, on average, take approximately 0.24 more CTE credits than women. CTE is least common for high math-test scorers and high socioeconomic status (SES) students, and more concentrated around the bottom and middle of the testing and SES distributions. Students identified as special education students also take more CTE credits (although this difference might not be as large as one might expect), as do students less sure about whether they plan to earn a bachelor's degree or higher. Perhaps most surprising, though, are the descriptive findings on race. Contrary to previous research, White students average the most CTE courses, with White students taking more CTE credits than Black students (by 0.28 credits) and Hispanic students (by 0.617 credits) nearly an entire CTE course more than Black or Hispanic students. Asian students take by far the fewest CTE courses.

These differences by student characteristics appear to be driven partially by differences in where schools are located. For example, students at rural schools take 3.38 CTE credits on average, compared to students at urban schools who only averaged 2.5 CTE credits. Students in the southern United States also take more CTE courses on average than students across the rest of the country, with students in the West

**Table 4.1. CTE Credits Taken by Student and School Characteristics**

| | Mean CTE Credits | Standard Deviation | Population Size |
|---|---|---|---|
| **All Students** | **2.899** | **2.361** | **4,150,569** |
| ***Student Characteristics*** | | | |
| Males | 3.016 | 2.398 | 2,092,840 |
| Females | 2.780 | 2.316 | 2,057,729 |
| High Math Test Scorers (Top 25%) | 2.384 | 2.126 | 863,102 |
| Medium Math Test Scorers (Middle 50%) | 3.039 | 2.362 | 1,762,961 |
| Low Math Test Scorers (Bottom 25%) | 3.059 | 2.514 | 1,280,587 |
| High Socioeconomic Status (Top 25%) | 2.314 | 2.028 | 736,422 |
| Medium Socioeconomic Status (Middle 50%) | 3.066 | 2.380 | 2,081,674 |
| Low Socioeconomic Status (Bottom 25%) | 2.964 | 2.450 | 1,332,473 |
| Non-Special Education | 2.852 | 2.852 | 3,509,719 |
| Special Education | 3.158 | 2.604 | 640,850 |
| Very Sure about Graduating from High School | 2.930 | 2.338 | 3,395,812 |
| Not Sure about Graduating from High School | 2.698 | 2.409 | 650,992 |
| Expects to Earn a Bachelor's Degree or Higher | 2.804 | 2.237 | 2,345,742 |
| Does Not Expect to Earn a Bachelor's Degree | 3.036 | 2.588 | 881,206 |
| White | 3.138 | 2.470 | 2,157,004 |
| Black | 2.854 | 2.290 | 564,219 |
| Hispanic | 2.521 | 2.143 | 909,065 |
| Asian | 2.257 | 2.192 | 145,980 |
| ***School Characteristics*** | | | |
| Public | 3.013 | 2.386 | 3,853,284 |
| Private | 1.427 | 1.301 | 297,285 |
| Urban | 2.456 | 2.112 | 1,322,744 |
| Suburban | 2.675 | 2.258 | 1,383,844 |
| Rural | 3.375 | 2.486 | 956,059 |
| Northeastern United States | 2.960 | 2.470 | 722,282 |
| Midwestern United States | 2.946 | 2.285 | 920,448 |
| Southern United States | 3.275 | 2.464 | 1,558,075 |
| Western United States | 2.192 | 1.990 | 949,764 |
| Large (Top 25%) | 2.609 | 2.219 | 1,206,626 |
| Medium-Size (Middle 50%) | 3.222 | 2.426 | 1,660,458 |
| Small (Bottom 25%) | 3.014 | 2.431 | 947,340 |

*Source:* The High School Longitudinal Study of 2009 (HSLS:09). Washington, DC: US Department of Education, Institute of Education Sciences, National Center for Education Statistics.

taking more than a full credit less than their peers in the South. These findings challenge a historical narrative that CTE primarily targets minority students; instead, these results suggest that, although taking CTE courses is quite widespread, White, rural and southern students take the greatest number of CTE courses, on average. Finally, as might be expected, students at private schools take far fewer CTE courses than students at public schools; indeed, students at private schools took the fewest

CTE courses of any of the subpopulations studied. Although this survey cannot definitively answer whether student demand for CTE differs across school location and context, or whether *access* to CTE drives these differences (a question ripe for future study), it is clear that taking CTE courses looks quite different based on where students attend high school.

## Methods

Next, given that many of the factors discussed above are highly correlated, I employ ordinary least squares (OLS) regression models to identify factors that are particularly predictive in terms of how students will engage with CTE courses. Table 4.2 shows the coefficients and significance levels for seven different logistic regression models.

Column 1 represents the results of an OLS regression in which the dependent variable is a binary indicator for whether a student earned three or more CTE credits (a policy-relevant level of exposure, as prominent advocacy groups such as Jobs for the Future, the Association for Career and Technical Education, and multiple states currently push for or require three credit hours to identify CTE concentrators). To delineate between the substantive CTE exposure indicated by CTE-concentrator status and those with minor or no CTE exposure, I exclude students who took between 1.5 and 2.5 CTE credits. These students are effectively in a CTE gray zone, as they might be considered concentrators in some states but not in others. Comparing students taking 3+ CTE credits to those taking one or fewer allows for a contrast between students with clear, substantive time spent in CTE classes and otherwise similar students who engaged with CTE in only minor ways or not at all.

As the first columns of table 4.2 show, many of the student and school characteristics are significantly predictive of CTE concentration. Male students are more likely to be CTE concentrators than otherwise similar females by 7.9 percentage points. Conversely, Black and Hispanic students are substantially less likely to take CTE courses, all else remaining constant. This fits with the descriptive findings presented earlier and provides further reasons to be skeptical of concerns that race-based tracking is a primary driver of taking CTE courses in modern American high schools. Surprisingly, given the long-standing role of CTE in special education, students' special education status fails to significantly predict CTE concentration.

Students are predicted to take more CTE courses as their ninth-grade math scores rise, up to a certain point—the highest achievers are less likely to take as many CTE courses. These patterns could make sense if students who are certain of their postsecondary plans and academic ability choose to focus their energy solely on a college-preparatory curriculum, if they engage in advanced classes such as Advanced Placement or International Baccalaureate, or if they did not feel any pressure to learn skills preparing them for the workforce, feeling confident about their chances in college. Perhaps relatedly, students from higher SES backgrounds are also less likely to take larger numbers of CTE courses; SES becomes especially negatively predictive

**Table 4.2. OLS Regression Results: Predictors of Selection as CTE Concentrator and Select Outcomes of Interest**

| | Selection | Outcomes | | |
|---|---|---|---|---|
| | CTE Concentrator (3+ Credits) | Ever Dropped or Stopped Out of HS | Earned "On-Time" HS Diploma | Enrolled in College Fall After "On-Time" HS Graduation |
| **Student-Level Characteristics** | | | | |
| Male | .079** | .012 | −.016+ | −.075** |
| Race (reference category: White) | | | | |
|   Black | −.052* | −.012 | −.009 | .029 |
|   Latinx | −.067** | −.028* | .023* | .046** |
|   Asian | −.065+ | −.001 | .005 | .080** |
| Special Ed | .025 | .031* | −.022* | −.054** |
| Socioeconomic Status | −.043** | −.029** | .033** | .096** |
| Socioeconomic Status Squared | −.031** | .014** | .019** | −.001 |
| Ninth-Grade Math Test | .072** | −.018** | .015** | −.064** |
| Ninth-Grade Math Test Squared | −.032** | −.004 | −.005 | .006 |
| Expect to Complete a Bachelor's Degree or Higher | −.028+ | −.005 | .026** | .011** |
| Total Credits Taken | .032** | −.024** | .027** | .017** |
| **School-Level Characteristics** | | | | |
| Private School | −.431** | −.026+ | .010 | .076** |
| Student Enrollment Size | −.001* | −.001** | .001** | .001 |
| School Location (reference category: Suburban) | | | | |
|   Urban | −.039 | .009 | −.006 | −.011 |
|   Rural | .061* | −.020 | .010 | −.032* |
| School Region (reference category: Northeast) | | | | |
|   Midwest | −.056+ | −.029* | .018 | .007 |
|   South | .056* | .046** | −.034** | −.057** |
|   West | −.046 | −.042** | .014 | .017 |
| *Observations* | 11,900 | 16,303 | 16,303 | 16,303 |
| *Population Represented* | 3,074,548 | 4,150,651 | 4,150,651 | 4,150,651 |
| $R^2$ | .334 | .289 | .382 | .236 |

Significance levels: **$p < .01$, *$p < .05$, +$p < .1$.

*Source*: The High School Longitudinal Study of 2009 (HSLS:09). Washington, DC: US Department of Education, Institute of Education Sciences, National Center for Education Statistics.

**Table 4.3. Balance Check: Comparing CTE Concentrators with Matched Comparison Groups**

| | Nearest Neighbor | | Nearest 5 Neighbors | | Epanechnikov Kernel | |
|---|---|---|---|---|---|---|
| | CTE Concentrators | Matched Comparison | CTE Concentrators | Matched Comparison | CTE Concentrators | Matched Comparison |
| **Student-Level Characteristics** | | | | | | |
| Male | .487 | .491 | .487 | .495 | .487 | .489 |
| Race (reference category: White) | | | | | | |
| Black | .099 | .097 | .099 | .098 | .099 | .097 |
| Latinx | .159 | .140** | .159 | .144* | .159 | .145+ |
| Asian | .074 | .084+ | .074 | .082 | .074 | .082 |
| Special Ed | .140 | .134 | .140 | .144 | .140 | .141 |
| Socioeconomic Status | .025 | .109** | .025 | .098** | .025 | .083** |
| Socioeconomic Status Squared | .539 | .541 | .539 | .540 | .539 | .544 |
| Ninth-Grade Math Test | .081 | .190** | .081 | .185** | .081 | .172** |
| Ninth-Grade Math Test Squared | .846 | .773** | .846 | .796** | .846 | .794* |
| Expect to Complete Bachelor's Degree or Higher | .608 | .637** | .608 | .631* | .608 | .632** |
| Total Credits Taken | 26.326 | 26.562** | 26.316 | 26.522* | 26.316 | 26.436 |

## School-Level Characteristics

| | | | | | |
|---|---|---|---|---|---|
| **Private School** | .082 | .087 | .082 | .086 | .085 |
| Student Enrollment Size | 1,305 | 1,298 | 1,305 | 1,280+ | 1,270* |
| School Location (reference category: Suburban) | | | | | |
| Urban | .260 | .264 | .260 | .260 | .254 |
| Rural | .371 | .374 | .371 | .379 | .377 |
| School Region (reference category: Northeast) | | | | | |
| Midwest | .271 | .300** | .271 | .287+ | .284 |
| South | .418 | .419 | .418 | .423 | .417 |
| West | .155 | .125** | .155 | .129** | .133* |
| R (variance ratio) | 1.28 | 1.17 | 1.17 | | 1.17 |

Significance levels: **p < .01, *p < .05, + p < .01.

Note: "CTE Concentrators" indicate those taking at least 3 credits in a designated CTE field.
Comparison students are those who took 1 CTE credit or less, matched to CTE Concentrators using the characteristics in table 4.3 through the three propensity score matching procedures listed here.

Source: Data from US Department of Education NCES, High School Longitudinal Study of 2009.

near the top of the SES distribution. Attendance at a private school is the strongest predictor against CTE concentration, whereas school location also provides significant predictive power; attending rural schools or schools in the South increases the likelihood of a concentration of CTE courses.

Finally, all models include a control for the number of total credits taken. Because transcript data are only collected at a single time, HSLS does not allow for a consideration of *when* in their high school career students engaged with CTE or *when* students dropped out, stopped out, or took fewer classes. As such, this study includes a control for the total number of credits taken, to guard against attributing any returns to CTE to simply taking more CTE classes *as a function* of taking more classes overall. This means that the estimates presented in this chapter should be thought of as a lower-bound estimate on the potential effects of CTE, given that any impact CTE has through its ability to increase the number of courses students take in high school will not be seen in these findings.

Turning next to outcomes, I use propensity score matching to compare outcomes for CTE concentrators to students who were similarly likely to concentrate in CTE but did not do so. Using the models from table 4.2, each student is assigned a propensity score (the likelihood of being a CTE concentrator based on observable characteristics). I can then compare CTE concentrators to students with similar propensity to be a concentrator.[2] By creating propensity scores, I can also identify non-concentrators who were highly unlikely to ever become CTE concentrators. In order to ensure that estimates come from students who could have plausibly become CTE concentrators, I exclude students with the lowest propensity scores in order to use a more valid matched comparison group, reducing concerns that estimates are biased by students who were extremely unlikely to ever opt into CTE.

---

2. To successfully employ a propensity score matching model, two conditions must be satisfied in the identification of predictive variables (Rubin, 2001; Shadish, Clark, & Steiner, 2008). First, predictors must not simply be "off-the-shelf" but, instead, must be predictive of selection into treatment. The preceding discussion aims to satisfy this condition. Through school characteristics, student academic achievement, aspirations and expectations, demographics, and family background (including a composite measure of SES that incorporates both family income and parental education), this chapter argues that the characteristics in table 4.2 can satisfactorily predict which students will select into treatment at the four levels of dosage discussed here.

The second condition required of these predictors is that they also predict the outcomes of interest. Columns 2–4 present the results of OLS regressions of the same predictors on the study's three outcomes—whether a student ever dropped or stopped out of high school, whether a student earned a high school diploma by the fall after "on-time" graduation, and whether a student enrolled in college by the fall after "on-time" (four-year) high school graduation. Table 4.2 shows that many of these predictors are not only predictive of taking CTE courses, but also the three outcomes.

Next, I identify an optimal number of blocks for which the mean propensity score is not statistically different between treatment and control students; this provides a test of balance as suggested by Rosenbaum and Rubin (1984). I use three matching propensity score-matching methods—nearest neighbor matching, nearest five neighbors matching, and Epanechnikov Kernel matching to identify matched comparison students for each "treatment" student. Table 4.3 tests the degree to which these matches were successful, showing that, on the whole, all three matching procedures created comparison samples that are extremely similar to the treatment sample on observed characteristics. For each of the three matching methods, the matches produce variance ratios between 1.17 and 1.28, close to the optimal match of 1 and well within the range of 0.5–2 commonly suggested by Rubin (2001).

## Results and Discussion

Forming matched comparison groups allows for the assumption that, in the absence of the "treatment" (in this case, higher levels of taking CTE courses), the two groups should have similar outcomes. Therefore, any differences in outcome can be considered as the treatment effects of CTE concentration. Table 4.4 shows these treatment effects as measured by the differences in outcomes for the treatment and matched comparison groups.

Table 4.4 offers mixed evidence to advocates of career and technical education. On the whole, CTE concentration appears to have no significant impact on dropout behavior or on-time high school graduation. As noted before, these estimates, which match students partially on the basis of the total number of credits taken in high school, should likely be considered as conservative estimates, because they limit CTE's ability to affect our outcomes through a potentially key mechanism—encouraging students to take more credits. CTE concentration *does* appear to reduce students' likelihood of attending college immediately after high school, with estimates from the three models suggesting 7.7 to 8.7 percentage point decreases in immediate college attendance. This may be expected, as some CTE programs explicitly prepare students for direct entry into the workforce. Nevertheless, these initial results do provide suggestive evidence that, at a nationally representative level, CTE concentration does seem to be sending students down different paths post–high school.

As an additional check, table 4.5 uses OLS to test similar outcomes from the propensity score-matching methods. Table 4.5 presents similar findings, with no evidence of significant impact on dropping out or receiving an on-time diploma, but a 6.6 percentage point decline in immediate college attendance.

These findings speak to a need for deeper understanding about the current state of CTE in America and how CTE has evolved from the vocational education of current generations. First, rather than considering CTE as a binary policy intervention that

**Table 4.4. Propensity Score Results: CTE Concentrators Compared to Matched Students**

| Outcomes | Nearest Neighbor | Nearest 5 Neighbors | Epanechnikov Kernel |
|---|---|---|---|
| Ever Dropped or Stopped Out of High School | .009 (.011) | .004 (.009) | .004 (.009) |
| Received High School Diploma by Fall After "Normal Time" | −.012 (.010) | −.014 (.009) | −.012 (.009) |
| Enrolled in College by Fall After "Normal Time" | −.084** (.015) | −.087** (.012) | −.077** (.012) |

Significance levels: **p < .01, *p < .05, + p < .01.

*Note*: "CTE Concentrators" indicate those taking at least 3 credits in a designated CTE field.
Comparison students are those who took 1 CTE credit or less, matched to CTE Concentrators using the characteristics in table 3 through the three propensity score matching procedures listed here.

*Source*: Data from US Department of Education NCES, High School Longitudinal Study of 2009.

**Table 4.5. OLS Regression Results: Effect of CTE Concentration**

| | Ever Dropped or Stopped Out of High School | Received High School Diploma by Fall After "Normal Time" | Enrolled in College by Fall After "Normal Time" |
|---|---|---|---|
| CTE Concentrator | −0.014 | 0.013 | −0.066*** |
| | (0.013) | (0.013) | (0.016) |
| Male | 0.014 | −0.018+ | −0.073*** |
| | (0.009) | (0.010) | (0.013) |
| Black | −0.014 | −0.010 | 0.039+ |
| | (0.015) | (0.016) | (0.023) |
| Hispanic | −0.022 | 0.026* | 0.042* |
| | (0.014) | (0.012) | (0.020) |
| Asian | 0.001 | 0.016 | 0.071** |
| | (0.019) | (0.021) | (0.027) |
| Socioeconomic Status | −0.034*** | 0.037*** | 0.090*** |
| | (0.006) | (0.006) | (0.010) |
| Socioeconomic Status Squared | 0.014* | −0.020*** | 0.001 |
| | (0.006) | (0.006) | (0.008) |
| Special Education | 0.018 | −0.009 | −0.041* |
| | (0.014) | (0.012) | (0.019) |
| Ninth-Grade Math Test | −0.017*** | 0.017** | 0.058*** |
| | (0.005) | (0.005) | (0.008) |
| Ninth-Grade Math Test Squared | 0.004 | −0.007+ | 0.006 |
| | (0.004) | (0.004) | (0.004) |
| Expect Bachelor's Degree or Higher | −0.004 | 0.027** | 0.114*** |
| | (0.009) | (0.010) | (0.016) |
| Total Credits Taken | −0.023*** | 0.025*** | 0.020*** |
| | (0.001) | (0.001) | (0.001) |
| Private School | −0.041* | 0.019 | 0.071*** |
| | (0.017) | (0.014) | (0.019) |
| Student Enrollment Size | −0.000*** | 0.000 | 0.000 |
| | (0.000) | (0.000) | (0.000) |
| Urban | 0.021 | −0.017 | −0.023 |
| | (0.014) | (0.014) | (0.018) |
| Rural | −0.019 | 0.007 | −0.020 |
| | (0.014) | (0.013) | (0.018) |
| Midwest | −0.034* | 0.018 | 0.031 |
| | (0.015) | (0.014) | (0.021) |
| South | 0.036* | −0.024+ | −0.039+ |
| | (0.014) | (0.012) | (0.020) |
| West | −0.057** | 0.017 | 0.026 |
| | (0.019) | (0.019) | (0.028) |
| *Observations* | 11,900 | 11,900 | 11,900 |
| *Population Represented* | 3,074,548 | 3,074,548 | 3,074,548 |
| $R^2$ | 0.306 | 0.400 | 0.243 |

Significance levels: **$p < .01$, *$p < .05$, + $p < .01$.

*Note*: "CTE Concentrator" indicates those taking at least 3 credits in a designated CTE field. Comparison students are those who took 1 CTE credit or less.

*Source*: Data from US Department of Education NCES, High School Longitudinal Study of 2009.

students either do or do not participate in, CTE is, to varying degrees, a component of the high school curriculum for a large percentage of American high schools, with more than 90% of students taking at least one CTE course. Nearly half (about 44% of students) take at least 3 credits in CTE under the federal definitions, with the average student taking 2.899 credits. Simply put, CTE is not a niche part of the curriculum that only impacts a select few students.

Moreover, a robust literature found that vocational education in previous generations primarily served low-income students, racially minoritized students, and students with disabilities, but this no longer appears to be the case. Although CTE continues largely to serve low-SES students, Black students and Hispanic students today are *less* likely to engage with CTE than their White peers. Students with disabilities are only descriptively more likely to engage with CTE, though this difference does not hold after accounting for other factors. Moreover, gender is a substantial predictor of CTE participation today, with male students taking disproportionately more CTE courses than female students. Indeed, although a diverse range of students engage with CTE, the American CTE concentrator of today is disproportionately male, white, rural, and southern.

These findings raise important questions for future research about *why* these patterns have changed, in particular, whether gaps in taking CTE courses are driven by differential supply or differential demand. Several plausible hypotheses deserve consideration. First, CTE today is especially common in rural America, and much more common in the southern states than in the rest of the country. These regional differences may drive differential participation, though racial and gender gaps hold even after accounting for these regional differences. Second, the legacy of race-based tracking and vocational education's role in limiting postsecondary access may have led to a backlash against CTE among racially minoritized populations, driving down their participation in ways not impacting White students. In addition, the national "college for all" movement may have differentially impacted CTE participation among different populations (Rosenbaum, 2001). Another possibility could be that as "vocational education" rebranded into "CTE" as part of a college and career readiness agenda and increased its focus on high-rigor, often STEM fields, CTE may be viewed as more appealing and perhaps more complementary to a college-preparatory curriculum, which could lead to changes in both supply and demand. These are just a few possibilities, but the reasons for these shifts in taking CTE courses deserve further attention and research. Given the increasing evidence base pointing toward the potential of positive outcomes from CTE, it may also be worth considering questions of access and equity in opportunities to participate in high-quality CTE.

Next, this study may allay concerns that CTE limits student opportunity by inhibiting their ability to obtain a high school diploma or attend college. The study finds no evidence of an increase in student stop-out behavior and no evidence of a decrease in on-time high school completion associated with CTE concentration. Due to the nature of the data collection, these estimates are likely lower-bound, conservative estimates, because total credits taken are controlled for in all models.

Indeed, one plausible way CTE might decrease dropout behavior and increase high school graduation is by keeping students more engaged in high school so that they choose to take more courses. Indeed, in additional results not shown here, if we allow for the total number of courses to vary, CTE concentration is positively associated with on-time high school graduation. CTE *is* associated with a decrease in college attendance immediately after high school, but this might be expected given the nature of many CTE programs that prepare students for direct entry into the workforce. Notably, though, the relatively modest estimated change in likelihood of college attendance does *not* seem to suggest that CTE broadly prevents college attendance for most CTE students. Although more evidence is needed, suggestive evidence from other studies has shown that CTE students may be especially likely to return to college and close college attendance gaps after a few years in the workforce, with postsecondary credentials often needed for advancement within many CTE fields (Bifulco, Fletcher, Oh, & Ross, 2014; Brunner, Dougherty, & Ross, 2019).

Although more work is needed to better understand causal effects of taking CTE courses and the mechanisms of those effects in American high schools, this study sheds light on the changing nature of engagement with CTE in American high schools at a nationwide level, highlighting the many ways that CTE in the modern era of "college and career readiness" differs from the vocational education of previous eras. This, alongside the growing research base on CTE, leads to several directions for future research, along with a number of recommendations for policy and practice.

## RECOMMENDATIONS FOR POLICY AND PRACTICE

As policy makers and school, district, and state leaders consider how CTE can best support their students, equity and quality should be at the root of conversations and decision making. CTE has, on the whole, shown great potential for promising outcomes for students, but CTE programs show enormous variation in their ability to set students on positive paths—particularly low-income students, students with disabilities, students who have struggled academically, and students from underrepresented backgrounds. This section proposes several items for policy makers and leaders in education to consider. Broadly speaking, these recommendations encourage a reframing of the debate around CTE. Rather than "Should we provide more or less CTE?," leaders should instead ask, "How can we ensure that our CTE programs are high quality and that students who can benefit have access to programs that will prepare them for success?"

### Define Intended Outcomes for Specific CTE Programs

Unlike many core academic classes, it is not clear that standardized tests are the strongest way to measure student learning in CTE. Instead, policy makers and educators should define the intended outcomes of a successful CTE student in each particular program of study, with the understanding that the outcomes of successful students may differ across fields as diverse as health care, IT, construction, mechatronics. One benefit of CTE is that it can prepare students for successful transitions into specific paths based on their unique skills and interest. Programs should consider leaning into these outcomes and making them explicit for students, families, and teachers. Intended outcomes may include (but are not limited to)

1. entry into a postsecondary program at a community college, technical college, or university in a field related to the CTE program;
2. meeting the requirements for industry-recognized certification and/or licensure for a related career; and
3. direct employment in a job that is directly tied to the CTE program of study (after completing a curriculum that has been informed by what employers say is needed to be prepared for direct entry).

By making explicit the "goal" of each specific CTE program, students and families can better understand the implications of different CTE programs, instructors can align their instruction to these goals, and teachers and counselors can have more focused conversations with students about how to prepare for life after high school. In addition, given that students may change career paths or decide to attend college, it is crucial that CTE students leave high school with a solid base of skills that will allow them the flexibility to transition back into school or other career paths.

## Build Partnerships to Strengthen CTE Programs

One of the most important aspects of CTE is that it helps students make connections between the classroom and the real world and helps them to see themselves in potential pathways after high school. In order to maximize these connections, CTE programs should work to build strong relationships with local partners that focus in related fields. This might include strategies such as

1. allowing students to take some CTE coursework at a local college (or to work with the college to offer coursework at the high school);
2. working with faculty in local postsecondary programs to ensure that the skills and knowledge taught in high school will prepare students to seamlessly enter into and be successful in related programs;
3. creating apprenticeships, internships, or other work-based opportunities for students to gain hands-on experience doing the types of work they might expect to do following completion of the CTE program; and
4. cultivating strong, active relationships with local industry leaders in related fields to ensure that the knowledge and skills taught in CTE classrooms are up-to-date and relevant and to build opportunities for students to interact with local industry leaders.

By creating these partnerships, CTE programs become more dynamic and relevant for students while also creating important real-world exposure that can help motivate students and also better understand their post–high school outcomes. Another tangible benefit is that these strategies can help students gain access to post–high school opportunities. If high school health-care students receive dual-enrollment credits that count toward an associate degree in nursing, that helps set them up for success not only in high school but in college. If students do a work-based learning program or have a CTE teacher who came from a local employer, this may help them network and show their worth to potential future employers in ways that can help them achieve a job directly related to their CTE program.

## Only Offer High-Quality, Relevant CTE Programs

Although more research is needed about how to define and measure quality in CTE, it is clear that not all CTE is created equal. Schools should work to make sure that their CTE programs are engaging and challenging and that they set students up for success with a clear pathway(s) after their time in high school. For some students, that may mean preparing them for entry into a community college program; for others, it might mean preparing students for well-paying jobs with growth potential. Most states now have state longitudinal data systems that link secondary, postsecondary, and employment data—states should consider analyses of outcomes for their different CTE programs, both at an aggregate and more local levels. At individual schools, this may take additional data collection by teachers and schools to better understand students' post–high school plans and early career experiences. Put simply, if most of the students in a business CTE program are working entry-level jobs in retail stores or in fast-food restaurants, then this in an indication that the CTE program is not preparing students for a specific career path in the way they are intended.

Relatedly, CTE programs should prepare students for jobs that are in demand in the local workforce, especially given that the large majority of students nationwide stay near home when entering the workforce. If a school offers a CTE program that does not currently set students up for a clear pathway, or if it sets students up for career paths that are not available in the local area, it is important to consider changes to those programs. Given the rapidly evolving workforce, it is natural that the most beneficial types of CTE should also evolve; schools should take care not to remain tied to programs that no longer serve students well; conversely, schools should be open to new programs as their local economy changes.

## Ensure Access to CTE for the Students Who Stand to Benefit Most

As this chapter has discussed, there are strong reasons to think that some students may benefit most from CTE. Particularly for students who have struggled in traditional classroom settings, and those who are not planning to enter college directly, CTE can be an especially important option to keep students engaged and on a clear path through graduation and into the crucial early years of young adulthood. As policy makers and school leaders work to increase the academic rigor of CTE programs and emphasize STEM programs, one potential concern is if these CTE programs become too popular, higher-income, higher-testing students might crowd out many of the students who might stand to benefit the most.

To protect against this, schools should take care that admissions criteria to popular CTE programs do not systematically exclude students who have struggled in traditional academic settings. Rejecting students with lower test scores, GPAs, and attendance rates may prevent many students who were disengaged in traditional classrooms but could benefit from a different learning style and from the real-world connections that CTE can provide. Although the push to enhance the academic rigor of CTE has been a positive development, educators must take caution to ensure that the highest-quality, most-rigorous CTE programs do not become out of reach for lower-income and academically lower-performing students.

## Focus on Equitable Participation in CTE

Throughout this chapter, a central theme has been that not all CTE is created equal. Because of this, a focus on equitable access to and participation in high-quality CTE programs is crucial if CTE wishes to live up to its potential. Policy makers and school leaders should demand transparency in the demographic representation of students not only in CTE programs as a whole, but in specific CTE programs. If CTE aims to be a tool to lift students out of poverty, to support students who did not have clear pathways into postsecondary education and well-paying careers, then all students must be able to access the highest-quality programs. As the range of programs (and related outcomes) in CTE is wider than ever in today's schools, great care must be taken that there are not "two tracks" within CTE—where one track is for "old vocational" programs, enrolling mostly lower-income students, students with disabilities, and racially minoritized students; and the other track consists of high-rigor, "new CTE" programs that set students up for high-earning careers and primarily enroll White students and those from upper-middle-class backgrounds.

Relatedly, the consistent evidence across settings that male students benefit from CTE more than female students—along with dramatically gendered participation in different CTE fields—raises difficult questions about why women are not enrolling in certain CTE fields and why their outcomes are not as strong after participating in CTE. School leaders and instructors should pay especially close attention to whether and how they make different programs accessible and desirable for all students, and one where all students can thrive. As a first step, schools must collect demographic data to understand their equity gaps and opportunities for growth. In particular, the findings in this chapter that Black and Hispanic students nationally are less likely than their White peers may provide reason for concern. School, district, and state leaders would be well-served by conducting analyses of participation in their own contexts.

As schools continue to consider how CTE can best serve their students, a number of key questions remain for researchers and policy makers to explore. Although evidence is growing that CTE *can* positively impact students, a greater understanding is needed about how, why, when, and for whom CTE can be beneficial, or conversely, when it might be detrimental for some students.

Perhaps most crucial is a better understanding of quality—both what high-quality CTE means, and how CTE programs' quality can be measured and evaluated. Much of the research base on the effectiveness of high school CTE relies on schools and programs that are oversubscribed and therefore are perceived by students and families to be desirable. However, less is known about which tactics and qualities make those programs and schools successful. Although quantitative CTE research has expanded, particularly from the growth in State Longitudinal Data Systems, more quantitative researchers are needed to examine questions in this field, along with more qualitative researchers asking questions about mechanisms and quality within CTE. Key questions about quality are ripe for further study, including:

- What are the markers of successful apprenticeships and other work-based learning programs, and how do these programs compare to in-class learning experiences? How can schools and leaders understand when different modes of learning are most appropriate?
- How should schools think about student "fit," both for CTE and for specific CTE programs in particular? How can we give students and families the opportunities to understand their different opportunities, and how can schools support them in making choices that best set them up for success?
- What should student assessment look like in CTE? How should we evaluate student success? What role should certification exams play, and how should this differ for different fields of study?
- What are the differences in student outcomes for different models of CTE delivery? How does CTE operate differently in whole-school CTE models, within comprehensive high schools, at local CTE centers, or via dual enrollment at local postsecondary institutions? Are certain models more or less appropriate for different students or fields of study?
- What makes a successful CTE teacher? How should education and training work for CTE teachers? How should their certification requirements differ from teachers in core academic subject areas? When should CTE teachers come from educator backgrounds versus from the industry of their CTE field? When coming from industry, how can schools attract, train, and retain CTE teachers?

A common thread in these questions is that all call for a deeper understanding of what happens *within* and *across* CTE programs and classrooms. Rather than evaluating outcomes of CTE as a whole, these questions call for more exploration of what works, what doesn't work, and for whom. This calls for a mix of quantitative and qualitative research, for engagement among researchers, policy makers, and practitioners. Working together, a deeper understanding will allow for greater access not just to CTE but, rather, an expansion of access to high-quality CTE, policies to scale best practices, and an understanding of where limited resources can do the most good. The opportunities are ripe for those wishing to pursue impactful research in this area.

Although these questions are directed at researchers, certain questions also would be beneficial for policy makers, school leaders, and teachers to consider. The research may not yet be clear on all of these questions, but they are still important questions for practitioners to consider and can help guide useful conversations about advancing practice and policy. Thinking deeply about key questions of quality, success metrics, student fit, and instructional success provides policy makers and practitioners with a useful set of considerations for their work in CTE.

## REFERENCES

Acevedo, P., Cruces, G., Gertler, P., & Martinez, S. (2020). How vocational education made women better off but left men behind. *Labour Economics, 65,* 101824.

ACT. *Ready for college and ready for work: Same or different?* (2015, March 12). ACT study: College and Workforce Training Readiness. https://www.act.org/content/act/en/research/pdfs/ready-for-collegeandreadyforworksameordifferent.html

Alfonsi, L., Bandiera, O., Bassi, V., Burgess, R., Rasul, I., Sulaiman, M., & Vitali, A. (2020). Tackling youth unemployment: Evidence from a labor market experiment in Uganda. *Econometrica, 88*(6), 2369–2414.

Anderson, J. (1982). The historical development of Black vocational education. In H. Kantor & D. B. Tyack (Eds.), *Work, youth and schooling: Historical perspectives on vocational education* (pp. 180–222). Redwood City, CA: Stanford University Press.

Barrera-Osorio, F., Kugler, A. D., & Silliman, M. I. (2020). *Hard and soft skills in vocational training: Experimental evidence from Colombia* (Working Paper No. 257548). National Bureau of Economic Research.

Bertrand, M., Mogstad, M., & Mountjoy, J. (2019). *Improving educational pathways to social mobility: Evidence from Norway's "reform 94"* (Working Paper No. 25679). National Bureau of Economic Research.

Bifulco, R., Fletcher, J., Oh, S. J., & Ross, S. L. (2014). Do high school peers have persistent effects on college attainment and other life outcomes? *Labour Economics, 29,* 83–90.

Bishop, J., & Mane, F. (2004). The impacts of career-technical education on high school labor market success. *Economics of Education Review, 23*(4), 381–402.

Blair, P. Q., Castagnino, T. G., Groshen, E. L., Debroy, P., Auguste, B., Ahmed, S., Diaz, F. G., & Bonavida, C. (2020). *Searching for STARs: Work experience as a job market signal for workers without bachelor's degrees* (Working Paper No. 26844). National Bureau of Economic Research.

Bonilla, S. (2020). The dropout effects of career pathways: Evidence from California. *Economics of Education Review, 75,* 101972.

Bowles, S., & Gintis, H. (1976). *Schooling in capitalist America: Educational reform and the contradictions of economic life.* New York: Basic.

Brunner, E., Dougherty, S., & Ross, S. (2019). *The effects of career and technical education: Evidence from the Connecticut technical high school system* (EdWorkingPaper No. 19-112). Annenberg Institute at Brown University. http://www.edworkingpapers.com/ai19-112

Carnevale, A. P., Strohl, J., Ridley, N., & Gulish, A. (2018). *Three educational pathways to good jobs: High school, middle skills, and bachelor's degree.* Georgetown University Center on Education and the Workforce. https://1gyhoq479ufd3yna29x7ubjn-wpengine.netdna-ssl .com/wp-content/uploads/3ways-FR.pdf

Carruthers, C. K., & Jepsen, C. (2021). Vocational education: An international perspective. In B. P. McCall (Ed.), *The Routledge handbook of the economics of education*, 343–380. Abingdon, UK: Routledge, Taylor & Francis Group.

Carruthers, C. K., & Sanford, T. (2018). Way station or launching pad? Unpacking the returns to adult technical education. *Journal of Public Economics, 165*, 146–159.

Cellini, S. (2006). Smoothing the transition to college? The effect of tech-ed programs on educational attainment. *Economics of Education Review, 25*(4), 394–411.

Cullen, J., Jacob, B., & Levitt, S. (2000). *The impact of school choice on student outcomes: An analysis of the Chicago public schools* (Working Paper No. 7888). National Bureau of Economic Research.

Deming, D., Hastings, J., Kane, T., & Staiger, D. (2011). *School choice, school quality, and postsecondary attainment* (Working Paper No. 17438). National Bureau of Economic Research.

Dougherty, S. (2018). The effect of career and technical education on human capital accumulation: Causal evidence from Massachusetts. *Education Finance and Policy, 13*(2), 119–148.

Dougherty, S., & Ecton, W. G. (2021). The economic effect of vocational education on student outcomes. *Oxford Research Encyclopedia of Economics and Finance.*

Dougherty, S., & Lombardi, A. (2016). From vocational education to career readiness: The ongoing work of linking education and the labor market. *Review of Research in Higher Education, 40*(1), 326–355.

Ecton, W. G., & Dougherty, S. (2021). *Heterogeneity in high school career and technical education outcomes* (EdWorkingPaper No. 21-492). Annenberg Institute at Brown University. https://www.edworkingpapers.com/sites/default/files/ai21-492.pdf

Gottfried, M., & Plasman, J. (2018). Linking the timing of career and technical education coursetaking with high school dropout and college-going behavior. *American Educational Research Journal, 55*(2), 325–336.

Gray, L., & Lewis, L. (2018). *Career and technical education programs in public school districts, 2016–2017.* National Center for Education Statistics. US Department of Education.

Grubb, W. N., & Lazerson, M. (1982). Education and the labor market: Recycling the youth problem. In H. Kantor and D. B. Tyack (Eds.), *Work, youth and schooling: Historical perspectives on vocationalism in American education* (pp. 110–141). Stanford, CA: Stanford University Press.

Grubb, W. N., & Lazerson, M. (2005). Vocationalism in higher education: The triumph of the education gospel. *Journal of Higher Education, 76*(1), 1–25.

Hall, C. (2012). The effects of reducing tracking in upper secondary school: Evidence from a large-scale pilot scheme. *Journal of Human Resources, 47*(1), 237–269.

Hampf, F., & Woessmann, L. (2017). Vocational vs. general education and employment over the life cycle: New evidence from PIAAC. *CESifo Economic Studies, 63*(3), 255–269.

Hanushek, E. A., Ruhose, J., & Woessmann, L. (2017). Knowledge capital and aggregate income differences: Development accounting for US states. *American Economic Journal: Macroeconomics, 9*(4), 184–224. https://doi.org/10.1257/mac.20160255

Hanushek, E., Woessmann, L., & Zhang, L. (2011). *General education, vocational education, and labor-market outcomes over the life-cycle.* Federal Reserve Bank of St. Louis.

Hemelt, S. W., Lenard, M. A., & Paeplow, C. G. (2019). Building bridges to life after high school: Contemporary career academies and student outcomes. *Economics of Education Review, 68,* 161–178.

Holzer, H. J., & Baum, S. R. (2017). *Making college work: Pathways to success beyond high school.* Washington, DC: Brookings Institution.

Hudson, L. (2014). *Trends in CTE coursetaking: Data point.* NCES 2014-117. National Center for Education Statistics. US Department of Education.

Kemple, J., & Willner, C. (2008). *Career academies: Long-term impacts on labor-market outcomes, educational attainment, and transitions to adulthood.* New York: MDRC.

Kreisman, D., & Stange, K. (2020). Vocational and career tech education in American high schools: The value of depth over breadth. *Education Finance and Policy, 15*(1), 11–44.

Levesque, K., Laird, J., Hensley, E., Choy, S., Cataldi, E., & Hudson, L. (2008). Career and technical education in the United States: 1990 to 2005 (NCES 2008-035). National Center for Education Statistics. US Department of Education.

Lucas, S. (1999). *Tracking inequality: Stratification and mobility in American high schools.* New York: Teachers College Press.

Maitra, P., & Mani, S. (2017). Learning and earning: Evidence from a randomized evaluation in India. *Labour Economics, 45*(C), 116–130.

Mishkind, A. (2014). Definitions of college and career readiness: An analysis by state. Washington, DC: American Institutes for Research.

Oakes, J. (1983). Limiting opportunity: Student race and curricular differences in secondary vocational education. *American Journal of Education, 91*(3), 328–355.

Plasman, J. S., & Gottfried, M. A. (2018). Applied STEM coursework, high school dropout rates, and students with learning disabilities. *Educational Policy, 32*(5), 664–696.

Plasman, J. S., Gottfried, M. A., & Klasik, D. J. (2021). Do career-engaging courses engage low-income students? *AERA Open, 7.*

Pugatch, T. (2014). Safety valve or sinkhole? Vocational schooling in South Africa. *IZA Journal of Labor & Development, 3*(1), 1–31.

Rosenbaum, J. E. (2001). *Beyond college for all: Career paths for the forgotten half.* New York: Russell Sage Foundation.

Rosenbaum, P. R., & Rubin, D. B. (1984). Reducing bias in observational studies using subclassification on the propensity score. *Journal of the American Statistical Association, 79*(387), 516–524.

Rubin, D. B. (2001). Using propensity scores to help design observational studies: Application to the Tobacco Litigation. *Health Services and Outcomes Research Methodology 2,* 169–188.

Shadish, W. R., Clark, M. H., & Steiner, P. M. (2008). Can nonrandomized experiments yield accurate answers? A randomized experiment comparing random and nonrandom assignments. *Journal of the American Statistical Association, 103*(484), 1334–1344.

Stevens, A. H., Kurlaender, M., & Grosz, M. (2019). Career technical education and labor market outcomes evidence from California community colleges. *Journal of Human Resources, 54*(4), 986–1036.

Stone, J. R., III, & Aliaga, O. A. (2005). Career and technical education and school-to-work at the end of the 20th century: Participation and outcomes. *Career and Technical Education Research, 30*(2), 123–142.

Sublett, C., Ecton, W., Klein, S., Atwell, A., & D'Amico, M. M. (2021). Community college alignment of workforce education and local labor markets. *Journal of Applied Research in the Community College, 28*(1), 13–29.

Theobald, R. J., Goldhaber, D. D., Gratz, T. M., & Holden, K. L. (2019). Career and technical education, inclusion, and postsecondary outcomes for students with learning disabilities. *Journal of Learning Disabilities, 52*(2), 109–119.

Tyack, D. (1974). *The one best system: A history of American urban education.* Cambridge, MA: Harvard University Press.

US Department of Education. (2015). *High school longitudinal study of 2009: 2013 update.* Institute of Education Sciences. National Center for Education Statistics. https://nces.ed.gov/surveys/hsls09/index.asp

White House, The. (2011, March 14). *President Obama calls on Congress to fix No Child Left Behind before the start of the next school year* [Press release]. https://obamawhitehouse.archives.gov/realitycheck/the-press-office/2011/03/14/president-obama-calls-congress-fix-no-child-left-behind-start-next-schoo

Yettick, H., Cline, F., & Young, J. (2012). Dual goals: The academic achievement of college prep students with career majors. *Journal of Career and Technical Education, 27*(2), 120–142.

Zilic, I. (2018). General versus vocational education: Lessons from a quasi-experiment in Croatia. *Economics of Education Review, 62*, 1–11.

# 5

# Turning Hurdles into Launch Pads: Improving Equity and Efficiency Through Increased High School Graduations in the United States

*Aidan Vining and David Weimer*

Educational attainment requires a high level of public and private (individual and family) investment. Accordingly, knowing the costs and benefits of various educational attainment credentials is important for good public policy (Jaeger & Page, 1996; Wolf & McShane, 2013). High school graduation is one of the most important of these credentials in the United States as are its equivalent in other countries (Neal, 1997; Vining & Weimer, 2019). For the 2018–19 academic year, the adjusted cohort graduation rates (ACGR) for public high schools ranged from 75% to 92% across US states (NECS, 2021). The ACGR is the percentage of public high school students who graduate with a regular diploma within four years of starting ninth grade.[1] These percentages for recent school years demonstrate that substantial numbers of students in the United States still leave high school without diplomas. The rate of high school graduation in the United States is particularly important for both efficiency and equity reasons, because as we demonstrate below, despite considerable improvement in graduation rates over time, significant deficits remain among minority groups and across income levels (Belfield & Levin, 2007; Murnane, 2013; Papay, Murnane, & Willett, 2015) that are considerably greater than the rates in other wealthy democracies (Hanushek, 2009).

This chapter addresses this variability by adopting a social value perspective, primarily in terms of cost-benefit analysis (CBA), but also considering cost-effectiveness analysis (CEA) research results that represent the best efficiency-relevant evidence available. Almost always, however, distributional impacts intersect with

---

1. "Students who enter ninth grade for the first time form a cohort for the graduating class. The cohort is 'adjusted' by adding any students who subsequently transfer into the cohort and subtracting any students who subsequently transfer out, emigrate to another country, or die." https://www.ojjdp.gov /ojstatbb/population/qa01502.asp?qaDate=2018. An obvious limitation of this data is that it only pertains to public schools and excludes all private schools.

efficiency when considering policies that impact the economically disadvantaged or particular minority groups (see Boardman, Greenberg, Vining, & Weimer, 2020). Even so, analysts often treat efficiency and equity separately, and certainly good reasons exist for doing so, as the relationship between them can be complex. Nonetheless, well-designed and well-focused programs can be both more efficient and more equitable than current policy, avoiding the need for trade-offs in policy choice (Okun, 1975; Weimer & Vining, 2009; Boardman et al., 2020). Policies that increase high school graduation rates among the disadvantaged, therefore, have the potential to increase both efficiency and equity. However, we also make the case that currently in the United States effort has been minimal on the ground (in social science terminology—social experiments) to test and comprehensively evaluate policies (preferably through CBA) that might improve graduation rates among disadvantaged groups (Greenberg & Robins, 1986; Greenberg & Barnow, 2014). This is the case despite the evidence of net benefits from increased graduation at the general population level.

The rest of the chapter is organized as follows:

- Section 2 summarizes the extant evidence on high school graduation by both minority status and income level. We recognize that these are not the only important distributional dimensions. Significant differences across geographic regions and states and within aggregated ethnic categories, such as the overall Asian American category, deserve attention, as do people with physical and cognitive disabilities, but these topics are beyond the scope of this chapter.
- Section 3 lays out the components of CBA and details their specific application to educational attainment.
- Section 4 builds on previous conceptual and (especially) empirical research to estimate the social value of an incremental high school graduation from the aggregate societal perspective.
- Section 5 considers factors that may be relevant to the value of high school graduation specifically for minority and economically disadvantaged students.
- Section 6 considers both policies that have been assessed with CBA or CEA and a wider range of interventions that hold promise for improving graduation rates for minority and disadvantaged students.
- Section 7 concludes with policy implications.

## AVAILABLE EVIDENCE ON ETHNICITY/RACE (MINORITY) AND INCOME DIFFERENCES

Despite substantial increases in the overall US national ACGR in recent years, significant differences remain in rates across minority and income groups. As table 5.1 shows, the overall graduation rate rose from 81% to 86% from the 2012–13 to the 2018–19 school year. In terms of minority groups, there certainly has been

**Table 5.1. Public School Adjusted Cohort Graduation Rate by Ethnic Group for the 2012 Through 2018 School Years (percent)**

| | 2012–2013 | 2013–2014 | 2014–2015 | 2015–2016 | 2016–2017 | 2017–2018 | 2018–2019 |
|---|---|---|---|---|---|---|---|
| Total | 81 | 82 | 83 | 84 | 85 | 85 | 86 |
| American Indian/ Alaska Native | 70 | 70 | 72 | 72 | 72 | 74 | 74 |
| Black | 71 | 73 | 75 | 76 | 78 | 79 | 80 |
| Hispanic | 75 | 76 | 78 | 79 | 80 | 81 | 82 |
| White | 87 | 87 | 88 | 88 | 89 | 89 | 89 |
| Asian/Pacific Islander | 89 | 89 | 90 | 91 | 91 | 92 | 93 |
| Economically Disadvantaged | 75 | 75 | 76 | 78 | 78 | 80 | 80 |

*Source:* Various years of *Trends in high school dropout and completion rates in the United States,* National Center for Educational Statistics. See, for example, McFarland, J., Cui, J., Holmes, J., & Wang, X. (2019). *Trends in high school dropout and completion rates in the United States: 2019* (NCES 2020-117). US Department of Education. Washington, DC: National Center for Education Statistics. Retrieved September 24, 2021, from https://nces.ed.gov/pubsearch

some progress. Specifically, over this period the ACGR percent for Black students has increased by 9 percentage points, the largest gain among the identified groups. Hispanic students also experienced a substantial gain of 7 percentage points. However, both of these groups started from relatively low ACGR rates so that substantial deficits compared to White and Asian/Pacific Islander students remain. Also, the gains for American Indian/Alaska Natives commenced at a low base and have only risen by 4 percentage points; consequently, these students have ACGRs that are considerably lower than other groups. Thus, except for Asian/Pacific Islander students, the identified minority groups continue to have ACGRs that are lower than majority White students.

The last row of table 5.1 shows ACGRs for economically disadvantaged students, defined as students eligible for free or reduced-price meals under the National School Lunch and Child Nutrition Program. Although the ACGR for these students has gone up 5 percentage points over the period, it remains substantially below the overall graduation rate. Indeed, the 2018–19 school year gap of 6 percentage points is the same as it was in the 2012–13 school year.

These data make clear that substantial disparities in ACGR continue, although the data do not permit partitioning of the disparities between those associated with minority status and those associated with economic disadvantage. We recognize that many factors likely contribute to the disparities. For example, there is evidence of the intergenerational effects of slavery on underinvestment in human capital (Bertocchi & Dimico, 2012; Jung, 2021). Further, differences in family formation, particularly the incidence of single-parent households, affect childhood development and human capital accumulation (McLanahan & Sawhill, 2015). The history of de jure and de facto discrimination against American minorities, especially Blacks and Native Americans, demonstrates sources of disparity beyond economic disadvantage alone.

In the context of schooling specifically, past discrimination against minorities almost certainly contributes to current disparity through a variety of family, neighborhood, and school access channels. Past discrimination in education contributes to lower levels of parental education. Past labor market discrimination contributes to lower levels of current family wealth. The legacy of residential redlining contributes to limits in access to high-quality schools and potentially contributes to adverse neighborhood effects (Zenou & Boccard, 2000).

## WHY DOES IT MATTER? THE SOCIAL VALUE OF HIGH SCHOOL COMPLETION

Education creates personal and social value insofar as it enhances individuals' productivity and relationships. Although measuring productivity and social flourishing is difficult, social scientists generally have focused on earnings as an outcome of interest because it reflects the value that markets place on the productive use of individuals' human capital. In this sense, higher earnings for higher levels of education reflect this greater productivity.

The social value of education consists not only of the private individual benefits but also benefits that accrue to all other members of society. Even ignoring the significant distributional considerations, assessing the social value of high school graduation is not straightforward for several reasons. Most important, investments in educational increments in both quantity (attainment) and quality (achievement) have multidimensional, long-run, and nonlinear impacts (Hanushek, 2009; Vining & Weimer, 2019). These impacts are difficult to estimate convincingly because often little data exists to distinguish between impacts of schooling increments from impacts that result from the innate cognitive and noncognitive abilities of individuals and the family support they do or do not receive (Card, 2001; Hanushek, Schwerdt, Wiederhold, & Woessmann, 2015).

To isolate the causal impact of educational attainment, it is necessary to separate out impacts that flow from individuals' innate ability. Further, because productivity gains and their associated social benefits accrue over the life of the individual, assessing the costs and benefits of education requires discounting to allow comparison with alternative public investments. Because of this long period of time over which education has impacts, the selected discount rate for analysis has a significant impact on the estimated net value of educational investments (Moore, Boardman, Vining, Weimer, & Greenberg, 2004).

The Washington State Institute for Public Policy (WSIPP, 2019) pioneered the systematic application of CBA at the state level. WSIPP initially developed a shadow price for the social value of a policy-induced high school graduation in Washington State—that is, how a marginal high school graduation affects society. Vining and Weimer (2019) updated and augmented the WSIPP estimates to the year 2019. They produced shadow price estimates of high school graduation, as well as further levels of educational attainment that are dependent on high school completion. They performed sensitivity analysis on the estimates using different social discount rates and various assumptions about productivity change, primarily those related to temporal technological progress (Black & Lynch, 2001).

Apart from its direct impact on individual productivity, education indirectly underlies many other aspects of productivity increases, such as those related to managerial employee quality (Black & Lynch, 2004). Finally, they estimated the benefits of education that do not accrue to the employed but, rather, to the rest of society (i.e., external benefits). We reprise these estimates and update them to 2021 dollars.

The social value of an additional high school graduation is most useful in the analysis of school and closely related policies that can directly affect the graduation rate. But graduation can also affect outcomes (and so policies) that have other socially valuable impacts, including those that reduce the level of juvenile and adult crime (McCollister, French, & Fang, 2010), reduce substance abuse (McCollister et al., 2017), reduce the need for foster care (Zerbe et al., 2009), and improve mental health. Even policies that affect early childhood development, such as preschool care, nutrition intake, and child protection, can also affect educational attainment later in life (Burger, 2010). Thus, the availability of a shadow price for high school graduation can enhance the feasibility of conducting CBAs and CEAs in a wide range of social policy areas.

## HIGH SCHOOL GRADUATION SHADOW PRICES FOR THE UNITED STATES

### Estimation Steps

Following the general approach pioneered by WSIPP, Vining and Weimer (2019) estimated a shadow price for an additional high school graduation. We briefly reprise the steps, summarized in table 5.2, that lead to the shadow price here and later expand the analysis to consider potential minority and (low) income "adjustments" that would make the estimates more appropriate for these subpopulations. Their nine steps to estimate the value of graduation are:

1. predict earning increments for individuals with increasing levels of educational attainment over their working lives;
2. include the value of fringe benefits in order to estimate the total economic value of compensation, that is, of total compensation;
3. adjust the value of compensation to account for the effect of predicted real economic growth over a life cycle;
4. adjust the compensation estimates to account for mortality risk during the working lives of individuals;
5. attempt to net out the effects of educational attainment that derives from individuals' initial cognitive and other endowments;

6. discount earning gain estimates to obtain estimates of the present values of both costs and benefits, and of net benefits;
7. specify some alternative paths to further levels of education that are contingent on high school graduation;
8. adjust estimates to account for the costs of education; and
9. add external impacts (either positive or negative externalities) that flow from changed productivity.

Some of these steps are relatively straightforward and uncontroversial, but others involve more substantial uncertainties that could benefit from more research and social experimentation. To take account of some of the key parameter uncertainties, means and standard deviations are estimated using Monte Carlo simulations.

### Estimation Issues

The analysis begins with estimates of age and education's specific estimates of earnings based on data from the March Supplement of the Community Population Survey for the years 2002 through 2014. Age-specific earning profiles were estimated for individuals with four levels of educational attainment: less than high school degree, high school degree, some college, and college graduation. Specifically, for ages 19 through 65, quadratic models with year fixed effects were estimated for each level of attainment. Because earnings do not fully capture the cost of labor to firms, differences in earnings alone underestimate the value of gains in productivity to society. In addition, estimates of the value of productivity gains from educational increments to the employed should be based on total compensation. The difference is significant between the value of earnings and total compensation: WSIPP derived an average ratio of total compensation to wages of 1.441. Boardman, Greenberg, Vining, & Weimer (2018) estimated the ratio to be somewhat higher at 1.462.

As it has historically, total compensation can be expected to grow in real terms over time as technological improvements increase the productivity of workers in aggregate. However, technological change has differential effects on the value of labor for workers at different levels of education (Moretti, 2004). For example, technological change that induces plant automation almost certainly reduces the relative value of the labor of less-educated workers compared to that of more-educated workers (Doms, Dunne, & Troske, 1997; Riddell & Song, 2017). We use the shadow price of a high school graduation to predict the value of additional current graduations. We base the compensation estimates on historical data and assume the continuation of the recent historical trends. Boardman et al. (2018) used the WSIPP data and estimated the relative change to be negative at –0.0062 for those without a high school diploma as against positive 0.0053 for those with a high school diploma; we make the same assumption.

Unfortunately, some individuals die before they reach retirement age, cutting off the productivity gains that derive from education or anything else. However,

**Table 5.2. Steps in Estimating Disadvantaged High School Graduation Shadow Price**

| Step | Task | Sources | Comment |
|------|------|---------|---------|
| 1 | Predict earnings over life cycle by level of education | Community Population Survey for the years 2002–2014 | Projections based on historical experience. |
| 2 | Adjust earnings for fringe benefits to get total compensation | Bureau of Labor Statistics (2017) | Projections based on historical experience. |
| 3 | Adjust total compensation for predicted real economic growth over life cycle | Washington State Institute of Public Policy (2018) | Projections based on historical experience. |
| 4 | Adjust estimates to take account of mortality risk over working life | United States Life Tables (2010) | Assumes mortality risk independent of education. |
| 5 | Net out effects of cognitive and other endowments from education attainment | Heckman, Humphries, & Veramendi (2015) | Relies on complex econometric estimates. Requires further research and evidence relating to disadvantaged. |
| 6 | Discount stream of gains from high school graduation to obtain present value | Moore, Boardman, Vining, Weimer, & Greenberg (2004); Boardman, Greenberg, Vining, & Weimer (2018) | Assumes retirement at age 65 ignoring benefits beyond working life. |
| 7 | Specify probabilities of alternative educational paths following high school graduation | Current Population Survey (2018) | Assumes current educational paths. Specify path ratios by ethnic group and income/wealth. |
| 8 | Adjust estimates to account for the costs of education | National Center for Education Statistics; Boardman et al. (2018) | Assumes recent costs. Update cost ratios and estimates frequently by ethnic group and income/wealth. |
| 9 | Account for the possible impacts from increased productivity on the rest of society | Breton (2010); Belfield, Hollands, & Levin (2011); Kang et al. (2016); Riddell & Song (2017) | Assumes productivity spillovers continue over working life and ignores improvements in consumption efficiency. |

Source: Adapted from Vining, A. R., & Weimer, D. L. (2019). The value of high school graduation in the United States: Per-person shadow price estimates for use in cost–benefit analysis. *Administrative Sciences*, 9(4), 81–96, Table 1.

the *causal* relationship between education and mortality is complex. Nonetheless, a higher education level almost certainly contributes to greater longevity and other positive behaviors and outcomes (the "health gradient"). Ignoring this relationship almost certainly results in underestimating the productivity gains deriving from education (Cutler & Lleras-Muney, 2010).

Superior cognitive, noncognitive, health, and other endowments make some individuals more productive than others at any level of education. Consequently, the difference in total compensation between high school non-completion versus completion leads to an overestimate of the causal effect of higher levels of educational attainment. WSIPP estimated the causal effect of cognitive and other endowments versus those attributable to education based on research done by Heckman and colleagues (Heckman, Humphries, & Veramendi, 2015). Boardman et al. (2018) applied the same set of factors to compare high school graduates to those who did not graduate. They used a causal effect of 50% (standard error of 17 percentage points) to adjust the present value of total compensation gains for those graduating from high school relative to the gains of those who drop out and imputed causal effects of 56% (standard error of 13 percentage points) and 42% (standard error of 11 percentage points) to the gains from some college relative to high school graduation and college degree or higher relative to some college, respectively. These standard errors were used in the Monte Carlo simulations.

Almost all social policies have costs and benefits that vary over time, which is certainly the case for many educational interventions; CBA values impacts occurring at different times in terms of net present value (NPV). NPVs of policies with long time horizons are quite sensitive to the selected social discount rate level (Moore, Boardman, & Vining, 2013). The present value of the benefits of high school graduation is usually discounted over the 18 to 65 age range, or a 47-year period. Consequently, higher discount rates substantially reduce the estimated value of high school completion.

The completion of high school opens pathways to further levels of education and, therefore, for additional gains in productivity that are contingent on completing high school. WSIPP used percentage estimates specific to Washington State: 26, 38, and 36 percentages, respectively, for those who do not go on for higher education after high school graduation, those who complete some college, and those who graduate from college. To develop a national US estimate, Boardman et al. (2018) estimated that 66% of graduating high school students pursued some additional higher education, which is quite a bit lower than the aggregate 74% found in Washington State.

Education involves some opportunity cost for the student and imposes resource costs on society, although this is not as significant as it is at further levels of education. WISPP assumed that schools would reap negligible real resource savings from each additional dropout. Boardman et al. (2018) made a similar assumption and estimated the present value of the resource cost of education by discounting the average annual cost of college for two-year colleges, for those with some college, and for four-year colleges for those who complete college degrees (Ginder, Kelly-

Reid, & Mann, 2016). Standard errors for these estimates were then used in the Monte Carlo simulations.

The higher earnings resulting from greater productivity can also indirectly create important external benefits. Students in school engage in less antisocial behavior and crime, make better consumption and fertility choices, and enhance intra-family productivity. The evidence shows school attainment normally does all of these (Haveman & Wolfe, 1984; Wolfe & Haveman, 2001; McMahon, 2018). Apart from the increased returns from work, Machin, Marie, and Vujić (2011) discuss two channels that contribute to reduced criminal behavior: the net "self-incapacitation" effect of time spent in school as against that spent in other activities, and the beneficial impacts of educational attendance on greater patience and risk aversion (Luallen, 2006; Anderson, 2014). Greater patience (a lower discount rate) has been shown to be associated with a higher rate of high school graduation (Castillo, Jordan, & Petrie, 2019). The WSIPP analysis drew upon several studies to specify a range of external benefits for a general-population student, expressed as a percentage of total compensation, ranging from 13% to 42%. WSIPP took 37% to be the modal value of these external benefits (Belfield, Hollands, & Levin, 2011). By definition, this average includes disadvantaged and minority groups, but obviously it is not tailored to factors that would alter the percentage for these subpopulations.

Taking account of the positive externalities of educational attainment raises several shadow price estimation questions that intersect with income and minority status:

1. First, with respect to the income gradient, is it reasonable to assume that externalities are proportional to total compensation across the income range?
2. Second, we have mentioned that targeted policies based on income, minority status, or the intersection of the two, may improve both efficiency and equity (we return to this point when we consider some potential policies for increasing graduation rates). Some benefits, such as reductions in crime, are a mix of private and external benefits. These benefits would come disproportionately from increases in total compensation going to lower-income individuals.
3. Third, there are also nonmarket benefits, or "internalities," that increase with education (Jones, Karoly, Crowley, & Greenberg, 2015). For example, educational attainment almost certainly enables people to be more informed consumers. Again, these benefits are both private and external, and they would likely partially accrue to incremental general-population graduates but may well be larger for various disadvantaged subpopulations.

## SHADOW PRICE ESTIMATES

### Benefits and Discount Rates

Implementing the steps outlined in section 4, table 5.3 shows estimates of the net benefits of a single high school graduation under different assumptions about the appropriate level of the social discount rate and excluding or including college costs and externalities. The main insight is that a high school graduation provides net benefits, even at the highest discount rate that we use (ranging from 2% to 7%, as shown in column 1).

Columns 2 and 3 show estimates of the shadow price of a policy-induced high school graduation in the United States under the shown discount rates. The top number in each cell of columns 2 and 3 is the point estimate using the modal values previously discussed. The second and third numbers show the means and the standard deviations from Monte Carlo simulations that specify distributions for several parameters, including the causality factors, college costs, and externalities. Column 2 shows shadow prices including only productivity gains and educational costs accruing to individuals—essentially the private returns of high school graduation. Most relevant from a CBA perspective, column 3, following the WSIPP estimation procedures, provided estimates that include the estimated positive externalities—the aggregate social returns from graduation as we discuss below.

Not surprisingly, the selected discount rate has a substantial impact on the ultimate estimated value of the shadow prices shown in columns 2 and 3. The US Office

**Table 5.3.  US High School Graduation Estimates: Alternative Discount Rates and Specifications, Point Estimates, and Monte Carlo Means (and Standard Deviations) in 1,000s of 2021 Dollars**

| (1) Real Discount Rate (%) | (2) Productivity With Education Costs | (3) Productivity With Education Costs and Externalities |
|:---:|:---:|:---:|
| 2 | 323 | 461 |
|   | 318 | 432 |
|   | (64.0) | (87.2) |
| 3 | 242 | 352 |
|   | 242 | 332 |
|   | (48.6) | (66.7) |
| 4 | 184 | 271 |
|   | 181 | 253 |
|   | (39.9) | (54.8) |
| 5 | 139 | 229 |
|   | 136 | 210 |
|   | (32.4) | (44.2) |
| 6 | 105 | 163 |
|   | 104 | 151 |
|   | (26.9) | (36.5) |
| 7 | 80 | 128 |
|   | 79 | 118 |
|   | (21.2) | (28.6) |

*Source*: Adapted from Table C17.1, Boardman, Greenberg, Vining, & Weimer (2018), p. 508, with additional calculations by authors.

of Management and Budget (OMB, 2021), which reviews the Regulatory Impact Analyses for major rules issued by administrative agencies, recommends that analyses use discount rates of 3% and 7% in calculating present values (values for these rates are shown in column 1 of table 5.3). The value of the shadow price at the lower 3% rate is almost three times its value at the higher 7% rate. It is worth mentioning that CBAs (and CEAs) of social programs often avoid overtly discussing the discount rate because they focus on, and often only report, the costs and benefits that occur on a one program-year basis. However, when an immediate impact, such as high school graduation, casts a long shadow into the future, such as educational attainment contributing to higher earnings over one's working life, an unstated discount rate is implicitly and inevitably embedded in the shadow price.

### Benefits Including Externalities

Vining and Weimer (2019) presented overall "general-population" estimates for a national program that would result in an additional 100 students graduating from high school using a 3% discount rate and including positive externalities. Converting their estimate to 2021 dollars, shadow price value of a *single* graduate including external benefits using the point estimate is $352,000; and the social monetized value of an additional hundred graduations produced a benefit estimate of $35.2 million ($352,000 times 100). The shadow price value of a single graduation based on Monte Carlo simulations was slightly lower at $332,000 and produced a slightly lower aggregate benefit estimate of $33.2 million, rather than $35.2 million.

As CBAs of social policies often involve many uncertain parameters, it is more appropriate to predict a distribution of net benefits using the Monte Carlo simulation approach rather than net benefits based on point estimates of parameters. These estimates were for a national average student in the general population and made no adjustments for income, wealth, or for particular racial or ethnic groups (Weimer & Vining, 2009). The implications for different groups can be particularly difficult to disentangle because inequity and discrimination can feed back into efficiency impact estimates in complex ways (Lang & Spitzer, 2020; Belfield, 2021).

### Applicability of the Estimates to Minority and Economically Disadvantaged Students

Our derivation of the shadow price for a high school graduation extrapolates historical earnings profiles. An implicit assumption underlying this approach is that these profiles provide reasonable estimates of differences in earnings across educational groups as people age. However, changes in the economy, such as globalization, automation, and gig work, imply uncertainly in the value of the shadow price that is not fully captured in the Monte Carlo simulations that account for parameter uncertainty. At the same time, discounting of predicted productivity in the future over quite a long time frame reduces somewhat the (NPV) impact of greater uncertainty for long-run changes on the estimated value of the shadow price.

Concern about the accuracy of basing predictions of future earnings on historical profiles is a major reason why we only calculate a shadow price for the general population. Estimating a shadow price by gender, for example, would require an analysis of changes in economic opportunity for women over recent decades (see, e.g., Blau & Kahn, 2017) and disentangling discrimination from voluntary nonparticipation. A similar concern applies to estimates of the shadow prices for minority groups. Racial discrimination undoubtedly continues to play a role in limiting economic opportunities for Blacks and other minorities (Quillian, Pager, Hexel, & Midtbøen, 2017; Kang, DeCelles, Tilcsik, & Jun, 2016; Pager & Shepherd, 2008). Fortunately, however, its role has certainly declined to some degree over the past 50 years, and various public policies may reduce it further. Using the nine-step procedure to estimate a separate shadow price for an additional graduation by a Black student based on historical earnings profiles would inevitably reflect high levels of historical disadvantage and discrimination. Consequently, rather than attempting to estimate separate shadow prices for specific minority groups or by income, we consider the factors that might lead us to believe that the shadow prices presented might be too high or too low for either minority or economically disadvantaged students.

As already noted, the externality benefits for economically disadvantaged students who do graduate from high school are likely to be relatively large. The result of performing step 9 is the assumption that the externality benefit per dollar earned falls between 13% and 42%. Haveman and Wolfe (1984) and Wolfe and Haveman (2001) estimated the combination of the increases in the earnings of very low-income workers and the external benefits from graduation to be closer to one dollar, or the same magnitude as compensation. However, it is difficult to partition the private benefits from the external benefits. If one were to adopt their order of magnitude size adjustment—assuming the earnings profiles apply—the estimated shadow prices summarized in table 5.3 are quite a bit too low for economically disadvantaged students.

The general population shadow price could underestimate the marginal impact of high school graduation for minority students because it compensates for lower initial levels of family and social capital. However, three factors suggest that the predicted general population earnings profiles could be optimistic about productivity gains for minority and economically disadvantaged students from high school graduation.

*First*, although current labor shortages may be reducing the impact of racial discrimination that have depressed employment opportunities for minority graduates, they still likely face fewer options when entering the labor market (Kang et al., 2016). In turn, historical discrimination reduces the employment-relevant social capital of these families and results in fewer current employment opportunities for both minority and economically disadvantaged graduates compared to the employment opportunities of the general population. This would result in less difference in earnings between non-graduation and graduation for minorities and the economically disadvantaged relative to the general population.

*Second*, minority and economically disadvantaged students may have lower levels of family capital relevant to gaining higher education than the general population. Both family income and parental education affect educational attainment. In 2018 the college enrollment rates were 42% for Whites, 37% for Blacks, 36% for Hispanics, 59% for Asians, 24% for Pacific Islanders, and 24% for American Indian/ Alaska Natives (US Department of Commerce, 2019). Family capital also affects the financial capability of students for continuing toward a degree. For example, among the cohort of 2009 ninth graders, the percentage that was enrolled in postsecondary education in 2016 was 78% for the highest socioeconomic quintile but only 28% for the lowest quintile (US Department of Education, 2019). For those entering college in 2013, the six-year graduation rate was 44.3% for Black students compared to 66.7% for White students (US Department of Education, 2021); this gap is likely related to the lower levels of family wealth—Black family wealth is only about 15% of White family wealth (Bhutta, Chang, Dettling, & Hsu, 2020).

*Third*, geographic constraints may limit employment market access. Some types of employment are less readily accessible in lower-income neighborhoods or in rural areas. Family and cultural ties often make moving to locations with better access to employment less attractive, and limited financial resources may make moving less feasible. The cultural ties may be particularly significant for American Indians, who may want to stay in reservation communities. All three factors, however, represent the impact of some form of historic or current discrimination.

A possible important caveat affects estimates of expected benefits for either the general student population or the economically disadvantaged. Implicit in the projected earnings profiles by educational attainment is the assumption of stable distributions of achievement within attainment categories going forward. The general population shadow price may overestimate the social value of high school graduations if policy-induced graduations for any number of reasons on the margin embody lower levels of achievement than the prior average. In the extreme, simply awarding diplomas would produce much smaller or zero productivity gains, reflecting the value of credentialing rather than the value of the knowledge and skills that it currently signals.

## INCREASING MINORITY AND DISADVANTAGED STUDENT GRADUATION

This chapter focuses on the potential size and scope of the economic benefits of high school graduation for students from lower-income families and various minority groups. It has not yet considered specific programs and policies that would reduce dropout rates or improve graduation for these socio-demographic groups. However, in view of the significant private and social benefits from increased graduation in aggregate, it is important to consider the extant empirical evidence on which programs and policies work for disadvantaged groups and also speculate about the programs or policies that might work but have not been tried, or have not been tried but not rigorously analyzed.

## CBA and CEA Evidence

In terms of "what works," we first focus on the CBA and CEA findings for the United States. These studies consider both impacts and the costs of the interventions that produce them; the CBAs directly assess efficiency, and the CEAs could do so using the shadow price for a high school graduation (Boardman & Vining, 2017). Our starting point for findings on programs that increase graduation rates is Hollands et al. (2014), who analyzed the What Works Clearinghouse (WWC) inventory of interventions that addressed high school incompletion and developed CEA ratios for studies where it was feasible to do so. We also briefly review subsequent WWC evidence since 2014, although we note that WCC evaluation procedures have been subject to serious criticism (Schoenfeld, 2006). Hollands et al. (2014) only analyzed five interventions that the WCC concluded had positive or potentially positive effects: Talent Search, JOBSTART, New Chance, National Guard Youth Challenge (NGYC), and Job Corps. In each case they calculated cost-effectiveness ratios by retrospectively developing program-cost estimates for the interventions, but also by augmenting some effectiveness measures. Hollands et al. (2014) provided a description of the five programs in their table 1 and summarized their CEA findings in their table 2. They acknowledge the significant comparability assumptions they had to make to standardize across interventions, as well as across sites within interventions.

Hollands et al. (2014) calculated CEA ratios for the five interventions, where the effectiveness measure is a high school graduation. We convert their 2010-dollar estimates to 2021 dollars. Talent Search is the only program among the five that pertains to in-school students who had not dropped out—that is, it is the only preventive intervention. They estimated the cost per graduation at $38,410, which is the lowest estimated cost per graduation of the five interventions. JOBSTART targeted socially and economically disadvantaged youths who had dropped out, so it is a remedial program with an estimated cost per graduation of $87,480. NGYC is also a remedial program that targeted 16- to 18-year-old youth who had dropped out or been expelled. Its estimated cost per graduation was $89,630. Job Corps is also a remedial program that targeted 16- to 24-year-old low-income individuals who had dropped out of high school. Its estimated cost per graduation is $164,870. New Chance targeted young mothers who had dropped out of high school. The estimated cost per graduation for this program is $240,380, which is, not surprisingly, the highest of the five interventions.

We note some features of the five interventions that limit their generalizability to an overall assessment of *potential* graduation enhancement policies for disadvantaged students. First, the WCC did not attempt to perform either CBA or CEA on the interventions—Hollands et al. (2014), after commendable effort, were only able to estimate CEA ratios retrospectively, as against a broader assessment of social value.

This is a serious limitation because of the potential multiplicity of socially relevant impacts that high school completion may generate.

Second, all five interventions were essentially counseling or training programs; as such, they represent a relatively narrow range of interventions compared to the universe of potential interventions. We think it is fair to conclude that none of the interventions included strong financial incentives to remain in, or return to, school, certainly relative to non-school (compatible) employment (but see Morissette, Chan, & Lu, 2015).

Third, four of the five programs concerned youth who had already dropped out of high school; thus, these remedial interventions did not focus on students who might be more easily incentivized on the margin to remain in school, as against returning to school. Consequently, we emphasize that analysis of the social costs and benefits of high school completion policies is not equivalent to analysis of the social costs and benefits of reversing dropping-out policies. Surprisingly little evidence is available on preventive interventions for disadvantaged groups.

Fourth, several of the programs had multiple sites across diverse environments. Extensive evaluation research shows that it is very difficult to ensure intervention homogeneity across heterogeneous sites so as to be able to derive clear lessons about what works (Qin, Deutsch, & Hong, 2021; Jackson et al., 2021). These limitations should be understood in the context of the legal constraints on directly targeting minority groups for remedial interventions (Dee & Penner, 2021).

Since Hollands et al. (2014) performed their CEA analysis, we have found only two additional published studies that directly estimate the economic value of high school graduation for various categories of disadvantaged students. Recovery High School (RHS) students graduated from high school at a 21 to 25 percentage point higher rate than did those in the matched comparison cohort. Weimer, Moberg, French, Tanner-Smith, and Finch (2019) estimated the incremental benefits of the RHS program by monetizing the increased probability of high school graduation and comparing it to the incremental costs. The analysis showed substantial positive net benefits from RHS participation with mean net benefits ranging from $16,100 to $51,9000 per participant compared to other substance use interventions. The benefit-to-cost ratios ranged from 3.0 to 7.2. The estimated increases in the probability of high school graduation were both large and statistically significant. A reduction in substance abuse appeared to be the major contributing factor to the observed increase in student graduation rates. From a policy perspective, the study has a limited application to the small set of students who return to high school after dropping out for treatment.

Another promising program aimed at a narrow segment of the high school population is the facilitation of day care for high school students who deliver children. Macchia, Therriault, and Wood (2021) conducted a CBA of a Florida program aimed at increasing graduation rates for pregnant high school students. Although the comprehensive online version of the program did not show evidence of substantial gains in graduation rates or positive net benefits, students who began the program but returned to face-to-face schooling with day-care support did see substantially increased graduation rates and positive net benefits. The authors suggest that the key to increasing graduation for this population is the availability of day care, perhaps through school-based day-care centers.

Although not directly relating to improving high school graduation, "college promise" programs are particularly informative on two important launch pad dimensions: on successfully motivating (particularly) young Black American students (but also other minority and low-income students) and partially doing so through strong incentives. Bartik, Herschbein, and Lachowska (2016) performed a sophisticated CBA of the "Kalamazoo Promise" Universal Scholarships program (focusing on benefit-cost ratios) that they consider provided "generous" incentives. They found that the program was (net) beneficial for all participants under many assumptions, but it was most beneficial for the disadvantaged (see their table 5). Although participants presumably were somewhat older than typical high school students, we believe that it offers suggestive evidence on possible programs that would incentivize disadvantaged students to stay in high school and graduate.

Unfortunately, school districts, which provide the most direct point of contact with students at risk of dropping out, have neither the incentive nor the resources to provide payments to students—the resource constraint is likely to be most severe in the school districts where minority and economically disadvantaged students are most at risk of dropping out. Consequently, financial incentive programs would likely have to be designed and funded by organizations or governments other than school districts.

## Promising Interventions That Have Not (Yet) Been Shown to Offer Positive Net Benefits

As there is a relative dearth of economic valuations of initiatives aimed at higher graduation rates, we turn to the broader social science evidence on programs that aim to reduce dropouts but have not directly addressed graduation as the measure of success (i.e., the graduation rate per se is not the dependent variable). Delaying dropping out not only increases the likelihood of graduation but also may yield benefits by increasing school attainment short of graduation as well as increasing achievement for those who do graduate.

A comprehensive review of evidence by De Witte, Cabus, Thyssen, Groot, and van den Brink (2013) identified a range of risk factors for dropping out and examines a range of interventions aimed at students, parents, and schools that could mitigate them. Surprisingly, De Witte and colleagues can find minimal evidence on promising interventions directly aimed at students. However, they do point to early identification and support for students with a variety of risk factors as being critical. The more recent research subsequent to their review suggests, for example, that even elementary school or preschool programs in high poverty areas can produce substantial decreases in dropout rates in high school (Lee-St. John et al., 2018; Bailey, Sun, & Timpe, 2021). De Witte and colleagues also note that identifying ninth-grade students who were not on track for graduation facilitates potential intervention by teachers and school administrators, and subsequent research reaches the same conclusion (Allensworth, 2013; Roderick, Kelley-Kemple, Johnson, & Ryan, 2021). They also imply that less use of grade retention, a major risk factor for dropping out, could reduce it. However, this is a more questionable conclusion because almost certainly some excluded factors affect both grade retention and dropping out; this potential ambiguity on causality suggests that it would be premature to draw policy implications.

Perhaps most promising, they identify peer and adult counseling programs that are potentially beneficial, especially for students from disadvantaged backgrounds (Hebert & Reis, 1999). More recent research also finds beneficial effects of counseling. For example, it appears that participation in group counseling increases earned credits (Chan, Kuperminc, Seitz, Wilson, & Khatib, 2020) and resilience (Kuperminc, Chan, Hale, Joseph, & Delbasso, 2020). Combining group counseling with financial incentives, both short-term assistance and funds that accumulate for use in postsecondary education, increased both graduation rates and college enrollment for children from low socioeconomic Canadian families living in public housing projects in Toronto (Oreopoulos, Brown, & Lavecchia, 2017).

De Witte and colleagues also suggest the importance of family environment for completing high school. However, they do not report evidence about interventions to improve family environment. We can speculate that public policies that raise the income of low-income families would have a positive effect on the schooling success of their children. However, estimating the magnitude of any such effects—which would likely depend on expectations about anticipated *permanent* increases in resources rather than experimental increases—poses a major policy challenge. Permanent increases would likely require federal policies, such as the refundable child tax credit, that do not vary by state. Nonetheless, using a differences-in-differences design, Yeung (2020) did find a relative reduction in dropout rates for students in states that accepted Medicaid expansion under the Affordable Care Act compared to those in states that did not. This is consistent with our speculation.

Finally, De Witte and colleagues considered school-based interventions and point to the importance of school environments that are specifically adapted to the needs of ethnically diverse students. Research provides evidence for two approaches to creating school environments that are welcoming to diverse students.

*First,* evidence shows that increasing the opportunity for students of color to have teachers of color produces desirable learning effects (Bristol & Martin-Fernandez, 2019). Exposure to same-race teachers reduces exclusionary discipline for Black students (Lindsay & Hart, 2017). The presence of students and teachers with the same race or ethnicity results in fewer unexcused absences for Latinx students (Gottfried, Kirksey, & Fletcher, 2022). The presence of same-race teachers at the advanced level increases the likelihood of enrollment in advanced-level courses by Black students (Hart, 2020). Most important, Gershenson, Hart, Hyman, Lindsay, and Papageorge

(2018) find substantial positive high school graduation and college enrollment effects for Black students in Tennessee and North Carolina who had interaction with at least one same-race teacher in grades K-3, suggesting that exposure to same-race teachers can be valuable at any grade.

*Second*, small schools aimed at disadvantaged students appear to produce substantial gains in graduation rates (Bloom, Unterman, Zhu, & Reardon, 2020). New York City created a large number of small schools, with entering classes of about 100 students, in disadvantaged neighborhoods that previously had large schools with low graduation rates. The impact of these schools can be estimated because they were not academically selective. Bloom and Unterman (2014) estimate that these schools increased graduation rates for disadvantaged students by more than 9 percentage points.

## CONCLUSIONS AND POLICY IMPLICATIONS

The importance of high school graduation to students is unambiguous, but its broader social value—and how to best achieve increases in high school graduation rates—are tougher questions. If, for example, raising graduation rates has a high social value, then there is an added justification for policies that can credibly increase them because the benefits will outweigh the cost.

As we have demonstrated here and elsewhere, completion of high school increases the productivity and total wages of students who graduate and results in additional benefits to the wider society. We can make this statement with confidence for the general population, but at this time we are less confident on the size of the benefits that would accrue to the economically and socially disadvantaged from completing high school. Depending on a number of crucial assumptions, these benefits could be somewhat smaller or a lot larger.

This uncertainty stems from a number of reasons. With a couple of exceptions, there has been very little social experimentation concerning the individual or social value of retention programs, as opposed to remedial programs for those who have left school, that attempt to improve the rate of high school graduation for disadvantaged groups. As far as we are aware, no experiments have focused on incentives targeted at students and their families compared to those going to agents such as teachers or counselors. Somewhat related, there has been little experimentation with direct (strong) financial or close to financial incentives, which economists think work in many other policy arenas (this would help discriminate between whether potential dropouts are damaged in some specific way . . . or just disadvantaged by individual and family poverty). Finally, it is intrinsically difficult to estimate and value productivity change from an additional disadvantaged student graduation in the presence of historical and current discrimination. However, even if our estimates for the general population overestimate those for minority and economically disadvantaged students by a factor of two or three, increasing their graduation rates from most plausible programs would still offer positive net benefits.

Finding ways to increase the graduation rates of minority and economically disadvantaged students offers prospects for hitting the rare "sweet spot" of increased equity and efficiency. Creating and evaluating interventions that can possibly hit the spot should be a high priority for social policy.

# REFERENCES

Allensworth, E. (2013). The use of ninth-grade early warning indicators to improve Chicago schools. *Journal of Education for Students Placed at Risk, 18*(1), 68–83.

Anderson, D. M. (2014). In school and out of trouble? The minimum dropout age and juvenile crime. *Review of Economics and Statistics, 96*, 318–331.

Bailey, M. J., Sun, S., & Timpe, B. (2021). Prep school for poor kids: The long-run impacts of Head Start on human capital and economic self-sufficiency. *American Economic Review, 111*(12), 3963–4001.

Bartik, T., Herschbein, B., & Lachowska, M. (2016). The merits of universal scholarships: Benefit–cost evidence from the Kalamazoo promise. *Journal of Benefit–Cost Analysis, 7*, 400–433.

Belfield, C. (2021). *The economic burden of racism from the U.S. education system.* National Education Policy Center.

Belfield, C., Hollands, F., & Levin, H. (2011). *What are the social and economic returns?* Campaign for Educational Equity. Teachers College, Columbia University.

Belfield, C., Clive, R., and Levin, H. M. (Eds.). (2007). *The price we pay: Economic and social consequences of inadequate education.* Brookings Institution Press,

Bertocchi, G., & Dimico, A. (2012). The racial gap in education and the legacy of slavery. *Journal of Comparative Economics, 40*(4), 581–595.

Bhutta, N., Chang, A. C., Dettling, L. J., & Hsu, J. W. (2020). *Disparities in wealth by race and ethnicity in the 2019 Survey of Consumer Finances.* Board of Governors of the Federal Reserve System. https://doi.org/10.17016/2380-7172.2797

Black, S. E., & Lynch, L. M. (2001). How to compete: The impact of workplace practices and information technology on productivity. *Review of Economics and Statistics, 83*(3), 434–445.

Black, S. E., & Lynch, L. M. (2004). What's driving the new economy? The benefits of workplace innovation. *Economic Journal, 114*(493), F97–F116.

Blau, F. D., & Kahn, L. M. (2017). The gender wage gap: Extent, trends, and explanations. *Journal of Economic Literature, 55*(3), 789–865.

Bloom, H. S., & Unterman, R. (2014). Can small high schools of choice improve educational prospects for disadvantaged students? *Journal of Policy Analysis and Management, 33*(2), 290–319.

Bloom, H. S., Unterman, R., Zhu, P., & Reardon, S. F. (2020). Lessons from New York City's small schools of choice about high school features that promote graduation for disadvantaged students. *Journal of Policy Analysis and Management, 39*(3), 740–771. https://doi.org/10.1002/pam.22192

Boardman, A., Greenberg, D., Vining, A., & Weimer, D. (2018). *Cost–benefit analysis: Concepts and practice* (5th ed.). New York: Cambridge University Press.

Boardman, A. E., Greenberg, D. H., Vining, A. R., & Weimer, D. L. (2020). Efficiency without apology: Consideration of the marginal excess tax burden and distributional impacts in benefit–cost analysis. *Journal of Benefit–Cost Analysis, 11*(3), 457–478.

Boardman, A., & Vining, A. (2017). There are many (well, more than one) paths to nirvana: The economic evaluation of social policies. In B. Greve (Ed.), *Handbook of social policy evaluation* (pp. 77–99). Cheltenham, UK, and Northampton, MA: Edward Elgar.

Bristol, T. J., and Fernandez, J. M. (2019). The added value of Latinx and Black teachers for Latinx and Black students: Implications for policy. *Policy Insights from the Behavioral and Brain Sciences, 6*(2), 147–153.

Burger, K. (2010). How does early childhood care and education affect cognitive development? An international review of the effects of early interventions for children from different social backgrounds. *Early Childhood Research Quarterly, 25*(2), 140–165.

Card, D. (2001). Estimating the return to schooling: Progress on some persistent econometric problems. *Econometrica, 69*(5), 1127–1160.

Castillo, M., Jordan, J. L., & Petrie, R. (2019). Discount rates of children and high school graduation. *Economic Journal, 129*(619), 1152–1181.

Chan, W. Y., Kuperminc, G. P., Seitz, S., Wilson, C., & Khatib, N. (2020). School-based group mentoring and academic outcomes in vulnerable high-school students. *Youth & Society, 52*(7), 1220–1237.

Cutler, D., & Lleras-Muney, A. (2010). Understanding differences in health behaviors by education. *Journal of Health Economics, 29*(1), 1–28.

Dee, T. S., & Penner, E. K. (2021). My brother's keeper? The impact of targeted educational supports. *Journal of Policy Analysis and Management, 40*(4), 1171–1196.

De Witte, K., Cabus, S., Thyssen, G., Groot, W., & van den Brink, H. M. (2013). A critical review of the literature on school dropout. *Educational Research Review, 10*, 13–28.

Doms, M., Dunne, T., & Troske, K. (1997). Workers, wages, and technology. *Quarterly Journal of Economics, 112*(1), 253–290.

Gershenson, S., Hart, C. M. D., Hyman, J., Lindsay, D., & Papageorge, N. W. (2018). *The long-run impacts of same-race teachers* (Working Paper No. 25254). National Bureau of Economic Research.

Ginder, S., Kelly-Reid, J., & Mann, F. (2016). *Postsecondary institutions and cost of attendance in 2015–16; degrees and other awards conferred, 2014–15; and 12-month enrollment, 2014–15: First look (provisional data)*. National Center for Education Statistics Report, NCES 2016-112rev. https://nces.ed.gov/pubs2016/2016112rev.pdf

Gottfried, M., Kirksey, J. J., Fletcher, T. L. (2022). Do high school students with a same-race teacher attend class more often? *Educational Evaluation and Policy Analysis, 44*(1), 149–169.

Greenberg, D., & Barnow, B. S. (2014). Flaws in evaluations of social programs: Illustrations from randomized controlled trials. *Evaluation Review, 38*(5), 359–387.

Greenberg, D. H., & Robins, P. K. (1986). The changing role of social experiments in policy analysis. *Journal of Policy Analysis and Management, 5*(2), 340–362.

Gubbels, J., van der Put, C. E., & Assink, M. (2019). Risk factors for school absenteeism and dropout: A meta-analytic review. *Journal of Youth and Adolescence, 48*, 1637–1667.

Hanushek, E. (2009). The economic value of education and cognitive skills. In G. Sykes, B. Schneider, & D. Plank (Eds.), *Handbook of education policy research* (pp. 39–56). New York: Routledge.

Hanushek, E. A., Schwerdt, G., Wiederhold, S., & Woessmann, L. (2015). Returns to skills around the world: Evidence from PIAAC. *European Economic Review, 73*, 103–130.

Hart, C. M. D. (2020). An honors teacher like me: Effects of access to same-race teachers on Black students' advanced-track enrollment and performance. *Educational Evaluation and Policy Analysis, 42*(2), 163–187.

Haveman, R., & Wolfe, B. (1984). Schooling and economic well-being: The role of nonmarket effects. *Journal of Human Resources, 19*(3), 377–407.

Hebert, T. P., & Reis, S. M. (1999). Culturally diverse high-achieving students in an urban high school. *Urban Education, 34*(4), 428–457.

Heckman, J., Humphries, J., & Veramendi, G. (2015). *The causal effects of education on earnings and health* (Unpublished manuscript). Department of Economics, University of Chicago.

Hollands, F., Bowden, A. B., Belfield, C., Levin, H. M., Cheng, H., Shand, R., Pan, Y., & Hanisch-Cerda, B. (2014). Cost-effectiveness analysis in practice: Interventions to improve high school completion. *Educational Evaluation and Policy Analysis, 36*(3), 307–326.

Jackson, C. K., Porter, S. C., Easton, J. Q., & Kiguel, S. (2020). *Who benefits from attending effective schools? Examining heterogeneity in high school impacts* (Working Paper No. 28194). National Bureau of Economic Research. http://www.nber.org/papers/w28194

Jaeger, D., & Page, M. (1996). Degrees matter: New evidence on sheepskin effects in the returns to education. *Review of Economics and Statistics, 78*, 733–740.

Jones, D. E., Karoly, L. A., Crowley, D. M., & Greenberg, M. T. (2015). Considering valuation of noncognitive skills in benefit–cost analysis of programs for children. *Journal of Benefit–Cost Analysis, 6*(3), 471–507.

Jung, Y. (2021). *Formation of the legacy of slavery: Evidence from the US South.* Available at SSRN 3966791. https://papers.ssrn.com/sol3/papers.cfm?abstract_id=3966791

Kang, S. K., DeCelles, K. A., Tilcsik, A., & Jun, S. (2015). Whitened résumés: Race and self-presentation in the labor market. *Administrative Science Quarterly, 61*(3), 469–502.

Kuperminc, G. P., Chan, W. Y., Hale, K. E., Joseph, H. L., & Delbasso, C. A. (2020). The role of school-based group mentoring in promoting resilience among vulnerable high school students. *American Journal of Community Psychology, 65*(1–2), 136–148.

Lang, K., & Kahn-Lang Spitzer, A. (2020). Race discrimination: An economic perspective. *Journal of Economic Perspectives, 34*(2), 68–89.

Lee-St. John, T. J., Walsh, M. E., Raczek, A. E., Vuilleumier, C. E., Foley, C., Heberle, A., Sibley, E., & Dearing, E. (2018). The long-term impact of systemic student support in elementary school: Reducing high school dropout. *AERA Open, 4*(4), 1–16.

Lindsay, C. A., & Hart, C. M. D. (2017). Exposure to same-race teachers and student disciplinary outcomes for Black students in North Carolina. *Educational Evaluation and Policy Analysis, 39*(3), 485–510.

Luallen, J. (2006). School's out . . . forever: A study of juvenile crime, at-risk youths and teacher strikes. *Journal of Urban Economics, 59*(1), 75–103.

Macchia, S. E., Therriault, D. J., & Wood, R. C. (2021). A cost-benefit analysis of a teen pregnancy program employed as a high school dropout intervention. *Planning & Changing, 50*(1), 20–36.

Machin, S., Marie, O., & Vujić, S. (2011, May 12). The crime reducing effect of education. *Economic Journal, 121*, 463–484.

McCollister, K., French, M., & Fang, H. (2010). The cost of crime to society: New crime-specific estimates for policy and program evaluation. *Drug and Alcohol Dependence, 108*(1–2), 98–109.

McCollister, K., Yang, X., Sayed, B., French, M., Leff, J., & Schackman, B. (2017). Monetary conversion factors for economic evaluations of substance use disorders. *Journal of Substance Abuse Treatment, 81*, 25–34.

McFarland, J., Cui, J., Holmes, J., & Wang, X. (2020, January). Trends in high school dropout and completion rates in the United States: 2019 (Compendium Report, NCES 2020-117). National Center for Education Statistics. US Department of Education. https://nces.ed.gov/pubs2020/2020117.pdf

McLanahan, S., & Sawhill, I. (2015). Marriage and child wellbeing revisited: Introducing the issue. *Future of Children, 25*(3), 3–9.

McMahon, W. (2018). The total return to higher education: Is there underinvestment for economic growth and development? *Quarterly Review of Economics and Finance, 70*, 90–111.

Moore, M., Boardman, A., & Vining, A. (2013). More appropriate discounting: The rate of social time preference and the value of the social discount rate. *Journal of Benefit–Cost Analysis 4*(1), 1–16.

Moore, M., Boardman, A., Vining, A., Weimer, D., & Greenberg, D. H. (2004). "Just give me a number!" Practical values for the social discount rate. *Journal of Policy Analysis and Management, 23*(4), 789–812.

Moretti, E. (2004). Estimating the social returns to higher education: Evidence from longitudinal and repeated cross-sectional data. *Journal of Econometrics, 121*, 175–212.

Morissette, R., Chan, P. C. W., & Lu, Y. (2015). Wages, youth employment, and school enrollment: Recent evidence from increases in world oil prices. *Journal of Human Resources, 50*(1), 222–253.

Murnane, R. (2013). US high school graduation rates: Patterns and explanations. *Journal of Economic Literature, 51*(2), 370–422.

National Center for Education Statistics (NCES). (2021). *High school graduation rates.* Department of Education. https://nces.ed.gov/fastfacts/display.asp?id=805

Neal, D. (1997). The effects of Catholic secondary schooling on educational attainment. *Journal of Labor Economics, 15*(1), 98–123.

Okun, A. M. (1975). *Efficiency and equity: The big tradeoff.* Washington, DC: Brookings Institution.

Oreopoulos, P., Brown, R. S., & Lavecchia, A. M. (2017). Pathways to education: An integrated approach to helping at-risk high school students. *Journal of Political Economy, 125*(4), 947–984.

Pager, D., & Shepherd, H. (2008). The sociology of discrimination: Racial discrimination in employment, housing, credit, and consumer markets. *Annual Review of Sociology, 34*, 181–209.

Papay, J., Murnane, R., & Willett, J. (2015). Income-based inequality in educational outcomes: Learning from state longitudinal data systems. *Educational Evaluation and Policy Analysis, 37*(1), 29S–52S.

Qin, X., Deutsch, J., & Hong, G. (2021). Unpacking complex mediation mechanisms and their heterogeneity between sites in a Job Corps evaluation. *Journal of Policy Analysis and Management, 40*(1), 158–190.

Quillian, L., Pager, D., Hexel, O., & Midtbøen, A. H. (2017). Meta-analysis of field experiments shows no change in racial discrimination in hiring over time. *Proceedings of the National Academy of Sciences, 114*(41), 10870–10875.

Riddell, W. C., & Song, X. (2017). The role of education in technology use and adoption: Evidence from the Canadian Workplace and Employee Survey. *International Labor Review, 70*(5), 1219–1253.

Roderick, M., Kelley-Kemple, T., Johnson, D. W., & Ryan, S. (2021, September). *The preventable failure: Improvements in high school graduation rates when high schools focused on the ninth grade year* (Working paper). University of Chicago Consortium on School Research. https://consortium.uchicago.edu/publications/the-preventable-failure

Schoenfeld, A. H. (2006). What doesn't work: The challenge and failure of the What Works Clearinghouse to conduct meaningful reviews of studies of mathematics curricula. *Educational Researcher, 35* (2006), 13–21.

US Bureau of Labor Statistics. (2017, March 17). *Employer costs for employee compensation—December 2016.* News Release USDL-17-0321, table A, p. 2.

US Department of Commerce, Census Bureau. (2000, 2010, & 2018, October Supplement). *Current Population Survey (CPS): Digest of Education Statistics 2019,* table 302.60.

US Department of Education. (2019). *Young adult educational and employment outcomes by family socioeconomic status.* National Center for Education Statistics. https://nces.ed.gov/programs/coe/indicator/tbe

U.S. Department of Education (2021). Digest of Education Statistics. Table 326.10. 2021 Tables and Figures. https://nces.ed.gov/programs/digest/d21/tables/dt21_326.10.asp. (Accessed November 19, 2022).

US Office of Management and Budget. (2003, September 17). *Circular A-4: Regulatory analysis.* https://obamawhitehouse.archives.gov/omb/circulars_a004_a-4/

Vining, A., & Weimer, D. (2010). An assessment of important issues concerning the application of benefit-cost analysis to social policy. *Journal of Benefit–Cost Analysis, 1*(1), 1–38.

Vining, A., & Weimer, D. (2019). The value of high school graduation in the United States: Per-person shadow price estimates for use in cost–benefit analysis. *Administrative Sciences, 9*(4), 81–96.

Washington State Institute for Public Policy. *Benefit–cost technical documentation.* (2019, December). https://www.wsipp.wa.gov/TechnicalDocumentation/WsippBenefitCostTechnicalDocumentation.pdf

Weimer, D. (2017). *Behavioral economics for cost–benefit analysis: Benefit validity when sovereign consumers seem to make mistakes.* New York: Cambridge University Press.

Weimer, D. L., Moberg, D. P., French, F., Tanner-Smith, E. E., & Finch, A. J. (2019). Net benefits of recovery high schools: Higher cost but increased sobriety and increased probability of high school graduation. *Journal of Mental Health Policy and Economics, 22*(3), 109–120.

Weimer, D., & Vining, A. (Eds.). (2009). *Investing in the disadvantaged: Assessing the benefits and costs of social policies.* Washington, DC: Georgetown University Press.

Wolf, P., & McShane, M. (2013). Is the juice worth the squeeze? A benefit/cost analysis of the District of Columbia Opportunity Scholarship program. *Education Finance and Policy, 8*(1), 74–99.

Wolfe, B., & Haveman, R. (2001). Accounting for the social and non-market benefits of education. In J. F. Helliwell (Ed.), *The contribution of human and social capital to sustained economic growth and well-being* (pp. 221–250). Vancouver: University of British Columbia Press.

Yeung, R. (2020). The effect of the Medicaid expansion on dropout rates. *Journal of School Health, 90*(10), 745–753.

Zenou, Y., & Boccard, N. (2000). Racial discrimination and redlining in cities. *Journal of Urban Economics, 48*(2), 260–285.

Zerbe, R. O., Plotnick, R. D., Kessler, R. C., Pecora, P. J., Hiripi, E., O'Brien, K., Williams, J., English, D., & White, J. (2009). Benefits and costs of intensive foster care services: The Casey Family programs compared to state services. *Contemporary Economic Policy, 27*(3), 308–320.

# Part II

## CHANGES NEEDED AT THE STATE AND LOCAL LEVEL TO MAKE POSITIVE RESULTS MORE WIDESPREAD

# 6

# Getting Past the Current Trade-Off Between Privacy and Equity in Educational Technology

*Ryan Baker*

Today, the best educational technologies can be very effective at engaging learners and increasing learning outcomes. Educational games such as Zoombinis (Asbell-Clarke et al., 2021), Physics Playground (Shute, Ventura, & Kim, 2013), and Dragonbox (Siew, Geofrey, & Lee, 2016) can make difficult concepts in computational thinking, physics, and mathematics accessible to students. Intelligent tutoring systems such as Mathia (Pane, Griffin, McCaffrey, & Karam, 2014) and ALEKS (Huang, Craig, Xie, Graesser, & Hu, 2016) help students learn mathematical reasoning skills, targeting students' time to material they have not yet learned and providing scaffolding for learning. Research on computer-supported collaborative learning has supported the enhancement of discussion forums where students learn together (Jeong, Hmelo-Silver, & Jo, 2019).

However, awareness is growing that educational technologies may not work equally effectively for all learners. Repeatedly, technologies and pedagogies that work effectively in some settings fail to function effectively when taken to new settings (Orr, 2015). Differences in implementation and usage between schools clearly play a large role in this phenomenon (Tipton & Olsen, 2018). However, there is also evidence that even the findings these technologies are developed based on may not generalize across all groups of students (Karumbaiah, Ocumpaugh, & Baker, 2021).

Within the broader span of educational technologies, the use of artificial intelligence in education is increasing. Artificially intelligent educational technologies can be highly effective at promoting learning (see review in VanLehn, 2011), but the algorithms that these systems depend upon can also have algorithmic biases (Baker & Hawn, 2021), despite the best intentions of their developers (Holstein, Wortman Vaughan, Daumé, Dudik, & Wallach, 2019). Algorithmic bias refers to the situation when an algorithm performs worse for members of some subsets of the population than others, meaning that the predictions and recommendations that follow from the algorithm may be harmful to some even if, on average, they are positive. Biases have been documented for many educational technologies (Baker & Hawn, 2021).

In order to reduce algorithmic bias, it is necessary to have data on student demographic membership and to retain data for long enough for student outcomes to be clear. However, increasing concerns about student privacy have led to an increasing push for educational technology vendors to not collect identifying data or demographic data, to discard this data after a year, or not to share this data.

Unfortunately, as this chapter will argue, the push to delete or never collect identifying and demographic data is likely to make it much more difficult to investigate inequities and to improve effectiveness for the learners being negatively impacted.

In this chapter, I will discuss each of these trends, considering the value of both protecting privacy and reducing algorithmic bias, and how specific privacy protection measures can hinder attempts to identify and address algorithmic bias. I will then discuss ways that new data analysis and data protection technologies may be able to improve the trade-off between these important values. Finally, the chapter offers recommendations for state educational agencies and school districts.

## THE PROMISE OF ARTIFICIALLY INTELLIGENT EDUCATIONAL TECHNOLOGY

The first two decades of the 21st century have seen the demonstration, validation, and scaling of several artificially intelligent educational technologies. A relatively large share of the expanded use of educational technology during the pandemic consisted of videoconferencing to support continued human teaching and learning management systems and/or courseware where students watched videos and completed or submitted assignments (Francom, Lee, & Pinkney, 2021). The user base of artificially intelligent educational technologies expanded as well.

Some of the key early visions for how artificial intelligence could be used in education suggested that learning systems could leverage the same strategies that expert tutors use in one-on-one in-person tutoring, coining the term *intelligent tutoring systems* for this type of technology (Merrill, Reiser, Ranney, & Trafton, 1992; Lepper, Woolverton, Mumme, & Gurtner, 1993; McArthur, Stasz, & Zmuidzinas, 1990). This led to visions of learning software as perceptive as teachers (Self, 1999) and expert tutors (Shute & Psotka, 1994). Popular science fiction books such as *Diamond Age* (Stephenson, 2003) envisioned one-to-one real-time learning experiences that would guide children through both their academic and life skills development, from early childhood into adulthood.

Although contemporary learning technologies are not yet as sophisticated as some of these researchers initially hoped (Baker, 2016), nonetheless these systems have been a substantial overall success. Contemporary scaled systems tend to each be successful at capturing a single (not always the same) dimension of the sophisticated systems envisioned decades ago (Baker, 2016).

The first intelligent tutoring system to clearly document efficacy in real-world classrooms and scale was the Cognitive Tutor (now called Mathia). Developed over more than a decade by cognitive psychologists at Carnegie Mellon University, Mathia now covers the majority of middle school and high school mathematics. Mathia has been the subject of many experimental and quasi-experimental studies, from its earliest usage in Pittsburgh (Koedinger, Anderson, Hadley, & Mark, 1997) to nationwide RCTs (Pane, McCaffrey, Slaughter, Steele, & Ikemoto, 2010; Pane et al., 2014). Recent studies have suggested that some Mathia curricula are highly effective (Pane et al., 2014); results have been mixed for other Mathia curricula (Pane et al., 2010). Implementation fidelity and teaching practices make a major difference for its effectiveness (Sales, Wilks, & Pane, 2016; Sales & Pane, 2020), and teachers tend to achieve better results once they are experienced at using it in their classrooms (Pane et al., 2014).

When used by experienced teachers in the fashion it was designed for, Mathia leads to deeper conceptual understanding of mathematics and better problem-solving skill, as well as better performance on standardized examinations. Mathia's success is dependent in part on its ability to recognize student knowledge in real time, information it uses to decide when to advance the student within its curriculum (Corbett, 2001).

Several other intelligent tutoring systems and related systems have also scaled and provided evidence for efficacy. ALEKS uses automated algorithms to determine which topics a student is prepared to work on (Cosyn, Uzun, Doble, & Matayoshi, 2021) and has been shown to reduce equity gaps (Huang et al., 2016) and to improve overall outcomes (Mojarad, Baker, Essa, & Stalzer, 2021) but also to be very dependent on proper implementation to work well (Phillips, Pane, Reumann-Moore, & Shenbanjo, 2020).

The intelligent simulation Inq-ITS can automatically detect multiple aspects of student science inquiry skill in line with the Next Generation Science Standards and uses this information to scaffold the development of those skills, leading to knowledge that generalizes across contexts (Li, Gobert, Dickler, & Moussavi, 2018). SQL-Tutor has been used by more than 100,000 students to learn database programming worldwide, using a complex model of domain knowledge to identify student errors (Mitrovic & Ohlsson, 2016). A range of other examples of the effectiveness of intelligent tutoring systems can now be found in the literature, with several recent meta-analyses (VanLehn, 2011; Steenbergen-Hu & Cooper, 2013; Ma, Adesope, Nesbit, & Liu, 2014; Kulik & Fletcher, 2016; Xu, Wijekumar, Ramirez, Hu, & Irey, 2019).

The artificially intelligent learning systems that are widely used in K-12 classrooms, both in the United States and internationally, typically rely on AI technology and algorithms from the 1990s or on more recent updates to the same paradigms of adaptivity made possible by those algorithms. The past two decades have seen an explosion of advancement in what can be detected about students in real time, including their disengaged behaviors (Baker & Rossi, 2013), emotion (D'Mello & Graesser, 2010), and self-regulated learning skills (Aleven, McLaren, Roll, & Koedinger, 2006;

Maldonado-Mahauad, Pérez-Sanagustín, Kizilcec, Morales, & Munoz-Gama, 2018). These algorithms capture aspects of behavior and student state that can be easy for humans to recognize but hard to explain, leading to the increased use of machine learning algorithms that learn to replicate human judgments. Several experimental lessons and systems have been developed that leverage these algorithms to adapt in real time to increase educational effectiveness. For example, affectively aware systems have been adapted to help frustrated students improve their self-efficacy (DeFalco et al., 2018), and systems respond to student disengagement by visualizing students' recent behavior for them (Arroyo et al., 2007; Xia, Asano, Williams, Qu, & Ma, 2020).

Another recent trend is toward systems that use *reinforcement learning* algorithms (reinforcement for the algorithm, not for the child) to learn how to teach more effectively. These systems experiment with their own decisions, figuring out which content and supports to offer to a specific student in a specific situation (Singla, Rafferty, Radanovic, & Heffernan, 2021). Although K-12 and undergraduate use of these systems is primarily in the early experimental stages (Ausin, Maniktala, Barnes, & Chi, 2020; MacLellan & Gupta, 2021), Amazon now uses algorithms of this nature to increase the time-efficiency of its online training materials for employees (Bassen et al., 2020). In general, adaptive learning technologies make it possible for systems to differentiate their learning support for different students, and reinforcement learning makes it faster for systems to figure out how to do so. Over the next decades, it seems reasonable to expect increasing usage of more sophisticated automated artificial intelligence in K-12 education in the United States and worldwide.

## THE RISK OF ALGORITHMIC BIAS

As the use of machine learning and reinforcement learning for education increases, some of the risks now known to exist for these types of algorithms emerge in education as well. Perhaps foremost among these risks is the risk of *algorithmic bias*, where a computer algorithm either replicates a bias found in human behavior and decision making, or through poor design actually learns to demonstrate new biases on its own. Algorithmic bias has been demonstrated in a range of contexts, from criminal justice (Angwin, Larson, Mattu, & Kirchner, 2016), to medicine (O'Reilly-Shah et al., 2020), to computer vision (Klare, Burge, Klontz, Bruegge, & Jain, 2012), to hiring (Garcia, 2016).

Algorithmic biases have also been documented in the educational use of algorithms. Algorithms have been documented to perform worse for specific demographic groups for a range of applications—predicting student dropout (Anderson, Boodhwani, & Baker, 2019), detecting emotion (Ocumpaugh, Baker, Gowda, Heffernan, & Heffernan, 2014), automated essay scoring (Bridgeman, Trapani, & Attali, 2012), and many others. Baker and Hawn (2021) review the published literature on algorithmic bias in education and find that biases manifest not only for variables known to be involved in algorithmic bias in general (race, ethnicity, and gender) but for a range of other variables (rural learners, native language, parental educational background, international students, military-connected students).

Baker and Hawn's review investigates which groups are impacted by algorithmic bias in education. Kizilcec and Lee (2021) demonstrate that much of this bias occurs due to flaws in the algorithms used. However, Karumbaiah (2021) argues that "upstream" sources of bias—stemming from data collection, study design, and the choice of theory—are an equally important source of bias. She notes that educational technologies are often designed using findings derived using data from well-represented populations, and that these findings may not apply to historically marginalized populations (Karumbaiah et al., 2021). As another example, upstream bias also emerges when AI algorithms are trained on small or unrepresentative samples, so the resulting predictions that look good on average are not actually as good for specific subsections of the population.

However, the findings reviewed by Baker and Hawn (2021) and by Karumbaiah (2021) can only be obtained in a context where researchers have access to student demographic variables. Despite the increasing magnitude of research on algorithmic bias in education, most research on educational algorithms does not study the impacts on different groups. In fact, as a recent review by Paquette and colleagues (2020) indicates, most research on educational algorithms does not even mention the demographic attributes of the populations contributing data, much less study whether there is differential effectiveness or impact.

It has been known for decades that our existing educational system produces poorer outcomes for members of historically marginalized communities (see review in Gordon, 2007). If the next generation of educational technologies is based on algorithms that are less effective for members of these communities, we will end up perpetuating, or even magnifying, these inequities. Similarly, if the next generation of educational technologies is based on research findings that only apply to non-marginalized populations, we will perpetuate, or even magnify, the inequities that exist. If we are to use advanced artificial intelligence technologies to benefit learners, we need to develop these technologies so that they work for all learners, particularly historically underserved learners. We can only do so by developing our models on diverse and representative populations of learners—and we can only be certain we have avoided algorithmic bias if we look for it. Doing so requires collecting large data sets that include demographic data and other measures of individual characteristics that serve as proxies for the full suite of preferences and differences between learners.

However, another ongoing trend puts this possibility at risk. This trend, entered into with generally very positive motivations and goals, nonetheless creates risks that the field and community of developers will develop a generation of educational technologies that are less effective for historically underrepresented learners. This trend is the push toward prioritizing privacy.

## THE PUSH TOWARD PRIORITIZING PRIVACY

Recent years have seen considerable concern about student privacy, both in academia (Slade & Prinsloo, 2013; Lynch, 2017; Klose, Desai, Song, & Gehringer, et al., 2020) and in public advocacy (NASSP, n.d.; Student Privacy Compass, 2021). Both researchers and public advocates have expressed concern about the increasing amount of educational data becoming available at scale and its uses for both commercial and scientific purposes. Klose et al. (2020) have noted that educational databases, when hacked, have been used for purposes such as identity theft. There has also been concern that educational data could be used to advertise services to students (Lynch, 2017; Golightly, 2020). Many have also speculated that long-term use of educational data could lead to decisions being made about individual years, or even decades, after a poor decision is made (Zeide, 2017).

Some have called for deidentification as a way to address these concerns (Ho, 2017), and key data sharing initiatives such as the Pittsburgh Science of Learning Center DataShop (Koedinger, Cunningham, Skogsholm, & Leber, et al., 2008) and the edX research data eXchange (edX, 2021) remove all student identifiers prior to data sharing. However, other researchers have noted that reidentification remains possible for data sets even after student identifiers have been removed, noting a case where a class could be identified based on when they took a field trip (Yacobsen, Fuhrman, Hershkovitz, & Alexandron, 2021). This has led some researchers to argue for the use of privacy-protection approaches where student demographic identity variables are removed from data as well (Klose et al., 2020), at minimum in cases where a student is not representative of the class or overall data set they are part of (Bayardo & Agrawal, 2005).

Others have sought to put stringent limitations on the sharing of deidentified data—for example, the Student Data Privacy Consortium's template agreement (2021) requires that each time a deidentified data set is shared, it must be approved by each local education agency. Although this agreement protects the school district's rights and oversight, the agreement also makes it very onerous to share large multi-school district data sets with a broad span of researchers. Going even further, some have argued for the deletion of all educational data for any purpose after the school semester has ended and the agreement not to use data for any secondary analysis purpose (Herold, 2017; see discussion in Laird, Quay-de la Vallee, & Mahesh, 2019).

As privacy initiatives go forward and school districts increasingly mandate that vendors do not collect or use demographic data or put into place agreements that make data sharing or usage onerous, there are likely reductions of risk to student privacy. This reduction of risk does not come for free, however; it is accompanied by an inability to test for and reduce algorithmic bias. In other words, the question is not whether AI will be biased at first—as the process of fine-tuning algorithms inevitably involves predictions that deviate from reality in ways that are correlated with individual characteristics—but whether we will have the systems in place to collect the information and the incentives to ensure that the information is used to reduce these biases and make AI algorithms better.

Requiring a vendor to delete student data, or making it difficult to share data, makes it harder to use data for inappropriate purposes. It also makes it much more difficult to hold that vendor accountable for algorithmic biases in its product. Many educational technology vendors have demonstrated responsibility in identifying algorithmic bias in their products, publishing evidence about these limitations and flaws and working with the scientific community to correct them (Bridgeman et al., 2012; Loukina & Buzick, 2017; Christie, Jarratt, Olson, & Taijala, 2019; Baker, Berning, & Gowda, 2020). Poorly designed data privacy agreements make it much harder for external researchers to participate in this process of critique, increasing the risk that algorithmic bias will reduce the effectiveness of educational technologies for historically underrepresented populations. The same is likely for requirements that prevent the collection and use of demographic and identity data—perhaps even more so, because rapid research processes could still find and correct algorithmic bias in data required to be deleted, but if data is never collected, it cannot be used.

The arguments around data privacy are often couched in the language of non-maleficence, the goal of doing no harm. Violations of student privacy create clear opportunities for harm, and this author has no intention of minimizing their importance. However, another non-maleficence goal should also be considered—the goal of preventing algorithmic bias. Educational technology should be effective for all students, in particular for students from historically marginalized populations. The noble goal of avoiding harm through privacy violations must be balanced with the goal of a fair and equitable educational system.

## ALTERNATIVE WAYS TO PROTECT PRIVACY WHILE IMPROVING ALGORITHMIC EFFECTIVENESS

The current situation appears to leave us with a difficult choice: should we take action to protect student privacy, or should we move instead in the direction of using data to identify and fix algorithmic biases? But perhaps the question should not be which of these non-maleficent values we prefer but, instead, whether there is a way to have both. Can we protect student privacy while also collecting and using the data that we need to avoid algorithmic biases?

Fortunately, it appears that we can. There are now approaches that enable us to collect, retain, and use the data we need to address algorithmic biases—while reducing (though not entirely eliminating) risks to privacy. Essentially, these approaches come down to carefully managing data rather than eliminating it (or the feasibility of using it) entirely.

School districts today retain a great deal of data on learners. This data is necessarily personally identifying—schools need to be able to track their students' grades, disciplinary incidents, and standardized examination scores. This data contains information that could be embarrassing or problematic if it were released—often much more so than the data held by educational technology vendors. School district data security is often imperfect—hacks, malware, and ransomware has plagued school districts in recent years (Lopez, 2021), much as they have impacted broader society. And yet, we neither call for school districts to discard all their data on an annual basis, nor prevent school districts from collecting demographic information, nor try to make it very difficult for school districts to let external researchers use that data for appropriate research uses. The risk of security breaches in educational vendors is real. At the same time, it is not immediately obvious that a company—which can be put out of business by lawsuits—has less of an interest in data security than a school district does.

The key is to develop secure ways to make data available for research without redacting that data to the point where it is no longer useful to test for algorithmic bias. There are legitimate concerns around data sharing, but the goal ultimately is the *use* of data, not sharing it. An example of this distinction can be seen in our data infrastructure (named MORF) at the University of Pennsylvania. We currently store our data from Massive Online Open Courses in a repository that enables research on complete, unredacted data while making it highly difficult (hopefully infeasible) to extract that data (Gardner, Andres, Brooks, & Baker, 2018). Our open-source infrastructure allows researchers to submit data analysis programs to the infrastructure; a wide range of data analysis programs (across programming languages and data analysis tools) can be used, but only a restricted set of output functions can be used. New output functions cannot be added to the system without careful hand review by the technical team. This functionality allows researchers to run a range of analyses on student data without exposing that student data directly to researchers, reducing the risk of privacy breaches.

Our prototype has been used to attempt to replicate a number of past findings and analyses of algorithms (Andres, Baker, Siemens, Gasevic, & Spann, 2017; Gardner, Yang, Baker, & Brooks, 2019). It is imperfect in terms of usability and has thus far been difficult for researchers to learn to use outside of our team and a small number of pilot universities. However, it establishes a paradigm where vendors and school districts could make their data available for analysis—analysis on algorithmic bias, using a full range of demographic and identity variables—with substantially reduced risk of data disclosure and privacy violation.

Our infrastructure may not be the eventual infrastructure adopted by this sector (first research projects seldom are), but this overall paradigm—analysis on secured servers, with no direct access to personal data—has the potential to find a better compromise between privacy and reducing algorithmic bias than solutions that emphasize one goal over the other.

## RECOMMENDATIONS FOR STATE EDUCATIONAL AGENCIES AND SCHOOL DISTRICTS

The need to find a trade-off between the non-maleficent goals of protecting privacy and avoiding algorithmic bias leads this author to offer a few recommendations to state educational agencies and school districts:

## Provide Demographic Data to Vendors for the Purpose of Checking for Algorithmic Bias

If a technology is leading to worse outcomes for some demographic groups or making worse predictions for those demographic groups, districts adopting that technology and community members need to know that (and we need to fix the problem). Of course, this data should be transmitted and stored in a secure fashion, but it is needed if we are to verify whether algorithmic bias is occurring.

## Incentivize Vendors to Conduct Algorithmic Bias Audits, or Conduct Them Directly

Where the expertise is available, school districts and state agencies can conduct audits for algorithmic bias. However, this may not be feasible in many cases: not every school district has the capacity to conduct an algorithmic bias audit. As the developer of the algorithm, it is generally easier for the vendor to do an algorithmic bias audit, if it has the necessary demographic data. Doing so makes for economies of scale. External researchers may also be able to conduct these audits, a practice often seen for evaluations of efficacy. Best practices for the audit should be used, of course, with measures and groups agreed to in advance, and evidence on how the analysis was conducted being open for inspection.

## Rather Than Asking Vendors to Delete Data, Ask Them to Secure It

The practice of requiring vendors to delete data at the end of every school year reduces the risk of privacy leaks but also makes it impossible to check for longer-term equity issues. Many algorithms' accuracy and impacts can only be determined using longitudinal data (i.e., the accuracy of a predictive analytics model), so data should be kept until it is clear it will no longer be needed for this purpose.

## Encourage Vendors to Adopt Data Infrastructures That Enable Privacy-Protecting Analyses

Accountability can be increased by allowing school district/state researchers and other external researchers to inspect and/or conduct algorithmic bias analyses. Doing so with current data infrastructures is often difficult to do securely, and the transfer of data creates privacy risks. Encouraging vendors to develop or adopt data infrastructure that enables analysis while securing data (like the aforementioned repository at the University of Pennsylvania) will enable a better trade-off between privacy and reducing algorithmic bias than is currently possible today.

## CONCLUSIONS

In this chapter, I have discussed the trade-off between two concerns, both coming from a value of non-maleficence: protecting privacy and preventing algorithmic bias. I have briefly reviewed the push toward protecting privacy in education and some of the unintended consequences that current steps to protect privacy may be causing. I have discussed the emerging evidence that algorithmic bias is a major challenge to the effectiveness of new AI technologies for education. These technologies are, in many cases, beneficial overall but may be less effective for specific groups of students due to algorithmic bias. Current steps to protect privacy may make it much more difficult to prevent algorithmic bias.

This chapter details why specific privacy protection measures may make it harder to identify or address algorithmic bias. It discusses the possibility that new approaches to data storage and use may help to create a better balance between protecting privacy and preventing algorithmic bias. These new data storage and analysis technologies are still in the early stages of research and development, but given the fast developments ongoing in data science, they may be available to vendors, school districts, and state education agencies fairly soon. In tandem, conducting research on which variables should be collected will help us to comprehensively prevent algorithmic bias. There remains a need for further study of which groups are impacted by algorithmic bias in which situations (Baker & Hawn, 2021). Simply making it possible to use the variables that are already being collected would make a positive difference; a move toward collecting a broader research-based range of variables will make it possible to prevent algorithmic bias more comprehensively.

Overall, the right approach to balancing privacy and equity remains open to question, but both goals must be attended to. Otherwise, the promise of artificial intelligence for education may instead result in educational technologies that amplify the inequities that already exist in our educational system.

## REFERENCES

Aleven, V., McLaren, B., Roll, I., & Koedinger, K. (2006). Toward meta-cognitive tutoring: A model of help seeking with a cognitive tutor. *International Journal of Artificial Intelligence in Education, 16*(2), 101–128.

Anderson, H., Boodhwani, A., & Baker, R. S. (2019). *Assessing the fairness of graduation predictions.* Proceedings of the 12th International Conference on Educational Data Mining, pp. 488–491.

Andres, J. M. L ., Baker, R. S., Siemens, G., Gasevic, D., & Spann, C. A. (2017). Replicating 21 findings on student success in online learning. *Technology, Instruction, Cognition, and Learning, 10*(4), 313–333.

Angwin, J., Larson, J., Mattu, S., & Kirchner, L. (2016, May 23). Machine bias: There's software used across the country to predict future criminals. And it's biased against blacks. *ProPublica.* https://www.propublica.org/article/machine-bias-risk-assessments-in-criminal -sentencing

Arroyo, I., Ferguson, K., Johns, J., Dragon, T., Meheranian, H., Fisher, D., Barto, A., Mahadevan, S., & Woolf, B. P. (2007, June). Repairing disengagement with non-invasive interventions. In *AIED* (Vol. 2007, pp. 195–202).

Asbell-Clarke, J., Rowe, E., Almeda, V., Edwards, T., Bardar, E., Gasca, S., & Scruggs, R. (2021). The development of students' computational thinking practices in elementary- and middle-school classes using the learning game, *Zoombinis*. *Computers in Human Behavior, 115*, 106587.

Ausin, M. S., Maniktala, M., Barnes, T., & Chi, M. (2020, July). *Exploring the impact of simple explanations and agency on batch deep reinforcement learning induced pedagogical policies*. International Conference on Artificial Intelligence in Education, pp. 472–485. Cham: Springer.

Baker, R. S. (2016). Stupid tutoring systems, intelligent humans. *International Journal of Artificial Intelligence and Education, 26*(2), 600–614.

Baker, R. S., Berning, A., & Gowda, S. M. (2020). Differentiating military-connected and non-military-connected students: Predictors of graduation and SAT score. *EdArXiv*. https://doi.org/10.35542/osf.io/cetxj

Baker, R. S., & Hawn, M. A. (2021). Algorithmic bias in education. *International Journal of Artificial Intelligence and Education*. https://osf.io/pbmvz/download?format=pdf

Baker, R. S. J. D., & Rossi, L. M. (2013). Assessing the disengaged behavior of learners. In R. Sottilare, A. Graesser, X. Hu, & H. Holden (Eds.), *Design recommendations for intelligent tutoring systems: Learner modeling* (Vol. 1, pp. 155–166). US Army Research Laboratory. https://www.upenn.edu/learninganalytics/ryanbaker/BakerRossi2013.pdf

Bassen, J., Balaji, B., Schaarschmidt, M., Thille, C., Painter, J., Zimmaro, D., Grimes, A., Fast, E., & Mitchell, J. C. (2020, April). *Reinforcement learning for the adaptive scheduling of educational activities*. Proceedings of the 2020 CHI Conference on Human Factors in Computing Systems, pp. 1–12.

Bayardo, R. J., & Agrawal, R. (2005). *Data privacy through optimal k-anonymization*. Proceedings of the 21st International Conference on Data Engineering (ICDE'05), 217–228.

Bridgeman, B., Trapani, C., & Attali, Y. (2012). Comparison of human and machine scoring of essays: Differences by gender, ethnicity, and country. *Applied Measurement in Education, 25*(1), 27–40.

Christie, S. T., Jarratt, D. C., Olson, L. A., & Taijala, T. T. (2019). *Machine-learned school dropout early warning at scale*. Proceedings of the International Conference on Educational Data Mining.

Corbett, A. (2001). Cognitive computer tutors: Solving the two-sigma problem. In M. Bauer, P. J. Gmytrasiewicz, & J. Vassileva (Eds.), *[Lecture Notes in Computer Science] User Modeling 2001* (Vol. 2109, pp. 137–147). Springer, Berlin, Heidelberg. https://doi.org/10.1007/3-540-44566-8_14

Cosyn, E., Uzun, H., Doble, C., & Matayoshi, J. (2021). A practical perspective on knowledge space theory: ALEKS and its data. *Journal of Mathematical Psychology, 101*, 102512.

DeFalco, J. A., Rowe, J. P., Paquette, L., Georgoulas-Sherry, V., Brawner, K., Mott, B. W., Baker, R. S., & Lester, J. C. (2018). Detecting and addressing frustration in a serious game for military training. *International Journal of Artificial Intelligence and Education, 28*(2), 152–193.

D'Mello, S. K., & Graesser, A. (2010). Multimodal semi-automated affect detection from conversational cues, gross body language, and facial features. *User Modeling and User-Adapted Interaction, 20*(2), 147–187.

edX. (2021). *Using the research data exchange data package*. Retrieved December 20, 2021, from https://edx.readthedocs.io/projects/devdata/en/latest/rdx/index.html

Francom, G. M., Lee, S. J., & Pinkney, H. (2021). Technologies, challenges and needs of K-12 teachers in the transition to distance learning during the COVID-19 pandemic. *TechTrends, 65*, 589–601.

Garcia, M. (2016). Racist in the machine: The disturbing implications of algorithmic bias. *World Policy Journal, 33*(4), 111–117.

Gardner, J., Andres, J. M., Brooks, C., & Baker, R. (2018). *MORF: A framework for predictive modeling and replication at scale with privacy-restricted MOOC data*. 2018 IEEE International Conference on Big Data (Big Data), 3235–3244. https://homes.cs.washington.edu/~jpgard/papers/icbd19.pdf

Gardner, J., Yang, Y., Baker, R., & Brooks, C. (2019). *Modeling and experimental design for MOOC dropout prediction: A replication perspective*. Proceedings of the 12th International Conference on Educational Data Mining, 49–58.

Golightly, D. (2020, June 26). Google, New Mexico AG spar over Chromebook student data collection. *Android Headlines*. https://www.androidheadlines.com/2020/02/google-new-mexico-attorney-general-lawsuit-student-data-collection-chromebook.html

Gordon, E. W., Paik, S. J., & Walberg, H. J. (2007). *Narrowing the achievement gap: Strategies for educating Latino, Black, and Asian students*. Berlin: Springer Science & Business Media.

Herold, B. (2017, June 30). Maryland dad wants June 30 to be "national student data deletion day." *Education Week*. https://www.edweek.org/technology/aryland-dad-wants-june-30-to-be-national-student-data-deletion-day/2017/06

Ho, A. (2017). *Advancing educational research and student privacy in the "Big Data" era*. Workshop on Big Data in Education: Balancing the Benefits of Educational Research and Student Privacy, pp. 1–18. Washington, DC: National Academy of Education.

Holstein, K., Wortman Vaughan, J., Daumé, H., Dudik, M., & Wallach, H. (2019). *Improving fairness in machine learning systems: What do industry practitioners need?* Proceedings of the 2019 CHI Conference on Human Factors in Computing Systems, 1–16.

Huang, X., Craig, S. D., Xie, J., Graesser, A., & Hu, X. (2016). Intelligent tutoring systems work as a math gap reducer in 6th grade after-school program. *Learning and Individual Differences, 47*, 258–265.

Jeong, H., Hmelo-Silver, C. E., & Jo, K. (2019). Ten years of computer-supported collaborative learning: A meta-analysis of CSCL in STEM education during 2005–2014. *Educational Research Review, 28*, 100284.

Karumbaiah, S. (2021). *The upstream sources of bias: Investigating theory, design, and methods shaping adaptive learning systems* [Unpublished doctoral dissertation]. University of Pennsylvania, Philadelphia.

Karumbaiah, S., Ocumpaugh, J., & Baker, R. S. (2021). Context matters: Differing implications of motivation and help-seeking in educational technology. To appear in *International Journal of Artificial Intelligence and Education*.

Kizilcec, R. F., & Lee, H. (2021). Algorithmic fairness in education. In W. Holmes & K. Porayska-Pomsta (Eds.), *Ethics in artificial intelligence in education*. Abingdon-on-Thames, UK: Taylor & Francis.

Klare, B. F., Burge, M. J., Klontz, J. C., Bruegge, R. W. V., & Jain, A. K. (2012). Face recognition performance: Role of demographic information. *IEEE Transactions on Information Forensics and Security, 7*(6), 1789–1801.

Klose, M., Desai, V., Song, Y., & Gehringer, E. (2020). *EDM and privacy: Ethics and legalities of data collection, usage, and storage.* Proceedings of the 13th International Conference on Educational Data Mining.

Koedinger, K. R., Anderson, J. R., Hadley, W. H., & Mark, M. A. (1997). Intelligent tutoring goes to school in the big city. *International Journal of Artificial Intelligence in Education, 8*(1), 30-43.

Koedinger, K., Cunningham, K., Skogsholm, A., & Leber, B. (2008). *An open repository and analysis tools for fine-grained, longitudinal learner data.* Proceedings of the 1st International Conference on Educational Data Mining.

Kulik, J. A., & Fletcher, J. D. (2016). Effectiveness of intelligent tutoring systems: A meta-analytic review. *Review of Educational Research, 86*(1), 42–78.

Laird, E., Quay-de la Vallee, H., & Mahesh, A. (2019). *Balancing the scale of student data deletion and retention in education.* Washington, DC: Center for Democracy and Technology. https://cdt.org/wp-content/uploads/2019/03/Student-Privacy-Deletion-Report.pdf

Lepper, M. R., Woolverton, M., Mumme, D. L., & Gurtner, J. (1993). Motivational techniques of expert human tutors: Lessons for the design of computer-based tutors. *Computers as Cognitive Tools,* 75–105.

Li, H., Gobert, J., Dickler, R., & Moussavi, R. (2018). *The impact of multiple real-time scaffolding experiences on science inquiry practices.* International Conference on Intelligent Tutoring Systems, pp. 99–109. Berlin: Springer.

Lopez, G. A. (2021). Investigating the ransomware infection rate of K12 school districts during the COVID pandemic. Electronic Theses, Projects, and Dissertations. 1317. https://scholarworks.lib.csusb.edu/etd/1317/

Loukina, A., & Buzick, H. (2017, December). *Use of automated scoring in spoken language assessments for test takers with speech impairments* (Research Report No. RR-17-42, pp. 1–10). Princeton, NJ: Educational Testing Service (ETS).

Lynch, C. F. (2017). Who prophets from big data in education? New insights and new challenges. *Theory and Research in Education, 15*(3), 249–271.

Ma, W., Adesope, O. O., Nesbit, J. C., & Liu, Q. (2014). Intelligent tutoring systems and learning outcomes: A meta-analysis. *Journal of Educational Psychology, 106*(4), 901–918.

MacLellan, C. J., & Gupta, A. (2021). *Learning expert models for educationally relevant tasks using reinforcement learning.* International Educational Data Mining Society.

Maldonado-Mahauad, J., Pérez-Sanagustín, M., Kizilcec, R. F., Morales, N., & Munoz-Gama, J. (2018). Mining theory-based patterns from Big Data: Identifying self-regulated learning strategies in Massive Open Online Courses. *Computers in Human Behavior, 80,* 179–196.

McArthur, D., Stasz, C., & Zmuidzinas, M. (1990). Tutoring techniques in algebra. *Cognition and Instruction, 7*(3), 197–244.

Merrill, D. C., Reiser, B. J., Ranney, M., & Trafton, J. G. (1992). Effective tutoring techniques: A comparison of human tutors and intelligent tutoring systems. *Journal of the Learning Sciences, 2*(3), 277–305.

Mitrovic, A., & Ohlsson, S. (2016). Implementing CBM: SQL-Tutor after fifteen years. *International Journal of Artificial Intelligence in Education, 26*(1), 150–159.

Mojarad, S., Baker, R. S., Essa, A., & Stalzer, S. (2021). Replicating studying adaptive learning efficacy using propensity score matching and inverse probability of treatment weighting. *Journal of Interactive Learning Research, 32*(3), 169–203.

National Association of Secondary School Principals (NASSP). (n.d.). *Student data privacy*. Retrieved December 20, 2021, from https://www.nassp.org/top-issues-in-education/position-statements/student-data-privacy/

Ocumpaugh, J., Baker, R., Gowda, S., Heffernan, N., & Heffernan, C. (2014). Population validity for Educational Data Mining models: A case study in affect detection. *British Journal of Educational Technology, 45*(3), 487–501.

O'Reilly-Shah, V. N., Gentry, K. R., Walters, A. M., Zivot, J., Anderson, C. T., & Tighe, P. J. (2020). Bias and ethical considerations in machine learning and the automation of perioperative risk assessment. *British Journal of Anaesthesia, 125*(6), 843–846.

Orr, L. L. (2015). 2014 Rossi award lecture: Beyond internal validity. *Evaluation Review, 39*(2), 167–178.

Pane, J. F., Griffin, B. A., McCaffrey, D. F., & Karam, R. (2014). Effectiveness of cognitive tutor algebra I at scale. *Educational Evaluation and Policy Analysis, 36*(2), 127–144.

Pane, J. F., McCaffrey, D. F., Slaughter, M. E., Steele, J. L., & Ikemoto, G. S. (2010). An experiment to evaluate the efficacy of cognitive tutor geometry. *Journal of Research on Educational Effectiveness, 3*(3), 254–281.

Paquette, L., Ocumpaugh, J., Li, Z., Andres, J. M. A. L., & Baker, R. S. (2020). Who's learning? Using demographics in EDM research. *Journal of Educational Data Mining, 12*(3), 1–30.

Phillips, A., Pane, J. F., Reumann-Moore, R., & Shenbanjo, O. (2020). Implementing an adaptive intelligent tutoring system as an instructional supplement. *Educational Technology Research and Development, 68*(3), 1409–1437.

Sales, A. C., & Pane, J. F. (2020). *The effect of teachers reassigning students to new cognitive tutor sections*. Proceedings of the 13th International Conference on Educational Data Mining.

Sales, A. C., Wilks, A., & Pane, J. F. (2016). *Student usage predicts treatment effect heterogeneity in the Cognitive Tutor Algebra I program*. Proceedings of the 9th International Conference on Educational Data Mining.

Self, J. (1999). The defining characteristics of intelligent tutoring systems research: ITSs care, precisely. *International Journal of Artificial Intelligence in Education, 10*(3–4), 350–364.

Shute, V. J., & Psotka, J. (1994). *Intelligent tutoring systems: Past, present, and future*. Technical Report, Armstrong Lab, Brooks Air Force Base. US Air Force.

Shute, V. J., Ventura, M., & Kim, Y. J. (2013). Assessment and learning of qualitative physics in Newton's Playground. *Journal of Educational Research, 106*(6), 423–430.

Siew, N. M., Geofrey, J., & Lee, B. N. (2016). Students' algebraic thinking and attitudes towards algebra: The effects of game-based learning using Dragonbox 12+ app. *Electronic Journal of Mathematics and Technology, 10*(2), 66–79.

Singla, A., Rafferty, A. N., Radanovic, G., & Heffernan, N. T. (2021). *Reinforcement learning for education: Opportunities and challenges*. Proceedings of the International Conference on Educational Data Mining.

Slade, S., & Prinsloo, P. (2013). Learning analytics: Ethical issues and dilemmas. *American Behavioral Scientist, 57*(10), 1510–1529.

Steenbergen-Hu, S., & Cooper, H. (2013). A meta-analysis of the effectiveness of intelligent tutoring systems on K–12 students' mathematical learning. *Journal of Educational Psychology, 105*(4), 970–987.

Stephenson, N. (2003). *The diamond age: Or, a young lady's illustrated primer*. Spectra.

Student Data Privacy Consortium. (2021). Standard Student Data Privacy Agreement (NDPA Standard Version 1.0) Version 1r7. https://cdn.ymaws.com/www.a4l.org/resource/resmgr/files/sdpc-publicdocs/final_sdpc_ndpa_v1-7.pdf

Student Privacy Compass. (2021, October 5). Student Privacy Primer. https://studentprivacy compass.org/resource/student-privacy-primer/

Tipton, E., & Olsen, R. B. (2018). A review of statistical methods for generalizing from evaluations of educational interventions. *Educational Researcher, 47*(8), 516–524.

VanLehn, K. (2011). The relative effectiveness of human tutoring, intelligent tutoring systems, and other tutoring systems. *Educational Psychologist, 46*(4), 197–221.

Xia, M., Asano, Y., Williams, J. J., Qu, H., & Ma, X. (2020, August). *Using information visualization to promote students' reflection on "gaming the system" in online learning.* Proceedings of the Seventh ACM Conference on Learning@Scale, pp. 37–49.

Xu, Z., Wijekumar, K., Ramirez, G., Hu, X., & Irey, R. (2019). The effectiveness of intelligent tutoring systems on K-12 students' reading comprehension: A meta-analysis. *British Journal of Educational Technology, 50*(6), 3119–3137.

Yacobson, E., Fuhrman, O., Hershkovitz, S., & Alexandron, G. (2021). De-identification is insufficient to protect student privacy, or—What can a field trip reveal? *Journal of Learning Analytics, 8*(2), 83–92.

Zeide, E. (2017). The structural consequences of big data-driven education. *Big Data, 5*(2), 164–172.

# 7

# Identifying, Establishing, and Distributing the Economic Value of the Classroom Teacher

*Christopher D. Brooks and Matthew G. Springer*

It is now commonly accepted that teachers are the single most important school-based resource for impacting student outcomes (Chetty, Friedman, & Rockoff, 2014b). This fact may seem unsurprising, given the amount of time students spend with their teachers, particularly in early grades, and the multifaceted role of teachers in students' lives as instructors, mentors, and community members.

Policy makers have tried to leverage this fact through the past 20 years of educational reforms focused on improving student outcomes through school-based resources, including reforms to teacher evaluation and accountability through measured student achievement. And yet, educational policies still often fail to reflect the tremendous value that teachers generate both for students and society because they do little to alter the pipelines through which teachers enter the workforce or use available incentives to reward effective teachers in the workforce.

This chapter will focus on how measuring the differential impacts of variously skilled teachers and constructing the highest-quality teacher workforce possible is tantamount to promoting educational opportunity, promoting economic growth, and preparing individuals to be engaged participants in a liberal democracy. We also explore whether educational policy is currently accomplishing this important task and what changes are needed to achieve these goals in the years ahead. We will do so by first examining the most robust estimates of teachers' long-term economic impacts on students. Then, we will examine how teacher compensation, evaluation, and retention policies often fail to recognize, prioritize, and maximize the value of teachers and what interventions can improve these aspects of the teacher labor market. We then turn to how the value of effective teaching is distributed across and within schools, surveying the literature on whether students have equitable, or even equal, access to effective teaching, and what policies work best to promote equitable access to effective teaching. Finally, we conclude with a brief summation of recommendations for policy makers and researchers.

## QUANTIFYING THE ECONOMIC VALUE OF TEACHERS

Measuring teacher quality is difficult due to a lack of available data and the multidimensional nature of their output—namely, the class atmosphere and the student. It is important, therefore, to decompose teacher contributions into the relevant outputs and focus on mapping available proxies to each output.

Conceptually, teacher outputs can be categorized along the two dimensions described in table 7.1: temporally, meaning short-term and medium/long-term

**Table 7.1.   Dimension and Examples of Teacher Production**

| | | Type | |
| --- | --- | --- | --- |
| | | *Test Score* | *Non-Test Score* |
| Temporal | Short Term | Definition: How a teacher impacts student achievement and learning growth within a school year, best captured by robust value-added models, which account for the influence of non-teacher controllable variables.<br><br>Examples:<br><br>• Student and classroom achievement<br>• Student and classroom growth | Definition: How a teacher impacts student behaviors and non-test score learning, such as GPA or skills such as interpersonal communication. Ideally but less frequently measured by value-added, and often best measured by quasi-experimental methods.<br><br>Examples:<br><br>• Suspensions<br>• Attendance<br>• Grades<br>• Socio-emotional skills |
| | Medium and Long Term | Definition: How a teacher impacts student learning in future years due to the additive or cumulative impact of a teacher's instruction. Later outcomes can be attributed to teachers using longitudinal panel data.<br><br>Examples:<br><br>• Future student achievement<br>• Future student growth | Definition: How a teacher impacts student behavior in subsequent years or in long-term outcomes, such as graduation rate. Later outcomes can be attributed to teachers using longitudinal panel data.<br><br>Examples:<br><br>• Graduation<br>• Attending College<br>• Income |

outcomes; and by production type, generally test score and non-test score outcomes. Although the outputs contained in any given category relate to and inform the outputs in the others, this conceptualization captures the types of impacts teachers can have on their students.

Translating the production quadrants in table 7.1 into a measurement that is interoperable across various educational resources and public spending is conceptually difficult. For instance, short-term test score gains or attendance improvement are easy to measure and can be normatively valuable to a society that intrinsically values education and student learning. But the goals of education are larger than this, focused on socio-democratic or personal and collective economic benefits of developing human capital (Labaree, 1997). For short-term productions to "matter," they must relate to the longer-term outcomes of the individual. Longer-term outcomes generally occur in adulthood, where ranges of behavior—such as attending college—or variables—such as income—are either directly or secondarily translatable into dollars. An example we will discuss includes the long-term income differences attributable to highly effective teachers, a measure easily put into dollars and, therefore, useful for directly assessing the monetary value of teachers relative to other policy interventions that generate economic value.

But longer-term outcomes also have their challenges. From a data perspective, linking school-year outcomes to adult outcomes requires a significant lag between when the teacher data is collected and when the adult outcomes are known. This, and the challenge of accessing these data, can make it difficult to demonstrate *causal* associations between a teacher's individual contribution to a student and lifelong outcomes. Likewise, determining which short-term outcomes can be causally attributed to teachers is also a challenge. For example, test scores on their own capture more than just a teacher's ability. Factors such as parental availability, income, and extracurricular opportunities can contribute to student performance and confound the attribution of student ability to teacher ability. However, as we will discuss, recent research has been able to address these challenges and create estimates that relate short-term impacts on test scores to longer-term measures of value in adulthood.[1]

The earliest work on the impact and value of teachers focused on short-term outcomes such as student test scores on state-mandated standardized assessments in reading and math. One of the more common ways to measure student learning growth and demonstrate heterogeneity in teacher ability is value-added models of teacher effectiveness. Value-added models use statistical techniques to account for

---

1. Value can be viewed from two perspectives. The first is the relative value of individual teachers to other teachers, which can be used in policies regarding the efficiency or equity of the distribution of teacher effectiveness. The second is the absolute aggregated value of teachers collectively, which can be used to gather the total impact that teachers have on society and the economy. Although decisions made in the former necessarily impact the latter, considering both the scale and distribution of value is important. For instance, if a district hires five highly effective teachers, the overall value that the district's teacher workforce produces increases. But if all five new teachers are working in the wealthiest, Whitest, or already highest achieving school within the district, the aggregate benefit of these new teachers will only be enjoyed by the on average more privileged students, creating gaps in present learning and long-term outcomes. This issue will be explored in greater detail later in the chapter.

measured and unmeasured characteristics of schools, teachers, and students. When appropriately implemented, value-added models can isolate the causal impact that an individual teacher has on a student's test score growth in a school year without misattributing learning changes to factors not associated with the teacher.

Value-added measures of teachers' effectiveness are widely used to identify if, and to what extent, teachers vary in their effectiveness to improve student test scores. If there were no variation in value added, implying that teachers are equally effective at raising student achievement, then aggregate educational production would be fixed, meaning that teacher labor market policies have no benefits. However, decades of value-added research have demonstrated significant variation in teacher ability to improve student test scores. To do so requires rich panel data that can pair students to teachers, provide information on their demographics, and capture past performance. Such longitudinal data sets have only been widely available in recent decades but have offered rich insights into the variance in teacher ability to promote student learning.

Hanushek and Rivkin (2010) concluded that going from a 25th percentile to a 75th percentile value-added teacher would be associated with an average increase in student achievement of .2 standard deviations, an impact in the same range as expensive interventions such as 10-student class size reduction (p. 268). Chetty et al. (2014b) equate the learning gains made under a 1st percentile teacher to be the equivalent of missing one-third of a school year with an average teacher. This means that within a given distribution of teacher ability, deselecting or improving the least-effective teachers could have large aggregate benefits.

But student test score growth is not inherently interesting if either (1) the effect of a teacher in a given year does not create lasting learning gains or if (2) the teacher's impact in one year does not relate to her actual ability in future years. A second stage of research into the impact of teachers on student outcomes was to explore the lasting medium-term effects of teachers on students in subsequent school years. For students, a high value-added teacher in one year has positive additive and cumulative effects on future student learning in subsequent years, with the negative learning impact of a less-effective teacher also being cumulatively impactful, regardless of future teacher effectiveness (Sanders & Rivers, 1996). Thus, learning growth in one year is, in fact, meaningfully capturing real gains in student ability. And for teachers, Cantrell and Kane (2013) found that in a randomized control trial, the gold standard for causal identification, value-added measures are the single best predictor of future student test score growth under a teacher, meaning they capture the intertemporal ability of a teacher to improve student learning. Thus, value added is capturing an aspect of a teacher's practice regarding her ability to improve student test scores that is somewhat stable over time.[2]

---

2. Although year-to-year value added has significant variation due to potential nonrandom sorting of teachers to students or variation in testing instruments (Sass, 2008), aggregating robust value-added estimates over time can create a stable and accurate estimate of teacher effectiveness that is robust to these variabilities (Koedel & Betts, 2011). Thus, multiple years of value-added data can inform schools about which teachers are best suited to raise student achievement and learning growth.

Insofar as learning in core subjects, measured by test scores, is valuable to a society, then teachers obviously generate meaningful outputs for students. And exposure to teachers with higher test score value added is associated with a decreased likelihood of teenage pregnancy, greater uptake in college attendance, and increased participation in 401k retirement savings programs (Chetty et al., 2014b). In addition, Jackson (2018) demonstrated a positive correlation between teacher value-added and a teacher's impact on reducing absences, suspensions, and grade retention.

But again, this is only important if students, and thus society at large, benefit from short-term test score gains in the medium and long term. Fortunately, test score value added is related to important long-term outcomes, where "value" is easier to capture.

At the microeconomic level, researchers have linked variation in teacher quality to variation in future earnings. The scope of longitudinal data required to track students from elementary school to the labor force is daunting. Hanushek (2011) circumvents this issue by instead taking data on the variation of teacher effectiveness and the difference in income attributable to cognitive skills as an adult to relate the impact a teacher has on student learning to long-term earnings. This model requires some assumption about the true variation in teacher quality and the exact returns of cognitive skill in the labor market. At conservative estimations of both, Hanushek (2011) concludes that a teacher one standard deviation above the mean generated $426,225 in lifetime earning every year in a class of 20 students. This means that a single year of instruction from a teacher one standard deviation above the mean would equate to $21,311 in lifetime earnings for an individual student.

More recent work by Chetty and colleagues (2014b) affirms the scope of value that Hanushek (2011) estimates. The authors link tax information and school district records to estimate the real-world differences in incomes attributable to variations in teacher effectiveness for more than one million students. This avoids the need for estimating at the true variations in teacher quality and returns to education in the workforce. The authors found that one school year with a teacher whose effectiveness is one standard deviation above the median is associated with an increase in lifetime earnings of 1.34%. This equates to approximately $39,000 more in lifetime earnings for a single student, relative to a student with an average teacher in a given year. For a class of 20 students in a single year, a teacher one standard deviation above median effectiveness is expected to increase the nondiscounted lifetime earnings for their students by $780,000. This means the effective teacher generates nearly a million dollars in future income *every year*, assuming effectiveness is generally temporally stable.[3] Or for an individual student, having a teacher one standard deviation above the median effectiveness in grades 3–8 would be expected to increase their lifetime earnings by around $234,000, assuming that the effect is additive.

---

3. Again, aggregating robust value-added estimates over time can create a stable and accurate estimate of teacher effectiveness that is robust to these variabilities (Koedel & Betts, 2011), although as discussed later in the chapter, there are significant temporal changes in effectiveness over time, with large positive gains experienced in the first five years of teaching and a tailing from efficacy after several decades of teaching.

Taken together, the micro- and macro-economic impacts of teachers are staggering, given that the average annual salary for public school teachers in the 2019–20 school year was $63,645 in the United States (NCES, 2020). Even a 50% increase of this average salary for effective teachers is relatively little compared to the surplus value they generate. Based purely on short-term test score improvement, research has demonstrated that teachers vary significantly in their ability to improve student learning. This variance creates measurable and substantive economic differences in the long run. Therefore, recruiting, training, hiring, and retaining the most effective teachers has massive benefits to the productivity of individuals and society.

However, emphasizing high test score value added has a major shortcoming, as it relies on annual student test scores. Test scores are generated primarily in math and reading in grades 3–8 and intermittently in high school testing. Obviously, teachers in non-tested subjects and grades also make substantive impacts on student lives and generate long-term value, but currently there is not the data infrastructure to measure the annual learning growth of students in non-tested classrooms. Expanding testing to more grades and subjects is not a perfect solution, as standardized testing may not make sense in some grade ranges or in certain subjects. We can infer that those non-tested teachers make impacts similar to their tested colleagues, but without a robust way to measure and differentiate the performance of these teachers, policies that prioritize high value-added teachers will exclude and ignore many educators.[4]

One promising but relatively understudied solution to this problem is using value-added techniques on non-test score student outcomes. Groundbreaking research in this space by Jackson (2018) used value-added techniques on an index of non-test score outcomes, including absences, suspensions, course grades, and grade repetition. They found that teachers vary significantly in their ability to impact these non-test score short-term outcomes. This index relies on data already collected by schools and are outcomes that any teacher could impact, regardless of the subject taught. Thus, non-test score measures offer a compelling way of expanding measures of teacher value generation outside the standardized testing structure.[5]

---

4. One alternative not discussed at length here is teacher observations and student surveys, which can be implemented in any classroom to capture the pedagogical processes of the teacher that may, in turn, be related to student learning and future outcomes. Although experimental research is finding that high-quality observation and student survey data can predict future student outcomes, these measures are unsurprisingly not as predictive as test-score value added (Kane, 2013). In addition, as we discuss later, a breadth of research has identified issues of observer bias related to teachers and the students they teach and inflated observation scores in high-stakes assessments, along with a low uptake in surveys due to teacher mistrust of the accuracy of student surveys and student concern over anonymity (for a review on measures of teacher evaluation and their shortcomings, see Brooks & Springer [2022]). Thus, we believe that the more promising direction for measuring the economic value of non-tested teachers is robust value-added models that use non-test score student outcomes.

5. Importantly, Jackson (2018) demonstrates that although teacher test score value added is positively correlated with non-test score value added, both value-added measures capture distinct variation in medium-term student outcomes, such as high school graduation. This means that measuring the non-test score value added of students not only expands which teachers can be evaluated but also meaningfully captures different skills about a teacher's practice besides test score value added.

As with short-term test score gains, improvements to attendance, suspension rates, and so on can be normatively valuable for society, but they are difficult to equate to generalized economic value. Jackson's work tackles this issue by showing that, conditional on test scores, having a teacher with a higher non-test score value added is associated with significant decreases in dropout rates and increases in graduation rates, total GPA, SAT uptake, and college attendance intentions. These medium-term outcomes can lead to substantial and measurable value for students. For instance, better SAT scores can open access to more selective colleges, holding all else constant. These selective colleges have significant and positive impacts on earnings for Black or Hispanic students and for students from less-educated households (Dale & Kreuger, 2011). Graduation and college attendance rates likewise have positive long-term impacts on income. High school graduates earn about $7,400 more annually and $297,000 more over a lifetime relative to high school dropouts, and college graduates earn a staggering $35,100 more annually and $1.4 million more in a lifetime (BLS, 2019).[6]

Given the scope of impacts that high school and college completion have on an individual on average, even a relatively small change in student trajectory caused by a teacher can be incredibly valuable to a student and society. Jackson's (2018) findings, when considering the classes of students that a teacher interacts with every year over the course of a career, indicate that the non-test score impacts on students are again of significant economic value. More work needs to be done to develop non-test score value added as a measure of teacher effectiveness and as a predictor of long-term student outcomes, with validation linking individual students to long-term tax records as in Chetty et al. (2014b) being ideal. But it remains a promising avenue for broadening the scope of the value-added techniques to untested subjects and expanding the ways in which we conceptualize and capture the impact of a teacher in a robust manner.

Overall, teachers vary significantly in their ability to improve short-term student outcomes, but they do make incredible impacts on students' lives. These impacts have been quantified in lifelong earnings, allowing policy makers to understand the expected average benefit of policies regarding teachers relative to its cost. Given the scope of value that teachers generate, it is therefore paramount for educational policy to reflect this value and place considerable effort in training, identifying, recruiting, retaining, and equitably distributing effective teachers to schools for the benefit of students individually and society generally.

---

6. Captured in these estimates are the significant positive association between dropping out of high school and incarceration rates (Monrad, 2007; Sum, Khatiwada, McLaughlin, & Palma, 2009) and most notably of all, between high school completion and health. Freudenberg and Ruglis (2007) surmise that education exerts greater influence on health than on income or occupation, with educational attainment being negatively correlated with early deaths and risk factors such as smoking or being overweight. And De Ridder et al. (2013) causally estimate that high school dropout is significantly associated with long-term sickness or disability in young adulthood, independent of individual or family health and SES as an adolescent.

# MAXIMIZING TEACHER VALUE:
## POLICY REFORMS TO COMPENSATION, RECRUITMENT, EVALUATION, AND RETENTION

Having established the economic value of teachers, we can now turn to whether education policy is well aligned with recognizing the value of teachers. We will also examine how labor market policies regarding compensation, recruitment, evaluation, and retention can be improved to raise the overall quality of the teacher workforce, reward teachers who make invaluable impacts on students' lives, and build a better educated and productive society. This section follows a two-part structure for each of the core issues in teacher labor market policy that we highlight. First, we examine how current policies come short of recognizing the value of teachers and how this value is produced. Second, we examine promising policies that would better align educational policy with maximizing teacher quality and promoting better educations and futures for students.

### The Problem: Teacher Compensation Policies Fail to Recognize the Value of Teachers

Research demonstrates that teachers are valuable, whereas the policies surrounding teacher evaluation, retention, and distribution largely fail to reflect this value. Take, for example, teacher salaries, which can be viewed from two perspectives. First, teacher compensation overall is relatively low compared to fields with comparable educational requirements, thus creating a disincentive for individuals to enter teaching. And second, teacher salaries do not incentivize high performance and do not reward the most effective teachers, which can contribute to issues of turnover, as the most valuable teachers do not see that value reflected in their salaries.

Research on the relative compensation of teachers finds a 6.5% wage penalty for teachers relative to similarly educated individuals (Han, 2021). These low salaries negatively impact recruitment and selection into teaching, thus limiting the supply of teachers, meaning that schools have fewer options when they wish to replace a teacher or hire a new one (Hough & Loeb, 2013).[7] This underpayment has been shown to contribute to selection into the teaching workforce (Hoxby & Leigh, 2004) and is likely contributive to the relatively lower academic ability of those who choose to teach (Goldhaber & Walch, 2014; Master, Sun, & Loeb, 2018; Podgursky, Monroe, & Watson, 2004), and the overrepresentation of female and White teachers, who may be differentially equipped to accept lower salaries (NCES Annual Reports, 2021a).[8]

---

7. These wage differences do not include the substantial amount of non-salary benefits that teachers receive. However, there is also evidence that teachers may not perceive the non-salary portions of their total compensation with the same weight as they do salaries (Johnston, 2020).

8. The overrepresentation of White teachers and female teachers is quite large (NCES Annual Reports, 2021a and 2021b) and problematic given that same-race and same-sex teachers have substantial positive impacts on students, especially for Black, low-income, and male students (race: Dee, 2001; Egalite, Kisida, & Winters, 2015; Lindsay & Hart, 2017. gender: Dee, 2007; Winters, Hughes, Swaim, & Pickering, 2013). Academic ability is not as strong a predictor of teacher performance (Bardach & Klassen, 2020), but studies on the topic may also be relatively underpowered for measuring smaller effect sizes at the extremes of the distribution given that most teachers are not at the top or bottom of the distribution.

Given the previously discussed surplus value that effective teachers can generate, this relative underinvestment in teacher salaries seems inefficient to the extent that it discourages potentially effective teachers from entering the classroom. Increasing teacher salaries to have parity with, or even a premium to, compensation of similarly educated individuals, could potentially improve the quality of the teacher labor supply due to increased interest and retention.[9] In recent years an uptick in teacher labor unrest across various states has led to more discussion and some increases in teacher compensation. However, there does not appear to be the political will to substantially change teacher compensation levels uniformly, as traditional educational reform attitudes prefer differentiated compensation systems that reward effective teachers, thus devoting resources to those generating the most economic value (Will, 2018). But teacher associations, in turn, are resistant to compensation structures that differentiate teachers based on student test score growth, which is discussed more in-depth below (West & Mykerezi, 2011).

But some salary differentiation does already exist among teachers. In addition to examining teacher wages relative to other fields, it is also worth considering whether current monetary differentiation favors more effective teachers. Collective bargaining favors differentiated compensation by qualifications or duties (West & Mykerezi, 2011). For example, nearly all districts pay traditional public-school teachers using a "step-and-lane" single salary schedule (Podgursky & Springer, 2007, 2011). A prototypical example is depicted in table 7.2 from a school district in Maryland, where steps indicate years of experience and lanes signify levels of educational attainment. Total compensation depends on the level of experience and level of education of the teacher, with some additional avenues based on professional or extracurricular duties that the individual takes on.

This system, which standardizes salaries for all teachers, was a progressive measure developed in the 20th century to ensure that female and minority teachers received equal compensation for their work (Kelley & Odden, 1995; Podgursky & Springer, 2007, 2011). By basing compensation on objective and measurable aspects of a teacher's career, the single salary schedule helped prevent the previously commonplace discretionary compensation system in which administrators discriminated against non-male and non-White teachers.

The goals of preventing discriminatory compensation structures through the use of measurable salary schedules is certainly good. But the unfortunate truth is that the

---

9. Although more can be said about recruitment and selection into teaching, this is not a primary focus of the chapter. This is because the best strategies for increasing the diversity and ability of potential teachers and having teacher preparation get them into classrooms as effective instructors are not entirely clear. Most preparation programs lack strong data sharing that links teacher preparation to future performance (Springer, Bastian, & Brooks, 2021). And as von Hippel and Bellows (2018) note, the differences in teacher effectiveness *within* preparation programs is significantly greater than the differences *between* programs, meaning that it is almost impossible to distinguish effective programs from less-effective programs. Alternative certification programs that circumvent traditional teacher colleges and thus expedite the process at a lower cost to the potential teacher have been shown to attract more minority and male recruits, and teaching candidates were comparable across test performance and college selectivity (Woods, 2016). But research also suggests these alternatively certified teachers also leave teaching at higher rates, a problem in its own right (Redding & Smith, 2016).

**Table 7.2. Step-and-Lane Salary Schedule in Carroll County Public Schools, MD (in US dollars)**

| Step | Lane 3 | Lane 4 | Lane 5 | Lane 6 |
|------|--------|--------|--------|--------|
| 1 | 48,840 | 50,352 | 54,161 | 55,947 |
| 2 | 49,876 | 51,703 | 55,565 | 57,343 |
| 3 | 50,912 | 53,054 | 56,969 | 58,739 |
| 4 | 51,947 | 54,406 | 58,373 | 60,135 |
| 5 | 52,983 | 55,757 | 59,777 | 61,531 |
| 6 | 54,021 | 57,108 | 61,183 | 62,929 |
| 7 | 55,645 | 59,167 | 63,243 | 64,988 |
| 8 | 57,272 | 61,225 | 65,300 | 67,046 |
| 9 | 58,897 | 63,284 | 67,360 | 69,106 |
| 10 | 60,521 | 65,341 | 69,419 | 71,162 |
| 11 | 62,147 | 67,400 | 71,475 | 73,221 |
| 12 | 63,772 | 69,460 | 73,535 | 75,281 |
| 13 | 65,398 | 71,517 | 75,593 | 77,338 |
| 14 | 67,023 | 73,576 | 77,652 | 79,398 |
| 15 | 68,648 | 75,635 | 79,711 | 81,456 |
| 16 | 70,273 | 77,693 | 81,769 | 83,514 |
| 17 | 71,898 | 79,752 | 83,828 | 85,574 |
| 18 | 73,523 | 81,811 | 85,886 | 87,632 |
| 19 | 75,147 | 83,869 | 87,946 | 89,691 |
| 20 | 75,147 | 86,687 | 90,003 | 91,748 |

| | |
|--------|--------------------------------|
| Lane 3 | Bachelor's Degree |
| Lane 4 | Master's Degree or Equivalent |
| Lane 5 | Master's + 30 |
| Lane 6 | Master's + 60 |

*Source:* Adapted from https://www.carrollk12.org/admin/hr/Documents/CCEA%20MASTER%20AGREEMENT%202022%20-%20website%20 copy.pdf

primary pecuniary incentives within traditional single salary schedules, experience and educational attainment, are not good predictors of whether a teacher will improve student learning. This, in turn, means that salary differentiation is not aligned with whether the teacher is effectively creating the long-term economic value that education generates for students.[10] The most recent and robust research on advanced degrees demonstrates inconsistent to null relationships between post-bachelor educational attainment and student achievement (Chingos & Peterson, 2011; Clotfelter,

---

10. That is not to say that reform necessitates the elimination of compensation based on experience and education. Nor do we suggest returning to discretionary compensation. Experience and education were good and logical attempts for trying to capture what would be valuable to reward in the teacher labor market in the time before robust data systems and modern statistical techniques, but in reality, they are not reflective of the value teachers generate. As we will discuss, incorporating more objective measures of student learning into compensation structure will better align salary differentiations in a manner that rewards and incentivizes effective teaching.

Ladd, & Vigdor, 2007a, 2007b; Ladd & Sorenson, 2015). Harris and Sass (2007) report suggestive evidence that in higher grades, math teachers are more effective after obtaining a master's degree than before, aligning with prior research that finds small but statistically significant gains in math achievement (Dee, 2004; Goldhaber & Brewer, 2000; Nye, Konstantopoulos, & Hedges, 2004) or science (Henry et al., 2014). However, such findings are far from consistent, and such nuance, as it may exist, is not reflected in the single salary schedule, which uniformly rewards degree attainment regardless of subject or grade.

Relatively speaking, experience is a far better predictor of student achievement than educational attainment, with research demonstrating that teachers improve significantly in their ability to raise student achievement in their first four years of teaching (Kini & Podolsky, 2016). Although some positive effect remains after these initial gains (Kraft & Papay, 2014; Ladd & Sorensen, 2017), effectiveness gains beyond the first years of teaching are substantively small. Although we have relatively less evidence supporting growth trajectory of late-career teachers, evidence suggests that effectiveness tails off late in a teacher's career (Ladd & Sorenson, 2017). These nonlinear relationships between experience and effectiveness are not reflected in the traditional teacher salary schedule, meaning that salary differences are not aligned with factors that consistently predict teacher effectiveness.

Compensation is a primary mechanism for incentivizing workers to enter and stay in a profession (Podgursky & Springer, 2007; Heinrich & Marschke, 2010). Thus, compensation can be used to attract and retain the most effective teachers who generate the most value for society. Although tying compensation directly to student learning growth is not necessarily required, the measures by which salaries are differentiated should at least be associated with growth in student learning. Educational attainment may be valuable to have within a profession, but it is not a good predictor of efficacy. And although rewarding commitment to the teaching profession may be normatively good, experience only substantially improves efficacy in the beginning years of teaching, a log curve that is generally not reflected in the linear experience pay scale. The primary way in which salaries are differentiated in teaching is not attached to the differences in effectiveness that are associated with substantial differences in student lifelong outcomes. Present policies largely fail to incentivize or reward teacher effectiveness, which creates a misalignment between local, state, and federal investment and the production of educational outcomes.

## Potential Policies for Improvement: Teacher Performance Incentives

In recent years, policy makers have attempted to address the shortcomings of teacher compensation systems by offering additional compensation to teachers through performance incentives. These policies generally give financial awards to teachers or schools that meet specific performance goals. These policies are built on principal-agent theory (Burgess & Ratto, 2003; Dixit, 2002) and motivational theories in organizational studies (Bajorek & Bevan, 2015; Podgursky & Springer, 2007).

In the former, schools are the principals, and performance pay incentives align monetary incentives of the agents, teachers, with the intended goal of education. By aligning monetary inputs toward production outputs by incentivizing student test score growth, effectiveness and efficiency increase. And in terms of motivational theory, rewarding these most effective teachers is expected to improve recruitment and retention of effective teachers and improve job satisfaction (e.g., Springer & Taylor, 2021).

The specific structure of performance pay programs can be quite varied. For example, incentives can complement traditional salary differentiation or supplant the single salary schedule entirely, making the primary salary differentiator student test score growth. Performance pay can also be done uniformly across all schools (e.g., Booker & Glazerman, 2009) or can be used to incentivize effective teachers to work in specific high-need schools that generally have fewer highly effective teachers on average (e.g., Clotfelter, Glennie, Ladd, & Vigdor, 2008a, 2008b; Swain, Rodriguez, & Springer, 2019). And incentives can exist for individual teachers (e.g., Goldhaber & Walch, 2012) or can be group incentives for grade, subject, or schoolwide performance (e.g., Goodman & Turner, 2011; Imberman & Lovenheim, 2015; Marsh et al., 2011; Springer & Winters, 2009; Springer et al., 2012).

A recent meta-analysis by Pham, Nguyen, and Springer (2020) synthesized 37 studies and found that merit pay programs were associated with a statistically significant 0.053 standard deviation increase in student test scores on average. The authors also found that programs in the United States tend to have smaller awards relative to total compensation, and studies take place over shorter time frames; correspondingly, the largest effects tend to come from outside the United States. The impact of these policies tended to be larger in elementary schools, when paired with professional development, and when awards are larger.

Pham et al. (2020) also find that these incentives raised teacher retention in the incentivized schools, which can help keep effective teachers in the profession and sort these teachers into specific schools where incentives exist (i.e., drawing the most-effective teachers to highest-need schools). Thus, compelling evidence shows that incentive pay programs, if well designed to have an adequately large reward and paired with professional development, appear to be promising interventions for raising student achievement by incentivizing effort and rewarding the most effective teachers.

However, despite the apparent success of these programs, they remain relatively underused in state and district compensation. A 2018 report by the National Council on Teacher Quality on performance pay found that 26 states had no requirements that districts pay teachers based on performance, with 16 suggesting and just 9 requiring differentiated salary based on performance (Ross & Worth, 2018). At the district level, Jarmolowski (2018) found that of the 124 large school districts examined, only 16 offered performance bonuses to highly rated teachers, with 31 additional districts freezing salary increases with ineffective teachers.

And even when these bonuses or salary withholdings occur, they are generally linked to state or district teacher evaluation systems that may not give much or any weight to measures such as student learning growth (NCTQ, 2016). Thus, the monetary incentives that do exist do not rely on direct measures of teacher impact on student learning that are most closely tied to future economic value generation. As we will discuss later, these evaluation systems often rely excessively on principal observations, which are generally inflated and, in some cases, biased against teachers of certain races or genders and against certain student class compositions.

Student-performance-based measures also have issues with opportunistic gaming at the individual or school level (Ballou & Springer, 2015), which deserve greater consideration in policy discourse. But these types of gaming are more circumstantial and should not be systematically correlated with individual characteristics such as teacher race or gender or the makeup of the class being taught. Basing compensation on measures that suffer from biases rooted in systemic perceptions of race, class, or ability runs the risk of reintroducing the subjective and biased compensation structures that were present prior to the now commonplace single salary step-and-lane compensation structure. Although linking compensation to teacher performance is a policy centered on aligning financial incentives for teachers to the economic value they produce, using teacher performance measures that are systemically biased against certain identities creates an unpalatable scenario worse than the inefficient but not biased single salary schedule system.[11]

Thus, although evidence demonstrates that well-funded and well-designed performance pay systems can raise student achievement, these policies remain relatively underused, particularly when considering the growing evidence supporting their effectiveness. Traditional avenues of teacher compensation comprise most of the salary differentiation among teachers. This misalignment fails to recognize that teachers are not all equally effective at raising student achievement and that teachers make meaningful and measurable lifelong impacts on their students, for better and for worse. Devoting additional public resources to teacher salaries overall and restructuring teacher compensation to create individual incentives to attract, retain, and reward the most effective teachers would go a long way to having education policy reflect the value of teachers in society and maximize the value of education in the United States.

---

11. Concern over potential bias in value-added models has led to considerable debate about value added as a means of evaluation. Rothstein (2009) demonstrates the nonrandom sorting of students to classrooms as a risk for bias. Sorting by time invariant characteristics can effectively be controlled for using multiple years of prior student test scores, but sorting along time-varying characteristics is a potential source of bias. However, work by Chetty et al. (2014b) and Bacher-Hicks, Kane, and Staiger (2014) demonstrates that in well-specified models that leverage the data commonly available to schools, the bias in value added attributable to such sorting is substantively small and statistically indistinguishable from 0, alleviating the concerns that Rothstein (2009) raised that systemic sorting of students to teachers creates significant bias that undermines the measurement validity of value-added measures. Comparable evidence for systemic and substantively meaningful bias due to sorting in well-specified models does not currently exist. Similar statistical techniques for controlling for bias generally do not exist for observational evaluations, and thus we prefer value-added as a stronger basis for teacher evaluation and differentiated compensation. For a more detailed discussion of bias and stability in value-added, see Brooks and Springer (2022) and Koedel, Mihaly, and Rockoff (2015).

## CHALLENGES IN EVALUATING AND RETAINING THE MOST EFFECTIVE AND VALUABLE TEACHERS

Compensations structures are not the only way in which policy fails to prioritize the value of teaching. The overall effectiveness of the teacher workforce is defined both by those who are teaching and by the pool of persons interested in, and capable of, teaching. Who is drawn into, or pushed out of, the potential pool of teachers is a matter of (1) recruitment, (2) evaluation, and (3) retention. All three frame the teacher labor supply and could be optimized to attract, recognize, and retain the most effective teachers, increasing the benefits of a highly educated society. In this section, we will examine the teacher labor market and how policies regarding recruitment, evaluation, and retention often fail to recognize the drivers of teacher effectiveness and, therefore, often fail to prioritize valuable teaching.

### The Problem: Teacher Evaluation Systems Neither Adequately Differentiate Teachers by Ability Nor Emphasize the Economic Value of Teachers

Teacher evaluation has changed drastically in the past decade for the better, although it is our opinion that these systems have a long way to go. We begin by offering a brief overview of the recent history of teacher evaluation reform before examining the ways in which it has largely fallen short of the ideal of reflecting the economic value of teachers.

In the past 15 years, researchers and policy makers have begun to question whether traditional methods of teacher evaluation were well aligned with the value teachers produce. Traditional evaluation relied almost exclusively on poorly structured observations by principals, because prioritizing effective teaching requires that state evaluation systems identify effective teachers. Alarmingly, Weisberg, Sexton, Mulhern, & Keeling (2009), in a groundbreaking report that came to be known as the Widget Effect Report, demonstrated that many systems had binary ratings of either satisfactory or unsatisfactory, making any nuance on the degree of effectiveness impossible to capture. In addition, Weisberg et al. (2009) showed that nearly every teacher was being rated as effective, meaning that even in evaluation systems with multiple categories, ratings were not differentiating teacher ability.[12] Not every teacher can be exceptional, but in rating them as such, any efforts to strategically reward and retain the best teachers were made useless.

In combination with the Obama administration's federal Race to the Top (RTTP, 2009), these revelations pushed states to incorporate value added into teacher evaluation systems and reform current observation systems to be more robust. These subsequent reform efforts led to a significant decrease in districts with binary teacher

---

12. In Denver Public Schools only 1.3% of teachers were rated as unsatisfactory. And even in districts where multiple categories of effectiveness existed, such as Chicago Public Schools, more than 90% of teachers were rated as superior or excellent, just .4% rated as unsatisfactory.

rating systems, increased weight given to student learning growth, and reforms to make observations a more rigorous practice.

Teacher evaluation reforms have been associated with learning gains in some places such as Cincinnati (Taylor & Tyler, 2012), Chicago (Steinberg & Sartain, 2015), and Washington, DC (Dee & Wyckoff, 2015; Dotter, Chaplin, & Bartlett, 2021). However, reformed systems can be quite heterogeneously implemented, and research on a nationally representative sample has found that these new teacher evaluation systems have not impacted student outcomes on average (Bleiberg, Brunner, Harbatkin, Kraft, & Springer, et al., 2021). Although this partially may be attributable to how actionable these new reform-based methods of teacher evaluation are for making hiring and firing decisions, which we will focus on in the next section, here we will focus on the current shortcoming of the methods of evaluation themselves and how they are misaligned with improving teacher quality.

Under reformed evaluation policies, administrator observations of teachers are still the key component of teacher evaluation. But old methods have been replaced by new rubrics, such as Charlotte Danielson's Framework for Teaching or the Classroom Assessment Scoring System (CLASS). These new rubrics focus on standardizing the domains in which teachers are evaluated. This is accomplished by creating multiple categories of effectiveness for each domain, structuring specific feedback in post-observation conferences, and having multiple observations throughout the year, steps for attempting to address the issues with the observation system highlighted in the Widget Effect Report (Weisberg et al., 2009). And five reform-based rubrics, including the Danielson Framework and CLASS, were validated in the Gates Foundation's Measures of Effective Teaching (MET) study. Kane, McCaffrey, Miller, and Staiger (2013) demonstrated in a randomized control trial that teachers with multiple observers who were rated more highly by the Danielson Framework also on average were better able to raise student achievement each year.

However, despite the validity of classroom observation rubrics in some circumstances, observation reforms have done little to align evaluation with the economic value of teachers or to fulfill their promise of offering feedback teachers can use to improve their practice. For example, Kraft and Gilmour (2017) investigated 24 states that reformed their observation rubrics in the wake of the Widget Effect Report. They found that despite adopting more robust observation systems, the percentage of teachers rated as unsatisfactory was still less than 1% in a majority of settings, and observers reported perceiving three times more teachers as below proficient than they rated as such. This finding calls into question whether teacher observations, when attached to high-stakes evaluation, are useful tools for differentiating teacher ability unless observers are better trained to avoid such biases.

In addition, evidence is building that teacher observation scores show significant bias. Some of these biases may be inherent in human-to-human observation. For instance, teacher observation scores have been shown to fall victim to the observer effect, meaning that teachers alter their behavior when being observed (McIntyre, 1980). And more recent research on observation-based evaluation generally has found that scores can depend on the type of lesson being taught (Mikeska, Holtzman, McCaffrey, Liu, & Shattuck, 2019) or the observer's mood (Floman, Hagelskamp, Brackett, & Rivers, 2017). But more problematic, growing evidence shows that classroom composition and teacher characteristics may bias teacher observation scores. Male teachers and those teaching higher proportions of low-income, low-achieving, or non-White students receive less-favorable ratings than teachers with comparable value added (Campbell & Ronfeldt, 2018; Drake, Auletto, & Cowen, 2019; Steinberg & Garrett, 2016).

Even if observations are not a differentiating or unbiased measure of effectiveness, observation could still be useful if the feedback teachers received helped improve practice. However, emerging research on the quality and practical value of feedback provided by post-observation meetings is lacking, and administrator feedback was not targeted at specific instructional practices for teachers within their subjects (Rigby et al., 2017). In addition, this feedback also lacks specific alignment to the areas that teachers are weaker in, fails to provide specific evidence for the rating, and is missing language regarding goal-setting that is actionable for teacher practice (Hunter & Springer, forthcoming). Overall, reformed observation rubrics have conceptually addressed some issues raised by the Widget Effect Report, but fundamentally, observations, the most prominent teacher evaluation method, largely fail to differentiate teacher ability or improve teacher practice. Thus, sole reliance on these methods neither gives schools the ability to hire and retain the most effective teachers nor leads to teachers improving their practice over time.

Of course, the potential remains for observations to meaningfully contribute to the evaluation of teachers. Specifically, improvements are needed in observer ability to differentiate high and low performers without bias. Higher-quality post-observation meetings are needed, with specific, constructive, and multidimensional feedback that can help teachers improve their practice over time. And of course, observations can be part of an evaluation regime and an important aspect of teacher evaluation when implemented well. But overreliance on observations that have the shortcomings outlined can lead to an imperfect picture of which teachers are most effective.

The disappointment of the reformed observation rubrics would be more palatable had value-added measures, which directly measure meaningful teacher ability, been deeply and lastingly incorporated into teacher evaluation programs, as it had appeared they might after Race to the Top. If evaluations were focused on teacher ability to raise student test scores, school decision makers would be better able to make informed decisions on retention and recruitment. But unfortunately, implementation of value-added measures into teacher evaluation systems was flawed for several reasons. First, many states now require student test score data in the teacher evaluation process, but very few explicitly require the use of value-added measures; when required, generally a small portion of the overall evaluation is determined by student learning growth (Aragon, 2016). And because value-added metrics have large variation year over year, it is a tool better suited for measuring teacher ability that is refined over time as more data becomes available (Loeb & Candelaria, 2012). A single year of value-added data is better suited for measuring true effectiveness only at the extremes of the ability distribution. Although much change has occurred in teacher evaluation, often the change was different than what reformers, who were focused on the value and importance of teachers, envisioned.

Finally, states have begun to move away from teacher evaluation reforms. A 2019 report by Ross and Walsh found that from 2009 to 2015, the number of states that used student growth measures in teacher evaluations increased from 15 to 43, but by 2019, this number had decreased to 34. Similarly, in 2015, 37 states required that state standardized test data be used in teacher evaluation; by 2019, only 26 states continued to do so. This shift away from student growth and testing indicates a policy environment less interested in incorporating the best available methods for measuring a teacher's impact on student learning in tested subjects and grades. And finally, in 2011, only 17 states had more than two rating categories for teachers. This number increased to 44 in 2015, but even this has seen a slight decrease to 41 by 2019.

These trends are quite alarming in light of the value that effective instructors have on society. Although the reformed evaluation systems that states developed may not have reached the ambitions reforms would have liked, they were progress toward a more robust evaluation process that rates teachers by their ability to improve students' learning. Rather than continue to move toward this, states appear increasingly interested in returning to old ways of evaluation, which can only make it harder for schools to identify effective teachers.

## The Solution: Evaluation Systems That Emphasize Robust Measures of Value Added

Because we believe and have cited evidence that well specified value-added scores across multiple years are the best predictor of teacher effectiveness as it relates to long-term student outcomes, we would argue that evaluation systems that give the preponderance of weight to value added would be best suited for aligning policies with the value of teachers.

During the aforementioned MET randomized control trial, researchers determined that blending value added, teacher observations, and student surveys yielded the teacher evaluation models most predictive of future student achievement (Cantrell & Kane, 2013). In that regard, many state systems are successfully incorporating multiple measures of teacher evaluation.

However, the specific weights that Cantrell and Kain identify are that evaluation systems should have an overwhelming majority of the evaluation rely on teacher value added (81% weight), with less weight being given to student surveys and observations.[13] As we noted, reformed systems still rely heavily on observation

---

13. These specific weights would be considered over fit to the specific data of the MET, but regardless provide reasonable estimates that systems with similar weighting would be better equipped to predict a teacher's future ability to improve test scores. In addition, this model is most predictive but is also least reliable year-to-year, again emphasizing the need for multiple years of performance data to home in on true teacher ability.

scores, which are inflated in high-stakes scenarios (Grissom & Loeb, 2017; Kraft & Gilmour, 2017; Weisberg et al., 2009), and can penalize high value-added teachers who are perceived as being low effort or outside the professional community (Harris, Ingle, & Rutledge, 2014). Harris et al. (2014) find only a weak positive correlation between observation scores and value added, and that principals rarely assign teachers to the level of effectiveness that their value added implies. Thus, a system that gives less weight to these observations would be expected to rate and differentiate teachers by ability and significantly change the composition of teacher effectiveness within schools if used for retention decisions.[14] Although reformed observation rubrics can be effective and should continue to be invested in and improved, the current preference for observation over student growth measures in many states fails to align teacher evaluations with the best measures of a teacher's impact on student learning. Reshaping teacher evaluation systems to integrate both testing and observations, and giving greater weight to the former, would make it easier for schools to identify and differentiate their most effective teachers.

### The Problem: Teacher Retention Is Low, Especially for Highly Effective Teachers, and School Leaders Have Limited Capacity for Removing Ineffective Teachers

Two key forms of retention are commonly discussed in the research literature: positive retention, wherein schools retain teachers because they have desirable characteristics, such as a high value-added score or identifying with a demographic group underrepresented in education; and negative retention, wherein schools push out less effective teachers and, ideally, replace them with relatively more effective teachers.[15] Done properly, the teacher labor market could retain effective teachers and push out the least effective, promoting student learning and the value-generation of teachers. Grissom and Bartanen (2018) refer to this as strategic retention. Unfortunately, poli-

---

14. One obvious problem with an evaluation system that relies primarily on value added is that this is only applicable to math and reading teachers in grades 3–8. We reiterate that this is a limitation of data, not the underlying methodology of value added, which should be able to predict an individual teacher's ability to impact any number of outcomes so long as the outcome data is connected to the teacher, student, and class and collected at regular intervals. The example we provided earlier was for the developing area of non-test score value added, which could potentially apply to any teacher in any grade, because behavioral and non-test outcomes are measurable for every student. When we imagine improved evaluation focused on value added, we are not exalting test-scores per se but, rather, the causal identification of teacher effects on students that are linked to long-term outcomes.

15. This naturally raises a concern over labor supply. If there are not enough teachers overall, then all teachers, even the ineffective ones, are needed in schools. Put differently, if there is not a supply of unemployed but available average to above-average teachers, then firing an ineffective teacher would likely lead to hiring a similarly ineffective teacher. The other policies discussed in this chapter, particularly around compensation, would likely expand the supply of available teachers. Currently, teacher shortages and a limited labor pool, particularly in STEM subjects, are frequently discussed (e.g., Garcia & Weiss, 2019; Han & Hur, 2021), but recent research also suggests that at least in some areas, the supply of teachers is large enough that, on average, the least-effective teachers can be replaced by more-effective teachers (Loeb, Miller, & Wyckoff, 2015; Sartain & Steinberg, 2021).

cies are lacking that generate this ideal situation of retaining the best teachers and replacing those least effective.

First, consider the extremely high rate of teacher turnover. A report by Carver-Thomas and Darling-Hammond (2017) found that 16% of teachers leave their positions each year, with about half of these leaving the profession entirely. These rates are even higher in schools where most students are non-White and in Title I schools.[16] However, a recent meta-analysis by Nguyen, Pham, Crouch, and Springer (2020) also found that more effective teachers are slightly less likely to leave, meaning that although turnover is high, and worse in some key staffing areas, such as non-White and STEM teachers, effective teachers are not systematically leaving teaching altogether. But when baseline turnover rates are so high, marginally better rates for effective teachers are still suboptimal, and clearly more needs to be done to retain effective teachers.

At the same time, not all attrition is bad, as turnover among the least-effective teachers and replacement with relatively more effective teachers is another way in which retention can be leveraged to raise student achievement and maximize the value of teaching.

At the core of positive and negative retention are school principals, whose role as leader and decision maker has significant influence on which teachers are hired, retained, and eventually given tenure. The most commonly cited reason for teachers leaving schools is problems with school leadership, and research has demonstrated that teachers are more likely to stay in schools where principals are more effective (Boyd et al., 2011; Grissom, 2011; Kraft, Marinell, & Yee, 2016). The most effective principals are those who are effective at having above-average retention rates, concentrated on the most-effective teachers, and simultaneously higher than average turnover rates for the least-effective teachers (Grissom & Bartanen, 2018).

Unfortunately, principals are not necessarily well equipped to do this important work of strategic labor management. First, there are not interventions for improving principals' practice. A recent systematic review by Grissom, Egalite, and Lindsay (2021) identified the practices that effective principals employ in their schools. These include data-driven engagement with teachers on their instructional practice, building a trusting and collaborative environment, facilitating collaboration between teachers, and managing personnel and resources strategically. But it is not clear how to get principals to adopt these practices. How best to get principals to leverage more objective measures of teacher effectiveness and use the strategies that Grissom et al. (2021) identified is a significant problem that requires further research.

In terms of teacher evaluation, research demonstrates that principals can identify teachers at the top and bottom 10%–20% of the ability distribution in a low-stakes environment (Jacob & Lefgren, 2008), despite on average preferring observation scores, personal opinions, and the opinions of colleagues and parents over test score and value-added data when making retention decisions (Goldring et al., 2015). If

---

16. Early survey results indicate that teachers report themselves more likely to leave after the onset of the COVID-19 pandemic (Zamarro, Camp, Fuchsman, & McGee, 2021).

principals could just retain those top teachers and push out those bottom teachers, massive dividends to the quality of teacher and overall student learning in each school would ensue.

However, the extent to which principals are able to make staffing decisions on all teachers, and whether principals view their role as prioritizing strategic retention, is a different matter. First, recall that in high-stakes evaluations, principal observation scores—their preferred data source when making retention decisions—are extremely inflated and fail to differentiate teachers (Kraft & Gilmour, 2017; Weisberg et al., 2009). In low-stakes environments, principals tend to give less-positive ratings to teachers on average, although scores are still high overall (Grissom & Loeb, 2017). The best practices for getting principals to act in the interest of student learning through strategic retention are not well understood, which is an area that needs greater attention from researchers, lawmakers, and practitioners.

And finally, principals are also inhibited in their ability to use strategic retention because they often do not have the ability to hire and fire teachers based on their performance. This is because teacher tenure, where present, offers strong job protection. Many states have implemented tenure reform in the wake of the Obama administration's Race to the Top initiative. These reforms generally changed the tenure process from being nearly automatic for a teacher in good standing with the required experience to a system where effectiveness needed to be demonstrated.[17] Although these improvements are good on paper, tenure offer rates are extremely high and still take relatively little time to obtain. Test score value added requires multiple years of teacher data to be a precise, more stable assessment of teacher ability, but many states only require three years of experience for tenure eligibility (ECS, 2020). If the window in which teachers can be freely dismissed based on performance is so short that the best metrics of evaluation are not precise, then strategic negative retention is nearly impossible. And only 10 states have explicit provisions wherein teachers can lose tenure status due to inadequate performance, meaning that once value added becomes a stable measure of ability, it cannot necessarily be used to inform retention.

Taken together, a lack of willingness and capability to remove the least-effective teachers and an overall turnover problem are failing to effectively keep the best teachers in schools. Understanding what steps are needed to address these issues is complicated.

### Potential Policies for Improvement: Tenure Reforms, Principal Accountability, and Increased Incentives

Because retention is a multifaceted issue of both positive and negative retention, several promising policies would help better align the teacher labor market to the valuable work teachers do.

---

17. Although as we have noted, this effectiveness is rarely heavily dependent on value-added metrics and is inflated by overly positive teacher evaluations.

First, we would reiterate the value that increased overall compensation and targeted performance-based compensation would have on the teacher workforce. If the opportunity cost of being a teacher were reduced or eliminated, and especially the most effective ones, then one would expect a greater interest in continuing to be a teacher. Although overall compensation increases are needed and would likely reduce attrition and turnover, performance-based compensation has the added benefit of differentiating compensation based on the value that individual teachers produce, meaning that having a substantial portion of salary differentiation be based on teacher performance would also create a disincentive for low value-added teachers to stay in teaching if they have other viable alternatives.

Next, we believe that interesting, valuable work in tenure system reform, if continued, could lead to significant improvements in strategic retention in schools. We argue that tenure systems should focus on giving job security to teachers who demonstrate a minimum level of effectiveness, measured by test score or non-test score value added, while encouraging attrition for the least-effective teachers. We reiterate that the best measure of teacher effectiveness is teacher value added, which we hope will expand to non-tested outcomes and thus be applied to all teachers, and expect that requiring a level of effectiveness, measured by value added rather than inaccurate high-stakes observations, would greatly improve the teacher workforce, as the lowest percentile of teachers would not receive non-probationary status and be relatively fixed in schools. This would require that tenure decisions take longer than three years, with probationary status being extendable if effectiveness has not been demonstrated to enable value added to be a stable measure of teacher ability.

Some promising examples of such interventions include tenure reform experiments in New York City (Loeb, Miller, & Wyckoff, 2015). In New York, different schemes were employed on an annual basis to see the impact that data-driven interventions have on principal tenure recommendations. From 2009 to 2014, these reforms included some combination of requiring principals to provide a rationale for tenure recommendations that ran counter to the district's data on teacher value added, parent and student surveys, or traditional evaluation scores in the past two years, identifying which teachers had exceptionally better or worse than average performances, or providing value-added data in a range of effectiveness categories that summarized the impact a teacher had on students.

Prior to these various changes, 94% of teachers in New York City were extended tenure offers. By the end of the observed period, just 56% were offered tenure. Most others were given a probationary extension, and a small but meaningful group of the least-effective teachers were not offered tenure. Under this reform, the 44% of teachers who did not receive tenure also had higher rates of attrition, meaning less-effective teachers were leaving at higher rates. On average, these teachers were replaced by more-effective teachers in subsequent years. By surfacing value-added data in the tenure process and forcing principals to justify when they go against data-driven strategic retention practices, the New York reforms offer promising insight into how relatively small changes to tenure could make big impacts on the long-term effectiveness of the teacher workforce.

Changes to the tenure process should also be paired with expanded requirements that teachers continue to demonstrate effectiveness throughout their career. Tenure offers important security against arbitrary dismissal. But well-specified and longitudinal performance data are not arbitrary grounds. We argue that demonstrated effectiveness by measures such as value added should be required to maintain tenure. Several states already allow teachers to be returned to probationary status if effectiveness is not demonstrated in consecutive years (ECS, 2020). Expanding these policies, and basing the return to probationary status on value added, would ensure that the privileges of job security are not misaligned with the importance of effective teaching.

Principals seem open to these changes in practice. Research on principal perceptions of these new teacher evaluation regimes have shown largely positive attitudes, with research finding that principals believe they can help improve instructional progress of teachers regardless of the evaluation regime (Young, Range, Hvidston, & Mette, 2015). Research on principal perceptions post-tenure reform in Tennessee found that principals were generally positive and believe that more data-driven tenure processes aided in keeping effective teachers and pushing out the least-effective teachers (Lomascolo & Angelle, 2019).

Tenure reforms have generally appeared to allow principals to leverage their position as instructional leaders and give them greater agency in ensuring that fewer ineffective teachers are retained in their schools, improving attitudes toward evaluation systems and tenure itself. This positive sensemaking and a deep understanding of strategic retention and the motivations for performance-based tenure reform are needed for substantial impact (Rodriguez, 2020). We only suggest that reforms go further in emphasizing teacher value added and continue to make principals use more objective measures of teacher effectiveness when making retention decisions.

Tenure is an important fixture for teachers' labor unions, offering legal protections that antidiscrimination laws do not always include, and does place a needed burden on employers to demonstrate justified grounds for dismissal that protects against arbitrary punitive measures (Kahlenberg, 2016). Such practices are a good thing. However, we believe that teacher performance is not an arbitrary ground for dismissal. Given the import of effective teachers on society, greater emphasis on performance in evaluation, compensation, and tenure would help align education policy with the value of teachers and be beneficial for society.

## EQUITY: HOW CAN WE GET THE MOST-EFFECTIVE TEACHERS TO WORK WITH THE LEAST-ADVANTAGED STUDENTS?

We have covered in detail the immense value highly effective teachers generate for individuals, and, inversely, how ineffective instruction can have negative long-term impacts on students. And we have discussed the ways that current teacher policies often fail to recognize and prioritize effective teaching, and potential avenues for increasing teacher effectiveness overall. Often, discussions of the value of teaching end at this point, in the generalities that structural reform to teacher labor market policies will lead to a more effective teacher workforce that, in turn, benefits individuals and society.

But as with any resource in society, raising overall teacher effectiveness in the labor supply does not eliminate heterogeneity in ability, nor does it mean that every student will have equal access to the most-effective teachers. As we have discussed, teachers are the single most important school-based resource for student learning. Although they may not be able to make up for the socioeconomic inequities that influence a student's development, we do know that high-poverty schools tend to have a harder time recruiting and retaining highly effective teachers. A review by Adamson and Darling-Hammond (2011) concluded that, on the state level, students of color in low-income schools are 3–10 times more likely "to have unqualified teachers than students in predominantly White schools." Loeb and Myung (2010) conclude that "teachers, on average, prefer schools with high-achieving, high-income, and white students (p. 474)," not the type of school where effective, experienced teachers are necessarily most needed.

More recent work has also examined between-school sorting of teachers by their value added and found similar results (e.g., Goldhaber, Quince, & Theobald, 2019; Hanselman, 2019; Isenberg et al., 2016; Rodriguez, Nguyen, & Springer, 2020). For example, a study by Goldhaber et al. (2019) investigated this inequitable access to effective teaching over a 20-year period in North Carolina and Washington State. In both states, the authors found that in every year where data are available, and across both value-added and non-test score qualification, economically disadvantaged students and Black, Hispanic, and Native American students were disproportionately exposed to lower-quality instruction relative to their higher-income or non-underrepresented racial/ethnic group peers, primarily due to the inequitable distribution of teachers across districts and across schools within districts.

This disproportionate access is a grim, if not surprising, reality, considering the immense value that effective teaching has on students in the long run. However, the present scope of sorting does not make as large a difference on student learning as one might expect. Hanselman (2019) estimates that the aggregate difference in learning opportunities between low-income and non-low-income students across grades K–8 is equivalent to approximately 10 weeks of math instruction and 5 weeks of math instruction in total. This indicates that overall heterogeneity in teacher quality is large for all students, and systemic sorting is relatively small compared to that range of quality. It also indicates that other factors contribute to learning gaps between poorer and more wealthy students, as this cumulative difference is smaller than overall socioeconomic achievement gaps.

However, closing these access gaps is nonetheless important—first, because unequal access to educational opportunity that reproduces an inequitable society, no matter how small, is wrong. Second, recognizing teachers as an impactful, valuable resource may also lead to disproportionate assignment of effective teachers toward low SES students to indirectly compensate for the differences in educational opportunity that a school may have no control over (e.g., long-term effects of living in poverty) and thus reduce achievement gaps and differences in long-term outcomes overall. Such policies, unfortunately, may be politically challenging to implement, but they could represent a means of generating more equal educational opportunity from a holistic sense that takes into account both school resources and the students' personal and home conditions.

So what can policy makers do to address unequal access to effective teachers across schools? Often the most obvious answer is to offer pecuniary incentives for teachers to sort themselves more equally or equitably across schools or districts, because now wealthier districts can pay teachers more and often lack within-district incentives to work in more disadvantaged schools. Research has found that even moderate incentives appear to be enough to recruit and retain effective or qualified teachers in high-need schools (Clotfelter, Glennie, Ladd, & Vigdor, 2008a, 2008b; Cowan & Goldhaber, 2018; Glazerman, Protik, Teh, Bruch, & Max, 2013; Springer, Swain, & Rodriguez, 2016).

For example, Springer et al. (2016) analyzed a Tennessee program offering $5,000 for teachers in the highest rating category to stay in schools in the bottom 5% of state standardized testing performance. The authors found that eligible schools saw a 13 percentage point increase in the proportion of teachers in the highest value-added category relative to comparably performing ineligible schools in the time post-implementation. When analyzing *participating* schools, this effect was a significant 27 percentage point increase in the proportion of the highest value-added teachers. A follow-up study on student achievement impacts of this program found that schools eligible for the program saw increased student test scores in subsequent years, indicating that the retention from the program led to improved student achievement (Swain, Rodriguez, & Springer, 2019).

A different randomized experiment by Glazerman et al. (2013), wherein the highest value-added teachers were offered $10,000 annually for two years to transfer to schools with the lowest average test scores, found similar results. The incentive led effective teachers to fill the positions at the disadvantaged schools, student test scores improved in the school, and retention rates were similar to peers at the school even after final payment.

Clearly policies that emphasize transfers to and retention in high-need schools are an effective means of promoting equal or equitable educational opportunities at relatively low costs. And these policies also demonstrate the applied merits of efficiently allocating resources to reward, incentivize, and motivate effective educators. But these types of incentives are not used or are underused by states and districts, leading to inequitable access to effective teaching across schools and districts that contributes to later systemic inequities across class and race/ethnicity.

Although inequitable access to effective teaching is mostly due to sorting of teachers across districts and across schools within districts, this sorting also occurs within schools as well. Research shows that lower SES students have less access to the most-effective teachers within their schools (Goldhaber, Quince, & Theobald, 2019; Hanselman, 2019; Isenberg et al., 2016). At its highest, Hanselman (2019) estimates that, on average, approximately one-quarter of the disparity in exposure to effective teaching is due to disproportional assignment within schools. And Rodriguez et al. (2020) found that in Tennessee, economically disadvantaged students are, on average, 44% less likely to be assigned to a highly effective teacher than their more advantaged peers in the same school.

The reasons for this inequitable within-school sorting include factors such as unequal parental influence and greater influence from experienced effective teachers on dictating their desired class rosters. Principals also may be unaware of the long-term negative impacts that repeated assignment to less-effective teachers have on students (Springer et al., forthcoming).

Addressing this disproportionate student-teacher sorting is relatively understudied, and interventions corollary to the repeatable and seemingly effective cash bonuses for between-school inequities have not been developed to date. However, we are part of a research team developing a project that we hope can disrupt the disproportionate likelihood of low-SES students being assigned to low value-added teachers in consecutive years. This intervention, called the Equitable Rostering Solution (ERS), is an algorithmic software intervention that leverages already collected data to generate optimized rosters for principals (Springer et al., forthcoming). By integrating valid, actionable evidence into the assignment process, we believe decision makers can be more empowered to prioritize equal access to effective teaching and maximize student performance by giving data-driven rationales for more equal educational opportunity. Although the efficacy of this specific program is still to be determined, we offer it as an example of much-needed interventions that can promote equitable within-school access to effective teaching.

In summary, when interest in teacher labor market policies and interventions arises, generally the focus is on improving aggregate quality; often a prevailing attitude is that a rising tide should lift all boats. Although this is true in aggregate, more purposeful, equity-motivated policies are required to ensure that these benefits are used to generate a more equal society and close persistent disparities in educational opportunities and outcomes. Increases in the quality of the teacher workforce, and rewarding effective teachers for their impact on society, can operate with the policy initiative outlined here to promote equal or equitable access to effective teachers and redistribute the benefits of education to those communities that historically have not been given access to the same privileges as the most advantaged.

## CONCLUSION AND RECOMMENDATIONS

In this chapter, we have shown the short-, medium-, and long-term impacts of teachers and demonstrated the immense value that highly effective teachers have on their students throughout life. Put in dollars, the returns on having a highly effective teacher for just one year are worth tens of thousands of dollars in lifetime income and hundreds of thousands of dollars in lifetime income for a class of students, relative to having an *average* teacher. Ineffective teachers likewise impact students' lifetime earnings negatively, leading Chetty et al. (2014b) to estimate that replacing a teacher in the bottom 5% of value added with an average teacher is associated with a $1.4 million increase in expected undiscounted lifetime earnings.

But teacher evaluation and compensation systems are rarely structured to reflect the tremendous value overall and the wide heterogeneity in teacher effectiveness within the teacher supply. If teaching is so valuable for society and students, then labor market policies should be structured to maximize the recruitment, identification, and retention of effective teachers and ensure that they are distributed fairly across schools.

Given the broad topic we covered—the quality and distribution of teacher workforce—policy areas are equally broad where improvement can better align education policy with the value of effective educators. Our recommendations, which we summarize succinctly below, are neither exhaustive nor necessarily interdependent. Small progress in recruitment, compensation, evaluation, retention, and distribution can be made in any number of ways, and each can address the larger challenges of recognizing, prioritizing, and improving the value and production of teachers in society. In each area, researchers, principals, district leaders, policy makers—and most important, teachers themselves—have critical roles to play in developing understanding of the value and importance of teachers and building policies that promote development of an effective teacher workforce that is valued, invested in, and distributed equitably throughout society.

We recommend for practitioners and policy stakeholders:

## Compensation

Both the overall compensation and the heterogeneity of compensation among teachers fail to reflect the impact effective educators have on students and the value this generates for society. First, we recommend that, at the very least, the differences in compensation between teachers and comparably educated individuals be eliminated. This would be expected to expand the pool of individuals interested in teaching, especially among those with higher-paying alternative options for employment that may possess in-demand skills that are needed in schools. Teacher preparation programs and schools themselves could then be more selective in whom they recruit and retain out of this larger pool.

Second, compensation should more explicitly reward more effective teachers. We outlined many studies wherein bonuses were awarded to high value-added teachers, but few states and districts have such programs that are aligned with objective measures of student learning. Such bonuses need not replace all of the traditional salary schedule, like raises based on experience, but should be substantive enough to offer significant additional compensation to the best teachers. Doing so would be expected to incentivize effort and, most important, help retain the best teachers in the teacher workforce who feel that their ability is rewarded. Likewise, focusing on performance may also lead to negative retention for those teachers less effective at raising student achievement who are not receiving bonuses, thus raising the overall quality of teachers.

## Evaluation

Recent progress in incorporating value-added measures and multiple effectiveness categories into teacher evaluation system reforms appear to be dwindling across the country (ECS, 2020). Our strongest recommendation is that states redouble efforts to incorporate test score value added as a primary component of teacher evaluation for those teachers on which multiple years of testing data are available, a change perhaps made more palpable by our vision for compensation reform.

Finally, the future of evaluation should introduce more objective measures of a teacher's causal contribution to student development that go beyond test scores in math and reading. The work we highlight by Jackson (2018) represents a concrete step forward in examining the non-test-score impacts of teachers on students that are applicable across grades and subjects and that relate to meaningful long-term student outcomes. Factors that include student behavior and discipline rates, attendance, and grade progression are all meaningful predictors of student success and are doubtless affected by teachers. Much more research is needed on non-test-score value added and its relationship to medium- and long-term student outcomes, but this incredibly promising avenue of research should inform the future of teacher evaluation as appetites for testing-focused accountability regimes wane politically.

## Retention

Although retention is, in part, tied to compensation and the opportunity cost of teaching relative to other fields, some policy and research recommendations can better promote a higher-quality teacher workforce. For negative retention, tenure time lines and policies are misaligned with the years of data required for value-added data to be an accurate and stable estimation of teacher ability to improve student test scores, and often teacher value-added metrics are given little or no consideration in the formal tenure process.

Our proposed changes get at this issue from a number of approaches. First, tenure decisions should be tied to demonstrated effectiveness, measured by value added. The example from New York City's reform described by Loeb et al. (2015) gave principals information about whether a teacher was effective by value added, and in some years required justification for recommendations of tenure that went against this evaluation data. These changes led to a drastic reduction in the number of tenure offers and more effective replacement of nontenured teachers. Similar policies should be adopted in other districts as a means of prioritizing effective teachers through strategic retention.

Second, probationary status should take longer than three years, or again, as seen in New York City tenure reform, should be extendable when teaching effectiveness has not been demonstrated to an adequate degree (Loeb et al., 2015). This would allow districts and school leaders to have more reliable value-added data to evaluate teachers.

Finally, more states need to allow for teachers to be returned to probationary status if they are ineffective over a period. Tenure can and should offer teachers legal protection requiring the state to demonstrate job deficiency. However, tenure laws should carve out robust objective measures of effectiveness as a reason for reinstating probationary status to ensure that ineffective educators are not given excessive protection that ultimately harms the students they teach.

## Distribution

Based on the discussed research, more policy focus is needed on how teachers are distributed across districts, across schools within districts, and within schools. We think of distribution as a means of promoting equity and giving the most disadvantaged students the greatest resources for educational opportunity, as social or material capital in other parts of their lives may be lacking in providing opportunity that leads to persistent and replicant socioeconomic disparities in the country. To that end, states can create incentive programs that monetarily reward effective teachers who move to higher-needs districts and stay. States can also try to equalize local salaries to prevent high-wealth districts from hiring away effective teachers from low-wealth districts. An example is the recently ended state supplement equity program in West Virginia, which required that for comparable teachers, differences in local salaries not be greater than 10% between the top-10 paying districts and the lowest paying district (WV Code § 18A-4-5 [2018]).

Districts, in turn, can create monetary incentives for teachers to work in their higher-need schools, such as the program studied by Springer et al. (2016) in Tennessee or Clotfelter et al. (2008a; 2008b) in North Carolina. The structure and design of such policies are context dependent and require adequate funding and implementation fidelity. But offering pecuniary incentive is the easiest way to push teachers toward high-need schools.

Finally, within schools, principals need to be better informed about the impact of teachers on individual students and the tendency for low-SES students to be sorted away from experienced, high value-added teachers. This information, paired with empowerment to then prioritize the import of assignment over other pressing matters in the process, such as teacher or parent wishes, can disrupt cycles of inequitable assignment. The software-based Equitable Rostering Solution is one such method of informing and empowering principals, but the need remains for other types of interventions to be developed for within-school sorting.

# REFERENCES

Adamson, F., & Darling-Hammond, L. (2011). *Speaking of salaries: What it will take to get qualified, effective teachers in all communities.* Center for American Progress.

Adnot, M., Dee, T., Katz, V., & Wyckoff, J. (2017). Teacher turnover, teacher quality, and student achievement in DCPS. *Educational Evaluation and Policy Analysis, 39*(1), 54–76. https://doi.org/10.3102/0162373716663646

Allegretto, S., & Mishel, L. (2020). *Teacher pay penalty dips but persists in 2019: Public school teachers earn about 20% less in weekly wages than nonteacher college graduates.* Economic Policy Institute. https://www.epi.org/publication/teacher-pay-penalty-dips-but-persists -in-2019-public-school-teachers-earn-about-20-less-in-weekly-wages-than-nonteacher -college-graduates/

Aragon, S. (2016). Response to information request on the use of student test scores in teacher evaluations. Education Commission of the States. https://www.ecs.org/wp-content /uploads/Use-of-Student-Test-Scores-in-Teacher-Evaluations.pdf

Bacher-Hicks, A., Kane, T., & Staiger, D. (2014). *Validating teacher effect estimates using changes in teacher assignments in Los Angeles* (Working Paper No. 20657). National Bureau of Economic Research. https://doi.org/10.3386/w20657

Bacolod, M. P. (2007). Do alternative opportunities matter? The role of female labor markets in the decline of teacher quality. *Review of Economics and Statistics, 89*(4), 737–751. https:// doi.org/10.1162/rest.89.4.737

Bajorek, Z. M., & Bevan, S. M. (2015). Performance-related-pay in the UK public sector: A review of the recent evidence on effectiveness and value for money. *Journal of Organizational Effectiveness: People and Performance, 2*(2), 94–109. https://doi.org/10.1108 /JOEPP-03-2015-0011

Ballou, D., & Springer, M. G. (2015). Using student test scores to measure teacher performance: Some problems in the design and implementation of evaluation systems. *Educational Researcher, 44*(2), 77–86. https://doi.org/10.3102/0013189X15574904

Bardach, L., & Klassen, R. M. (2020). Smart teachers, successful students? A systematic review of the literature on teachers' cognitive abilities and teacher effectiveness. *Educational Research Review, 30*, 100312. https://doi.org/10.1016/j.edurev.2020.100312

Bischoff, K., & Reardon, S. (2014). Residential segregation by income, 1970–2009. In J. R. Logan (Ed.), *Diversity and disparities: America enters a new century* (pp. 208–233). New York: Russell Sage Foundation. https://www.russellsage.org/sites/all/files/logan/logan_di versity_chapter7.pdf

Bleiberg, J., Brunner, E., Harbatkin, E. A., Kraft, M. A., & Springer, M. G. (2021). *The effect of teacher evaluation on achievement and attainment: Evidence from statewide reforms* (EdWorkingPaper No. 21-496). Annenberg Institute at Brown University. https://www .edworkingpapers.com/ai21-496

Booker, K., & Glazerman, S. (2009). *Effects of the Missouri career ladder program on teacher mobility.* Mathematica Policy Research. https://www.mathematica.org/publications/effects -of-the-missouri-career-ladder-program-on-teacher-mobility

Boyd, D., Grossman, P., Ing, M., Lankford, H., Loeb, S., & Wyckoff, J. (2011). The influence of school administrators on teacher retention decisions. *American Educational Research Journal, 48*(2), 303–333. https://doi.org/10.3102/0002831210380788

Brooks, C. D., & Springer, M. G. (2022). Evaluating teacher effectiveness: A review of historical developments and current trends. In B. P. McCall (Ed.), *The Routledge handbook of the economics of education* (p. 127). Abingdon, UK: Routledge, Taylor & Francis Group.

Burgess, S., Propper, C., & Wilson, D. (2007). The impact of school choice in England: Implications from the economic evidence. *Policy Studies, 28*(2), 129–143. https://doi.org/10.1080/01442870701309064

Burgess, S., & Ratto, M. (2003). The role of incentives in the public sector: Issues and evidence. *Oxford Review of Economic Policy, 19*(2), 285–300. https://doi.org/10.1093/oxrep/19.2.285

Campbell, S. L., & Ronfeldt, M. (2018). Observational evaluation of teachers: Measuring more than we bargained for? *American Educational Research Journal, 55*(6), 1233–1267. https://doi.org/10.3102/0002831218776216

Cantrell, S., & Kane, T. (2013). *Ensuring fair and reliable measures of effective teaching: Culminating findings from the MET Project's three-year study.* Bill and Melinda Gates Foundation.

Carver-Thomas, D., & Darling-Hammond, L. (2017). *Teacher turnover: Why it matters and what we can do about it.* Learning Policy Institute. https://doi.org/10.54300/454.278

Chaplin, D., Gill, B., Thompkins, A., & Miller, H. (2014). *Professional practice, student surveys, and value added: Multiple measures of teacher effectiveness in the Pittsburgh Public Schools.* Institute of Education Sciences. https://files.eric.ed.gov/fulltext/ED545232.pdf

Chetty, R., Friedman, J. N., & Rockoff, J. E. (2014b). Measuring the impacts of teachers II: Teacher value-added and student outcomes in adulthood. *American Economic Review, 104*(9), 2633–2679. https://doi.org/10.1257/aer.104.9.2633

Chingos, M. M., & Peterson, P. E. (2011). It's easier to pick a good teacher than to train one: Familiar and new results on the correlates of teacher effectiveness. *Economics of Education Review, 30*(3), 449–465. https://doi.org/10.1016/j.econedurev.2010.12.010

Clotfelter, C. T., Glennie, E. J., Ladd, H. F., & Vigdor, J. L. (2008a). Teacher bonuses and teacher retention in low-performing schools: Evidence from the North Carolina $1,800 teacher bonus program. *Public Finance Review, 36*(1), 63–87. https://doi.org/10.1177/1091142106291662

Clotfelter, C., Glennie, E., Ladd, H., & Vigdor, J. (2008b). Would higher salaries keep teachers in high-poverty schools? Evidence from a policy intervention in North Carolina. *Journal of Public Economics, 92*(5–6), 1352–1370. https://doi.org/10.1016/j.jpubeco.2007.07.003

Clotfelter, C., Ladd, H., & Vigdor, J. (2007b). *Teacher credentials and student achievement in high school: A cross-subject analysis with student fixed effects* (Working Paper No. 13617). National Bureau of Economic Research. https://doi.org/10.3386/w13617

Corcoran, S. P., Evans, W. N., & Schwab, R. M. (2004). Women, the labor market, and the declining relative quality of teachers. *Journal of Policy Analysis and Management, 23*(3), 449–470. JSTOR.

Cowan, J., & Goldhaber, D. (2018). Do bonuses affect teacher staffing and student achievement in high poverty schools? Evidence from an incentive for national board certified teachers in Washington State. *Economics of Education Review, 65,* 138–152. https://doi.org/10.1016/j.econedurev.2018.06.010

Dale, S., & Krueger, A. (2011). *Estimating the return to college selectivity over the career using administrative earnings data* (Working Paper No. 17159). National Bureau of Economic Research. https://doi.org/10.3386/w17159

Dee, T. S. (2001). *Teachers, race and student achievement in a randomized experiment* (Working Paper No. 8432). National Bureau of Economic Research.

Dee, T. S. (2004). Teachers, race, and student achievement in a randomized experiment. *Review of Economics and Statistics, 86*(1), 195–210. https://doi.org/10.1162/003465304323023750

Dee, T. S. (2007). Teachers and the gender gaps in student achievement. *Journal of Human Resources, 42*(3), 528–554.

Dee, T. S., & Wyckoff, J. (2015). Incentives, selection, and teacher performance: Evidence from IMPACT. *Journal of Policy Analysis and Management, 34*(2), 267–297. https://doi .org/10.1002/pam.21818

De Ridder, K. A. A., Pape, K., Cuypers, K., Johnsen, R., Holmen, T. L., Westin, S., & Bjørngaard, J. H. (2013). High school dropout and long-term sickness and disability in young adulthood: A prospective propensity score stratified cohort study (the Young-HUNT study). *BMC Public Health, 13*(1), 941. https://doi.org/10.1186/1471-2458-13-941

Dixit, A. (2002). Incentives and organizations in the public sector: An interpretative review. *Journal of Human Resources, 37*(4), 696–727. https://doi.org/10.2307/3069614

Dotter, D., Chaplin, D., & Bartlett, M. (2021). *Measuring the impacts of school reforms in the District of Columbia on student achievement (Issue Brief)*. Mathematica Policy Research. https://www.mathematica.org/publications/measuring-the-impacts-of-school-reforms-in -the-district-of-columbia-on-student-achievement

Drake, S., Auletto, A., & Cowen, J. M. (2019). Grading teachers: Race and gender differences in low evaluation ratings and teacher employment outcomes. *American Educational Research Journal, 56*(5), 1800–1833. https://doi.org/10.3102/0002831219835776

Education Commission of the States. (2020, July 29). *50-state comparison: Teacher employment contract policies*. https://www.ecs.org/50-state-comparison-teacher-employment-contract -policies/

Egalite, A. J., Kisida, B., & Winters, M. A. (2015). Representation in the classroom: The effect of own-race teacher assignment on student achievement. *Economics of Education Review, 45*(1), 44–52.

Feuer, M. J., Floden, R. E., Chudowsky, N., & Ahn, J. (2013). *Evaluation of teacher preparation programs: Purposes, methods, and policy options*. National Academy of Education. https://files.eric.ed.gov/fulltext/ED565694.pdf

Floman, J. L., Hagelskamp, C., Brackett, M. A., & Rivers, S. E. (2017). Emotional bias in classroom observations: Within-rater positive emotion predicts favorable assessments of classroom quality. *Journal of Psychoeducational Assessment, 35*(3), 291–301. https://doi .org/10.1177/0734282916629595

Freudenberg, N., & Ruglis, J. (2007). Reframing school dropout as a public health issue. *Preventing Chronic Disease, 4*(4), A107.

Garcia, E. (2020, February 12). *Schools are still segregated, and Black children are paying a price*. Economic Policy Institute. https://www.epi.org/publication/schools-are-still-segregated -and-black-children-are-paying-a-price/

García, E., & Weiss, E. (2019). *The teacher shortage is real, large and growing, and worse than we thought (The first report in "The Perfect Storm in the Teacher Labor Market" series)*. Economic Policy Institute.

Glazerman, S., Protik, A., Teh, B., Bruch, J., & Max, J. (2013). *Transfer incentives for high-performing teachers: Final results from a multisite randomized experiment*. National Center for Education Evaluation and Regional Assistance, Institute of Education Sciences, US Department of Education. https://files.eric.ed.gov/fulltext/ED544269.pdf

Goldhaber, D. D., & Brewer, D. J. (2000). Does teacher certification matter? High school teacher certification status and student achievement. *Educational Evaluation and Policy Analysis, 22*(2), 129–145. https://doi.org/10.3102/01623737022002129

Goldhaber, D., Quince, V., & Theobald, R. (2019). Teacher quality gaps in U.S. public schools: Trends, sources, and implications. *Phi Delta Kappan, 100*(8), 14–19. https://doi .org/10.1177/0031721719846883

Goldhaber, D., & Walch, J. (2012). Strategic pay reform: A student outcomes-based evaluation of Denver's ProComp teacher pay initiative. *Economics of Education Review, 31*(6), 1067–1083. https://doi.org/10.1016/j.econedurev.2012.06.007

Goldhaber, D., & Walch, J. (2014). Gains in teacher quality: Academic capabilities of the U.S. teaching force are on the rise. *Education Next, 14*(1), 38–45. https://www.educationnext .org/gains-in-teacher-quality/

Goldring, E., Grissom, J. A., Rubin, M., Neumerski, C. M., Cannata, M., Drake, T., & Schuermann, P. (2015). Make room value added: Principals' human capital decisions and the emergence of teacher observation data. *Educational Researcher, 44*(2), 96–104. https:// doi.org/10.3102/0013189X15575031

Goodman, S., & Turner, L. (2011). Does whole-school performance pay improve student learning? Evidence from the New York City schools. *Education Next, 11*(2), 67–71.

Grissom, J. A. (2011). Can good principals keep teachers in disadvantaged schools? Linking principal effectiveness to teacher satisfaction and turnover in hard-to-staff environments. *Teacher College Record, 113*(11), 2552–2585.

Grissom, J. A., & Bartanen, B. (2018). Strategic retention: Principal effectiveness and teacher turnover in multiple-measure teacher evaluation systems. *American Educational Research Journal, 56*(2), 514–555. https://doi.org/10.3102/0002831218797931

Grissom, J. A., Egalite, A. J., & Lindsay, C. A. (2021). *How principals affect students and schools: A systematic synthesis of two decades of research*. Wallace Foundation. https://www .wallacefoundation.org/knowledge-center/Documents/How-Principals-Affect-Students -and-Schools.pdf

Grissom, J. A., & Loeb, S. (2017). Assessing principals' assessments: Subjective evaluations of teacher effectiveness in low- and high-stakes environments. *Education Finance and Policy, 12*(3), 369–395. https://doi.org/10.1162/EDFP_a_00210

Han, D., & Hur, H. (2021). Managing turnover of STEM teacher workforce. *Education and Urban Society, 54*(2), 205–222. https://doi.org/10.1177/00131245211053562

Han, E. S. (2021). Teacher wage penalty and decrease in teacher quality: Evidence from career-changers. *Labor Studies Journal, 46*(3), 251–285. https://doi.org/10.1177 /0160449X20929083

Hanselman, P. (2019). Access to effective teachers and economic and racial disparities in opportunities to learn. *Sociological Quarterly, 60*(3), 498–534. https://doi.org/10.1080/0038 0253.2019.1625732

Hanushek, E. A. (2011). The economic value of higher teacher quality. *Economics of Education Review, 30*(3), 466–479. https://doi.org/10.1016/j.econedurev.2010.12.006

Hanushek, E. A., Piopiunik, M., & Wiederhold, S. (2019). The value of smarter teachers: International evidence on teacher cognitive skills and student performance. *Journal of Human Resources, 54*(4), 857–899. https://doi.org/10.3368/jhr.54.4.0317.8619R1

Hanushek, E. A., & Rivkin, S. G. (2010). Generalizations about using value-added measures of teacher quality. *American Economic Review, 100*(2), 267–271. http://www.aeaweb.org /articles.php?doi=10.1257/aer.100.2.267

Hanushek, E. A., Ruhose, J., & Woessmann, L. (2017). Knowledge capital and aggregate income differences: Development accounting for US states. *American Economic Journal: Macroeconomics, 9*(4), 184–224. https://doi.org/10.1257/mac.20160255

Harris, D. N., Ingle, W. K., & Rutledge, S. A. (2014). How teacher evaluation methods matter for accountability: A comparative analysis of teacher effectiveness ratings by principals and teacher value-added measures. *American Educational Research Journal, 51*(1), 73–112. https://doi.org/10.3102/0002831213517130

Harris, D. N., & Sass, T. R. (2007). *Teacher training, teacher quality, and student achievement* (Working Paper 3). National Center for Analysis of Longitudinal Data in Education Research. https://caldercenter.org/sites/default/files/1001059_Teacher_Training.pdf

Heinrich, C., & Marschke, G. (2010). Incentives and their dynamics in public sector performance management systems. *Journal of Policy Analysis and Management, 29*(1), 183–208.

Henry, G. T., Bastian, K. C., Fortner, C. K., Kershaw, D. C., Purtell, K. M., Thompson, C. L., & Zulli, R. A. (2014). Teacher preparation policies and their effects on student achievement. *Education Finance and Policy, 9*(3), 264–303. https://doi.org/10.1162/EDFP_a_00134

Hough, H. J., & Loeb, S. (2013). Can a district-level teacher salary incentive policy improve teacher recruitment and retention? (No. 13–4; Policy Brief, p. 16). Policy Analysis for California Education (PACE).

Hoxby, C. M., & Leigh, A. (2004). Pulled away or pushed out? Explaining the decline of teacher aptitude in the United States. *American Economic Review, 94*(2), 236–240. https://doi.org/10.1257/0002828041302073

Imberman, S. A., & Lovenheim, M. F. (2015). Incentive strength and teacher productivity: Evidence from a group-based teacher incentive pay system. *Review of Economics and Statistics, 97*(2), 364–386. https://doi.org/10.1162/REST_a_00486

Isenberg, E., Max, J., Gleason, P., Johnson, M., Deutsch, J., & Hansen, M. (2016, October 27). *Do low-income students have equal access to effective teachers? Evidence from 26 districts.* Mathematica Policy Research. https://www.mathematica.org/publications/do-low-income-students-have-equal-access-to-effective-teachers-evidence-from-26-districts-es

Jacob, B. A., & Lefgren, L. (2008). Can principals identify effective teachers? Evidence on subjective performance evaluation in education. *Journal of Labor Economics, 26*(1), 101–136. https://doi.org/10.1086/522974

Jarmolowski, H. (2018). *How teacher evaluations impact compensation.* National Council on Teacher Quality (NCTQ). https://www.nctq.org/blog/Performance-Pay:-How-Teacher-Evaluations-Impact-Compensation

Johnston, A. C. (2020). *Teacher preferences, working conditions, and compensation structure* (IZA Discussion Papers, No. 13121). Institute of Labor Economics (IZA), Bonn. https://www.econstor.eu/bitstream/10419/216433/1/dp13121.pdf

Kahlenberg, R. D. (2016). Teacher tenure has a long history and, hopefully, a future. *Phi Delta Kappan, 97*(6), 16–21. https://doi.org/10.1177/0031721716636866

Kane, T., McCaffrey, D., Miller, T., & Staiger, D. (2013). *Have we identified effective teachers? Validating measures of effective teaching using random assignment* (MET Project, p. 52). Bill and Melinda Gates Foundation. https://files.eric.ed.gov/fulltext/ED540959.pdf

Kelley, C., & Odden, A. (1995). *Reinventing teacher compensation systems.* Consortium for Policy Research in Education, Finance Briefs. https://eric.ed.gov/?id=ED387910

Kini, T., & Podolsky, A. (2016). *Does teaching experience increase teacher effectiveness? A review of the research.* Learning Policy Institute. https://files-eric-ed-gov.libproxy.lib.unc.edu/fulltext/ED606426.pdf

Koedel, C., & Betts, J. R. (2011). Does student sorting invalidate value-added models of teacher effectiveness? An extended analysis of the Rothstein Critique. *Education Finance and Policy, 6*(1), 18–42. https://doi.org/10.1162/EDFP_a_00027

Koedel, C., Mihaly, K., & Rockoff, J. E. (2015). Value-added modeling: A review. *Economics of Education Review, 47*, 180–195. https://doi.org/10.1016/j.econedurev.2015.01.006

Kraft, M., & Gilmour, A. (2017). Revisiting *The Widget Effect*: Teacher evaluation reforms and the distribution of teacher effectiveness. *Educational Researcher, 46*(5), 234–249.

Kraft, M. A., Marinell, W. H., & Shen-Wei Yee, D. (2016). School organizational contexts, teacher turnover, and student achievement: Evidence from panel data. *American Educational Research Journal, 53*(5), 1411–1449. https://doi.org/10.3102/0002831216667478

Kraft, M. A., & Papay, J. P. (2014). Can professional environments in schools promote teacher development? Explaining heterogeneity in returns to teaching experience. *Educational Evaluation and Policy Analysis, 36*(4), 476–500. https://doi.org/10.3102/0162373713519496

Labaree, D. F. (1997). Public goods, private goods: The American struggle over educational goals. *American Educational Research Journal, 34*(1), 39–81. https://doi.org/10.3102/00028312034001039

Ladd, H., & Sorensen, L. (2015). *Do master's degrees matter? Advanced degrees, career paths, and the effectiveness of teachers* (p. 36). National Center for Analysis of Longitudinal Data in Education Research. https://caldercenter.org/publications/do-master%E2%80%99s-degrees-matter-advanced-degrees-career-paths-and-effectiveness-teachers

Ladd, H. F., & Sorensen, L. C. (2017). Returns to teacher experience: Student achievement and motivation in middle school. *Education Finance and Policy, 12*(2), 241–279.

Lindsay, C. A., & Hart, C. M. D. (2017). Exposure to same-race teachers and student disciplinary outcomes for Black students in North Carolina. *Educational Evaluation and Policy Analysis, 39*(3), 485–510.

Loeb, S., & Candelaria, C. A. (2012). *How stable are value-added estimates across years, subjects and student groups?* (Knowledge Brief 3). Carnegie Foundation for the Advancement of Teaching. https://files.eric.ed.gov/fulltext/ED537430.pdf

Loeb, S., Miller, L. C., & Wyckoff, J. (2015). Performance screens for school improvement: The case of teacher tenure reform in New York City. *Educational Researcher, 44*(4), 199–212. https://doi.org/10.3102/0013189X15584773

Loeb, S., & Myung, J. (2010). Economic approaches to teacher recruitment and retention. In *International encyclopedia of education* (3rd ed., pp. 473–480). Elsevier. https://doi.org/10.1016/B978-0-08-044894-7.01251-3

Lomascolo, D. J., & Angelle, P. S. (2019). Teacher tenure in Tennessee: An examination of principal perceptions post–Race to the Top. *NASSP Bulletin, 103*(2), 98–117. https://doi.org/10.1177/0192636519830766

Marsh, J. A., Springer, M. G., McCaffrey, D. F., Yuan, K., Epstein, S., Koppich, J., Kalra, N., DiMartino, C., & Peng, A. (X.). (2011). A big apple for educators: New York City's experiment with schoolwide performance bonuses: Final evaluation report. RAND Corporation. https://www.rand.org/pubs/monographs/MG1114.html

Master, B., Sun, M., & Loeb, S. (2018). Teacher workforce developments: Recent changes in academic competitiveness and job satisfaction of new teachers. *Education Finance and Policy, 13*(3), 310–332. https://doi.org/10.1162/edfp_a_00215

McIntyre, D. J. (1980). Teacher evaluation and the observer effect. *National Association of Secondary School Principals, 64*(434), 36–40. https://journals.sagepub.com/doi/pdf/10.1177/019263658006443408

Mikeska, J. N., Holtzman, S., McCaffrey, D. F., Liu, S., & Shattuck, T. (2019). Using classroom observations to evaluate science teaching: Implications of lesson sampling for measuring science teaching effectiveness across lesson types. *Science Education, 103*(1), 123–144. https://doi.org/10.1002/sce.21482

Monrad, M. (2007, September). High school dropout: A quick stats fact sheet (p. 4). National High School Center at the American Institutes for Research. https://files.eric.ed.gov /fulltext/ED501066.pdf

NCES. (2020). Estimated average annual salary of teachers in public elementary and secondary schools: Selected years, 1959–60 through 2019–20. Digest of Education Statistics, 2020. National Center for Education Statistics. https://nces.ed.gov/programs/digest/d20 /tables/dt20_211.50.asp

NCES Annual Reports. (2021a). *Characteristics of public school teachers*. National Center for Education Statistics. https://nces.ed.gov/programs/coe/indicator/clr

NCES Annual Reports. (2021b). *Racial/ethnic enrollment in public schools*. National Center for Education Statistics. https://nces.ed.gov/programs/coe/indicator/cge

NCTQ. (2016). *The national picture: State teacher evaluation policies (2015)* (p. 102). National Council on Teacher Quality. https://www.nctq.org/dmsView/Evaluation_Timeline_Brief _AllStates

NCTQ. (2019). *State of the states 2019: Teacher and principal evaluation policy*. National Council on Teacher Quality. https://www.nctq.org/pages/State-of-the-States-2019:-Teacher-and -Principal-Evaluation-Policy

Nguyen, T. D., Pham, L. D., Crouch, M., & Springer, M. G. (2020). The correlates of teacher turnover: An updated and expanded meta-analysis of the literature. *Educational Research Review, 31*, 100355. https://doi.org/10.1016/j.edurev.2020.100355

Nixon, A., Packard, A., & Douvanis, G. (2010). Non-renewal of probationary teachers: Negative retention. *Education, 131*(1), 43–53.

Nye, B., Konstantopoulos, S., & Hedges, L. V. (2004). How large are teacher effects? *Educational Evaluation and Policy Analysis, 26*(3), 237–257. https://doi.org/10.3102 /01623737026003237

Pham, L. D., Nguyen, T. D., & Springer, M. G. (2020). Teacher merit pay: A meta-analysis. *American Educational Research Journal, 58*(3), 527–566. https://doi.org/10.3102 /0002831220905580

Podgursky, M., Monroe, R., & Watson, D. (2004). The academic quality of public school teachers: An analysis of entry and exit behavior. *Economics of Education Review, 23*(5), 507–518.

Podgursky, M. J., & Springer, M. G. (2007). Teacher performance pay: A review. *Journal of Policy Analysis and Management, 26*(4), 909–950. https://doi.org/10.1002/pam.20292

Podgursky, M., & Springer, M. (2011). Teacher compensation systems in the United States K-12 public school system. *National Tax Journal, 64*(1), 165–192. https://doi .org/10.17310/ntj.2011.1.07

Podolsky, A., Kini, T., & Darling-Hammond, L. (2019). Does teaching experience increase teacher effectiveness? A review of US research. *Journal of Professional Capital and Community, 4*(4), 286–308. https://doi.org/10.1108/JPCC-12-2018-0032

Reardon, S. F., Weathers, E. S., Fahle, E. M., Jang, H., & Kalogrides, D. (2021). Is separate still unequal? New evidence on school segregation and racial academic achievement gaps (CEPA Working Paper No. 19-06, p. 60). Stanford Center for Education Policy Analysis. https://vtechworks.lib.vt.edu/bitstream/handle/10919/97804/SeparateStillEqual .pdf?sequence=1&isAllowed=y

Redding, C., & Smith, T. M. (2016). Easy in, easy out: Are alternatively certified teachers turning over at increased rates? *American Educational Research Journal, 53*(4), 1086–1125. https://doi.org/10.3102/0002831216653206

Rigby, J. G., Larbi-Cherif, A., Rosenquist, B. A., Sharpe, C. J., Cobb, P., & Smith, T. (2017). Administrator observation and feedback: Does it lead toward improvement in inquiry-oriented math instruction? *Educational Administration Quarterly, 53*(3), 475–516. https://doi.org/10.1177/0013161X16687006

Rodriguez, L. A. (2020). Understanding tenure reform: An examination of sense-making among school administrators and teachers. *Teachers College Record: The Voice of Scholarship in Education, 122*(11), 1–42. https://doi.org/10.1177/016146812012201112

Rodriguez, L. A., Nguyen, T. D., & Springer, M. G. (2020). Revisiting teacher quality gaps: Geographic disparities in access to highly effective teachers across Tennessee (Working paper). New York: New York University.

Ross, E., & Walsh, K. (2019). *State of the states 2019: Teacher and principal evaluation policy* (p. 21). National Council on Teacher Quality. https://www.nctq.org/pages/State-of-the -States-2019:-Teacher-and-Principal-Evaluation-Policy

Ross, E., & Worth, C. (2018). *Databurst: Strategic teacher compensation* (p. 4). National Council on Teacher Quality. https://www.nctq.org/dmsView/Strategic_Compensation_Databurst

Rothstein, J. (2009). Student sorting and bias in value-added estimation: Selection on ob-servables and unobservables. *Education Finance and Policy, 4*(4), 537–571. https://doi .org/10.1162/edfp.2009.4.4.537

Salary equity among the counties; state salary supplement, WV Code § 18A-4-5. (2018). https://law.justia.com/codes/west-virginia/2018/chapter-18a/article-4/section-18a-4-5/

Sanders, W. L., & Rivers, J. C. (1996). Cumulative and residual effects of teachers on future student academic achievement (p. 14). University of Tennessee Value-Added Research and Assessment Center. https://www.beteronderwijsnederland.nl/files/cumulative%20and%20 residual%20effects%20of%20teachers.pdf

Sartain, L., & Steinberg, M. (2021). *Can personnel policy improve teacher quality? The role of evaluation and the impact of exiting low-performing teachers* (EdWorkingPaper No. 21-486). Annenberg Institute at Brown University. https://www.edworkingpapers.com/ai21-486

Sass, T. R. (2008). The stability of value-added measures of teacher quality and implications for teacher compensation policy (p. 8) [4]. CALDER (National Center for Analysis of Longitudinal Data in Education Research). https://files.eric.ed.gov/fulltext/ED508273.pdf

Springer, M. G., Bastian, K. C., & Brooks, C. (2021). *The unpacking is underway: Current and future directions for teacher preparation data systems* (p. 10). National Institute for Excel-lence in Teaching. https://www.niet.org/assets/ResearchAndPolicyResources/9afb58ea2d /unpacking-underway-current-future-directions-teacher-preparation-data-systems-springer -bastian-brooks.pdf

Springer, M. G., Halpin, P. F., Springer, J. A., Stuit, D. A., Cohen-Vogel, L., & Brooks, C. D. (2023). Disproportional assignment: The need for strategic student-teacher rostering practices. In T. Downes & K. Killeen (Eds.), *Recent advancements in education finance and policy.* Charlotte, NC: Information Age Publishing.

Springer, M. G., Pane, J. F., Le, V.-N., McCaffrey, D. F., Burns, S. F., Hamilton, L. S., & Stecher, B. (2012). Team pay for performance: Experimental evidence from the Round Rock pilot project on team incentives. *Educational Evaluation and Policy Analysis, 34*(4), 367–390. https://doi.org/10.3102/0162373712439094

Springer, M. G., Swain, W. A., & Rodriguez, L. A. (2016). Effective teacher retention bonuses: Evidence from Tennessee. *Educational Evaluation and Policy Analysis, 38*(2), 199–221. https://doi.org/10.3102/0162373715609687

Springer, M. G., & Taylor, L. L. (2021). Compensation and composition: Does strategic compensation affect workforce composition? *Journal of Education Human Resources, 39*(2), 101–164. https://doi.org/10.3138/jehr-2020-0029

Springer, M. G., & Winters, M. A. (2009, April). *The NYC teacher pay-for-performance program: Early evidence from a randomized trial* (p. 48). Center for Civic Innovation at the Manhattan Institute. https://files.eric.ed.gov/fulltext/ED505911.pdf

Startz, D. (2017, May 11). Education programs and (un)selective colleges. *Brown Center Chalkboard* (blog). Washington, DC: Brookings Institution. https://www.brookings.edu/blog/brown-center-chalkboard/2017/05/11/education-programs-and-unselective-colleges/

Steinberg, M. P., & Garrett, R. (2016). Classroom composition and measured teacher performance: What do teacher observation scores really measure? *Educational Evaluation and Policy Analysis, 38*(2), 293–317. https://doi.org/10.3102/0162373715616249

Steinberg, M. P., & Sartain, L. (2015). Does teacher evaluation improve school performance? Experimental evidence from Chicago's Excellence in Teaching project. *Education Finance and Policy, 10*(4), 535–572. https://doi.org/10.1162/EDFP_a_00173

Sum, A., Khatiwada, I., McLaughlin, J., & Palma, S. (2009). *The consequences of dropping out of high school.* Boston: Northeastern University. https://www.prisonpolicy.org/scans/The_Consequences_of_Dropping_Out_of_High_School.pdf

Swain, W. A., Rodriguez, L. A., & Springer, M. G. (2019). Selective retention bonuses for highly effective teachers in high poverty schools: Evidence from Tennessee. *Economics of Education Review, 68*, 148–160. https://doi.org/10.1016/j.econedurev.2018.12.008

Taylor, E. S., & Tyler, J. H. (2012). The effect of evaluation on teacher performance. *American Economic Review, 102*(7), 3628–3651. https://doi.org/10.1257/aer.102.7.3628

US Bureau of Labor Statistics. (2021). *Education pays.* https://www.bls.gov/emp/chart-unemployment-earnings-education.htm

von Hippel, P. T., & Bellows, L. (2018, May 8). Rating teacher-preparation programs. *Education Next, 18*(3), 34–41. https://www.educationnext.org/rating-teacher-preparation-programs-value-added-make-useful-distinctions/

Weisberg, D., Sexton, S., Mulhern, J., & Keeling, D. (2009). *The widget effect: Our national failure to acknowledge and act on differences in teacher effectiveness* (p. 48). The New Teacher Project. https://tntp.org/assets/documents/TheWidgetEffect_2nd_ed.pdf

West, K. L., & Mykerezi, E. (2011). Teachers' unions and compensation: The impact of collective bargaining on salary schedules and performance pay schemes. *Economics of Education Review, 30*(1), 99–108. https://doi.org/10.1016/j.econedurev.2010.07.007

Will, M. (2018, September 28). From "rotten apples" to martyrs: America has changed its tune on teachers. *Education Week.* https://www.edweek.org/teaching-learning/from-rotten-apples-to-martyrs-america-has-changed-its-tune-on-teachers/2018/09

Winters, M. A., Haight, R. C., Swaim, T. T., & Pickering, K. A. (2013). The effect of same-gender teacher assignment on student achievement in the elementary and secondary grades: Evidence from panel data. *Economics of Education Review, 34*(C), 69–75.

Woods, J. R. (2016, May). *Mitigating teacher shortages: Alternative teacher certification* (p. 7). Education Commission of the States. https://www.ecs.org/wp-content/uploads/Mitigating-Teacher-Shortages-Alternative-Certification.pdf

Young, S., Range, B. G., Hvidston, D. J., & Mette, I. M. (2015). Teacher evaluation reform: Principals' beliefs about newly adopted teacher evaluation systems. *Planning and Changing, 46*(1/2), 158–174.

Zamarro, G., Camp, A., Fuchsman, D., & McGee, J. (2021). *Understanding how COVID-19 has changed teachers' chances of remaining in the classroom* (EDRE Research Brief No. 2021–01). University of Arkansas. https://edre.uark.edu/_resources/pdf/teacher_turnover_covid.pdf

# 8

# Ensuring All Children Succeed with Social-Emotional Learning

*Nicole A. Elbertson, Mark A. Brackett, Tangular A. Irby, and Krista L. Smith*

The term social and emotional learning (SEL) originated in 1994 with a focus on embedding the teaching and learning of related skills into preschool through high school education (Elias et al., 1997; Greenberg et al., 2003; Kress & Elias, 2006). SEL is defined as the process by which all young people and adults acquire and apply the knowledge, skills, and attitudes to develop healthy identities, manage emotions and achieve personal and collective goals, feel and show empathy for others, establish and maintain supportive relationships, and make responsible and caring decisions (CASEL, 2003). Since its inception, SEL has been researched broadly, and scientific evidence supports its effectiveness in positively impacting academic, personal, mental health, and social outcomes for students and adults (Durlak, Weissberg, Dymnicki, Taylor, & Schellinger, 2011; Domitrovich, Durlak, Staley, & Weissberg, 2017; Mahoney et al., 2021).

SEL can be a powerful lever for cultivating compassionate, just, engaging, inclusive, and mentally healthy communities where all educators and students can flourish. Importantly, SEL alone cannot solve long-standing and deep-seated inequities in the education system. Nevertheless, well-designed SEL programs and approaches that are implemented using a continuous improvement process can help us to examine biases, reflect on and address the impact of racism, understand cultural differences, and cultivate practices and policies that close opportunity gaps and create more inclusive and thriving school communities. To date, however, data is limited on which SEL programs and approaches work for whom. A forthcoming meta-analysis by Cipriano and colleagues will be the first to address which specific SEL content yields the best outcomes for which students (i.e., of different abilities, race, sexual and gender identities, and socioeconomic status; Cipriano et al., in press). These researchers also are exploring whether SEL interventions for students in grades K through 12 enhance student SEL competencies and associated outcomes, and whether intervention effects are associated with specific attitudes or skills that SEL targets.

With ever-increasing educator burnout, youth mental health needs, and hate crimes, especially during the years spent in the COVID-19 pandemic, the need for SEL to be implemented equitably and in inclusive learning environments—where all students and educators feel respected, appreciated, and affirmed in their individual talents, identities, and cultural and religious values and backgrounds—is much needed. In 2020 there were more than 8,000 reported hate crimes in the United States—the most in 12 years, according to the FBI (Federal Bureau of Investigation, 2021). This is likely an underestimate given the many challenges of reporting. The distribution by motive was: 61.8% of crimes were against race, ethnicity, or ancestry; 20% against sexual orientation; 13.3% against religion; and the remaining against gender, gender identity, or disability.

The pandemic intensified an already growing crisis in youth mental health. In the fall of 2020, the American Academy of Pediatrics, the Children's Hospital Association, and the American Academy of Child and Adolescent Psychiatry declared an emergency in child and adolescent mental health (American Academy of Pediatrics, 2021). During March through October 2020, the proportion of mental health-related visits to the emergency departments in hospitals increased by 24% among US children aged 5 to 11 years and 31% among adolescents aged 12 to 17 years, compared with 2019 (Radhakrishnan, Leeb, & Bitsko et al., 2022). The evidence for this is clear. In February 2022, a report showed that an astounding 55% of educators—regardless of age or experience—were thinking about leaving the profession earlier than they had planned (Walker, 2022). The poll also found that a disproportionate percentage of Black (62%) and Hispanic/Latino (59%) educators, already underrepresented in the teaching profession, were looking to depart from the profession.

Given all of this, educators, school and district leaders, and parents have realized the need to teach social and emotional skills and ask: where do we begin?

It all begins with us—the adults in students' lives. It begins with knowing our students—their interests and perspectives, their cultural backgrounds, the sources of their fears and insecurities and their curiosity and joy. In other words, we need to know our students' stories, including the knowledge and wisdom they have accumulated, the questions they have, the strengths and challenges they bring with them every day when they enter the school building and the classroom. Further, in order to support all youth in realizing their full potential, the adults who are involved in and influencing student lives also must be educated in SEL. Often, the missing piece in high-quality SEL is adult development. If children are to develop social and emotional skills, all of the adults around them need these skills, too. In fact, many teachers feel they need more time than they currently have to learn about and teach SEL (Lee, 2019).

We all have biases and beliefs about certain groups based on a number of factors, and these biases consciously and unconsciously impact our behavior in and out of the classroom (Tenenbaum & Ruck, 2007). Our beliefs or stereotypes about race, ethnicity, ability, and gender identity are shaped by "nurture," including what we learned from parents and peers, the music we listened to, the TV shows we watched, and the news we read. For example, research demonstrates racial in-group or own-race advantages and racial biases in perceiving faces and facial expressions (see Meissner & Brigham, 2001, for a review). Thus, when educators are teaching students from racial and ethnic backgrounds different from their own, they are likely to make more errors in emotion recognition. This can translate into attributing the wrong emotion or a negative emotion to a student because of a stereotype about that child's race or ethnic background. For example, anger bias (the tendency for someone to assume a behavior is an expression of anger) might explain why Black children are suspended more than White children for the same behaviors (Halberstadt et al., 2020). Research suggests that racial bias also can extend to unfair grading. In one experiment, White and female teachers evaluated the same second-grade writing sample more harshly when clues indicated that it had been written by a Black boy versus a White boy (Quinn, 2021).

When SEL is implemented with an equity lens, educators learn to question their own power and privilege, their beliefs about individuals and groups, and the impact of these beliefs on their relationships and student success. Such questioning has the potential to assist teachers in avoiding the fallacies of their biases and in supporting youth of color and low-resourced students in more equitable ways (Castagno, 2013; Jagers, Rivas-Drake, & Borowski, 2018). As a core principle of SEL, bringing awareness to diversity in any given school or classroom is not to further highlight the ways in which we are different but to appreciate the variety of stories and perspectives that students and educators alike bring to the table. When educators open their hearts and minds to understanding their own biases, it allows the unfamiliar to become familiar and sparks curiosity instead of judgment—all of which can help to dismantle barriers and enhance supports. Expanding our perspectives in this way is one step toward providing more equitable educational opportunities to our students.

In the following two sections, we (1) use one SEL approach, RULER, as a case study to illustrate how an equity lens can be embedded into SEL training and content; and (2) provide an overview of best practices that have been identified to support inclusive and equitable implementation of SEL programming in schools.

## RULER AS A CASE STUDY

For the purposes of illustrating concretely the role of equity in designing and implementing SEL efforts, we present a case study with RULER, a CASEL SELect approach to SEL (CASEL, 2012) developed at the Yale Center for Emotional Intelligence. Here, we provide a brief overview of RULER so that we can integrate examples throughout the remainder of the chapter of how an equity lens can be used to inform the design of an SEL approach, including its adaptations over time.

RULER is an evidence-based approach to SEL that supports entire school communities in understanding the value of emotions, building the skills of emotional intelligence, and creating and maintaining positive school climates. Over the past decade, evidence has accumulated for RULER's positive impact on students' emotional intelligence skills, social problem-solving ability, work habits, and grades; on classroom and school climate, including fewer instances of bullying; and on teacher stress, burnout, and instructional support for students (Brackett, Bailey, Hoffmann, & Simmons, 2019).

RULER is a pre-K-12 approach to SEL designed to integrate the teaching of social and emotional skills into a whole school or district. Its foundations lie in emotional intelligence theory (Salovey & Mayer, 1990; Mayer & Salovey, 1997), multiple theories of emotional development (e.g., Denham, 1998; Saarni, 1999), and ecological systems theory (Bronfenbrenner, 1979; Bronfenbrenner & Morris, 2006; see Brackett, Elbertson, & Rivers, 2015, for an overview of theories that have been applied to SEL). Importantly, RULER was designed to focus on a set of skills related to positive youth outcomes that can be developed through experience, practice, and adult modeling. Accordingly, the name, RULER, was created based on research and theory indicating that children and the adults in their lives will be more effective when they are able to Recognize, Understand, Label, Express, and Regulate emotions, hence the acronym, RULER (Brackett, Bailey, Hoffmann, & Simmons, 2019; Brackett et al., 2011; Maurer, Brackett, & Plain, 2004).

RULER begins when members of a school community adopt an "emotions matter" mind-set by acknowledging the value of emotions in our everyday effectiveness—from attention and learning, to decision making and creative problem solving, to forming and maintaining relationships, and our overall mental and physical well-being. RULER continues when school leaders, educators, students, and their parents and caregivers learn about and practice the five RULER skills of emotional intelligence: by recognizing emotions in oneself and others, understanding the causes and consequences of emotions, labeling emotions with a nuanced vocabulary, expressing emotions in accordance with cultural norms and social context, and regulating emotions with helpful strategies to achieve greater well-being.

The RULER skills are embedded and reinforced with four key tools, which are introduced to all stakeholders in the school community:

1. *The Emotional Intelligence Charter* builds and sustains positive emotional climates by creating agreed-upon norms for how people in a school, classroom, home, or other community or group want to feel and how they can help each other to experience those feelings.
2. *The Mood Meter* is a graph with two dimensions: pleasantness and energy, where users plot themselves to determine how they are feeling and if they would like to stay or shift. This tool enhances self- and social awareness and supports the development of a nuanced emotion vocabulary and a range of strategies for regulating emotion.

3. *The Meta-Moment* provides a process for pausing to respond to emotional situations with strategies that align with one's best self and that support healthy relationships and personal well-being.
4. *The Blueprint* serves as a guide for reflecting on conflict and restoring affected communities by supporting the development of empathy, perspective taking, and conflict resolution skills.

As the goal of RULER is to make the approach an enduring part of a school's culture, RULER is introduced in phases. Adoption begins with staff personal and professional learning and continues with classroom instruction for students from early childhood through high school, including family engagement and education. The classroom components of RULER were designed with students' social, emotional, and cognitive developmental needs at the center. In addition, RULER uses a spiral design (Johnston, 2012) such that each year students develop a more advanced understanding of emotion concepts and their application. RULER is also guided by the tenets of trauma-informed practices and culturally responsive pedagogy (Walkley & Cox, 2013) and, as such, encourages its implementation to be learned-centered and accounts for the diverse experiences and cultures of all stakeholders.

The importance of creating safe and inclusive learning environments where all learners thrive is at the core of RULER. RULER is based on the premise that all emotions matter and that individuals experience and manage emotions uniquely based on their identities and backgrounds. At present, RULER has been implemented in more than 3,500 highly diverse public and private schools in rural, suburban, and large cities across the United States and in other countries, including Australia, Canada, Chile, China, England, Italy, Mexico, Panamá, and Spain.

RULER tools focus on building positive emotional connections across differences, creating awareness around the range of our own emotions and the emotions of others, managing emotions with our best selves, building perspective-taking skills and empathy, resolving conflict, and restoring communities affected by conflict. We, the developers of RULER, acknowledge that the best approach to ensuring that RULER serves diverse students and educators is ongoing and iterative.

## BEST PRACTICES IN EQUITABLE IMPLEMENTATION OF SEL

Research suggests that SEL is one way to address and prevent economic inequities. However, approaches to SEL vary considerably in terms of how they address equity and culturally responsive pedagogy (Durlak et al., 2011; Jagers, Rivas-Drake, & Williams, 2019). Decades of research confirm that from culture to culture, social and emotional norms, which are at the heart of SEL teaching, vary tremendously. Emotions are interpreted, expressed, and managed differently, and patterns in relationships and social interactions differ depending on culture, including region, socioeconomic status, language, religion, race, and other factors (Hoffman, 2009).

Approaches to SEL must account for these differences so that the principles and tools provided can be adapted for unique environments, individuals, and groups. Arguably, universal developmental needs exist for self-awareness, self-management, social awareness, relationship skills, and responsible decision making (Denham & Weissberg, 2004). Still, the approach to developing these skills, the ways in which they are modeled, and the adults who are teaching them must take into account cultural diversity in values, attitudes, behavior, and meanings of SEL-related concepts.

Even when SEL approaches are designed to reach diverse students in equitable ways, schools and educators differ in their interpretation and implementation of these approaches (Jagers et al., 2018). Variability in the SEL approaches themselves and the ways in which they are implemented affects whether students experience the positive outcomes the approaches are designed to achieve. Thus, we ask: how can SEL best support students of diverse backgrounds, experiences, and needs to reach their full potential? Research points program developers and implementers to do the following.

## Commit to Making Equitable SEL a Priority

If we truly value and commit to any idea or goal, then we devote time, resources, and energy to it. To ensure that we are serving students' social and emotional needs in an equitable manner, we must spend time thoughtfully crafting and evaluating plans for implementing SEL. Many schools and districts have an SEL coordinator or planning committee. These individuals or groups, and specialized subgroups or subcommittees within these groups, can work together to ensure that SEL strategies are inclusive, accessible, and implemented in ways that reach all students. As school leaders and educators, we also must devote time and energy to getting to know our students and their unique backgrounds, perspectives, and needs with nonjudgmental observation and attentive listening and learning. Then, using that information as a starting point, we can give careful thought to how we meet them where they are. At the Yale Center for Emotional Intelligence (YCEI), in recent years, we have devoted increasing time and funds to ensuring that RULER is both designed and implemented with equity at its core, including hiring a third party to review all RULER content to ensure that it is inclusive, equitable, and representative and relatable to a broad range of students.

## Hire and Maintain a Diverse Staff to Instruct and Model SEL

Common sense tells us and research supports that people with diverse backgrounds, experiences, and perspectives contribute uniquely and synergistically to the successful rollout of new initiatives (Blazar & Lagos, 2021). However, research also tells us and history shows us that deeply entrenched systems of inequity have continuously enforced barriers to educational opportunities and inclusion for people with diverse backgrounds and experiences (Gillborn, 2008). Preliminary research even suggests that the culturally responsive practices and growth mind-sets that teachers of color bring into the classroom benefit students socially, emotionally, and academically (Blazar, 2021). Moreover, students with various racial, cultural, and ideological backgrounds learn best when they are given the opportunity to connect with the backgrounds of the adults in their schools (Castagno, 2013). Thus, in the United States, where the overwhelming majority of teachers are White women, White students, on average, experience closer and more caring relationships with their teachers than Black students (Cherng & Halpin, 2016; Hussar et al., 2020). Research has also exposed the less-effective relationships teachers generally have with students from lower SES and students of color than with White students (Allen, Scott, & Lewis, 2013; Yeager, Purdie-Vaughns, Hooper, & Cohen, 2017). Such findings underline the need to recruit and sustain educators with diverse backgrounds for teaching in general, including and perhaps especially SEL due to its focus on social interactions and emotions.

## Get to Know Students to Ensure That Lessons and Examples Are Relevant and Meaningful

Students learn best when new information is meaningful and relevant to their lived experiences and when they can apply what they learn to their lives (Zins, Bloodworth, Weissberg, & Walberg, 2007). Further, when new information is connected to concepts students already know, they remember it better (Simonsmeier, Flaig, Deiglmayr, Schalk, & Schneider, 2022). The only way to truly use students' own experiences as a jumping-off point and to know whether content is working for them is to get to know them—their stories, backgrounds, and their cultures—and to have trusting relationships with them so that they weigh in on what works. To do this, we can engage in small groups, conduct 1:1 discussions, and administer pretests to learn more about who our students are and what they know. We also can connect our students' prior knowledge and skills to instruction as a strategy to help them access new content and retain information. This knowledge also can be used to help build positive student-teacher relationships and increase student engagement when connected to instructional practices such as allowing for student choice (Pianta, Hamre, & Allen, 2012; Patall, Cooper, & Wynn, 2010).

In its early years, RULER often provided one book, video, or scenario to make a point or teach a lesson. Quickly, we learned that the approach needed to be more flexible. Not only did we need to provide more than one example for lessons, but we needed to provide guidance for educators to select reading material and situations to which students could relate. In fact, over time we have learned that the best suggestions for stories and situations to which to apply RULER principles come from students themselves. Although it can be a great exercise in empathy and taking perspective to learn about characters and narratives that are not our own, we tend to pay more attention and have increased motivation to learn when material is useful and relevant to real-life circumstances and challenges (Gueldner, Feuerborn, & Merrell, 2020). This is critical for culturally and linguistically diverse student populations that especially benefit from teaching practices that are responsive and relevant (Castro-Olivo, 2014).

We—program developers and implementers/educators—cannot assume we are the knowers. We must anchor learning in student knowledge, using their experiences as jumping-off points for new information. In turn, students are gradually equipped with the competencies to react less to external factors of their diverse settings and backgrounds and more in alignment with their core beliefs and values and sense of responsibility for their actions (Durlak et al., 2011; Bear & Watkins, 2006).

### Acknowledge Ethnocentrism and Bias in SEL Programs and Practices and Correct for Them

All programs and practices are developed by a group of humans—and humans are innately biased based on their temperament and lived experiences. Many SEL programs are developed by psychologists and educators within the United States— written in English, from an American point of view (Jagers et al., 2018). This means terms rely on our vernacular. This alone has many implications because language shapes our experiences, and different cultures use nuanced languages to describe their feelings (Kövecses, 2003). One way to correct for these types of biases is by having educators, students, and their families provide input on program development and feedback on its content and implementation so that SEL approaches can be tailored to best fit unique communities.

An example of this came up for the authors in the application of RULER's Meta-Moment across diverse populations. The tool focuses on identifying and leveraging one's "best self" to manage emotions in the moment. In teaching the tool, we emphasize that the best self varies considerably from person to person, depending on the roles in one's life, one's values, desired reputation, and goals. Yet, in working with thousands of educators and hundreds of thousands of students to help them identify their own best selves, we began to understand safety, diverse role models, and other variables at play. With regard to safety, we realized that acting in a way aligned with one's "best self" is often a luxury and is not possible when our safety is threatened (e.g., a teen whose best self is nonviolent but who will be targeted by violence if he does not prove himself with violence).

As implementers of SEL programs, we must keep these issues of context in mind and remember not to push ideals based on our own or majority culture. For instance, although one individual's best self may be slower to react with anger, another's might be someone who acts more readily in anger by standing up to someone who hurts him. Similarly, one person's best self may be kinder and giving; another's best self might be more assertive with clearer boundaries and courage to say no more often. Another example occurs as students attempt to form or identify a best self and consider family or celebrity role models. When these role models have certain qualities, we, as educators, may be tempted to judge (e.g., a family member with a criminal record or a celebrity with a reputation of using illicit drugs). However, rather than reject the role model, we can be curious and help students identify the specific qualities of the individual that they would like to emulate.

## Ensure That SEL Is Not Misused to Control Marginalized Groups

Any well-intentioned tool can be misused without proper guidance and training on how to use that tool effectively. If our goal is to ensure that benefits are maximized and harm is prevented, then we must be diligent about training people to be aware of ways in which an SEL approach can be used in careful alignment with our goals and how it can be misused intentionally or unintentionally. We must constantly evaluate which students are being reached (or left out) in terms of the materials and examples used to teach and pay close attention to the principles of culturally responsive pedagogy. Adults working with students can carefully monitor how students receive SEL and its impact on their learning, behavior, and well-being (Cipriano, Schlichtmann, Riley, Naples, & Eveleigh, in press).

## Choose Words Carefully

We have already established that language is important because it is both a product and an influencer of our experiences. Thus, it is important to consider the native languages of students and their families as well as the nuances and semantics of the words and phrases we use throughout SEL content. What's more, in an increasingly divided political and socioeconomic world, some words or concepts may shut people down to listening and learning. For instance, certain parents or caregivers may be reluctant to support SEL if it is described to focus on value formation (which many believe should happen in the home) or spending limited school time talking about feelings instead of academics. Instead, we can explain that SEL supports and reinforces positive value systems that begin in the home. We can emphasize that SEL principles and practices embed seamlessly into core academic subjects and center on skills to support student attention and learning. We can mention research that shows that students learn best and are more motivated and engaged when they have positive and supportive relationships with their teachers and peers, which is a focus of SEL.

Still, other words may seem judgmental or self-righteous. In contrast, certain words imply nonjudgment and inclusivity. For example, in its initial form, we defined the RULER skill of labeling as "having and using a sophisticated vocabulary." Soon after releasing that definition out into the world, we received questions about why words must be "sophisticated." Immediately, we realized it is not the sophistication of the word (e.g., despondent versus sad, jubilant versus happy) but the granularity—that we have an abundance of words to describe nuanced experiences (sad versus disappointed, excited versus happy).

With regard to judgment, we initially defined the RULER skill of expressing emotion as "showing emotions appropriately," which implies right or wrong—that there is a correct way of expressing. We have since refined the definition to "expressing emotions in accordance with cultural norms and social context."

As an example of inclusivity, in our discussion of healthy emotion regulation strategies, we have changed instances of the word "exercise" or "working out," which often conjure images of lifting weights at a gym or running a marathon, to simply "physical activity," a more expansive term that includes whatever way individuals choose to move their bodies for health.

### Ensure Accessibility of All Tools, Strategies, and Content

Without attention to accessibility for diverse learners, we may inadvertently exclude certain students from the benefits of SEL. SEL approaches, particularly universal interventions, are designed with the majority in mind and may fall short in supporting educators in creating flexible solutions to meet diverse students' needs (Rappolt-Schlichtmann, Cipriano, Robinson, & Boucher, in press). Research shows that students who are minoritized based on race, language, sexuality, and/or ability report feeling more anxious, stigmatized, socially isolated, depressed, and lower in self-esteem (Artiles, Dorn, & Bal, 2016; Annamma & Morrison, 2018; Cruz-Gonzalez, Shrout, Alvarez, Hostetter, & Alegría, 2021). Students with disabilities and those who have experienced trauma or who live in economically disadvantaged communities tend to have lower social and emotional skills, including challenges in forming and maintaining relationships, recognizing and managing emotions, and knowing their own strengths and needs (Cipriano et al., 2021). Most approaches to SEL explicitly target these outcomes and skills, making it even more important that we reach minoritized students.

Another challenge with accessibility is that most SEL programs employ learning strategies that assume levels of reading, writing, and other skills that students with disabilities or learning differences may not have (Rappolt-Schlichtmann et al., in press). Many SEL approaches rely on these academic and social skills as the basis for teaching SEL. For instance, students with receptive language disorders will likely have difficulty learning new vocabulary around emotions because they struggle with language learning in general. Students with autism will likely struggle in discussions around emotion perception and on how people express their emotions because they tend not to notice emotion in others. SEL design and instruction must account for different student backgrounds, skills, languages, and modes of perception.

Finally, SEL tools and strategies must be designed with diverse modes of perception in mind. Students with visual or hearing impairments will be excluded if ideas are represented in only one way (pictures without text descriptions, audio without transcripts). Students with physical abilities will be excluded if handwriting or standing to join a group are required. We must provide examples and strategies that are relevant and accessible to students beyond the majority.

In RULER, we have taken this into consideration by adding notes throughout our learning units on adapting lessons based on diverse learners, adding text descriptions and transcripts for audio and visuals, and ensuring accessibility in the design of digital tools and platforms. We also have seen schools create various adaptations of our tools and strategies, including tactile versions of the Mood Meter in braille and other textures, symbols for the colored quadrants for those with color blindness, and faces and other visuals rather than or in addition to words to represent emotions within the quadrants. SEL programs must be developed with accessibility as a guide and provide notes that explain accommodations and flexibility in their design; implementers of SEL can think carefully about how aspects of SEL approaches can be adapted to ensure that all learners benefit.

## Consider Using SEL as a Means to Transform Inequitable Settings and Systems

Importantly, schools and districts across the nation recently have made or revisited commitments to DEI, including a focus on antiracism or other justice-oriented civic engagement. Leading SEL experts have shown how SEL can be used to support DEI initiatives through a framework called transformative SEL (Jagers et al., 2019). This specific form of SEL "emphasizes the development of identity, agency, belonging, curiosity, and collaborative problem-solving within the CASEL framework" with core features that include partnerships between youth and adults focused on sharing power and decision making; integration of race, class, and culture into academic content; reflections on personal and social identities, prejudices, and biases; and the disruption of inequities and co-construction of equitable and just solutions (Jagers et al., 2019). Schools looking to focus on transformative SEL consider the most marginalized within school communities and use data-based decision making to plan for SEL implementation that represents the needs and strengths of the community (see, e.g., Cipriano et al., in press).

## Partner with Parents, Caregivers, and the Community

Learning about relationships and feelings starts in the home well before students learn SEL in school. It's important to acknowledge the instrumental role parents, caregivers, and the community play in providing the foundation for SEL. SEL is designed to build on the lessons students bring in from their lives at home—and to reinforce their knowledge and build on it. As SEL implementers, we can engage parents and caregivers in the work, ask them for their thoughts and feedback, educate and inform them on plans to integrate SEL throughout the school, and provide ways they can support student learning of SEL at home.

Over the past decade, family engagement and education have become more prominent in RULER. We started with part of our classroom lessons that focus on teaching feelings words, including an activity that students take home to an adult family member (or other trusted adult) in which they have conversations about the feeling (i.e., how it is experienced, times when the student and adult have experienced the feeling). Since then, we have added sample presentations and letters for school leaders and educators to share with parents and caregivers as well as tip sheets, webinars, worksheets, and other learning opportunities for adult family members. Over time, we also have been translating our family resources in various languages, as we realize the importance of having resources for parents in their first language.

### Be Curious and Open to Feedback

The contexts in which learning takes place and the individuals within them change constantly. For this reason alone, it is important that we give careful thought and consideration to feedback on our programming and its implementation. We can look for grains of truth in even the harshest critique and engage in dialogue when there may be a lack of understanding. Although it is easy for feedback to prompt uncomfortable emotions that cloud responsive approaches, accepting how feedback and suggestions make us feel allows the opportunity to embody a growth mind-set and chip away at the discouraging power discomfort may have over us and our effective implementation of SEL, to the benefit of students and educators alike (Michalec & Wilson, 2021; Zins et al., 2007). As a result, we can engage in deep dialogues to modify our strategies over time as students, the adults in their lives, and the contexts surrounding us all change and grow. Focus groups, surveys, emails, and thousands of conversations with school leaders, educators, students, and their families have informed all aspects of RULER and the many changes we have made over time.

### Use SEL for Prevention as Well as Intervention

Recent world shifts from the pandemic exposed a lack of readiness as a society to tackle certain challenges effectively because we are typically problem-oriented rather than preventive in our approaches to crises. Introducing students to knowledge and providing practice on skills focused on understanding and managing their own emotions and relationships sets them up for success in managing the obstacles, expected and unexpected, that come with life. SEL interventions work best when we continuously assess protective and risk factors of the communities we serve, rather than only responding to crises when they arise (Taylor, Oberle, Durlak, & Weissberg, 2017). Since the beginning of the pandemic in early 2020, demand for RULER has increased sharply, likely due to new or reinforced perceived need in investing in the mental health of students and the adults in their lives. Although we are thrilled to broaden the reach of RULER skills and principles, we hear from schools that trained in RULER before the pandemic that the lessons and competences RULER taught helped them to survive and even thrive within periods of intense uncertainty, social isolation, and other challenges of the pandemic. We only wish more school and district leaders, educators, students, and families could have had this armory of skills built up before we entered into the pandemic.

**Monitor All SEL Efforts Over Time and Strive for Continuous Improvement**

Once we choose an SEL approach, we must set aside regular time to monitor its progress, assess its collective impact and its impact on individual students and staff, and to make changes along the way. Schools, students, the adults in their lives, and the larger context of learning and life are in constant flux. From educator and school leader turnover to evolving technology, to shifting school or district priorities, to big changes in the world at large (pandemics, natural disasters, mass shootings, etc.), an ever-changing world calls for constant evaluation and continuous improvement. As students and their interests grow and change, we must continue to prioritize learning about them and whether our existing approaches to SEL still make sense.

With RULER, we encourage schools to engage in both formal and informal research. Meetings with and surveys of students and all adults in their lives can gauge attitudes, beliefs, opinions, and perceived outcomes of an approach to SEL. Educators instructing SEL can provide information on their confidence and comfort with SEL programming, attitudes toward program components and its value, commitment to program goals, beliefs in program efficacy, and recommendations for improvement. Questions for students can ask about their overall impression of the SEL program including its relevance and impact on their lives. For RULER, we have spent the past several years conducting research and developing tools that schools can use to assess educator well-being, school climate, student emotional skills, and other evidence of impact.

## CONCLUSION AND POLICY IMPLICATIONS

Although nearly three decades have been dedicated to developing SEL initiatives to support the healthy development of students and adults, we are still learning. Continuous improvement in the SEL space includes conducting research and collecting data to determine who is and who is not being served well. Importantly, this research and data can inform the practice and policy changes necessary to ensure that the social and emotional needs of all members of our school communities are addressed.

What is our path forward in terms of policy? Equity-focused SEL policies can be viewed from school, state, and federal levels and can include evaluation of SEL program effectiveness. At the school level, schools and districts can move from punitive discipline policies to restorative practices, which include a participatory learning and decision-making process. A child who is suspended even once is much more likely to become disconnected from school, drop out, or enter the criminal justice system. Hence, moving from these forms of discipline to learning and restoring has long-term consequences. States also play a critical role in helping to ensure that all students have consistent opportunities to engage in high-quality SEL. State leaders can establish SEL learning standards, benchmarks, guidelines, and goals, as well as provide funding and professional development support to districts and schools. As one example, states permit or ban corporal punishment (proven to have adverse outcomes for children), which is still allowed in 19 states in the United States.

Finally, federal policies play a key role in creating conditions that support statewide and districtwide implementation of SEL. The Every Student Succeeds Act (ESSA) authorizes K-12 policy in support of high-quality education and is widely seen as the primary funding source for social, emotional, academic, and civic/career efforts in schools. Provisions in ESSA, for example, support SEL through a broader definition of student success that includes "nonacademic" indicators such as student engagement or school safety, a broader approach to professional development, and handing over power to states and districts to create their school improvement plans, which can include SEL. Last, the $123 billion infusion to K-12 education in the American Rescue Plan (ARP) Act of 2021 represents an unprecedented opportunity to invest in SEL to ensure equitable outcomes for all children.

SEL, when delivered through an equity lens, creates opportunities to uncover and address inequitable practices and systems. The world is constantly changing, and undoubtedly, we will be faced with the impact of having experienced recent and ongoing traumatic events, from the pandemic to war and everything in between, all of which may contribute to the rise in teacher turnover rates, the youth mental health crisis, and hate crimes. Now more than ever, leaning into SEL strategies—tools, skills, and a common language around emotions and relationships—can help us as we navigate these challenges. To provide optimal support, these strategies must be developed and implemented with careful thought and attention to ensuring that they meet all students and adults where they are and support them in equitable ways.

## REFERENCES

Allen, A., Scott, L. A., & Lewis, C. W. (2013). Racial microaggressions and African American and Hispanic students in urban schools: A call for culturally affirming education. *Interdisciplinary Journal of Teaching and Learning, 3*(2), 117–129.

American Academy of Pediatrics (2021, October). *AAP-AACAP-CHA Declaration of a national emergency in child and adolescent mental health.* https://www.aap.org/en/advocacy/child-and-adolescent-healthy-mental-development/aap-aacap-cha-declaration-of-a-national-emergency-in-child-and-adolescent-mental-health/

Annamma, S., & Morrison, D. (2018). Identifying dysfunctional education ecologies: A DisCrit analysis of bias in the classroom. *Equity & Excellence in Education, 51*(2), 114–131. https://doi.org/10.1080/10665684.2018.1496047

Artiles, A. J., Dorn, S., & Bal, A. (2016). Objects of protection, enduring nodes of difference: Disability intersections with "other" differences, 1916 to 2016. *Review of Research in Education, 40*(1), 777–820.

Bear, G. G., & Watkins, J. M. (2006). Developing self-discipline. In G. G. Bear & K. M. Minke (Eds.), *Children's needs III: Development, prevention, and intervention* (pp. 29–44). National Association of School Psychologists.

Blazar, D. (2021). *Teachers of color, culturally responsive teaching, and student outcomes: Experimental evidence from the random assignment of teachers to classes* (EdWorkingPaper No. 21-501). Annenberg Institute at Brown University. https://doi.org/10.26300/jym0-wz02

Blazar, D., & Lagos, F. (2021). *Professional staff diversity and student outcomes: Extending our understanding of race/ethnicity-matching effects in education* (EdWorkingPaper No. 21-500). Annenberg Institute at Brown University. https://edworkingpapers.com/sites/default/files /ai21-500.pdf

Brackett, M. A., Bailey, C. S., Hoffmann, J. D., & Simmons, D. N. (2019). RULER: A theory-driven, systemic approach to social, emotional, and academic learning. *Educational Psychologist, 54*(3), 144–161. https://doi.org/10.1080/00461520.2019.1614447

Brackett, M. A., Elbertson, N. A., & Rivers, S. E. (2015). Applying theory to the development of approaches to SEL. In J. A. Durlak, C. E. Domitrovich, R. P. Weissberg, & T. P. Gullotta (Eds.), *Handbook of social and emotional learning: Research and practice* (pp. 20–32). Guilford.

Brackett, M. A., & Kremenitzer, J. P., with Maurer, M., Carpenter, M., Rivers, S. E., & Elbertson, N. A. (Eds.). (2011). *Creating emotionally literate classrooms: An introduction to the RULER approach to social and emotional learning.* National Professional Resources.

Bronfenbrenner, U. (1979). *The ecology of human development: Experiments by nature and design.* Cambridge, MA: Harvard University Press.

Bronfenbrenner, U., & Morris, P. (2006). The bioecological model of human development. In R. M. Lerner & W. Damon (Eds.), *Handbook of child psychology: Theoretical models of human development* (6th ed., Vol. 1, pp. 793–828). New York: John Wiley.

CASEL (Collaborative for Academic, Social, and Emotional Learning). (2003). *Safe and sound: An educational leader's guide to evidence-based social and emotional learning programs.* Illinois edition.

CASEL. (2012). *2013 CASEL guide: Effective social and emotional learning programs: Preschool and elementary school edition.* https://ed.buffalo.edu/content/dam/ed/alberti/docs/CASEL -Guide-SOCIAL-EMOTIONAL-LEARNING.pdf

Castagno, A. E. (2013). Multicultural education and the protection of whiteness. *American Journal of Education, 120*(1), 101–128.

Castro-Olivo, S. M. (2014). Promoting social-emotional learning in adolescent Latino ELLs: A study of the culturally adapted Strong Teens program. *School Psychology Quarterly, 29*(4), 567–577. https://doi.org/10.1037/spq0000055

Cherng, H. Y. S., & Halpin, P. F. (2016). The importance of minority teachers: Student perceptions of minority versus white teachers. *Educational Researcher, 45*(7), 407–420. https:// doi.org/10.3102/0013189X16671718

Cipriano, C., Naples, L. H., Zieher, A., Durlak, J., Eveleigh, A., Funaro, M., Strambler, M., Ponnock, A., McCarthy, M. F., & Chow, J. (2021). The state of evidence for social and emotional learning: A contemporary meta-analysis of universal school-based SEL interventions. *Child Development.* https://osf.io/r246m

Cipriano, C., Schlichtmann, G., Riley, J., Naples, L., & Eveleigh, A. (In press). Supporting transformative SEL implementation with a collaboratory for equity and inclusion. In K. Schonert-Reichl, M. Strambler, & S. Rimm-Kaufman (Eds.), *Social and emotional learning in action: Creating systemic change in schools.* New York: Guilford.

Common Core State Standards Initiative (CCSSI). (2010). *National Governors Association Center for Best Practices and Council of Chief State School Officers.* http://www.corestandards .org/assets/CCSSI_Math%20Standards.pdf.

Cruz-Gonzalez, M., Shrout, P. E., Alvarez, K., Hostetter, I., & Alegría, M. (2021). Measurement invariance of screening measures of anxiety, depression, and level of functioning in a US sample of minority older adults assessed in four languages. *Frontiers in Psychiatry, 12,* 129. https://doi.org/10.3389/fpsyt.2021.579173

Denham, S. A. (1998). *Emotional development in young children.* Guilford.

Denham, S. A., & Weissberg, R. P. (2004). Social-emotional learning in early childhood: What we know and where to go from here. In E. Chesebrough, P. King, T. P. Gullotta, & M. Bloom (Eds.), *A blueprint for the promotion of prosocial behavior in early childhood* (pp. 13–50). New York: Kluwer/Plenum.

Domitrovich, C. E., Durlak, J. A., Staley, K. C., & Weissberg, R. P. (2017). Social-emotional competence: An essential factor for promoting positive adjustment and reducing risk in school children. *Child Development, 88*(2), 408–416.

Durlak, J. A., Weissberg, R. P., Dymnicki, A. B., Taylor, R. D., & Schellinger, K. B. (2011). The impact of enhancing students' social and emotional learning: A meta-analysis of school-based universal interventions. *Child Development, 82*(1), 405–432. https://doi.org/10.1111/j.1467-8624.2010.01564.x

Durlak, J. A., & Wells, A. M. (1997). Primary prevention mental health programs for children and adolescents: A meta-analytic review. *American Journal of Community Psychology, 25,* 115–152.

Elias, M. J., Zins, J. E., Weissberg, R. P., Frey, K. S., Greenberg, M. T., Haynes, N. M., Kessler, R., Schwab-Stone, M. E., & Shriver, T. P. (1997). *Promoting social and emotional learning: Guidelines for educators.* Association for Supervision and Curriculum Development.

Federal Bureau of Investigation. (2021, October 25). *FBI releases updated 2020 hate crime statistics* [Press release]. https://www.fbi.gov/news/pressrel/press-releases/fbi-releases-updated-2020-hate-crime-statistics

Gillborn, D. (2008). *Racism and education: Coincidence or conspiracy?* New York: Routledge.

Greenberg, M. T., Weissberg, R. P., O'Brien, M. U., Zins, J. E., Fredericks, L., Resnik, H., & Elias, M. J. (2003). Enhancing school-based prevention and youth development through coordinated social, emotional, and academic learning. *American Psychologist, 58*(6), 466–474.

Gueldner, B. A., Feuerborn, L. L., & Merrell, K. W. (2020). *Social and emotional learning in the classroom: Promoting mental health and academic success.* New York: Guilford.

Halberstadt, A. G., Cooke, A. N., Garner, P. W., Hughes, S. A., Oertwig, D., & Neupert, S. D. (2020). Racialized emotion recognition accuracy and anger bias of children's faces. *Emotion, 22*(3), 403–417. Advance online publication. https://doi.org/10.1037/emo0000756

Hoffman, D. M. (2009). How (not) to feel: Culture and the politics of emotion in the American parenting advice literature. *Discourse: Studies in the Cultural Politics of Education, 30*(1), 15–31. https://doi.org/10.1080/01596300802643058

Hussar, B., Zhang, J., Hein, S., Wang, K., Roberts, A., Cui, J., Smith, M., Mann, F. B., Barmer, A., & Dilig, R. (2020). *The condition of education 2020.* NCES 2020-144. National Center for Education Statistics. US Department of Education.

Jagers, R. J., Rivas-Drake, D., & Borowski, T. (2018). *Equity & social and emotional learning: A cultural analysis.* CASEL Assessment Work Group Brief series.

Jagers, R. J., Rivas-Drake, D., & Williams, B. (2019). Transformative social and emotional learning (SEL): Toward SEL in service of educational equity and excellence. *Educational Psychologist, 54*(3), 162–184. https://doi.org/10.1080/00461520.2019.1623032

Johnston, H. (2012). The Spiral Curriculum. Research into Practice. *Education Partnerships, Inc.*

Kövecses, Z. (2003). *Metaphor and emotion: Language, culture, and body in human feeling.* Cambridge, UK: Cambridge University Press.

Kress, J. S., & Elias, M. J. (2006). School-based social and emotional learning programs. In K. A. Renninger & I. E. Sigel (Eds.), *Handbook of child psychology* (6th ed., Vol. 4, pp. 592–618). New York: Wiley.

Lee, L. (2019, November 26). Lacking training, teachers develop their own SEL solutions. *Edutopia.* https://www.edutopia.org/article/lacking-training-teachers-develop-their-own-sel-solutions

Mahoney, J. L., Weissberg, R. P., Greenberg, M. T., Dusenbury, L., Jagers, R. J., Niemi, K., Schlinger, M., Schlund, J., Shriver, T. P., VanAusdal, K., & Yoder, N. (2021). Systemic social and emotional learning. *American Psychologist, 76*(7), 1128–1142. https://pubmed.ncbi.nlm.nih.gov/33030926/

Maurer, M., Brackett, M. A., & Plain, F. (2004). *Emotional literacy in the middle school: A 6-step program to promote social, emotional, and academic learning.* National Professional Resources/Dude.

Mayer, J. D., & Salovey, P. (1997). What is emotional intelligence? In P. Salovey and D. J. Sluyter (Eds.), *Emotional development and emotional intelligence: Educational implications* (pp. 3–34). New York: Basic. https://psycnet.apa.org/record/1997-08644-001

Meissner, C. A., & Brigham, J. C. (2001). Thirty years of investigating the own-race bias in memory for faces: A meta-analytic review. *Psychology, Public Policy, and Law, 7*(1), 3–35. https://doi.org/10.1037/1076-8971.7.1.3

Michalec, P., & Wilson, J. L. (2021). Truth hidden in plain sight: How social-emotional learning empowers novice teachers' culturally responsive pedagogy in Title I schools. *Journal of Education.* https://doi.org/10.1177/0022057421991866

Patall, E. A., Cooper, H., & Wynn, S. R. (2010). The effectiveness and relative importance of choice in the classroom. *Journal of Educational Psychology, 102*(4), 896. https://doi.org/10.1037/a0019545

Pianta, R. C., Hamre, B. K., & Allen, J. P. (2012). Teacher-student relationships and engagement: Conceptualizing, measuring, and improving the capacity of classroom interactions. In S. Christenson, A. Reschly, & C. Wylie (Eds.), *Handbook of research on student engagement* (pp. 365–386). Boston, MA: Springer. https://doi.org/10.1007/978-1-4614-2018-7_17

Quinn, D. M. (2021). How to reduce racial bias in grading: New research supports a simple, low-cost teaching tool. *Education Next, 21*(1), 72–78.

Radhakrishnan, L., Leeb, R. T., Bitsko, R. H., et al. (2022, February 25). Pediatric emergency department visits associated with mental health conditions before and during the COVID-19 pandemic—United States, January 2019–January 2022. *Morbidity and Mortal Weekly Report (MMWR), 71*(8), 319–324. https://www.cdc.gov/mmwr/volumes/71/wr/mm7108e2.htm

Rappolt-Schlichtmann, G., Cipriano, C., Robinson K., & Boucher, A. (In press). Universal design for social and emotional learning. In K. R. Harris & S. Robinson (Eds.), *Universal design for learning in the classroom: Practical application* (2nd ed.). New York: Guilford.

Saarni, C. (1999). *The development of emotional competence.* New York: Guilford.

Salovey, P., & Mayer, J. D. (1990). Emotional intelligence. *Imagination, Cognition and Personality, 9*(3), 185–211.

Simonsmeier, B. A., Flaig, M., Deiglmayr, A., Schalk, L., & Schneider, M. (2022). Domain-specific prior knowledge and learning: A meta-analysis. *Educational Psychologist, 57*(1), 31–54. https://doi.org/10.1080/00461520.2021.1939700

Taylor, R. D., Oberle, E., Durlak, J. A., & Weissberg, R. P. (2017). Promoting positive youth development through school-based social and emotional learning interventions: A meta-analysis of follow-up effects. *Child Development, 88*(4), 1156–1171. https://doi .org/10.1111/cdev.12864

Tenenbaum, H. R., & Ruck, M. D. (2007). Are teachers' expectations different for racial minority than for European White students? A meta-analysis. *Journal of Educational Psychology, 99*(2), 253–273. https://doi.org/10.1037/0022-0663.99.2.253

Walker, T. (2022, February 1). Survey: Alarming number of educators may soon leave the profession. *NEA News.* https://www.nea.org/advocating-for-change/new-from-nea/survey -alarming-number-educators-may-soon-leave-profession

Yeager, D. S., Purdie-Vaughns, V., Hooper, S. Y., & Cohen, G. L. (2017). Loss of institutional trust among racial and ethnic minority adolescents: A consequence of procedural injustice and a cause of life-span outcomes. *Child Development, 88*(2), 658–676.

Zins, J. E., Bloodworth, M. R., Weissberg, R. P., & Walberg, H. J. (2007). The scientific base linking social and emotional learning to school success. *Journal of Educational and Psychological Consultation, 17*(2–3), 191–210. https://doi.org/10.1080/10474410701413145

# 9

# Only Systemic Change Will Do

*F. Mike Miles*

Although many of the chapters in this book have already pointed out substantial challenges, this chapter takes a systems-level approach to conceptualizing the future of K-12 education and how to design it for an ever-changing workplace.

The Year 2035 workplace will be fundamentally different from the one that currently exists, and our public education system is not prepared to educate students for that future. The numerous reform efforts over the past two decades have not been able to change the trajectory for significant numbers of students living in poverty.[1] Beyond COVID, the gaps and inequities will be exacerbated by the continual advance of technology and a workplace that requires stronger skills and places a premium on creativity and critical thinking.[2] Even the schools and districts that have heretofore enjoyed strong academic progress now need to rethink what students have to know and do and build teacher capacity to deliver instruction in different ways. Time is against all of us.

We are at a critical nexus in education. The next 10 years will either reinforce the current, largely failed public education system, or we will see the growth of different education systems that will better prepare students for a Year 2035 workplace and world. Because of the renewed interest in addressing inequities and the infusion of much-needed federal and state dollars to address learning loss due to COVID, public education has an opportunity to truly "reimagine education" and change the current trajectory for millions of students. Leaders can learn how to work more systemically and make the bold changes that will significantly improve student achievement and

---

1. See data from the National Assessment of Educational Progress (NAEP) at https://nces.ed.gov. For example, in 2019 (prior to COVID), only 14% of Black students scored "Proficient" in 8th-grade reading; 20 years earlier, 12% of Black students reached the same achievement level.

2. See, for example, Makridis, Hickman, Manning, and Duckworth. (2022). *Earnings Are Greater and Increasing in Occupations That Require Intellectual Tenacity*. SSRN working paper.

performance outcomes *and* help spur innovation to prepare students for a Year 2035 workplace and world.

The key challenge for school districts will be at the system level. If education leaders do not make systemic changes, it is unlikely that they will be able to close the opportunity gap or innovate in ways that will prepare students for the future.

On the whole, district leaders need training on what systemic change means and what it looks like. They should be provided with analyses of the strength of their reform efforts and the degree to which those efforts will result in meaningful and sustained growth.

## IGNORING SYSTEM PRINCIPLES

The current education system and how schools operate has failed to meaningfully narrow achievement gaps.[3] Moreover, in some cases, achievement gaps have increased.[4]

Unfortunately, even school leaders who are "reform minded" usually implement new programs or double down on existing methods in nonsystemic ways. Take, for example, the problem of low teacher salaries and the numerous attempts to change how teachers are compensated. After COVID and using one-time monies from the federal government (ESSER funding), most districts will "reform" their compensation system by giving a larger percentage increase to salaries and provide additional or larger stipends to teachers in hard-to-fill positions. These "larger-than-usual" adjustments to salaries appear every five to six years and are celebrated for a short while, but they do little to change the relative value of entering the teaching profession and have not impacted student achievement outcomes. This is so because the typical salary adjustment is an incremental change to a fundamentally flawed compensation system.

Most businesses undoubtedly would agree with the statement that "no organization can maximize its effectiveness if what it values is disconnected from how it compensates its employees." That statement is also true for any effective organization, including schools. Yet almost all schools and districts base their compensation plan on a "salary schedule" that gives higher salaries for years of experience and college credits but not for student achievement and performance outcomes. Teachers who have taught for 20 years receive a higher salary than those who have taught five years even if the teacher who has taught for five years is able to raise student achievement and the 20-year teacher is not.

And yet, this is not the first time that the flaws inherent in a tenure-based compensation system have been identified. In fact, despite the many known problems with the typical salary schedule and clear—although few—examples of ways to both

---

3. See, for example, Hanushek, Peterson, Talpey, and Woessmann, The Achievement Gap Fails to Close, *Education Next* (Summer 2019, Volume 19).

4. National Center on Education and the Economy, *The Widening Achievement Gap in the U.S.*, http://ncee.org, November 6, 2020.

raise average salaries and get better outcomes, relatively few school systems have moved away from a compensation plan based on years of experience and college credit. No change to the salary schedule will make much difference to student outcomes if the change does not address the underlying systemic principle noted above. Yet, educators are likely to continue these arguments well into the future with no significant change to how teachers are compensated. Why?

The same inability to make systemic change can be said of many recent efforts to address educational inequities brought into stark relief by COVID. Many schools and districts will allocate more money for technology resources and try to balance out various "programs" such as STEM or performance arts among different demographic groups within their school or district. These efforts will help a little, but they will not significantly address the achievement or opportunity gap because they do not address other system principles.

For example, effective organizations prioritize scarce resources. Thus schools should prioritize allocation of highly effective teachers. But most schools and districts do not have an effective system to place their highest performing teachers with their lowest performing students, even though they know that the most important resource—more than any piece of equipment or any program—is an effective teacher. Indeed, the most important action any school or district could take to tackle the inequity in schools is to distribute their highest performing teachers to their lowest performing schools.

If the examples above are obvious in any way, it begs the question as to why schools cannot or will not change in ways to achieve significantly different student outcomes.

## A DIFFERENT SYSTEM

Every system by definition has interconnected parts that together operate in a way that attains a certain result. Further, according to some system thinkers, "every system is perfectly designed to get the results it gets."[5] When it comes to schools, the concept fits too: we have been using the same education system for decades and have been getting the same achievement outcomes. Yes, successes have come here and there with varying aspects of the education system over the past couple of decades, but on the whole the education system has not changed. As a result, the outcomes have been stagnant at best and deteriorating at worst since the early 1980s.

Not much has changed in the way schools operate since then. The school calendar, the way teachers are paid, the brick-and-mortar base, the graduation requirements, what we want students to learn, and so on, are largely identical to the 1980s. This presents another reason why current school systems have failed:

---

5. Dr. Paul Batalden, professor emeritus of the Dartmouth Institute, is given credit for this quotation. However, the quotation's origin is in dispute, with Edwards Deming of the Deming Institute also being credited with creating it.

the system has not changed even though the context and purpose of schools have changed. Technological advances and cultural shifts have changed what the workplace looks like and what skills and competencies are needed for the future workplace and world. But schools and districts continue to tweak the parts of the old system even though those minor adjustments will not achieve outcomes that a changing world and workplace call for.

Districts are operating like Blockbuster in the late 1990s. Blockbuster doubled down on its model and practices and failed to change even though it was obvious by the year 2000 that the future would push demand for videos online. Most school systems are "Blockbusters," refusing to make systemic changes.

In the end, if every system is perfectly designed to get the outcomes it gets, then we need to build a different system to get different results.


## KEY OBSTACLES TO SYSTEMIC CHANGE

Although systemic change is necessary, most school and district leaders have reasons why they do not undertake transformation and settle instead on incremental changes to the current system. A few of those reasons are outlined below.


### The Navarré Point

In the human body (and other multicellular organisms) some cells, which are "mini-systems," undergo the process of apoptosis or programmed cell death. Cell apoptosis occurs when the cell's purpose has been fulfilled, such as in embryonic development or when the cell has been damaged or needs to be replaced with newer cells. From a systems lens, it appears that the cells undergoing apoptosis recognize when their "system" is no longer serving its original purpose or when its dysfunction may harm the larger body.

Analogously, school systems should also recognize when the system is no longer getting the outcomes it needs or when it is dysfunctional. Of course, no one is suggesting that schools or districts "self-destruct" but, rather, undertake systemic reform. Unfortunately, in education no mechanism typically signals the need for transformation and forces renewal. Indeed, it appears that the opposite phenomenon occurs in schools and probably most organizations. Instead of making critical, systemic changes, most school and district organizations continue to operate in traditional ways, allowing long-standing, enduring problems to continue.

These organizations have reached what this author calls the "Navarré Point": when the system's original purpose or outcomes lose importance, giving way to a stronger impulse to protect collective self-interests or maintain current system processes regardless of outcomes. Schools that have reached the Navarré Point will not implement a new evaluation system if it means that current teachers will receive a lower evaluation score (even if the lower score is more accurate or warranted). They will be loath to change the salary schedule, hold people accountable for student outcomes, cut programs that have not produced expected results, or distribute more effective teachers to lower performing groups of students. In these cases, people employed in or by the old system are strongly invested in the current way of doing things and feel that a change threatens their self-interests.

It is important to note that nothing inherently is wrong with people trying to preserve what they have invested in or protect their interests. But leaders need to recognize when their organization has reached that point and then place a premium on outcomes and the overarching interests of the students. If starting a transformation effort, they also need to understand that the Navarré Point concept will be one of the major obstacles to their efforts.

## Other Obstacles

Even if education leaders recognize that they need to make fundamental changes, the challenges are daunting and can be costly. Besides the Navarré Point, transformative school and district leaders will also face these obstacles:

### Constraints of an Interconnected System

Systemic change is difficult because, by definition, the parts of the system are interdependent. Changing one important part of the system usually necessitates changing other parts in significant ways. Take, for example, trying to change the way teachers are evaluated. Developing a more rigorous and fair evaluation system probably would require more instructional support for teachers. One probably would have to provide additional instructional feedback, offer different professional development, train administrators, and adjust the administrator evaluation system, adjust human resources policies, revise the teacher recruitment process, create a new data collection and evaluation platform, and possibly adjust significant parts of the compensation plan.

### Status Quo Bias

Any real change to the system will have to overcome status quo bias, the inertia in the system to continue to stay on its present path. Every past program, process, or initiative has concomitant processes and procedures that people have gotten used to and have integrated into their work or routine. Having been through numerous program changes and various nonsystemic initiatives, educators often believe that change makes little difference in the outcomes and thus resist what appears to be change for its own sake. The onus is on the change agent to show that the effect of the change will enable the organization to reach improved or different outcomes.

*Risk Aversion*

Systemic change is complex, difficult, and fraught with risks. The benefits for students may be huge, but the potential costs to leaders may be enormous. If nothing else, systemic change undoubtedly will prompt vocal criticism and social media "craziness." As the current system has little accountability for outcomes, school and district leaders often can advance in their careers by simply "going along to get along." Tackling systemic change, conversely, requires courage and a willingness to act at the risk of negatively affecting one's career.

*Failure to Assess the Future*

Finally, systemic change is rarely undertaken because of the inability or unwillingness of leaders to adequately assess the future and outline the outcomes the system should attain to prepare students and teachers for that future. No one can predict the future, but leaders must do (or obtain) the research and analysis to assess trends and the changing cultural and work landscape. Few leaders in the traditional system are willing to put any stakes in the ground as to what the future will hold for our students or current operations. Thus, schools continue to operate the way they have always operated despite the changing context, just as Blockbuster did. But if schools and districts do not tie their actions to a likely future, then any path forward will do. And that path forward is likely to be the one they have always been on.

A school system can make many mistakes, the majority of them not fatal. Instead, school systems fail because they do not adhere to system principles or implement changes in systemic ways. The obstacles are daunting, and the status quo has the overwhelming advantage. There is a reason why the needle on student achievement has hardly moved in the past 20 years despite the attention that No Child Left Behind and Race to the Top efforts placed on education: we are making incremental changes to an outdated system, but collectively we do not have the capacity or the will to fundamentally change it.

Can public education change? Is there a way to make fundamental changes to a system while not bringing it to a complete stop and starting over from scratch? Yes.

We must start by educating a new generation of leaders to think and work systemically. Changing the entire district system in fundamental ways may be too much to ask of most education leaders and politicians, but changing key parts of the system and working in systemic ways is doable and necessary to develop an education system that will significantly narrow achievement gaps and prepare students for a Year 2035 workplace and world.

## HOW TO CHANGE THE SYSTEM

Real system change begins with the big ideas and core concepts. An organization can lay the groundwork for systemic change by taking five steps.

The first step is for leaders to assess their organization's alignment with key principles and operating concepts that will enable it to work effectively to accomplish challenging goals.

At its core, an effective system is founded on key principles, adherence to which will enable an organization to accomplish challenging goals tied to an inspiring vision. Although these principles may vary depending upon the goals and vision, most educational organizations should have similar principles (as their goals and vision are usually similar). And every school district is adhering to some group of principles, either purposely identified or aligned with the vision and mission of the district.

An organization's operating principles ultimately manifest themselves in policy and behaviors. Imagine the difference in operations with a district that

- adheres to a principle of accountability for outcomes versus accountability for process or compliance requirements;
- believes that compensation should be tied to what the system values most versus years of experience;
- prioritizes the provision of resources to student academic needs versus providing relatively equal per pupil funding; and
- follows the principle that unsatisfactory and ineffective teachers should be removed versus one that adheres to a principle of protecting employees from removal despite the academic harm to children.

For the truly innovative, imagine the difference in how schools would have to operate if districts rigorously aligned their organizational operations and behaviors to the following principles:

- Learning should be increasingly focused on how to think and how to learn (versus "what" to learn and think).
- Learning should happen everywhere and anytime.
- School governance should be designed with three arms (branches) that check and balance one another.

Review also the principles of an innovative charter network and imagine the types of school actions and behaviors that would be evident if the schools were designed around those principles.

It may be too much to ask of any traditional district to embrace the latter examples, but the first several listed above (and there are others) are important for any district to consider. Further, it is highly unlikely that any district currently struggling academically will change its situation dramatically without adherence to several of the principles that form the foundation for most effective organizations.

If nothing else, districts should understand and identify the existing principles—stated and unstated—that undergird their organization and account for the operational behaviors and actions. Some will not have the capacity or strict objectivity to conduct a review of their system. Independent education organizations will have to help.

# EIGHT PRINCIPLES OF A NEW EDUCATION SYSTEM

## Learning Happens Everywhere and Anytime

In the new education system, learning happens everywhere. Education instruction and services are brought closer to students (to their communities and homes). When and where students learn is also much more variable and tied to student needs and interests.

## Learning Is Personalized, and Students Own Their Learning

We need an education system that shifts the focus from what schools require to what families demand. Ownership of student learning belongs to the student. Individual learning plans are tied to more than academic needs and include support for the growth of the whole child and his social-emotional needs.

## Parents Have Access to an Expanded Number of Choices of Schools and Programs

Parents are aware of and have access to an expanded number of choices of schools and programs. The system is designed to respond to the needs of families.

## The System Offers a New Employee Value Proposition, and Compensation Is Tied to What the System Values Most

Compensation is tied to what the organization values. Time to innovate and to make improvements to the system are built into employees' worktime. Jobs and career paths across the system are reimagined. The leaders and distinguished employees of the system determine minimum qualifications and competencies required for employment and bear the responsibility for growing the abilities of their employees at all levels.

## Learning Increasingly Is Focused on How to Think and How to Learn

What students need to know and do increasingly is focused on "how to think" and the competencies needed for a Year 2035 workplace and society. Students also learn how to learn. Those who govern the system adjust what students need to learn based on changing workforce requirements, community interests, and societal changes.

## The School, Community, and Family Provide Students With a Set of Required Experiences, Not Just Specific Courses

The education system not only provides students instruction in core subjects but also is designed to provide students key, relevant experiences that add to their understanding of their interests, varying perspectives, and the world.

## Community Groups Are Tapped to Educate Students in Many Non-Core Subjects

Community groups bear the responsibility for educating students in many non-core subjects.

## Governing Entities Check and Balance One Another and Encourage Innovation

The new education system uses a governance model that ensures that those who establish policies do not also operate the system's schools, departments, or functions. Governing bodies in the new system are charged with aligning the system to the principles and continuous innovation.

Effective organizations pay attention to the changing context and the future. The second step is to research and analyze trends that describe a likely future and then assess its impact on the work that the school or district is doing. This exercise does not have to be too elaborate, but one's description of what students need to know and be able to do in 2035 needs to be informed by experts, including businesspeople. Again, if one does not tie key goals and priorities to a likely future, then any path forward will do. And that path most likely will be the one the school or district has always been on.

Once a vision of future workplace competencies and skills is created, it is likely that that vision will suggest changes that need to be made and actions that need to be taken to ensure that students eventually can be successful. It is unlikely that the conduct of this exercise will result in most educators believing a district's current priorities and actions will meet the needs of a 2035 workplace and world.

In the third step, outline the outcomes and intermediate goals that the district or school will hold itself accountable for achieving to prepare students for the future described in the second step. Then identify how the current school or district will have to operate differently—how the system will have to change—to be able to accomplish those outcomes and goals. The third step should be done without regard to the current or self-imposed constraints.

The fourth step is to create and implement a new system in the school or in part of the district. The unit of change must be the entire school or a group of schools. It cannot be one part of the school or an incremental change; otherwise, momentum will not reach the inflection point that is needed, namely because:

- *Innovation or change to any system will be constrained by the other parts of the system upon which it is dependent or interconnected.* A failure to address the interdependence in a purposeful way will lead to inefficiency and ineffectiveness.
- *An incremental change to one part of a complex system will not be systemic and will have minimal positive impact on outcomes.* Indeed, such a change may just perpetuate inefficiencies or dysfunction in the rest of the system.

For any existing district or network of schools with more than a handful of schools, the best strategy for implementing systemic change may be a combination of the "split screen" approach, written by Ted Kolderie, and the "proof point" strategy.[6] Using a split-screen strategy, a district would not attempt to make systemic changes district-wide but would implement transformative changes in a part of the district while continue to make incremental improvements in the rest of the district. Once the schools operating on the new system principles achieve the outcomes and succeed, they will become proof points to allow the district to implement systemic change in even more schools over a period of time.

The fifth step is to mitigate the Navarré Point and other obstacles, and it is done iteratively with the fourth step. Systemic change will impact people's interests—some positively and some negatively. But systemic change will be more palatable and more effective if leaders take into account Navarré Point effects and try to mitigate the negative consequences. For example, in 2013 the Dallas Independent School District implemented a rigorous pay-for-performance system that fundamentally changed how teachers were evaluated and compensated. Knowing that teachers in the existing system would strongly try to protect their current salaries, the district's plan included provisions that no teacher's salary would ever go below current earnings regardless of performance.[7]

Another example would be to devise plans that include a "self-destruct" or planned ending point for certain programs or initiatives. The onus then would be on the leaders to justify why a change should be continued rather than the change continuing by default.

Perhaps the best example of mitigating Navarré Point effects can be found in the governance bylaws of Third Future Schools (TFS), a small network of charter schools that operate in Colorado and Texas. In their system, the Network's Council, comprising five independent members, may require the CEO and board to spend up to 5% of the budget on innovation as the council defines it. This unique power exists because the authors of the bylaws understood that one day the leaders of Third Future Schools may be so invested in the network's model and system that they may fail to recognize their own Navarré Point and fail to make substantive changes even though a future context may require them.

---

6. Ted Kolderie, *The Split Screen Strategy: How to Turn Education into a Self-improving System.* St. Paul, MN: Beaver's Pond Press, 2015.

7. Former Dallas Superintendent Mike Miles designed the pay-for-performance system in 2013. See his concept papers titled *Teacher Excellence Initiative Overview*, September 2013, and *Teacher Excellence Initiative: Strategic Compensation*, September 2013.

# AT THE OPERATIONAL LEVEL

Working systemically means operating or implementing key actions in ways that address the interdependent functions of the organization. Given the many immediate operational challenges school leaders face day-to-day, concepts such as "vision" and "system principles" usually are reserved for retreats and book studies. To be sure, systems thinking is not something most educators are trained on or pay attention to. Many find it hard to align an action plan or improvement plan with core principles. Others, having spent entire careers in the current system, find it difficult to imagine another way to operate or have no experience with alignment to a different set of principles.

At the operational level, then, it may be helpful to outline key "look fors" to determine whether a district's changes or reform initiatives will be implemented systemically and thus have a better chance of being successful over the long run. (See also rubric on pages 207–212.)

The following five areas are basic components for "nascent and progressing" systems that can be assessed in a system review.

## A Focus on Outcomes

Do clear performance and achievement outcomes for the employees at every level describe what success looks like? Is every new initiative or significant increase in expenditures tied to measurable results?

To what degree is the success of the organization tied to compliance measures versus outcomes?

Do leaders understand and make a distinction between implementing a process or program versus outcomes for performance or achievement?

## Alignment Throughout the Organization

Do the goals and key actions of the schools and district-level departments reflect and support the district's key actions and performance metrics? Is there a District Action Plan that drives the work of the district and the major actions of the schools? Are the key district actions tied to the success of the schools, and does success at the school and department levels ensure goal attainment at the district level?

## Accountability

To what degree is there accountability for effective performance and outcomes at all levels? What are the consequences of accountability? If the consequence of poor performance is a weaker evaluation that does not mean anything practically, then there is no accountability for poor performance. To what extent does the accountability algorithm call for collective accountability and individual accountability?

## Support

To what degree are teachers and implementers of initiatives provided relevant and effective support, including professional development, on-the-job coaching, resources, and so forth? Is the support aligned with the evaluation system and performance outcomes?

## Monitoring Progress

Does the district have a process or method to monitor the system for continuous improvement?

More "proficient" organizations address the components outlined above and also address the following issues.

## Budget Priorities

Does the budget align with the system principles and the key actions? Are the budget and resources prioritized and differentiated based on student needs?

## Compensation and Incentives

Is there close alignment between what the organization values and how it compensates its employees? Does the organization incentivize the behaviors most closely aligned with the goals and outcomes that have been outlined and that will lead to success?

## Capacity

Does the system have a clearly articulated plan to grow staff capacity to accomplish the goals? Are professional development and coaching tightly aligned with the evaluation system?

## Leadership Density

Does the organization invest in the development of leaders at multiple levels? Is there a purposeful plan to grow leadership density?

For more "advanced" organizations:

## System Principles

Are fundamental system principles identified, and are the behaviors and way of operating aligned with those principles?

## Vision for the Future

Is there a vision for the district, and are the key actions and behaviors aligned with that vision? Does the vision paint a picture of the future and what success looks like in that future?

## The Pace of Change

Do leaders determine the pace of change based on relevant variables such as the urgency of the situation, the capacity of the staff and current leadership team, the maturity of the processes already in place, and the degree to which the culture is high performing?

## Adaptability

Is the system purposely designed to continue to adapt and innovate?

## A Model for Systemic Reform

Does the district use a systems model to help align the work and make the various key actions more cohesive?

## THE PACE OF CHANGE

First, we need to address the pace of change or the speed with which we should bring about reform. Our profession is fond of saying that leaders need to "go slow to go fast." In many cases, where districts are looking for minor and continuous improvement, this strategy makes sense. As a blanket rule, however, that strategy is very problematic.

For districts seeking transformational impact, decision makers should determine the pace of change based on

- the urgency of the situation,
- the capacity of the staff and current leadership team,
- the maturity of the processes already in place, and
- the degree to which the culture is high performing.

The most important of those variables is the urgency of the situation in which the district or network finds itself. Struggling schools needs to approach reform with a clear sense of urgency, and our leaders not only need to understand and believe that the situation is urgent but must also convince the staff and community of that. Fifty million students are currently in America's schools. At our current pace of improvement, more than half of those students will reach the Year 2030 unable to read or do math at the proficient level. And as pointed out elsewhere in this chapter, the growing strength of artificial intelligence and technological advances will most likely worsen the traditional achievement gap or create a new gap—a Year 2030 competencies gap. This will be so unless we have the courage to do something drastically different.

Third Future Schools can reimagine education in fundamental ways in a relatively short period of time if it

- makes a case for urgency and inspires people with a vision to meet the challenge;
- works systemically, understanding how the key system components fit together and addressing the leverage points in each area first;
- drafts effective reform plans that are challenging, make sense, and have a strong chance of success if implemented well; and
- develops a high-performance culture that can implement effectively and holds itself accountable for challenging performance outcomes.

## REIMAGINED SCHOOLS?

Over the past year, during the pandemic, many education leaders talked about returning to reimagined schools. The pandemic revealed already extant inequities in the system, and addressing these inequities post-COVID gained new advocates. As noted in the introduction to this book, student outcomes were already deteriorating, and the public education system before the pandemic was not working well. Many agreed that if districts returned to "normal," they would miss an opportunity to innovate or at least make long-overdue changes. But only systemic change will truly lead to significantly different outcomes. Incremental or programmatic changes will simply return the current system to "normal," with enduring challenges frustrating yet another group of education leaders.

Although most of the ideas in this chapter are "high-level" or conceptual, school or district leaders can take specific steps to operate systemically or to think through a "split screen" strategy. The System Review Rubric on the following pages will help leaders assess the degree to which they are working systemically and the strength of their underlying system principles. At a minimum, the rubric provides educators at all levels a template to figure out what questions to ask and to vet ideas to determine how they will impact substantive change. Simply going through the rubric will be beneficial, helping leaders think more systemically and keeping them open to transformation. Ideally, it will help a design team think through system principles and the operational path forward for a school or district trying to prepare students for a Year 2035 workplace and world.

The following is a "minimum criteria" rubric. A school or district operating at the Nascent system (table 9.1) level must meet the characteristics or criteria outlined below for that beginning level. An organization operating at the next higher level, Progressing (table 9.2) must meet the criteria of the Nascent level and the minimum criteria of the Progressing level. The Proficient (table 9.3) and Advanced levels (table 9.4) follow the same pattern. Note that the Proficient and Advanced levels address additional system components.

**Table 9.1. Nascent Level**

| System Component | Characteristics | Notes |
|---|---|---|
| A focus on outcomes | • Clear and specific performance and achievement outcomes are identified.<br>• Key actions, new initiatives, and significant increases in expenditures are tied to measurable results.<br>• Key actions to accomplish the outcomes are articulated.<br>• Indicators of success and specific metrics are outlined.<br><br>➢ The metrics and outcomes are closely aligned.<br>➢ Attaining the outlined metrics ensures attainment of the performance or achievement outcome. | • Every major initiative, program, area of focus, key action, or significant expenditure should be tied to clear outcomes and metrics that describe success.<br>• The district should focus on approximately five to six significant overarching outcomes. |
| Alignment throughout the organization | ➢ The outcomes and key actions of the district are aligned throughout the organization.<br>➢ The outcomes and key actions of the schools and district-level departments reflect and support the district's outcomes and key actions.<br>➢ District key actions are tied to the success of the schools, and success at the school and department levels ensure goal attainment at the district level. | • The District Action Plan is the operational document that drives the work of the district and the major actions of the schools.<br>• The District Action Plan must be developed prior to the School Action Plans (or school improvement plans) in order for the two to be aligned.<br>• Alignment of major goals and key actions is not mutually exclusive of differentiated needs, targeted support, or autonomy for some actions. |
| Accountability for achievement and performance | • The person or persons responsible for accomplishing each key action are identified. | |
| Support | • All key actions are purposely tied to relevant and effective support, including professional development, relevant resources, on-the-job coaching, technical assistance, and so forth. | • Accountability without support breeds a climate of fear. |

**Table 9.2. Progressing Level**

| System Component | Characteristics | Notes |
|---|---|---|
| Focus on outcomes | • Most goals and outcomes address the key functions and purpose of the organizations.<br>• Key actions include ones to improve the quality of instruction. | • Outcomes and key actions address the variables that matter most to the district's success and vision. |
| Alignment throughout the organization | • Outcomes and metrics are aligned with the person or department's purpose and responsibilities.<br>• Roles and responsibilities and division of labor are clearly defined; however, processes are in place to ensure close coordination between individuals and departments. | • Lines of decision making should reflect the levels of responsibility. |
| Accountability for achievement and performance | • There is both group and individual accountability for achievement and performance metrics.<br>• Reasonable consequences are identified for failing to meet performance or achievement outcomes (and incentives or rewards for meeting challenging goals). | • At a minimum, success or failure should impact a person's evaluation.<br>• Each system must develop reasonable consequences based on its own context; however, without accountability there are no consequences (and organizations should not pretend that there is accountability just because they say there is).<br>• Leaders should have the most accountability, but everyone whose actions directly (and in some cases, indirectly) contribute to the success or failure of a performance metric should receive the relevant and proportional consequence. |
| Support | • Purposeful and effective support is provided for every metric for which someone is being held accountable. | |
| Monitoring progress | • Data and objective information are used to monitor progress of individuals and departments in meeting the goals and outcomes.<br>• Processes are in place to gather and analyze data from monitoring progress, and that information is used by individuals and departments to make midcourse corrections and to work more effectively. | • Information from monitoring progress should be provided at least quarterly. |

**Table 9.3. Proficient Level**

| System Component | Characteristics | Notes |
|---|---|---|
| Budget priorities | • The identified priorities for the district (and schools) are reflected in the budget.<br><br>  ➤ The district and school action plans are designed based on goals and outcomes and the concomitant needs assessment.<br><br>• The budget development process ensures alignment with the instructional and operational priorities.<br><br>  ➤ The district uses a process whereby department and school budgets vary annually depending on the priorities and key actions outlined for the year (such as a modified zero-based budgeting process).<br><br>• Budget allocations generally reflect the needs of various groups of students and are therefore differentiated. | • This requires the district to identify priorities and key actions prior to drafting the budget.<br>• One way to allocate funds based on student needs is to use a weighted formula (and not a strict per-pupil formula). |
| Compensation and incentives | • Employees are compensated for behaviors and outcomes that the system values most.<br><br>  ➤ The compensation plan is aligned with the evaluation system and what the organization values most.<br><br>• The organization provides incentives or rewards that encourage people to meet the wanted performance and achievement outcomes.<br><br>  ➤ Incentives or rewards are purposely designed to help the system achieve the outcomes it values most. | • No organization can maximize its effectiveness if what it values is disconnected from how it compensates its employees.<br>• Evaluation systems can be incentive based, pay-for-performance, differentiated salary levels based on proven competencies, and so forth. |

(continued)

**Table 9.3.** (*Continued*)

| System Component | Characteristics | Notes |
|---|---|---|
| Capacity | • The organization has a clearly articulated plan to grow staff capacity to accomplish the goals.<br>• Professional development and coaching are tightly aligned with the evaluation system.<br><br>➤ School leaders provide real-time feedback and coaching to continuously improve staff capacity. | • The most effective way to improve staff capacity is to provide on-the-job coaching and to build a culture of instructional feedback. |
| Leadership density | • The organization invests in the development of leaders at multiple levels.<br><br>➤ A purposeful plan is in place to grow leadership density.<br><br>• Teacher and administrator "leadership" is assessed in the evaluation system.<br><br>➤ Employees are trained in the specific leadership characteristics the organization expects.<br><br>• The organization provides leadership opportunities to those who want to improve their leadership competencies. | • The greater the leadership density, the more the organization will adhere to the core beliefs and create a high-performance culture. |

**Table 9.4. Advanced Level**

| System Component | Characteristics | Notes |
|---|---|---|
| System principles | • Fundamental system principles are identified.<br><br>  ➢ The organization adopts principles that align with its vision and mission.<br><br>• The organization develops and follows operational principles that are aligned with the overarching system principles. | • Every system operates on a set of principles and beliefs that guide behavior and actions.<br>• It is important to identify those that are helpful to accomplishing challenging goals and those that present barriers.<br>• The system cannot change significantly (and thus the outcomes will not change significantly) if the underlying principles do not change. |
| Actionable vision of the future | • The organization has a clear vision, and the key actions and behaviors are aligned with that vision.<br><br>  ➢ The vision paints a picture of the future and what success looks like in that future.<br><br>• The organization makes changes to its system and to the way it operates based on its vision. | • If leaders do not put stakes in the ground as to what the future holds and where they are trying to go, then any path forward will do. |
| Pace of change | • Leaders determine the pace of change based on relevant variables such as the urgency of the situation, the capacity of the staff and current leadership team, the maturity of the processes already in place, and the degree to which the culture is high performing. | • The notion of "go slow to go fast" may be appropriate in some circumstances, but generally provides even more advantage to the status quo.<br>• Instead, leaders need to go at the necessary pace based on the urgency of the situation, the capacity of the staff and current leadership team, the maturity of the processes already in place, and the degree to which the culture is high performing. |

(*continued*)

**Table 9.4.** **(*Continued*)**

| System Component | Characteristics | Notes |
|---|---|---|
| Innovation and adaptability | • The system is purposely designed to continue to adapt and innovate.<br>• Leaders are aware of the "innovator's dilemma" and are willing to establish goals and realize a vision that may not be assessed by current metrics (but nevertheless have other rigorous metrics by which to measure success). | • For example, in one charter school network, the "Council" may require the expenditure of up to 5% of the budget on innovation as they define it.<br>• If districts are to prepare students for a fundamentally different world or workplace, they must be willing to invest in initiatives or system changes that will help them accomplish some goals that are not currently measured in the accountability framework. |
| Model for systemic reform | • The district uses a systems model to help align the work and make the various key actions more cohesive and more understandable.<br>• The model addresses the system components outlined in this rubric.<br>• The model is not too complex and can be operationalized. | • Most school and district leaders, unfamiliar with working systemically, would benefit from a systems model that can chart a course for them and help guide the work. |

## REFERENCES

Deming, E. (with Cahill, K. E., & Allan, K. L.). (2018). *Out of the crisis.* Cambridge, MA: MIT Press (original work published 1982).

Hanushek, E., Peterson, P., Talpey, L., & Woessmann, L. (2019). The achievement gap fails to close. *Education Next, 19*(3).

Hastings, R., & Meyer, E. (2020). *No rules rules: Netflix and the culture of reinvention.* New York: Penguin.

Kolderie, T. (2015). *The split screen strategy: How to turn education into a self-improving system.* St. Paul, MN: Beaver's Pond.

Makridis, C. A., Hickman, L., Manning, B., & Duckworth, A. L. (2022). *Earnings are greater and increasing in occupations that require intellectual tenacity* (SSRN Working paper).

Miles, F. M. (September 2013a). Teacher Excellence Initiative Concept Paper.

Miles, F. M. (September 2013b). Teacher Excellence Initiative: Strategic Compensation.

Miles, F. M. (Revised June 2021). Third Future Schools Concept Paper.

National Assessment of Educational Progress (NAEP). (n.d.). National Center for Education Statistics. https://www.nagb.gov/naep/about-naep.html

National Center on Education and the Economy. (2020, November 6). The widening achievement gap in the U.S. https://ncee.org

# References

Acemoglu, D., & Restrepo, P. (2018). The race between man and machine: Implications of technology for growth, factor shares, and employment. *American Economic Review, 108*(6), 1488–1542.

Acevedo, P., Cruces, G., Gertler, P., & Martinez, S. (2020). How vocational education made women better off but left men behind. *Labour Economics, 65,* 101824.

ACT. (2015, March 12). *Ready for college and ready for work: Same or different?* ACT study: College and Workforce Training Readiness. https://www.act.org/content/act/en/research /pdfs/ready-for-collegeandreadyforworksameordifferent.html

Adamson, F., & Darling-Hammond, L. (2011). *Speaking of salaries: What it will take to get qualified, effective teachers in all communities.* Center for American Progress.

Adnot, M., Dee, T., Katz, V., & Wyckoff, J. (2017). Teacher turnover, teacher quality, and student achievement in DCPS. *Educational Evaluation and Policy Analysis, 39*(1), 54–76. https://doi.org/10.3102/0162373716663646

Afterschool Alliance. (2016). *America after 3 pm special report: Afterschool in communities of concentrated poverty.* Washington, DC.

Agostinelli, F., Doepke, M., Sorrenti, G., & Zilibotti, F. (2020). *When the great equalizer shuts down: Schools, peers, and parents in pandemic times* (Working Paper No. 28264). National Bureau of Economic Research.

Ainsworth, M. (1967). *Infancy in Uganda.* Baltimore: Johns Hopkins.

Ainsworth, M., & Bowlby, J. (1965). *Childcare and the growth of love.* London: Penguin.

Akerlof, G. A., Yellen, J. L., & Katz, M. L. (1996). An analysis of out-of-wedlock childbearing in the United States. *Quarterly Journal of Economics, 111*(2), 277–317. https://doi .org/10.2307/2946680

Aleven, V., McLaren, B., Roll, I., & Koedinger, K. (2006). Toward meta-cognitive tutoring: A model of help seeking with a cognitive tutor. *International Journal of Artificial Intelligence in Education, 16*(2), 101–128.

Alfonsi, L., Bandiera, O., Bassi, V., Burgess, R., Rasul, I., Sulaiman, M., & Vitali, A. (2020). Tackling youth unemployment: Evidence from a labor market experiment in Uganda. *Econometrica, 88*(6), 2369–2414.

Allegretto, S., & Mishel, L. (2020). *Teacher pay penalty dips but persists in 2019: Public school teachers earn about 20% less in weekly wages than nonteacher college graduates.* Economic Policy Institute. https://www.epi.org/publication/teacher-pay-penalty-dips-but-persists-in-2019-public-school-teachers-earn-about-20-less-in-weekly-wages-than-nonteacher-college-graduates/

Allen, A., Scott, L. A., & Lewis, C. W. (2013). Racial microaggressions and African American and Hispanic students in urban schools: A call for culturally affirming education. *Interdisciplinary Journal of Teaching and Learning, 3*(2), 117–129.

Allensworth, E. (2013). The use of ninth-grade early warning indicators to improve Chicago schools. *Journal of Education for Students Placed at Risk, 18*(1), 68–83.

Almlund, M., Duckworth, A. L., Heckman, J. J., Kautz, T. D. (2011). Personality psychology and economics. In E. Hanushek, S. Machin, & L. Woessmann (Eds.), *Handbook of the economics of education* (Vol. 4, pp. 1–181). Amsterdam: Elsevier.

Amato, P. R. (2005). The impact of family formation change on the cognitive, social, and emotional well-being of the next generation. *Future of Children, 15*(2), 75–96.

Amato, P. R. (2010). Research on divorce: Continuing trends and new developments. *Journal of Marriage and Family, 72*(3), 650–666.

Amato, P. R., & Keith, B. (1991). Consequences of parental divorce for children's well-being: A meta-analysis. *Psychological Bulletin, 10*, 26–46.

American Academy of Pediatrics (2021, October). *AAP-AACAP-CHA Declaration of a national emergency in child and adolescent mental health.* https://www.aap.org/en/advocacy/child-and-adolescent-healthy-mental-development/aap-aacap-cha-declaration-of-a-national-emergency-in-child-and-adolescent-mental-health/

Anderson, D. M. (2014). In school and out of trouble? The minimum dropout age and juvenile crime. *Review of Economics and Statistics, 96*, 318–331.

Anderson, H., Boodhwani, A., & Baker, R. S. (2019). *Assessing the fairness of graduation predictions.* Proceedings of the 12th International Conference on Educational Data Mining, pp. 488–491.

Andres, J. M. L., Baker, R. S., Siemens, G., Gasevic, D., & Spann, C. A. (2017). Replicating 21 findings on student success in online learning. *Technology, Instruction, Cognition, and Learning, 10*(4), 313–333.

Anderson, J. (1982). The historical development of Black vocational education. In H. Kantor & D. B. Tyack (Eds.), *Work, youth and schooling: Historical perspectives on vocational education* (pp. 180–222). Redwood City, CA: Stanford University Press.

Angwin, J., Larson, J., Mattu, S., & Kirchner, L. (2016, May 23). Machine bias: There's software used across the country to predict future criminals. And it's biased against blacks. *ProPublica.* https://www.propublica.org/article/machine-bias-risk-assessments-in-criminal-sentencing

Annamma, S., & Morrison, D. (2018). Identifying dysfunctional education ecologies: A DisCrit analysis of bias in the classroom. *Equity & Excellence in Education, 51*(2), 114–131. https://doi.org/10.1080/10665684.2018.1496047

Apsler, R. (2009). After-school programs for adolescents: A review of evaluation research. *Adolescence, 44*, 1–19.

Aragon, S. (2016). Response to information request on the use of student test scores in teacher evaluations. Education Commission of the States. https://www.ecs.org/wp-content/uploads/Use-of-Student-Test-Scores-in-Teacher-Evaluations.pdf

Arroyo, I., Ferguson, K., Johns, J., Dragon, T., Meheranian, H., Fisher, D., Barto, A., Mahadevan, S., & Woolf, B. P. (2007, June). Repairing disengagement with non-invasive interventions. In *AIED* (Vol. 2007, pp. 195–202).

Artiles, A. J., Dorn, S., & Bal, A. (2016). Objects of protection, enduring nodes of difference: Disability intersections with "other" differences, 1916 to 2016. *Review of Research in Education, 40*(1), 777–820.

Asbell-Clarke, J., Rowe, E., Almeda, V., Edwards, T., Bardar, E., Gasca, S., & Scruggs, R. (2021). The development of students' computational thinking practices in elementary- and middle-school classes using the learning game, *Zoombinis. Computers in Human Behavior, 115*, 106587.

Astone, N. M., & McLanahan, S. S. (1991). Family structure, parental practices, and high school completion. *American Sociological Review, 56*, 309–320.

Ausin, M. S., Maniktala, M., Barnes, T., & Chi, M. (2020, July). *Exploring the impact of simple explanations and agency on batch deep reinforcement learning induced pedagogical policies.* International Conference on Artificial Intelligence in Education, pp. 472–485. Cham: Springer.

Autor, D. H. (2014). Skills, education, and the rise of earnings inequality among the "other 99 percent." *Science, 344*(6186), 843–851.

Autor, D. H., & Dorn, D. (2013). The growth of low-skill service jobs and the polarization of the US labor market. *American Economic Review, 103*(5), 1553–1597.

Axford, N., Bjornstad, G., Matthews, J., Whybra, L., Berry, V., Ukoumunne, O. C., Hobbs, T., Wrigley, Z., Brook, L., Taylor, R., Eames, T., Kallitsoglou, A., Blower, S., & Warner, G. (2021). The effectiveness of a community-based mentoring program for children aged 5–11 years: Results from a randomized controlled trial. *Prevention Science, 22*(1), 100–112.

Bacher-Hicks, A., Kane, T., & Staiger, D. (2014). *Validating teacher effect estimates using changes in teacher assignments in Los Angeles* (Working Paper No. 20657). National Bureau of Economic Research. https://doi.org/10.3386/w20657

Bacolod, M. P. (2007). Do alternative opportunities matter? The role of female labor markets in the decline of teacher quality. *Review of Economics and Statistics, 89*(4), 737–751. https://doi.org/10.1162/rest.89.4.737

Bailey, D. H., Duncan, G. J., Cunha, F., Foorman, B. R., & Yeager, D. S. (2020). Persistence and fade-out of educational-intervention effects: Mechanisms and potential solutions. *Psychological Science in the Public Interest, 21*(2), 55–97.

Bailey, M. J., Sun, S., & Timpe, B. (2021). Prep school for poor kids: The long-run impacts of Head Start on human capital and economic self-sufficiency. *American Economic Review, 111*(12), 3963–4001.

Bajorek, Z. M., & Bevan, S. M. (2015). Performance-related-pay in the UK public sector: A review of the recent evidence on effectiveness and value for money. *Journal of Organizational Effectiveness: People and Performance, 2*(2), 94–109. https://doi.org/10.1108/JOEPP-03-2015-0011

Baker, R. S. (2016). Stupid tutoring systems, intelligent humans. *International Journal of Artificial Intelligence and Education, 26*(2), 600–614.

Baker, R. S., Berning, A., & Gowda, S. M. (2020). Differentiating military-connected and non-military-connected students: Predictors of graduation and SAT score. *EdArXiv.* https://doi.org/10.35542/osf.io/cetxj

Baker, R. S., & Hawn, M. A. (2021). Algorithmic bias in education. *International Journal of Artificial Intelligence and Education.* https://osf.io/pbmvz/download?format=pdf

Baker, R. S., & Rossi, L. M. (2013). Assessing the disengaged behavior of learners. In R. Sottilare, A. Graesser, X. Hu, & H. Holden (Eds.), *Design recommendations for intelligent tutoring systems: Learner modeling* (Vol. 1, pp. 155–166). US Army Research Laboratory. https://www.upenn.edu/learninganalytics/ryanbaker/BakerRossi2013.pdf

Ballou, D., & Springer, M. G. (2015). Using student test scores to measure teacher performance: Some problems in the design and implementation of evaluation systems. *Educational Researcher, 44*(2), 77–86. https://doi.org/10.3102/0013189X15574904

Bardach, L., & Klassen, R. M. (2020). Smart teachers, successful students? A systematic review of the literature on teachers' cognitive abilities and teacher effectiveness. *Educational Research Review, 30*, 100312. https://doi.org/10.1016/j.edurev.2020.100312

Barnard, J., Frangakis, C. E., Hill, J. L., & Rubin, D. B. (2003). Principal stratification approach to broken randomized experiments: A case study of school choice vouchers in New York City. *Journal of the American Statistical Association, 98*(462), 299–323.

Barrera-Osorio, F., Kugler, A. D., & Silliman, M. I. (2020). *Hard and soft skills in vocational training: Experimental evidence from Colombia* (Working Paper No. 257548). National Bureau of Economic Research.

Bartik, T., Herschbein, B., & Lachowska, M. (2016). The merits of universal scholarships: Benefit–cost evidence from the Kalamazoo promise. *Journal of Benefit–Cost Analysis, 7*, 400–433.

Bassen, J., Balaji, B., Schaarschmidt, M., Thille, C., Painter, J., Zimmaro, D., Grimes, A., Fast, E., & Mitchell, J. C. (2020, April). *Reinforcement learning for the adaptive scheduling of educational activities.* Proceedings of the 2020 CHI Conference on Human Factors in Computing Systems, pp. 1–12.

Bayardo, R. J., & Agrawal, R. (2005). *Data privacy through optimal k-anonymization.* Proceedings of the 21st International Conference on Data Engineering (ICDE'05), 217–228.

Bear, G. G., & Watkins, J. M. (2006). Developing self-discipline. In G. G. Bear & K. M. Minke (Eds.), *Children's needs III: Development, prevention, and intervention* (pp. 29–44). National Association of School Psychologists.

Becker, G. S. (1964). *Human capital: A theoretical and empirical analysis with special reference to education.* Chicago: University of Chicago Press.

Becker, G. S. (1981). *A treatise on the family.* Cambridge, MA: Harvard University Press.

Becker, G. S. (1994). *Human capital: A theoretical and empirical analysis with special reference to education* (3rd edition). Chicago: University of Chicago Press.

Becker, H. J., & Epstein, J. L. (1982). Parent involvement: A survey of teacher practices. *Elementary School Journal, 83*(2), 85–102.

Bedrick, J., & Burke, L. (2018). *Surveying Florida scholarship families: Experiences and satisfaction with Florida's tax-credit scholarship program.* EdChoice. https://www.edchoice.org/wp-content/uploads/2018/10/2018-10-Surveying-Florida-Scholarship-Families-byJason-Bedrick-and-Lindsey-Burke.pdf

Bedrick, J., & Tarnowski, E. (2021, August 19). *How big was the year of educational choice?* Education Next. https://www.educationnext.org/how-big-was-the-year-of-educational-choice/

Belfield, C. (2021). *The economic burden of racism from the U.S. education system.* National Education Policy Center.

Belfield, C., Hollands, F., & Levin, H. (2011). *What are the social and economic returns?* Campaign for Educational Equity, Teachers College, Columbia University.

Belfield, C., Clive, R., and Levin, H. M. (Eds.) (2007). *The price we pay: Economic and social consequences of inadequate education.* Brookings Institution Press,

Bergman, P. (2019). Nudging technology use: Descriptive and experimental evidence from school information systems. *Education Finance and Policy, 15*(4), 623–647.

Bernardi, F., & Boertien, D. (2017). Non-intact families and diverging educational destinies: A decomposition analysis for Germany, Italy, the United Kingdom and the United States. *Social Science Research, 63*, 181–191.

Bernardi, F., & Radl, J. (2014). The long-term consequences of parental divorce for children's educational attainment. *Demographic Research, 30*(61), 1653–1680.

Bertocchi, G., & Dimico, A. (2012). The racial gap in education and the legacy of slavery. *Journal of Comparative Economics, 40*(4), 581–595.

Bertrand, M., Mogstad, M., & Mountjoy, J. (2019). *Improving educational pathways to social mobility: Evidence from Norway's "reform 94"* (Working Paper No. 25679). National Bureau of Economic Research.

Betts, A., & Thai, K-P. (2022). *Handbook of research on innovative approaches to early childhood development and school readiness.* Age of Learning.

Betts, J. R., & Tang, Y. E. (2019). The effects of charter schools on student achievement. In M. Berends, R. J. Waddington, & J. Schoenig (Eds.), *School choice at the crossroads: Research perspectives* (pp. 67–89). New York: Routledge.

Bhutta, N., Chang, A. C., Dettling, L. J., & Hsu, J. W. (2020). *Disparities in wealth by race and ethnicity in the 2019 Survey of Consumer Finances.* Board of Governors of the Federal Reserve System. https://doi.org/10.17016/2380-7172.2797

Bifulco, R., Fletcher, J., Oh, S. J., & Ross, S. L. (2014). Do high school peers have persistent effects on college attainment and other life outcomes? *Labour Economics, 29*, 83–90.

Biglan, A., Metzler, C. W., Wirt, R., Ary, D., Noell, J., Ochs, L., French, C., & Hood, D. (1990). Social and behavioral factors associated with high-risk sexual behaviors among adolescents. *Journal of Behavioral Medicine, 13*(3), 245–261.

Birmingham, J., Pechman, E. M., Russell, C. A., & Mielke, M. (2005). *Shared features of high-performing after-school programs: A follow-up to the TASC evaluation.* Policy Studies Associates.

Bischoff, K., & Reardon, S. (2014). Residential segregation by income, 1970–2009. In J. R. Logan (Ed.), *Diversity and disparities: America enters a new century* (pp. 208–233). New York: Russell Sage Foundation. https://www.russellsage.org/sites/all/files/logan/logan_di versity_chapter7.pdf

Bishop, J., & Mane, F. (2004). The impacts of career-technical education on high school labor market success. *Economics of Education Review, 23*(4), 381–402.

Black, S. E., & Lynch, L. M. (2001). How to compete: The impact of workplace practices and information technology on productivity. *Review of Economics and Statistics, 83*(3), 434–445.

Black, S. E., & Lynch, L. M. (2004). What's driving the new economy? The benefits of work-place innovation. *Economic Journal, 114*(493), F97–F116.

Blair, P. Q., Castagnino, T. G., Groshen, E. L., Debroy, P., Auguste, B., Ahmed, S., Diaz, F. G., & Bonavida, C. (2020). *Searching for STARs: Work experience as a job market signal for workers without bachelor's degrees* (Working Paper No. 26844). National Bureau of Economic Research.

Blau, F. D., & Kahn, L. M. (2017). The gender wage gap: Extent, trends, and explanations. *Journal of Economic Literature, 55*(3), 789–865.

Blazar, D. (2021). *Teachers of color, culturally responsive teaching, and student outcomes: Experimental evidence from the random assignment of teachers to classes* (EdWorkingPaper No. 21-501). Annenberg Institute at Brown University. https://doi.org/10.26300/jym0-wz02

Blazar, D., & Lagos, F. (2021). *Professional staff diversity and student outcomes: Extending our understanding of race/ethnicity-matching effects in education* (EdWorkingPaper No. 21-500). Annenberg Institute at Brown University. https://edworkingpapers.com/sites/default/files/ai21-500.pdf

Bleiberg, J., Brunner, E., Harbatkin, E. A., Kraft, M. A., & Springer, M. G. (2021). *The effect of teacher evaluation on achievement and attainment: Evidence from statewide reforms* (EdWorkingPaper No. 21-496). Annenberg Institute at Brown University. https://www.edworkingpapers.com/ai21-496

Bloom, H. S., & Unterman, R. (2014). Can small high schools of choice improve educational prospects for disadvantaged students? *Journal of Policy Analysis and Management, 33*(2), 290–319.

Bloom, H. S., Unterman, R., Zhu, P., & Reardon, S. F. (2020). Lessons from New York City's small schools of choice about high school features that promote graduation for disadvantaged students. *Journal of Policy Analysis and Management, 39*(3), 740–771. https://doi.org/10.1002/pam.22192

Bloome, D. (2017). Childhood family structure and intergenerational income mobility in the United States. *Demography, 54*(2), 541–569.

Boardman, A., Greenberg, D., Vining, A., & Weimer, D. (2018). *Cost–benefit analysis: Concepts and practice* (5th ed.). New York: Cambridge University Press.

Boardman, A. E., Greenberg, D. H., Vining, A. R., & Weimer, D. L. (2020). Efficiency without apology: Consideration of the marginal excess tax burden and distributional impacts in benefit–cost analysis. *Journal of Benefit–Cost Analysis, 11*(3), 457–478.

Boardman, A., & Vining, A. (2017). There are many (well, more than one) paths to nirvana: The economic evaluation of social policies. In B. Greve (Ed.), *Handbook of social policy evaluation* (pp. 77–99). Cheltenham, UK, and Northampton, MA: Edward Elgar.

Bonilla, S. (2020). The dropout effects of career pathways: Evidence from California. *Economics of Education Review, 75*, 101972.

Booker, K., & Glazerman, S. (2009). *Effects of the Missouri career ladder program on teacher mobility.* Mathematica Policy Research. https://www.mathematica.org/publications/effects-of-the-missouri-career-ladder-program-on-teacher-mobility

Bowen, D. H., & Trivitt, J. R. (2014). Stigma without sanctions: The (lack of) impact of private school vouchers on student achievement. *Education Policy Analysis Archives, 22*(87), 1–22.

Bowles, S., & Gintis, H. (1976). *Schooling in capitalist America: Educational reform and the contradictions of economic life.* New York: Basic.

Boyd, D., Grossman, P., Ing, M., Lankford, H., Loeb, S., & Wyckoff, J. (2011). The influence of school administrators on teacher retention decisions. *American Educational Research Journal, 48*(2), 303–333. https://doi.org/10.3102/0002831210380788

Boyer, K. A. M. (2010). *Investigating differences among Asian American youth participating and not participating in grant-funded high school after-school programs* [Doctoral dissertation]. California State University. https://scholarworks.calstate.edu/downloads/ks65hd43b

Brackett, M. A., Bailey, C. S., Hoffmann, J. D., & Simmons, D. N. (2019). RULER: A theory-driven, systemic approach to social, emotional, and academic learning. *Educational Psychologist, 54*(3), 144–161. https://doi.org/10.1080/00461520.2019.1614447

Brackett, M. A., Elbertson, N. A., & Rivers, S. E. (2015). Applying theory to the development of approaches to SEL. In J. A. Durlak, C. E. Domitrovich, R. P. Weissberg, &

T. P. Gullotta (Eds.), *Handbook of social and emotional learning: Research and practice* (pp. 20–32). Guilford.

Brackett, M. A., & Kremenitzer, J. P., with Maurer, M., Carpenter, M., Rivers, S. E., & Elbertson, N. A. (Eds.). (2011). *Creating emotionally literate classrooms: An introduction to the RULER approach to social and emotional learning.* National Professional Resources.

Breton, Theodore. 2010. Schooling and National Income: How Large Are the Externalities? Revised Estimates. *Education Economics, 18*(1): 455–456.

Bridgeman, B., Trapani, C., & Attali, Y. (2012). Comparison of human and machine scoring of essays: Differences by gender, ethnicity, and country. *Applied Measurement in Education, 25*(1), 27–40.

Bristol, T. J., and Fernandez, J. M. (2019). The added value of Latinx and Black teachers for Latinx and Black students: Implications for policy. *Policy Insights from the Behavioral and Brain Sciences, 6*(2), 147–153.

Bronfenbrenner, U. (1979). *The ecology of human development: Experiments by nature and design.* Cambridge, MA: Harvard University Press.

Bronfenbrenner, U., & Morris, P. (2006). The bioecological model of human development. In R. M. Lerner & W. Damon (Eds.), *Handbook of child psychology: Theoretical models of human development* (6th ed., Vol. 1, pp. 793–828). New York: John Wiley.

Brooks, C. D., & Springer, M. G. (2022). Evaluating teacher effectiveness: A review of historical developments and current trends. In B. P. McCall (Ed.), *The Routledge handbook of the economics of education* (p. 127). Abingdon, UK: Routledge, Taylor & Francis Group.

Burgess, S., Propper, C., & Wilson, D. (2007). The impact of school choice in England: Implications from the economic evidence. *Policy Studies, 28*(2), 129–143. https://doi.org/10.1080/01442870701309064

Brunner, E., Dougherty, S., & Ross, S. (2019). *The effects of career and technical education: Evidence from the Connecticut technical high school system* (EdWorkingPaper No. 19-112). Annenberg Institute at Brown University. http://www.edworkingpapers.com/ai19-112

Brynjolfsson, E., & McAfee, A. (2014). *The second machine age: Work, progress, and prosperity in a time of brilliant technologies.* Norton.

Burger, K. (2010). How does early childhood care and education affect cognitive development? An international review of the effects of early interventions for children from different social backgrounds. *Early Childhood Research Quarterly, 25*(2), 140–165.

Burgess, S., & Ratto, M. (2003). The role of incentives in the public sector: Issues and evidence. *Oxford Review of Economic Policy, 19*(2), 285–300. https://doi.org/10.1093/oxrep/19.2.285

Burning Glass Technologies. (2018). Different skills, different gaps: Measuring and closing the skills gap. https://www.economicmodeling.com/2018/03/14/skills-gap-different-skills-different-gaps/

Campbell, B., & Manning, J. (2018). *The rise of victimhood culture: Microaggressions, safe spaces, and the new culture wars.* New York: Palgrave/Macmillan.

Campbell, D. E., Layman, G. C., & Green, J. C. (2021). *Secular surge: A new fault line in American politics.* New York: Cambridge University Press.

Campbell, S. L., & Ronfeldt, M. (2018). Observational evaluation of teachers: Measuring more than we bargained for? *American Educational Research Journal, 55*(6), 1233–1267. https://doi.org/10.3102/0002831218776216

Cantrell, S., & Kane, T. (2013). *Ensuring fair and reliable measures of effective teaching: Culminating findings from the MET Project's three-year study.* Bill and Melinda Gates Foundation.

Carbonaro, W. J. (1998). A little help from my friend's parents: Intergenerational closure and educational outcomes. *Sociology of Education, 71*, 295–313.

Carbone, P. M. (2010). *The effects of an after-school tutoring program on the Pennsylvania System of School Assessment* (Publication No. 3399823) [Doctoral dissertation]. Youngstown State University, Youngstown, OH. ProQuest Dissertations.

Card, D. (2001). Estimating the return to schooling: Progress on some persistent econometric problems. *Econometrica, 69*(5), 1127–1160.

Carnevale, A. P., Strohl, J., Ridley, N., & Gulish, A. (2018). *Three educational pathways to good jobs: High school, middle skills, and bachelor's degree.* Georgetown University Center on Education and the Workforce. https://1gyhoq479ufd3yna29x7ubjn-wpengine.netdna-ssl.com/wp-content/uploads/3ways-FR.pdf

Carnoy, M., Adamson, F., Chudgar, A., Luschei, T. F., and Witte, J. F. (2007). Vouchers and Public School Performance: A Case Study of the Milwaukee Parental Choice Program. Retrieved from Economic Policy Institute website: https://www.epi.org/publication/book_vouchers

Carr, E. M. (2015). Afterschool program interventions that support the academic achievement, behavior, and engagement of at-risk student populations. University of Houston-Clear Lake. http://proxy.library.vcuEdu/login?url=https://search.proquest.com/docview/305175724?accountid=14780

Carr, M. (2011). The Impact of Ohio's EdChoice on Traditional Public School Performance. *Cato Journal, 31*(2), 257–284.

Carruthers, C. K., & Jepsen, C. (2021). Vocational education: An international perspective. In B. P. McCall (Ed.), *The Routledge handbook of the economics of education,* 343–380. Abingdon, UK: Routledge, Taylor, & Francis Group.

Carruthers, C. K., & Sanford, T. (2018). Way station or launching pad? Unpacking the returns to adult technical education. *Journal of Public Economics, 165*, 146–159.

Carver-Thomas, D., & Darling-Hammond, L. (2017). *Teacher turnover: Why it matters and what we can do about it.* Learning Policy Institute. https://doi.org/10.54300/454.278

CASEL (Collaborative for Academic, Social, and Emotional Learning). (2003). *Safe and sound: An educational leader's guide to evidence-based social and emotional learning programs.* Illinois edition.

CASEL. (2012). *2013 CASEL guide: Effective social and emotional learning programs: Preschool and elementary school edition.* https://ed.buffalo.edu/content/dam/ed/alberti/docs/CASEL-Guide-SOCIAL-EMOTIONAL-LEARNING.pdf

Castagno, A. E. (2013). Multicultural education and the protection of whiteness. *American Journal of Education, 120*(1), 101–128.

Castillo, M., Jordan, J. L., & Petrie, R. (2019). Discount rates of children and high school graduation. *Economic Journal, 129*(619), 1152–1181.

Castro, M., Expósito-Casas, E., López-Martín, E., Lizasoain, L., Navarro-Asencio, E., & Gaviria, J. (2015). Parental involvement on student academic achievement: A meta-analysis. *Educational Research Review, 14*(1), 33–46.

Castro-Olivo, S. M. (2014). Promoting social-emotional learning in adolescent Latino ELLs: A study of the culturally adapted Strong Teens program. *School Psychology Quarterly, 29*(4), 567–577. https://doi.org/10.1037/spq0000055

Catt, A. D., & Rhinesmith, E. (2017). *Why Indiana parents choose: A cross-sector survey of parents' views in a robust school choice environment.* EdChoice. https://files.eric.ed.gov/fulltext/ED579213.pdf

Cavanagh, S. E., & Huston, A. C. (2006). Family instability and children's early problem behavior. *Social Forces, 85,* 575–605.

Cavanagh, S. E., Schiller, K. S., & Riegle-Crumb, C. (2006). Marital transitions, parenting, and schooling: Exploring the link between family-structure history and adolescents' academic status. *Sociology of Education, 79*(4), 329–354.

Cellini, S. (2006). Smoothing the transition to college? The effect of tech-ed programs on educational attainment. *Economics of Education Review, 25*(4), 394–411.

Chakrabarti, R. (2008). Can increasing private school participation and monetary loss in a voucher program affect public school performance? Evidence from Milwaukee. *Journal of Public Economics, 92*(5–6), 1371–1393.

Chakrabarti, R. (2013). Vouchers, public school response, and the role of incentives: Evidence from Florida. *EconomicIinquiry, 51*(1), 500–526.

Chan, W. Y., Kuperminc, G. P., Seitz, S., Wilson, C., & Khatib, N. (2020). School-based group mentoring and academic outcomes in vulnerable high-school students. *Youth & Society, 52*(7), 1220–1237.

Chaplin, D., Gill, B., Thompkins, A., & Miller, H. (2014). *Professional practice, student surveys, and value added: Multiple measures of teacher effectiveness in the Pittsburgh Public Schools.* Institute of Education Sciences. https://files.eric.ed.gov/fulltext/ED545232.pdf

Chase, R., & Valorose, J. (2010). *Child care use in Minnesota: Report of the 2009 statewide household child care survey.* Wilder Research.

Cheng, A., Henderson, M. B., Peterson, P. E., & West, M. R. (2021). Cost-benefit information closes aspiration gaps—if parents think their child is ready for college. *Education Economics, 29*(3), 233–251.

Cheng, A., Hitt, C., Kisida, B., & Mills, J. N. (2017). "No excuses" charter schools: A meta-analysis of the experimental evidence on student achievement. *Journal of School Choice, 11*(2), 209–238.

Cherng, H. Y. S., & Halpin, P. F. (2016). The importance of minority teachers: Student perceptions of minority versus white teachers. *Educational Researcher, 45*(7), 407–420. https://doi.org/10.3102/0013189X16671718

Chetty, R., Friedman, J. N., & Rockoff, J. E. (2014a). Measuring the impacts of teachers I: Evaluating bias in teacher value-added estimates. *American Economic Review, 104*(9), 2593–2632. https://www.aeaweb.org/articles?id=10.1257/aer.104.9.2593

Chetty, R., Friedman, J. N., & Rockoff, J. E. (2014b). Measuring the impacts of teachers II: Teacher value-added and student outcomes in adulthood. *American Economic Review, 104*(9), 2633–2679. https://doi.org/10.1257/aer.104.9.2633

Chetty, R., Hendren, N., Jones, M. R., & Porter, S. R. (2020). Race and economic opportunity in the United States: An intergenerational perspective. *Quarterly Journal of Economics 135*(2), 711–783.

Chingos, M. M., & Peterson, P. E. (2011). It's easier to pick a good teacher than to train one: Familiar and new results on the correlates of teacher effectiveness. *Economics of Education Review, 30*(3), 449–465. https://doi.org/10.1016/j.econedurev.2010.12.010

Chittum, J. R., Jones, B. D., Akalin, S., & Schram, Á. B. (2017). The effects of an afterschool STEM program on students' motivation and engagement. *International Journal of STEM Education, 4*(1), 1–16.

Christakis, D. A., Van Cleve, W., & Zimmerman, F. J. (2020). Estimation of US children's educational attainment and years of life lost associated with primary school closures during the coronavirus disease 2019 pandemic. *JAMA Network Open, 3*(11), e2028786–e2028786. doi:10.1001/jamanetworkopen.2020.28786

Christie, S. T., Jarratt, D. C., Olson, L. A., & Taijala, T. T. (2019). *Machine-learned school dropout early warning at scale.* Proceedings of the International Conference on Educational Data Mining.

Cipriano, C., Naples, L. H., Zieher, A., Durlak, J., Eveleigh, A., Funaro, M., Strambler, M., Ponnock, A., McCarthy, M. F., & Chow, J. (2021). The state of evidence for social and emotional learning: A contemporary meta-analysis of universal school-based SEL interventions. *Child Development.* https://osf.io/r246m

Cipriano, C., Schlichtmann, G., Riley, J., Naples, L., & Eveleigh, A. (In press). Supporting transformative SEL implementation with a collaboratory for equity and inclusion. In K. Schonert-Reichel, M. Strambler, & S. Rimm-Kaufman (Eds.), *Social and emotional learning in action: Creating systemic change in schools.* New York: Guilford.

Clotfelter, C. T., Glennie, E. J., Ladd, H. F., & Vigdor, J. L. (2008a). Teacher bonuses and teacher retention in low-performing schools: Evidence from the North Carolina $1,800 teacher bonus program. *Public Finance Review, 36*(1), 63–87. https://doi.org/10.1177/1091142106291662

Clotfelter, C., Glennie, E., Ladd, H., & Vigdor, J. (2008b). Would higher salaries keep teachers in high-poverty schools? Evidence from a policy intervention in North Carolina. *Journal of Public Economics, 92*(5–6), 1352–1370. https://doi.org/10.1016/j.jpubeco.2007.07.003

Clotfelter, C., Ladd, H., & Vigdor, J. (2007). *Teacher credentials and student achievement in high school: A cross-subject analysis with student fixed effects* (Working Paper No. 13617). National Bureau of Economic Research. https://doi.org/10.3386/w13617

Coleman, J. S. (1988). Supplement: Organizations and institutions: Sociological and economic approaches to the analysis of social structure: Social capital in the creation of human capital. *American Journal of Sociology, 94*, 95–120. https://www.jstor.org/stable/i329085

Common Core State Standards Initiative (CCSSI). (2010). National Governors Association Center for Best Practices and Council of Chief State School Officers. http://www.corestandards.org/assets/CCSSI_Math%20Standards.pdf.

Corbett, A. (2001). Cognitive computer tutors: Solving the two-sigma problem. In M. Bauer, P. J. Gmytrasiewicz, & J. Vassileva (Eds.), *[Lecture Notes in Computer Science] User Modeling 2001* (Vol. 2109, pp. 137–147). Springer, Berlin, Heidelberg. https://doi.org/10.1007/3-540-44566-8_14

Corcoran, R. P., Cheung, A. C. K., Kim, E., & Xie, C. (2018). Effective universal school-based social and emotional learning programs for improving academic achievement: A systematic review and meta-analysis of 50 years of research. *Educational Research Review, 25*, 56–72.

Corcoran, S. P., Evans, W. N., & Schwab, R. M. (2004). Women, the labor market, and the declining relative quality of teachers. *Journal of Policy Analysis and Management, 23*(3), 449–470. JSTOR.

Cortes, K. E., Fricke, H., Loeb, S., Song, D. S., & York, B. N. (2021). Too little or too much? Actionable advice in an early-childhood text messaging experiment. *Education Finance and Policy, 16*(2), 209–232. https://doi.org/10.1162/edfp_a_00304

Cosyn, E., Uzun, H., Doble, C., & Matayoshi, J. (2021). A practical perspective on knowledge space theory: ALEKS and its data. *Journal of Mathematical Psychology, 101*, 102512.

Cowan, J., & Goldhaber, D. (2018). Do bonuses affect teacher staffing and student achievement in high poverty schools? Evidence from an incentive for national board certified teachers in Washington State. *Economics of Education Review, 65,* 138–152. https://doi .org/10.1016/j.econedurev.2018.06.010

Cowen, J. M. (2008). School choice as a latent variable: Estimating the "complier average causal effect" of vouchers in Charlotte. *Policy Studies Journal, 36*(2), 301–315.

Cruz-Gonzalez, M., Shrout, P. E., Alvarez, K., Hostetter, I., & Alegría, M. (2021). Measurement invariance of screening measures of anxiety, depression, and level of functioning in a US sample of minority older adults assessed in four languages. *Frontiers in Psychiatry, 12,* 129. https://doi.org/10.3389/fpsyt.2021.579173

Cullen, J., Jacob, B., & Levitt, S. (2000). *The impact of school choice on student outcomes: An analysis of the Chicago public schools* (Working Paper No. 7888). National Bureau of Economic Research.

Cunha, F., & Heckman, J. (2007). The technology of skill formation. *American Economic Review, 97*(2), 31–47.

Cunha, F., Heckman, J., & Schennach, S. (May 2010). Estimating the technology of noncognitive skill formation. *Econometrica, 78*(3), 883–931. http://www.econometricsociety.org/

Cutler, D., & Lleras-Muney, A. (2010). Understanding differences in health behaviors by education. *Journal of Health Economics, 29*(1), 1–28.

Dale, S., & Krueger, A. (2011). *Estimating the return to college selectivity over the career using administrative earnings data* (Working Paper No. 17159). National Bureau of Economic Research. https://doi.org/10.3386/w17159

Dardas, L. A., van de Water, B., & Simmons, L. A. (2018). Parental involvement in adolescent depression interventions: A systematic review of randomized clinical trials. *International Journal of Mental Health Nursing, 27*(2), 555–570.

DeAngelis, C. A. (2017). Do self-interested schooling selections improve society? A review of the evidence. *Journal of School Choice, 11*(4), 546–558.

DeAngelis, C. A., & Dills, A. K. (2021). The effects of school choice on mental health. *School Effectiveness and School Improvement, 32*(2), 326–344.

DeAngelis, C. A., & Holmes Erickson, H. (2018). What leads to successful school choice programs? A review of the theories and evidence. *Cato Journal, 38*(1), 247–263.

DeAngelis, C. A., & Makridis, C. (2021). Are school reopening decisions related to union influence? *Social Science Quarterly, 102*(5), 2266–2284.

DeAngelis, C. A., & Makridis, C. (2022). Are school reopening decisions related to funding? Evidence from over 12,000 districts during the COVID-19 pandemic. *Journal of School Choice, 16*(3), 454–476.

DeAngelis, C. A., & McCluskey, N. P. (Eds.). (2020). *School choice myths: Setting the record straight on education freedom.* Cato Institute.

DeAngelis, C. A., & Wolf, P. J. (2019). Private school choice and crime: Evidence from Milwaukee. *Social Science Quarterly, 100*(6), 2302–2315.

DeAngelis, C. A., & Wolf, P. J. (2020). Private school choice and character: More evidence from Milwaukee. *Journal of Private Enterprise, 35*(3), 13–48.

Deaton, A. (2013). *The great escape: Health, wealth, and the origins of inequality.* Princeton University Press.

Dee, T. S. (2001). *Teachers, race and student achievement in a randomized experiment* (Working Paper No. 8432). National Bureau of Economic Research.

Dee, T. S. (2004). Teachers, race, and student achievement in a randomized experiment. *Review of Economics and Statistics, 86*(1), 195–210. https://doi.org/10.1162/003465304323023750

Dee, T. S. (2007). Teachers and the gender gaps in student achievement. *Journal of Human Resources, 42*(3), 528–554.

Dee, T., Huffaker, E., Phillips, C., & Sagara, E. (2021). *The revealed preferences for school reopening: Evidence from public-school disenrollment* (Working Paper No. 29156). National Bureau of Economic Research.

Dee, T. S., & Penner, E. K. (2021). My brother's keeper? The impact of targeted educational supports. *Journal of Policy Analysis and Management, 40*(4), 1171–1196.

Dee, T. S., & Wyckoff, J. (2015). Incentives, selection, and teacher performance: Evidence from IMPACT. *Journal of Policy Analysis and Management, 34*(2), 267–297. https://doi .org/10.1002/pam.21818

DeFalco, J. A., Rowe, J. P., Paquette, L., Georgoulas-Sherry, V., Brawner, K., Mott, B. W., Baker, R. S., & Lester, J. C. (2018). Detecting and addressing frustration in a serious game for military training. *International Journal of Artificial Intelligence and Education, 28*(2), 152–193.

De Lange, M., Dronkers, J., & Wolbers, M. H. J. (2014). Single-parent family forms and children's educational performance in a comparative perspective: Effects of school's share of single-parent families. *School Effectiveness and School Improvement, 25*(3), 329–350. https:// doi.org/10.1080/09243453.2013.809773

Delucchi, G. R. (2010). *An evaluation of an after-school program for low-income elementary and middle school students.* Fordham University. http://proxi.library.vcu.edu/login ?accountid=14780

Deming, D. J. (2011). Better schools, less crime? *Quarterly Journal of Economics, 126*(4), 2063–2115.

Deming, D., Hastings, J., Kane, T., & Staiger, D. (2011). *School choice, school quality, and postsecondary attainment* (Working Paper No. 17438). National Bureau of Economic Research.

Deming, E. (with Cahill, K. E., & Allan, K. L.). (2018). *Out of the crisis.* Cambridge, MA: MIT Press (original work published 1982).

Denham, S. A. (1998). *Emotional development in young children.* Guilford.

Denham, S. A., & Weissberg, R. P. (2004). Social-emotional learning in early childhood: What we know and where to go from here. In E. Chesebrough, P. King, T. P. Gullotta, & M. Bloom (Eds.), *A blueprint for the promotion of prosocial behavior in early childhood* (pp. 13–50). New York: Kluwer/Plenum.

De Ridder, K. A. A., Pape, K., Cuypers, K., Johnsen, R., Holmen, T. L., Westin, S., & Bjørngaard, J. H. (2013). High school dropout and long-term sickness and disability in young adulthood: A prospective propensity score stratified cohort study (the Young-HUNT study). *BMC Public Health, 13*(1), 941. https://doi.org/10.1186/1471-2458-13-941

De Witte, K., Cabus, S., Thyssen, G., Groot, W., & van den Brink, H. M. (2013). A critical review of the literature on school dropout. *Educational Research Review, 10*, 13–28.

Dills, A. K., & Hernández-Julián, R. (2011). More choice, less crime. *Education Finance and Policy, 6*(2), 246–266.

Dishion, T. J., Patterson, G. R., Stoolmiller, M., & Skinner, M. L. (1991). Family, school, and behavioral antecedents to early adolescent involvement with antisocial peers. *Developmental Psychology, 27*(1), 172–180.

Dixit, A. (2002). Incentives and organizations in the public sector: An interpretative review. *Journal of Human Resources, 37*(4), 696–727. https://doi.org/10.2307/3069614

D'Mello, S. K., & Graesser, A. (2010). Multimodal semi-automated affect detection from conversational cues, gross body language, and facial features. *User Modeling and User-Adapted Interaction, 20*(2), 147–187.

Dobbie, W., & Fryer, R. G., Jr. (2015). The medium-term impacts of high-achieving charter schools. *Journal of Political Economy, 123*(5), 985–1037.

Doherty, W. J., Willoughby, B. J., & Wilde, J. L. (2015). Is the gender gap in college enrollment influenced by nonmarital birth rates and father absence? *Family Relations, 65*(2), 263–274.

Domitrovich, C. E., Durlak, J. A., Staley, K. C., & Weissberg, R. P. (2017). Social-emotional competence: An essential factor for promoting positive adjustment and reducing risk in school children. *Child Development, 88*(2), 408–416.

Doms, M., Dunne, T., & Troske, K. (1997). Workers, wages, and technology. *Quarterly Journal of Economics, 112*(1), 253–290.

Doss, C., Fahle, E. M., Loeb, S., & York, B. N. (2019). More than just a nudge supporting kindergarten parents with differentiated and personalized text messages. *Journal of Human Resources, 54*(3), 567–603.

Dotter, D., Chaplin, D., & Bartlett, M. (2021). *Measuring the impacts of school reforms in the District of Columbia on student achievement (Issue Brief)*. Mathematica Policy Research. https://www.mathematica.org/publications/measuring-the-impacts-of-school-reforms-in -the-district-of-columbia-on-student-achievement

Dougherty, S. (2018). The effect of career and technical education on human capital accumulation: Causal evidence from Massachusetts. *Education Finance and Policy, 13*(2), 119–148.

Dougherty, S., & Ecton, W. G. (2021). The economic effect of vocational education on student outcomes. *Oxford Research Encyclopedia of Economics and Finance*.

Dougherty, S., & Lombardi, A. (2016). From vocational education to career readiness: The ongoing work of linking education and the labor market. *Review of Research in Higher Education, 40*(1), 326–355.

Downs, A. (1967). *Inside bureaucracy*. Boston: Little, Brown.

Drake, S., Auletto, A., & Cowen, J. M. (2019). Grading teachers: Race and gender differences in low evaluation ratings and teacher employment outcomes. *American Educational Research Journal, 56*(5), 1800–1833. https://doi.org/10.3102/0002831219835776

Dreyer, K. J. (2011). *An examination of academic outcomes for students who attend a school based afterschool program*. University of Pittsburgh. http://proxy.library.vcu .edu/login?url=https://search.proquest.com/docview/746583937?accountid=14780

Dronkers, J., Veerman, G. M., & Pong, S. (2017). Mechanisms behind the negative influence of single parenthood on school performance: Lower teaching and learning conditions? *Journal of Divorce & Remarriage, 58*(7), 471–486.

Duncan, G. J., & Murnane, R. (Eds.). (2011). *Whither opportunity? Rising inequality, schools, and children's life chances*. New York: Russell Sage Foundation.

Dunn, J. D. (2008). *Complex justice: The case of Missouri v. Jenkins*. Chapel Hill: University of North Carolina Press.

Durlak, J. A. (Ed.) (2015). *Handbook of social and emotional learning: Research and practice*. Guilford Publications.

Durlak, J. A., & Wells, A. M. (1997). Primary prevention mental health programs for children and adolescents: A meta-analytic review. *American Journal of Community Psychology, 25*, 115–152.

Durlak, J. A., Weissberg, R. P., Dymnicki, A. B., Taylor, R. D., & Schellinger, K. B. (2011). The impact of enhancing students' social and emotional learning: A meta-analysis of school-based universal interventions. *Child Development, 82*(1), 405–432. https://doi .org/10.1111/j.1467-8624.2010.01564.x

Durlak, J. A., Weissberg, R. P., & Pachan, M. (2010). A meta-analysis of after-school programs that seek to promote personal and social skills in children and adolescents. *American Journal of Community Psychology*, (3–4), 294–309.

Dynarski, M., James-Burdumy, S., Moore, M., Rosenberg, L., Deke, J., & Mansfield, W. (2004). *When schools stay open late: The national evaluation of the 21st-Century Community Learning Centers program—New findings*. US Department of Education.

Dynarski, M., Moore, M., Mullens, J., Gleason, P., James-Burdumy, S., Rosenberg, L., Pistorino, C., Silva, T., Deke, J., Mansfield, W., Heaviside, S., & Levy, D. (2003). *When schools stay open late: The national evaluation of the 21st-Century Community Learning Centers program: First year findings*. US Department of Education. http://www.educationnewyork.com/files/firstyear.pdf

Ecton, W. G., & Dougherty, S. (2021). *Heterogeneity in high school career and technical education outcomes* (EdWorkingPaper No. 21-492), Annenberg Institute at Brown University. https://www.edworkingpapers.com/sites/default/files/ai21-492.pdf

EdChoice (2021, April 14). *The 123s of school choice: What the research says about private school choice programs in America* [PowerPoint slides]. SlideShare. https://www.edchoice.org/wp-content/uploads/2021/04/2021-123s-SlideShare_FINAL.pdf

Edin, K., & Kefalas, M. (2005). Unmarried with children. *Contexts, 4*(2), 16–22. https://doi.org/10.1525/ctx.2005.4.2.16

Education Commission of the States. (2020, July 29). *50-state comparison: Teacher employment contract policies*. https://www.ecs.org/50-state-comparison-teacher-employment-contract-policies/

edX. (2021). *Using the research data exchange data package*. Retrieved December 20, 2021, from https://edx.readthedocs.io/projects/devdata/en/latest/rdx/index.html

Egalite, A. J., & Catt, A. D. (2020). Competitive Effects of the Indiana Choice Scholarship Program on Traditional Public School Achievement and Graduation Rates. Working Paper 2020-3. EdChoice.

Egalite, A. J., Kisida, B., & Winters, M. A. (2015). Representation in the classroom: The effect of own-race teachers on student achievement. *Economics of Education Review, 45*(1), 44–52.

Egalite, A. J., & Mills, J. N. (2021). Competitive impacts of means-tested vouchers on public school performance: Evidence from Louisiana. *Education Finance and Policy, 16*(1), 66–91.

Elias, M. J., Zins, J. E., Weissberg, R. P., Frey, K. S., Greenberg, M. T., Haynes, N. M., Kessler, R., Schwab-Stone, M. E., & Shriver, T. P. (1997). *Promoting social and emotional learning: Guidelines for educators*. Association for Supervision and Curriculum Development.

ESSA (Every Student Succeeds Act). I § 1001-1601. (2015a). https://www.everystudentsucceedsact.org/title-i-improving-basic-school-programs-operated-by-state-and-local-educational-agencies

ESSA (Every Student Succeeds Act). Title IV § 4201–4206. (2015b). https://www.everystudentsucceedsact.org/title-iv-21st-century-schools

Federal Bureau of Investigation. (2021, October 25). *FBI releases updated 2020 hate crime statistics* [Press release]. https://www.fbi.gov/news/pressrel/press-releases/fbi-releases-updated-2020-hate-crime-statistics

Feuer, M. J., Floden, R. E., Chudowsky, N., & Ahn, J. (2013). *Evaluation of teacher preparation programs: Purposes, methods, and policy options*. National Academy of Education. https://files.eric.ed.gov/fulltext/ED565694.pdf

Figlio, D., & Hart, C. (2014). Competitive effects of means-tested school vouchers. *American Economic Journal: Applied Economics, 6*(1), 133–156.

Figlio, D. N., Hart, C., & Karbownik, K. (2021). *Effects of scaling up private school choice programs on public school students* (No. 14342). Institute of Labor Economics (IZA).

Figlio, D., & Karbownik, K. (2016). Evaluation of Ohio's EdChoice Scholarship Program: Selection, Competition, and Performance Effects. Thomas B. Fordham Institute.

Figlio, D. N., & Rouse, C. E. (2006). Do accountability and voucher threats improve low-performing schools? *Journal of Public Economics, 90*(1-2), 239–255.

Fink, B. L. (2011). *The effect of a seventh grade after school leadership program on the developmental assets, academic achievement, and behavior of non-thriving students* (Publication No. 3465) [Doctoral dissertation]. University of Nebraska at Omaha. Digital Commons at University of Nebraska at Omaha. https://digitalcommons.unomaha.edu/cgi/viewcontent.cgi?article=4472&context=studentwork

First Five Years Fund. (2022). Child Care & Development Block Grant (CCDBG). https://www.ffyf.org/issues/ccdbg/

Flanders, W. (2020). *Politics in the pandemic: The role of unions in school reopening decisions.* Wisconsin Institute for Law & Liberty. https://will-law.org/wp-content/uploads/2020/12/reopening-brief.pdf

Flanders, W. (2021). Opting out: Enrollment trends in response to continued public school shutdowns. *Journal of School Choice, 15*(3), 331–43.

Floman, J. L., Hagelskamp, C., Brackett, M. A., & Rivers, S. E. (2017). Emotional bias in classroom observations: Within-rater positive emotion predicts favorable assessments of classroom quality. *Journal of Psychoeducational Assessment, 35*(3), 291–301. https://doi.org/10.1177/0734282916629595

Forster, G. (2008). Promising Start: An Empirical Analysis of How EdChoice Vouchers Affect Ohio Public Schools. School Choice Issues in the State. Friedman Foundation for Educational Choice.

Forster, G. (2008). Lost Opportunity: An Empirical Analysis of How Vouchers Affected Florida Public Schools. School Choice Issues in the State. Retrieved from: http://www.edchoice.org/wp-content/uploads/2015/09/Lost-Opportunity-How-Vouchers-Affected-Florida-Public-Schools.pdf

Francesconi, M., & Heckman, J. J. (2016). Child development and parental investment: Introduction. *The Economic Journal, 126*(596), F1–F27.

Francom, G. M., Lee, S. J., & Pinkney, H. (2021). Technologies, challenges and needs of K-12 teachers in the transition to distance learning during the COVID-19 pandemic. *TechTrends, 65*, 589–601.

Franklin, C. (2017). *Effects of the afterschool program on student achievement of students with disabilities in a rural Georgia middle school* (Publication No. 1500) [Doctoral dissertation]. Liberty University, Lynchburg, VA. Scholars Crossing: Institutional Repository of Liberty University. https://digitalcommons.liberty.edu/cgi/viewcontent.cgi?article=2556&context=doctoral

Freudenberg, N., & Ruglis, J. (2007). Reframing school dropout as a public health issue. *Preventing Chronic Disease, 4*(4), A107.

Friedman, M. (1955). The role of government in education. Collected Works of Milton Friedman Project records. Hoover Institution Archives, Stanford, CA.

Gamoran, A., Miller, H. K., Fiel, J. E., & Valentine, J. L. (2011). Social capital and student achievement: An intervention-based test of theory. *Sociology of Education, 94*(4), 294–315.

Garcia, E. (2020, February 12). *Schools are still segregated, and Black children are paying a price.* Economic Policy Institute. https://www.epi.org/publication/schools-are-still-segregated -and-black-children-are-paying-a-price/

García, E., & Weiss, E. (2019). *The teacher shortage is real, large and growing, and worse than we thought (The first report in "The Perfect Storm in the Teacher Labor Market" series).* Economic Policy Institute.

García, J. L., Heckman, J. J., Leaf, D. E., & Prados, M. J. (2020). Quantifying the life-cycle benefits of an influential early-childhood program. *Journal of Political Economy, 128*(7), 2502–2541. https://doi.org/10.108

Garcia, M. (2016). Racist in the machine: The disturbing implications of algorithmic bias. *World Policy Journal, 33*(4), 111–117.

Gardner, J., Andres, J. M., Brooks, C., & Baker, R. (2018). *MORF: A framework for predictive modeling and replication at scale with privacy-restricted MOOC data.* 2018 IEEE International Conference on Big Data (Big Data), 3235–3244. https://homes.cs.washington .edu/~jpgard/papers/icbd19.pdf

Gardner, J., Yang, Y., Baker, R., & Brooks, C. (2019). *Modeling and experimental design for MOOC dropout prediction: A replication perspective.* Proceedings of the 12th International Conference on Educational Data Mining, 49–58.

Geary, Daniel. (2015). *Beyond civil rights: The Moynihan report and its legacy.* Philadelphia: University of Pennsylvania Press.

Gershenson, S., Hart, C. M. D., Hyman, J., Lindsay, D., & Papageorge, N. W. (2018). *The long-run impacts of same-race teachers* (Working Paper No. 25254). National Bureau of Economic Research.

Geven, S., & van de Werfhorst, H. G. (2020). The role of intergenerational networks in students' school performance in two differentiated educational systems: A comparison of between- and within-individual estimates. *Sociology of Education, 93*(1), 40–64.

Gilkerson, J., Richards, J. A., Warren, S. F., Montgomery, J. K., Greenwood, C. R., Kimbrough Oller, D., Hansen, H. L., & Paul, T. D. (2017). Mapping the early language environment using all-day recordings and automated analysis. *American Journal of Speech-Language Pathology, 26*(2), 248–265. https://doi.org/10.1\044/2016\_AJSLP-15-0169

Gillborn, D. (2008). *Racism and education: Coincidence or conspiracy?* New York: Routledge.

Gillborn, D., Warmington, P., & Demack, S. (2017). QuantCrit: Education, policy, "Big Data" and principles for a critical race theory of statistics. *Race Ethnicity and Education, 21*(2), 158–179.

Ginder, S., Kelly-Reid, J., & Mann, F. (2016). *Postsecondary institutions and cost of attendance in 2015–16; degrees and other awards conferred, 2014–15; and 12-month enrollment, 2014–15: First look (provisional data).* National Center for Education Statistics Report, NCES 2016-112rev. https://nces.ed.gov/pubs2016/2016112rev.pdf

Girod, M., Martineau, J., & Yong, Z. (2004). After-school computer clubhouses and at-risk teens. *American Secondary Education, 32*(3), 63–76.

Glazerman, S., Protik, A., Teh, B., Bruch, J., & Max, J. (2013). *Transfer incentives for high-performing teachers: Final results from a multisite randomized experiment.* National Center for Education Evaluation and Regional Assistance, Institute of Education Sciences, US Department of Education. https://files.eric.ed.gov/fulltext/ED544269.pdf

Goldhaber, D. D., & Brewer, D. J. (2000). Does teacher certification matter? High school teacher certification status and student achievement. *Educational Evaluation and Policy Analysis, 22*(2), 129–145. https://doi.org/10.3102/01623737022002129

Goldhaber, D., Quince, V., & Theobald, R. (2019). Teacher quality gaps in U.S. public schools: Trends, sources, and implications. *Phi Delta Kappan, 100*(8), 14–19. https://doi .org/10.1177/0031721719846883

Goldhaber, D., & Walch, J. (2012). Strategic pay reform: A student outcomes-based evaluation of Denver's ProComp teacher pay initiative. *Economics of Education Review, 31*(6), 1067–1083. https://doi.org/10.1016/j.econedurev.2012.06.007

Goldhaber, D., & Walch, J. (2014). Gains in teacher quality: Academic capabilities of the U.S. teaching force are on the rise. *Education Next, 14*(1), 38–45. https://www.educationnext .org/gains-in-teacher-quality/

Goldring, E., Grissom, J. A., Rubin, M., Neumerski, C. M., Cannata, M., Drake, T., & Schuermann, P. (2015). Make room value added: Principals' human capital decisions and the emergence of teacher observation data. *Educational Researcher, 44*(2), 96–104. https:// doi.org/10.3102/0013189X15575031

Golightly, D. (2020, June 26). Google, New Mexico AG spar over Chromebook student data collection. *Android Headlines*. https://www.androidheadlines.com/2020/02/google-new -mexico-attorney-general-lawsuit-student-data-collection-chromebook.html

Goodman, S., & Turner, L. (2011). Does whole-school performance pay improve student learning? Evidence from the New York City schools. *Education Next, 11*(2), 67–71.

Gordon, E. W., Paik, S. J., & Walberg, H. J. (2007). *Narrowing the achievement gap: Strategies for educating Latino, Black, and Asian students*. Berlin: Springer Science & Business Media.

Gottfredson, D. C., Cross, A., & Soulé, D. A. (2007). Distinguishing characteristics of effective and ineffective after-school programs to prevent delinquency and victimization. *Criminology & Public Policy, 6*(2), 289–318.

Gottfredson, D. C., Cross, A. B., Wilson, D. M., Connell, N., & Rorie, M. (2010). *A randomized trial of the effects of an enhanced after-school program for middle-school students*. Final Report submitted to the US Department of Education Institute for Educational Sciences.

Gottfredson, D. C., Gottfredson, G. D., & Weisman, S. A. (2001). The timing of delinquent behavior and its implications for after-school programs. *Criminology & Public Policy, 1*, 61–86.

Gottfried, M., Kirksey, J. J., Fletcher, T. L. (2022). Do high school students with a same-race teacher attend class more often? *Educational Evaluation and Policy Analysis, 44*(1), 149–169.

Gottfried, M., & Plasman, J. (2018). Linking the timing of career and technical education coursetaking with high school dropout and college-going behavior. *American Educational Research Journal, 55*(2), 325–336.

Granger, R. (2010). Understanding and improving effectiveness of after-school practice. *American Journal of Community Psychology, 45*(3–4), 441–446. https://pubmed.ncbi.nlm .nih.gov/20238158/

Granger, R. C., Durlak, J., Yohalem, N., & Reisner, E. (2007). *Improving after-school program quality* (Working paper). William T. Grant Foundation.

Grannis, K. S., & Sawhill, I. V. (2013). *Improving children's life chances: Estimates from the Social Genome Model*. Washington, DC: Brookings Institution.

Gray, N. L., Merrifield, J. D., & Adzima, K. A. (2016). A private universal voucher program's effects on traditional public schools. *Journal of Economics and Finance, 40*(2), 319–344.

Gray, L., & Lewis, L. (2018). *Career and technical education programs in public school districts, 2016–2017*. National Center for Education Statistics. US Department of Education.

Greenberg, D., & Barnow, B. S. (2014). Flaws in evaluations of social programs: Illustrations from randomized controlled trials. *Evaluation Review, 38*(5), 359–387.

Greenberg, D. H., & Robins, P. K. (1986). The changing role of social experiments in policy analysis. *Journal of Policy Analysis and Management, 5*(2), 340–362.

Greenberg, M. T., Weissberg, R. P., O'Brien, M. U., Zins, J. E., Fredericks, L., Resnik, H., & Elias, M. J. (2003). Enhancing school-based prevention and youth development through coordinated social, emotional, and academic learning. *American Psychologist, 58*(6), 466–474.

Greene, J. P. (2001). An Evaluation of the Florida A-Plus Accountability and School Choice Program. Retrieved from Manhattan Institute website: http://www.manhattan-institute .org/pdf/cr_aplus.pdf

Greene, J. P. (2001). Vouchers in Charlotte. *Education Next, 1*(2), 55–60. https://www.edu cationnext.org/vouchersincharlotte/

Greene, J. P., & Forster, G. (2002). Rising to the Challenge: The Effect of School Choice on Public Schools in Milwaukee and San Antonio. Civic Bulletin.

Greene, J. P., & Marsh, R. H. (2009). The Effect of Milwaukee's Parental Choice Program on Student Achievement in Milwaukee Public Schools. SCDP Comprehensive Longitudinal Evaluation of the Milwaukee Parental Choice Program. Report# 11. School Choice Demonstration Project.

Greene, J. P., Peterson, P. E., & Du, J. (1999). Effectiveness of school choice: The Milwaukee experiment. *Education and Urban Society, 31*(2), 190–213.

Greene, J. P., & Winters, M. A. (2004). Competition passes the test: still more evidence from Florida that public schools improve when threatened with the loss of students and money. *Education Next, 4*(3), 66–72.

Greene, J. P., & Winters, M. A. (2007). An Evaluation of the Effect of DC's Voucher Program on Public School Achievement and Racial Integration After One Year. *Journal of Catholic Education, 11*(1), pp. 83–101. http://dx.doi.org/10.15365/joce.1101072013

Grissom, J. A. (2011). Can good principals keep teachers in disadvantaged schools? Linking principal effectiveness to teacher satisfaction and turnover in hard-to-staff environments. *Teacher College Record, 113*(11), 2552–2585.

Grissom, J. A., & Bartanen, B. (2018). Strategic retention: Principal effectiveness and teacher turnover in multiple-measure teacher evaluation systems. *American Educational Research Journal, 56*(2), 514–555. https://doi.org/10.3102/0002831218797931

Grissom, J. A., Egalite, A. J., & Lindsay, C. A. (2021). *How principals affect students and schools: A systematic synthesis of two decades of research.* Wallace Foundation. https://www .wallacefoundation.org/knowledge-center/Documents/How-Principals-Affect-Students -and-Schools.pdf

Grissom, J. A., & Loeb, S. (2017). Assessing principals' assessments: Subjective evaluations of teacher effectiveness in low- and high-stakes environments. *Education Finance and Policy, 12*(3), 369–395. https://doi.org/10.1162/EDFP_a_00210

Grolnick, W. S., Farkas, M. S., Sohmer, R., Michaels, S., & Valsiner, J. (2007). Facilitating motivation in adolescents: Effects of an after-school program. *Journal of Applied Developmental Psychology, 28*(4), 332–344.

Grossman, J. B., & Bulle, M. J. (2006). Review of what youth programs do to increase the connectedness of youth with adults. *Journal of Adolescent Health, 39*(6), 788–799.

Grossman, M., Reckhow, S., Strunk, K., & Turner, M. (2021). *All states close but red districts reopen: The politics of in-person schooling during the COVID-19 pandemic* (EdWorkingPaper No. 21-355). Annenberg Institute at Brown University. https://www.edworkingpapers .com/sites/default/files/ai21-355.pdf

Grubb, W. N., & Lazerson, M. (1982). Education and the labor market: Recycling the youth problem. In H. Kantor and D. B. Tyack (Eds.), *Work, youth and schooling: Historical perspectives on vocationalism in American education* (pp. 110–141). Stanford, CA: Stanford University Press.

Grubb, W. N., & Lazerson, M. (2005). Vocationalism in higher education: The triumph of the education gospel. *Journal of Higher Education, 76*(1), 1–25.

Gubbels, J., van der Put, C. E., & Assink, M. (2019). Risk factors for school absenteeism and dropout: A meta-analytic review. *Journal of Youth and Adolescence, 48*, 1637–1667.

Gueldner, B. A., Feuerborn, L. L., & Merrell, K. W. (2020). *Social and emotional learning in the classroom: Promoting mental health and academic success.* New York: Guilford.

Haidt, J. (2006). *The happiness hypothesis: Finding modern truth in ancient wisdom.* New York: Basic.

Haidt, J. (2012). *The righteous mind: Why good people are divided by politics and religion.* New York: Pantheon.

Halberstadt, A. G., Cooke, A. N., Garner, P. W., Hughes, S. A., Oertwig, D., & Neupert, S. D. (2020). Racialized emotion recognition accuracy and anger bias of children's faces. *Emotion, 22*(3), 403–417. Advance online publication. https://doi.org/10.1037/emo0000756

Hall, C. (2012). The effects of reducing tracking in upper secondary school: Evidence from a large-scale pilot scheme. *Journal of Human Resources, 47*(1), 237–269.

Hamilton, T. G. (2019). *Immigration and the remaking of Black America.* New York: Russell Sage Foundation.

Hammons, C. (2002). The Effects of Town Tuitioning in Vermont and Maine. School Choice Issues in Depth. Retrieved from: https://www.edchoice.org/wp-content/uploads/2019/03/The-Effects-of-Town-Tuitioning-in-Vermont-and-Maine.pdf

Hampf, F., & Woessmann, L. (2017). Vocational vs. general education and employment over the life cycle: New evidence from PIAAC. *CESifo Economic Studies, 63*(3), 255–269.

Han, D., & Hur, H. (2021). Managing turnover of STEM teacher workforce. *Education and Urban Society, 54*(2), 205–222. https://doi.org/10.1177/00131245211053562

Han, E. S. (2021). Teacher wage penalty and decrease in teacher quality: Evidence from career-changers. *Labor Studies Journal, 46*(3), 251–285. https://doi.org/10.1177/0160449X20929083

Hanselman, P. (2019). Access to effective teachers and economic and racial disparities in opportunities to learn. *Sociological Quarterly, 60*(3), 498–534. https://doi.org/10.1080/00380253.2019.1625732

Hanushek, E. A. (1994). Money might matter somewhere: A response to Hedges, Laine, and Greenwald. *Educational Researcher, 23*(4), 5–8.

Hanushek, E. (2009). The economic value of education and cognitive skills. In G. Sykes, B. Schneider, & D. Plank (Eds.), *Handbook of education policy research* (pp. 39–56). New York: Routledge.

Hanushek, E. A. (2011). The economic value of higher teacher quality. *Economics of Education Review, 30*(3), 466–479. https://doi.org/10.1016/j.econedurev.2010.12.006

Hanushek, E., Peterson, P., Talpey, L., & Woessmann, L. (2019). The achievement gap fails to close. *Education Next, 19*(3).

Hanushek, E. A., Piopiunik, M., & Wiederhold, S. (2019). The value of smarter teachers: International evidence on teacher cognitive skills and student performance. *Journal of Human Resources, 54*(4), 857–899. https://doi.org/10.3368/jhr.54.4.0317.8619R1

Hanushek, E. A., & Rivkin, S. G. (2010). Generalizations about using value-added measures of teacher quality. *American Economic Review, 100*(2), 267–271. http://www.aeaweb.org/articles.php?doi=10.1257/aer.100.2.267

Hanushek, E. A., Ruhose, J., & Woessmann, L. (2017). Knowledge capital and aggregate income differences: Development accounting for US states. *American Economic Journal: Macroeconomics, 9*(4), 184–224. https://doi.org/10.1257/mac.20160255

Hanushek, E. A., Schwerdt, G., Wiederhold, S., & Woessmann, L. (2015). Returns to skills around the world: Evidence from PIAAC. *European Economic Review, 73*, 103–130.

Hanushek, E., Woessmann, L., & Zhang, L. (2011). *General education, vocational education, and labor-market outcomes over the life-cycle.* Federal Reserve Bank of St. Louis.

Härkönen, J., Lindberg, M., Karlsson, L., Karlsson, H., & Scheinin, N. M. (2018). Education is the strongest socio-economic predictor of smoking in pregnancy. *Addiction, 113*(6), 1117–1126. https://doi.org/10.1111/add.14158

Harper, C. C., & McLanahan, S. S. (2004). Father absence and youth incarceration. *Journal of Research on Adolescence, 14*(3), 369–397. https://doi.org/10.1111/j.1532-7795.2004.00079.x

Harris, D. N., Ingle, W. K., & Rutledge, S. A. (2014). How teacher evaluation methods matter for accountability: A comparative analysis of teacher effectiveness ratings by principals and teacher value-added measures. *American Educational Research Journal, 51*(1), 73–112. https://doi.org/10.3102/0002831213517130

Harris, D. N., & Sass, T. R. (2007). *Teacher training, teacher quality, and student achievement* (Working Paper 3). National Center for Analysis of Longitudinal Data in Education Research. https://caldercenter.org/sites/default/files/1001059_Teacher_Training.pdf

Harris, D., Ziedan, E., & Hassig, S. (2021). *The effects of school reopenings on COVID-19 hospitalizations.* National Center on Education Access and Choice. https://www.reachcentered.org/uploads/technicalreport/The-Effects-of-School-Reopenings-onCOVID-19-Hospitalizations-REACH-January-2021.pdf

Hart, C. M. D. (2020). An honors teacher like me: Effects of access to same-race teachers on Black students' advanced-track enrollment and performance. *Educational Evaluation and Policy Analysis, 42*(2), 163–187.

Hartney, M. T., & Finger, L. K. (2021). Politics, markets, and pandemics: Public education's response to COVID-19. *Perspectives on Politics, 20*(2), 457–473. doi:https://doi.org/10.1017/S1537592721000955

Haskins, R., & Sawhill, I. V. (2016). The decline of the American family: Can anything be done to stop the damage? *Annals of the American Academy of Political and Social Science, 667*(1), 8–34. https://doi.org/10.1177/0002716216663129

Hastings, R., & Meyer, E. (2020). *No rules rules: Netflix and the culture of reinvention.* New York: Penguin.

Haveman, R., & Wolfe, B. (1984). Schooling and economic well-being: The role of nonmarket effects. *Journal of Human Resources, 19*(3), 377–407.

Hawrilenko, M., Kroshus, E., Tandon, P., & Christakis, D. (2021). The association between school closures and child mental health during COVID-19. *JAMA Network Open, 4*(9), e2124092.

Hebert, T. P., & Reis, S. M. (1999). Culturally diverse high-achieving students in an urban high school. *Urban Education, 34*(4), 428–457.

Heckman, J., Humphries, J., & Veramendi, G. (2015). *The causal effects of education on earnings and health* (Unpublished manuscript). Department of Economics, University of Chicago.

Hedges, L. V., Laine, R. D., & Greenwald, R. (1994). An exchange: Part I: Does money matter? A meta-analysis of studies of the effects of differential school inputs on student outcomes. *Educational Researcher, 23*(3), 5–14. https://www.jstor.org/stable/1177220?ref reqid=excelsior%3A57baa9f3941e8c2060acb35245097637&seq=1#metadata_info_tab _contents

Heinrich, C., & Marschke, G. (2010). Incentives and their dynamics in public sector performance management systems. *Journal of Policy Analysis and Management, 29*(1), 183–208.

Hemelt, S. W., Lenard, M. A., & Paeplow, C. G. (2019). Building bridges to life after high school: Contemporary career academies and student outcomes. *Economics of Education Review, 68*, 161–178.

Henderson, M. B., Peterson, P. E., & West, M. R. (2021). Pandemic parent survey finds perverse pattern: Students are more likely to be attending school in person where Covid is spreading more rapidly: Majority of students receiving fully remote instruction; private-school students more likely to be in person full time. *Education Next, 21*(2), 34–48.

Henry, G. T., Bastian, K. C., Fortner, C. K., Kershaw, D. C., Purtell, K. M., Thompson, C. L., & Zulli, R. A. (2014). Teacher preparation policies and their effects on student achievement. *Education Finance and Policy, 9*(3), 264–303. https://doi.org/10.1162/EDFP_a_00134

Herold, B. (2017, June 30). Maryland dad wants June 30 to be "national student data deletion day." *Education Week.* https://www.edweek.org/technology/aryland-dad-wants-june-30-to -be-national-student-data-deletion-day/2017/06

Hess, F. M. (2017). *Letters to a young education reformer.* Cambridge, MA: Harvard Education Press.

Hidi, S., & Renninger, K. A. (2006). The four-phase model of interest development. *Educational Psychologist, 41*(2), 111–127.

Hill, Z., Spiegel, M., Gennetian, L., Hamer, K., Brotman, L., & Dawson-McClure, S. (2021). Behavioral economics and parent participation in an evidence-based parenting program at scale. *Prevention Science, 22*, 891–902.

Ho, A. (2017). *Advancing educational research and student privacy in the "Big Data" era.* Workshop on Big Data in Education: Balancing the Benefits of Educational Research and Student Privacy, pp. 1–18. Washington, DC: National Academy of Education.

Hoffman, D. M. (2009). How (not) to feel: Culture and the politics of emotion in the American parenting advice literature. *Discourse: Studies in the Cultural Politics of Education, 30*(1), 15–31. https://doi.org/10.1080/01596300802643058

Hollands, F., Bowden, A. B., Belfield, C., Levin, H. M., Cheng, H., Shand, R., Pan, Y., & Hanisch-Cerda, B. (2014). Cost-effectiveness analysis in practice: Interventions to improve high school completion. *Educational Evaluation and Policy Analysis, 36*(3), 307–326.

Holmes Erickson, H. (2017). How do parents choose schools, and what schools do they choose? A literature review of private school choice programs in the United States. *Journal of School Choice, 11*(4), 491–506.

Holstein, K., Wortman Vaughan, J., Daumé, H., Dudik, M., & Wallach, H. (2019). *Improving fairness in machine learning systems: What do industry practitioners need?* Proceedings of the 2019 CHI Conference on Human Factors in Computing Systems, 1–16.

Holzer, H. J., & Baum, S. R. (2017). *Making college work: Pathways to success beyond high school.* Washington, DC: Brookings Institution.

Honein, M. A., Barrios, L. C., & Brooks, J. T. (2021, January 26). Data and policy to guide opening schools safely to limit the spread of SARS-CoV-2 infection. *JAMA Network.* https://jamanetwork.com/journals/jama/fullarticle/2775875

Hough, H. J., & Loeb, S. (2013). Can a district-level teacher salary incentive policy improve teacher recruitment and retention? (No. 13–4; Policy Brief, p. 16). Policy Analysis for California Education (PACE).

Howell, W. G., Wolf, P. J., Campbell, D. E., & Peterson, P. E. (2002). School vouchers and academic performance: Results from three randomized field trials. *Journal of Policy Analysis and Management, 21*(2), 191–217.

Hoxby, C. M. (2002). How School Choice Affects the Achievement of Public School Students. In Paul T. Hill (Ed.), *Choice with Equity* (pp. 141–78). Retrieved from https://books.google.com/books?id=IeUk3myQu-oC&lpg=PP1&pg=PA141

Hoxby, C. M., & Leigh, A. (2004). Pulled away or pushed out? Explaining the decline of teacher aptitude in the United States. *American Economic Review, 94*(2), 236–240. https://doi.org/10.1257/0002828041302073

Hu, X., Craig, S. D., Bargagliotti, A. E., Graesser, A. C., Okwumabua, T., Anderson, C., Cheney, K. R., & Sterbinsky, A. (2012). The effects of a traditional and technology-based after-school program on 6th grade student's mathematics skills. *Journal of Computers in Mathematics and Science Teaching, 31*(1), 17–38.

Huang, X., Craig, S. D., Xie, J., Graesser, A., & Hu, X. (2016). Intelligent tutoring systems work as a math gap reducer in 6th grade after-school program. *Learning and Individual Differences, 47*, 258–265.

Hudson, L. (2014). *Trends in CTE coursetaking: Data point*. NCES 2014-117. National Center for Education Statistics. US Department of Education.

Hurd, N., & Deutsch, N. (2017). SEL-focused after-school programs. *Future of Children, 27*(1), 95–115.

Hussar, B., Zhang, J., Hein, S., Wang, K., Roberts, A., Cui, J., Smith, M., Mann, F. B., Barmer, A., & Dilig, R. (2020). *The condition of education 2020*. NCES 2020-144. National Center for Education Statistics. US Department of Education.

Imberman, S. A., & Lovenheim, M. F. (2015). Incentive strength and teacher productivity: Evidence from a group-based teacher incentive pay system. *Review of Economics and Statistics, 97*(2), 364–386. https://doi.org/10.1162/REST_a_00486

Isenberg, E., Max, J., Gleason, P., Johnson, M., Deutsch, J., & Hansen, M. (2016, October 27). *Do low-income students have equal access to effective teachers? Evidence from 26 districts*. Mathematica Policy Research. https://www.mathematica.org/publications/do-low-income-students-have-equal-access-to-effective-teachers-evidence-from-26-districts-es

Jabbar, H., Fong, C. J., Germain, E., Li, D., Sanchez, J., Sun, W. L., & Devall, M. (2019). The competitive effects of school choice on student achievement: A systematic review. *Educational Policy, 36*(2), 247–281. https://doi.org/10.1177/0895904819874756

Jackson, C. K. (2020). Does school spending matter? The new literature on an old question. In L. Tach, R. Dunifon, & D. L. Miller (Eds.), *Confronting inequality: How policies and practices shape children's opportunities* (pp. 165–186). American Psychological Association. https://doi.org/10.1037/0000187-008

Jackson, C. K., Porter, S. C., Easton, J. Q., & Kiguel, S. (2020). *Who benefits from attending effective schools? Examining heterogeneity in high school impacts* (Working Paper No. 28194). National Bureau of Economic Research. http://www.nber.org/papers/w28194

Jacob, B. A., & Lefgren, L. (2008). Can principals identify effective teachers? Evidence on subjective performance evaluation in education. *Journal of Labor Economics, 26*(1), 101–136. https://doi.org/10.1086/522974

Jaeger, D., & Page, M. (1996). Degrees matter: New evidence on sheepskin effects in the returns to education. *Review of Economics and Statistics, 78*, 733–740.

Jagers, R. J., Rivas-Drake, D., & Borowski, T. (2018). *Equity & social and emotional learning: A cultural analysis.* CASEL Assessment Work Group Brief series.

Jagers, R. J., Rivas-Drake, D., & Williams, B. (2019). Transformative social and emotional learning (SEL): Toward SEL in service of educational equity and excellence. *Educational Psychologist, 54*(3), 162–184. https://doi.org/10.1080/00461520.2019.1623032

Jarmolowski, H. (2018). *How teacher evaluations impact compensation.* National Council on Teacher Quality (NCTQ). https://www.nctq.org/blog/Performance-Pay:-How-Teacher-Evaluations-Impact-Compensation

Jarratt, K. (2014). *Mathematics achievement outcomes for middle school students attending school-based afterschool mathematics programs* [Doctoral dissertation]. Union University, Jackson, TN.

Jarvis, J. A., Otero, C., Poff, J. M., Dufur, M. J., & Pribesh, S. L. (2021). Family structure and child behavior in the United Kingdom. *Journal of Child and Family Studies.* https://doi.org/10.1007/s10826-021-02159-z

Jeong, H., Hmelo-Silver, C. E., & Jo, K. (2019). Ten years of computer-supported collaborative learning: A meta-analysis of CSCL in STEM education during 2005–2014. *Educational Research Review, 28*, 100284.

Jeynes, W. H. (2007). The relationship between parental involvement and urban secondary school student academic achievement: A meta-analysis. *Urban Education, 42*(1), 82–110.

Johnston, A. C. (2020). *Teacher preferences, working conditions, and compensation structure* (IZA Discussion Papers, No. 13121). Institute of Labor Economics (IZA), Bonn. https://www.econstor.eu/bitstream/10419/216433/1/dp13121.pdf

Johnston, H. (2012). The Spiral Curriculum. Research into Practice. *Education Partnerships, Inc.*

Jones, B. R. (2014). *An after-school program and its effect on the math and reading performance levels of the standardized testing and reporting (STAR) for identified at-risk students* [Doctoral dissertation]. Capella University, Minneapolis, MN.

Jones, D. E., Karoly, L. A., Crowley, D. M., & Greenberg, M. T. (2015). Considering valuation of noncognitive skills in benefit–cost analysis of programs for children. *Journal of Benefit–Cost Analysis, 6*(3), 471–507.

Jones, J. N., & Deutsch, N. L. (2011). Relational strategies in after-school settings: How staff–youth relationships support positive development. *Youth & Society, 43*(4), 1381–1406. https://search.proquest.com/docview/1497967944/abstract/F46A90DBC46A47D6PQ/1

Jordan, C., Parker, J., Donnelly, D., & Rudo, Z. (Eds.) (2009). *Building and managing quality afterschool programs. A practitioner's guide.* Austin, TX: SEDL.

Jung, Y. (2021). *Formation of the legacy of slavery: Evidence from the US South.* Available at SSRN 3966791. https://papers.ssrn.com/sol3/papers.cfm?abstract_id=3966791

Justice Policy Institute. (2020). Sticker Shock 2014–2020: The Cost of Youth Incarceration.

Kahlenberg, R. D. (2016). Teacher tenure has a long history and, hopefully, a future. *Phi Delta Kappan, 97*(6), 16–21. https://doi.org/10.1177/0031721716636866

Kane, T. (2004). *The impact of after-school programs: Interpreting the results of four recent evaluations* (Working paper). William T. Grant Foundation.

Kane, T., McCaffrey, D., Miller, T., & Staiger, D. (2013). *Have we identified effective teachers? Validating measures of effective teaching using random assignment* (MET Project, p. 52). Bill and Melinda Gates Foundation. https://files.eric.ed.gov/fulltext/ED540959.pdf

Kang, S. K., DeCelles, K. A., Tilcsik, A., & Jun, S. (2016). Whitened résumés: Race and self-presentation in the labor market. *Administrative Science Quarterly, 61*(3), 469–502.

Karumbaiah, S. (2021). *The upstream sources of bias: Investigating theory, design, and methods shaping adaptive learning systems* [Unpublished doctoral dissertation]. University of Pennsylvania, Philadelphia.

Karumbaiah, S., Ocumpaugh, J., & Baker, R. S. (2021). Context matters: Differing implications of motivation and help-seeking in educational technology. To appear in *International Journal of Artificial Intelligence and Education.*

Kaufmann, E. (2019, March 18). Americans are divided by their views on race, not race itself. *New York Times.* https://www.nytimes.com/2019/03/18/opinion/race-america-trump.html

Kearney, M. S., & Levine, P. B. (2017). *The economics of non-marital childbearing and the "marriage premium for children"* (Working Paper No. 23230). National Bureau of Economic Research.

Kelley, C., & Odden, A. (1995). *Reinventing teacher compensation systems.* Consortium for Policy Research in Education, Finance Briefs. https://eric.ed.gov/?id=ED387910

Kelly, J. P., & Scafidi, B. (2013). More than scores: An analysis of why and how parents choose private schools. Indianapolis, IN: Friedman Foundation for Educational Choice (EdChoice). https://www.edchoice.org/wp-content/uploads/2015/07/More-Than-Scores.pdf

Kemple, J., & Willner, C. (2008). *Career academies: Long-term impacts on labor-market outcomes, educational attainment, and transitions to adulthood.* New York: MDRC.

Kennedy, E., & Smolinsky, L. (2016). Math circles: A tool for promoting engagement among middle school minority males. *EURASIA Journal of Mathematics, Science and Technology Education, 12*(4), 717–732.

Kessler-Sklar, S. L., & Baker, A. J. L. (2000). School district parent involvement policies and programs. *Elementary School Journal, 101*(1), 100–118.

Kim, Y-I., & Jang, S. J. (2018). Final evaluation report: A randomized controlled trial of the effectiveness of a responsible fatherhood program: The case of TYRO dads. *Faculty Publications—Department of World Languages, Sociology & Cultural Studies, 53.*

Kim, Y., Mok, S. Y., & Seidel, T. (2020). Parental influences on immigrant students' achievement-related motivation and achievement: A meta-analysis. *Educational Research Review, 30*(100327), 1–19.

Kini, T., & Podolsky, A. (2016). *Does teaching experience increase teacher effectiveness? A review of the research.* Learning Policy Institute. https://files-eric-ed-gov.libproxy.lib.unc.edu/fulltext/ED606426.pdf

Kizilcec, R. F., & Lee, H. (2021). Algorithmic fairness in education. In W. Holmes & K. Porayska-Pomsta (Eds.), *Ethics in artificial intelligence in education.* Abingdon-on-Thames, UK: Taylor & Francis.

Klare, B. F., Burge, M. J., Klontz, J. C., Bruegge, R. W. V., & Jain, A. K. (2012). Face recognition performance: Role of demographic information. *IEEE Transactions on Information Forensics and Security, 7*(6), 1789–1801.

Klose, M., Desai, V., Song, Y., & Gehringer, E. (2020). *EDM and privacy: Ethics and legalities of data collection, usage, and storage.* Proceedings of the 13th International Conference on Educational Data Mining.

Koedel, C., & Betts, J. R. (2011). Does student sorting invalidate value-added models of teacher effectiveness? An extended analysis of the Rothstein Critique. *Education Finance and Policy, 6*(1), 18–42. https://doi.org/10.1162/EDFP_a_00027

Koedel, C., Mihaly, K., & Rockoff, J. E. (2015). Value-added modeling: A review. *Economics of Education Review, 47,* 180–195. https://doi.org/10.1016/j.econedurev.2015.01.006

Koedinger, K. R., Anderson, J. R., Hadley, W. H., & Mark, M. A. (1997). Intelligent tutoring goes to school in the big city. *International Journal of Artificial Intelligence in Education, 8*(1), 30-43.

Koedinger, K., Cunningham, K., Skogsholm, A., & Leber, B. (2008). *An open repository and analysis tools for fine-grained, longitudinal learner data.* Proceedings of the 1st International Conference on Educational Data Mining.

Kolderie, T. (2015). *The split screen strategy: How to turn education into a self-improving system.* St. Paul, MN: Beaver's Pond.

Kövecses, Z. (2003). *Metaphor and emotion: Language, culture, and body in human feeling.* Cambridge, UK: Cambridge University Press.

Kraft, M., & Gilmour, A. (2017). Revisiting *The Widget Effect*: Teacher evaluation reforms and the distribution of teacher effectiveness. *Educational Researcher, 46*(5), 234–249.

Kraft, M. A., Marinell, W. H., & Shen-Wei Yee, D. (2016). School organizational contexts, teacher turnover, and student achievement: Evidence from panel data. *American Educational Research Journal, 53*(5), 1411–1449. https://doi.org/10.3102/0002831216667478

Kraft, M. A., & Papay, J. P. (2014). Can professional environments in schools promote teacher development? Explaining heterogeneity in returns to teaching experience. *Educational Evaluation and Policy Analysis, 36*(4), 476–500. https://doi.org/10.3102/0162373713519496

Kreisman, D., & Stange, K. (2020). Vocational and career tech education in American high schools: The value of depth over breadth. *Education Finance and Policy, 15*(1), 11–44.

Kremer, K. P., Maynard, B. R., Polanin, J. R., Vaughn, M. G., & Sarteschi, C. M. (2015). Effects of after-school programs with at-risk youth on attendance and externalizing behaviors: A systematic review and meta-analysis. *Journal of Youth and Adolescence, 44,* 616–636. https://doi.org/10.1007/s10964-014-0226-4

Kress, J. S., & Elias, M. J. (2006). School-based social and emotional learning programs. In K. A. Renninger & I. E. Sigel (Eds.), *Handbook of child psychology* (6th ed., Vol. 4, pp. 592–618). New York: Wiley.

Krishnamurthi, A., Ballard, M., & Noam, G. G. (2014). *Examining the impact of afterschool STEM programs.* Washington, DC: Afterschool Alliance.

Kulik, J. A., & Fletcher, J. D. (2016). Effectiveness of intelligent tutoring systems: A meta-analytic review. *Review of Educational Research, 86*(1), 42–78.

Kuperminc, G. P., Chan, W. Y., Hale, K. E., Joseph, H. L., & Delbasso, C. A. (2020). The role of school-based group mentoring in promoting resilience among vulnerable high school students. *American Journal of Community Psychology, 65*(1–2), 136–148.

Labaree, D. F. (1997). Public goods, private goods: The American struggle over educational goals. *American Educational Research Journal, 34*(1), 39–81. https://doi.org/10.3102/00028312034001039

Ladd, H., & Sorensen, L. (2015). *Do master's degrees matter? Advanced degrees, career paths, and the effectiveness of teachers* (p. 36). National Center for Analysis of Longitudinal Data in Education Research. https://caldercenter.org/publications/do-master%E2%80%99s-degrees-matter-advanced-degrees-career-paths-and-effectiveness-teachers

Ladd, H. F., & Sorensen, L. C. (2017). Returns to teacher experience: Student achievement and motivation in middle school. *Education Finance and Policy, 12*(2), 241–279.

Laird, E., Quay-de la Vallee, H., & Mahesh, A. (2019). *Balancing the scale of student data deletion and retention in education.* Washington, DC: Center for Democracy and Technology. https://cdt.org/wp-content/uploads/2019/03/Student-Privacy-Deletion-Report.pdf

Lang, K., & Kahn-Lang Spitzer, A. (2020). Race discrimination: An economic perspective. *Journal of Economic Perspectives, 34*(2), 68–89.

Larson, R. W., & Kleiber, D. A. (1993). Structured leisure as a context for the development of attention during adolescence. *Loisir et Société/Society and Leisure, 16*(1), 77–98.

Lauer, P. A., Akiba, M., Wilkerson, S. B., Apthorp, H. S., Snow, D., & Martin-Glenn, M. (2004, January). The effectiveness of out-of-school-time strategies in assisting low-achieving students in reading and mathematics: A research synthesis. Denver, CO: Mid-continent Research for Education and Learning.

Lauer, P. A., Akiba, M., Wilkerson, S. B., Apthorp, H. S., Snow, D., & Martin-Glenn, M. L. (2006). Out-of-school-time programs: A meta-analysis of effects for at-risk students. *Review of Educational Research, 76*(2), 275–313.

Lee, L. (2019, November 26). Lacking training, teachers develop their own SEL solutions. *Edutopia.* https://www.edutopia.org/article/lacking-training-teachers-develop-their-own-sel-solutions

Lee-St. John, T. J., Walsh, M. E., Raczek, A. E., Vuilleumier, C. E., Foley, C., Heberle, A., Sibley, E., & Dearing, E. (2018). The long-term impact of systemic student support in elementary school: Reducing high school dropout. *AERA Open, 4*(4), 1–16.

Lepper, M. R., Woolverton, M., Mumme, D. L., & Gurtner, J. (1993). Motivational techniques of expert human tutors: Lessons for the design of computer-based tutors. *Computers as Cognitive Tools, 75*–105.

Lerman, R. I., Price, J., & Wilcox, W. B. (2017). Family structure and economic success across the life course. *Marriage & Family Review, 53*(8), 744–758.

Lester, A., Chow, J., & Melton, T. (2020). Quality is critical for meaningful synthesis of afterschool program effects: A systemic review and meta-analysis. *Journal of Youth and Adolescence, 49*, 369–382. https://doi.org/10.1007/s10964-019-01188-8

Levesque, K., Laird, J., Hensley, E., Choy, S., Cataldi, E., & Hudson, L. (2008). Career and technical education in the United States: 1990 to 2005 (NCES 2008-035). National Center for Education Statistics. US Department of Education.

Levin, H. M., & McEwan, P. J. (2003). Cost-effectiveness analysis as an evaluation tool. In *International handbook of educational evaluation* (pp. 125–152). Berlin: Springer, Dordrecht.

Lewinsohn, P. M., Seeley, J. R., Roberts, R. E., & Allen, N. B. (1997). Center for Epidemiological Studies-Depression Scale (CES-D) as a screening instrument for depression among community-residing older adults. *Psychology and Aging, 12*(2), 277–287.

Li, H., Gobert, J., Dickler, R., & Moussavi, R. (2018). *The impact of multiple real-time scaffolding experiences on science inquiry practices.* International Conference on Intelligent Tutoring Systems, pp. 99–109. Berlin: Springer.

Lindblom, C. E., & Cohen, D. K. (1979). *Usable knowledge: Social science and social problem solving.* New Haven, CT: Yale University Press.

Lindsay, C. A., & Hart, C. M. D. (2017). Exposure to same-race teachers and student disciplinary outcomes for Black students in North Carolina. *Educational Evaluation and Policy Analysis, 39*(3), 485–510.

Loeb, S., & Candelaria, C. A. (2012). *How stable are value-added estimates across years, subjects and student groups?* (Knowledge Brief 3). Carnegie Foundation for the Advancement of Teaching. https://files.eric.ed.gov/fulltext/ED537430.pdf

Loeb, S., Miller, L. C., & Wyckoff, J. (2015). Performance screens for school improvement: The case of teacher tenure reform in New York City. *Educational Researcher, 44*(4), 199–212. https://doi.org/10.3102/0013189X15584773

Loeb, S., & Myung, J. (2010). Economic approaches to teacher recruitment and retention. In *International encyclopedia of education* (3rd ed., pp. 473–480). Elsevier. https://doi.org/10.1016/B978-0-08-044894-7.01251-3

Lomascolo, D. J., & Angelle, P. S. (2019). Teacher tenure in Tennessee: An examination of principal perceptions post–Race to the Top. *NASSP Bulletin, 103*(2), 98–117. https://doi.org/10.1177/0192636519830766

Lopez, G. A. (2021). Investigating the ransomware infection rate of K12 school districts during the COVID pandemic. Electronic Theses, Projects, and Dissertations. 1317. https://scholarworks.lib.csusb.edu/etd/1317/

Lopoo, L. M., & DeLeire, T. (2014). Family structure and the economic wellbeing of children in youth and adulthood. *Social Science Research, 43*(C), 30–44. https://pubmed.ncbi.nlm.nih.gov/24267751/

Loukina, A., & Buzick, H. (2017, December). *Use of automated scoring in spoken language assessments for test takers with speech impairments* (Research Report No. RR-17-42, pp. 1–10). Princeton, NJ: Educational Testing Service (ETS).

Luallen, J. (2006). School's out . . . forever: A study of juvenile crime, at-risk youths and teacher strikes. *Journal of Urban Economics, 59*(1), 75–103.

Lucas, S. (1999). *Tracking inequality: Stratification and mobility in American high schools.* New York: Teachers College Press.

Luce, F. C. (2018). *The effects of an after-school program on sixth-grade students' PARCC scores in a high-poverty urban location in New Jersey* [Doctoral dissertation]. Saint Peter's University, Jersey City, NJ. http://search.proquest.com/docview/2092265378/abstract/934CF09625EA4E4FPQ/1

Lukianoff, G., & Haidt, J. (2018). *The coddling of the American mind.* New York: Penguin.

Lynch, C. F. (2017). Who prophets from big data in education? New insights and new challenges. *Theory and Research in Education, 15*(3), 249–271.

Ma, W., Adesope, O. O., Nesbit, J. C., & Liu, Q. (2014). Intelligent tutoring systems and learning outcomes: A meta-analysis. *Journal of Educational Psychology, 106*(4), 901–918.

Macchia, S. E., Therriault, D. J., & Wood, R. C. (2021). A cost-benefit analysis of a teen pregnancy program employed as a high school dropout intervention. *Planning & Changing, 50*(1), 20–36.

Machin, S., Marie, O., & Vujić, S. (2011, May 12). The crime reducing effect of education. *Economic Journal, 121*, 463–484.

MacLellan, C. J., & Gupta, A. (2021). *Learning expert models for educationally relevant tasks using reinforcement learning.* International Educational Data Mining Society.

Mader, N. S. (2010). School Choice, Competition, and Academic Quality: Essays on the Milwaukee Parental Choice Program [Doctoral dissertation]. ProQuest.

Mahoney, J. L., Weissberg, R. P., Greenberg, M. T., Dusenbury, L., Jagers, R. J., Niemi, K., Schlinger, M., Schlund, J., Shriver, T. P., VanAusdal, K., & Yoder, N. (2021). Systemic social and emotional learning. *American Psychologist, 76*(7), 1128–1142. https://pubmed.ncbi.nlm.nih.gov/33030926/

Maitra, P., & Mani, S. (2017). Learning and earning: Evidence from a randomized evaluation in India. *Labour Economics, 45*(C), 116–130.

Makridis, C. A. (2020). Do right-to-work laws work? Evidence on individuals' well-being and economic sentiment. *Journal of Law and Economics, 62*(4), 713–745. https://www.journals.uchicago.edu/doi/10.1086/707081

Makridis, C. A., Hickman, L., Manning, B., & Duckworth, A. L. (2022). *Earnings are greater and increasing in occupations that require intellectual tenacity* (SSRN Working paper).

Makridis, C., Piano, C., & DeAngelis, C. (2022). *The effects of school closures on homeschooling and mental health: Evidence from the COVID-19 pandemic.* Available at SSRN 4001953.

Maldonado-Mahauad, J., Pérez-Sanagustín, M., Kizilcec, R. F., Morales, N., & Munoz-Gama, J. (2018). Mining theory-based patterns from Big Data: Identifying self-regulated learning strategies in Massive Open Online Courses. *Computers in Human Behavior, 80*, 179–196.

Maranto, R. (2015). Did the teachers destroy the school? Public entrepreneurship as creation and adaptation. *Journal of School Leadership, 25*(1), 69–101.

Maranto, R., & Crouch, M. (2014, April 20). Ignoring an inequality culprit: Single-parent families. *Wall Street Journal.* http://online.wsj.com/news/articles/SB10001424052702303603904579493612156024266

Maranto, R., Franklin, J., & Camuz, K. (2014). Immigrant advantage: What makes Dove Science Academy fly? In R. A. Fox & N. K. Buchanan (Eds.), *Proud to be different: Ethnocentric niche charter schools in America*, 103–124. Lanham, MD: Rowman & Littlefield Education.

Maranto, R., & McShane, M. Q. (2012). *President Obama and education reform: The personal and the political.* New York: Palgrave/Macmillan.

Maranto, R., & Ritter, G. (2014). Why KIPP is not corporate: KIPP and social justice. *Journal of School Choice, 8*(2) (April–June), 237–257.

Maranto, R., Shakeel, M. D., and Rhinesmith, E. (2018). "Immigrant educational entrepreneurs: Measuring the performance of Turkish-founded charter schools." In C. L. Glenn (Ed.), *Muslim educators in American communities* (pp. 207–220). Charlotte, NC: IAP.

Maranto, R., & Shuls, J. V. (2011). Lessons from KIPP Delta. *Phi Delta Kappan, 93*, 52–56.

Maranto, R., van Raemdonck, D. C., & Vasile, A. (2016). The educational-industrial complex in comparative perspective. *International Journal of Educational Reform, 25*(3), 236–248.

Maranto, R., & Wai, J. (2020). Why intelligence is missing from American education policy and practice, and what can be done about it. *Journal of Intelligence, 8*(1). https://www.mdpi.com/2079-3200/8/1/2/htm

Marianno, B. D., Hemphill, A., & Loures-Elias, A. S. (2022). Power in a pandemic: Teachers' unions and their responses to school reopening. *AERA Open, 8.* https://journals.sagepub.com/doi/10.1177/23328584221074337

Marsh, J. A., Springer, M. G., McCaffrey, D. F., Yuan, K., Epstein, S., Koppich, J., Kalra, N., DiMartino, C., & Peng, A. (X.). (2011). A big apple for educators: New York City's experiment with schoolwide performance bonuses: Final evaluation report. RAND Corporation. https://www.rand.org/pubs/monographs/MG1114.html

Master, B., Sun, M., & Loeb, S. (2018). Teacher workforce developments: Recent changes in academic competitiveness and job satisfaction of new teachers. *Education Finance and Policy, 13*(3), 310–332. https://doi.org/10.1162/edfp_a_00215

Matysiak, A., Styrc, M., & Vignoli, D. (2014). The educational gradient in marital disruption: A meta-analysis of European research findings. *Population Studies, 68*(2), 197–215.

Maurer, M., Brackett, M. A., & Plain, F. (2004). *Emotional literacy in the middle school: A 6-step program to promote social, emotional, and academic learning.* National Professional Resources/Dude.

Mayer, J. D., & Salovey, P. (1997). What is emotional intelligence? In P. Salovey and D. J. Sluyter (Eds.), *Emotional development and emotional intelligence: Educational implications* (pp. 3–34). New York: Basic. https://psycnet.apa.org/record/1997-08644-001

Mayer, S. E. (1997). *What money can't buy: Family income and children's life chances.* Cambridge, MA: Harvard University Press.

McArthur, D., Stasz, C., & Zmuidzinas, M. (1990). Tutoring techniques in algebra. *Cognition and Instruction, 7*(3), 197–244.

McCollister, K., French, M., & Fang, H. (2010). The cost of crime to society: New crime-specific estimates for policy and program evaluation. *Drug and Alcohol Dependence, 108*(1–2), 98–109.

McCollister, K., Yang, X., Sayed, B., French, M., Leff, J., & Schackman, B. (2017). Monetary conversion factors for economic evaluations of substance use disorders. *Journal of Substance Abuse Treatment, 81*, 25–34.

McCombs, J. S., Whitaker, A. A., & Yoo, P. Y. (2017). *The value of out-of-school time programs.* Santa Monica, CA: Rand Corporation.

McEachin, A., Lauen, D. L., Fuller, S. C., & Perera, R. M. (2020, June). Social returns to private choice? Effects of charter schools on behavioral outcomes, arrests, and civic participation. *Economics of Education Review, 76*, 101983.

McFarland, J., Cui, J., Holmes, J., & Wang, X. (2020, January). Trends in high school dropout and completion rates in the United States: 2019 (Compendium Report, NCES 2020-117). National Center for Education Statistics. US Department of Education. https://nces.ed.gov/pubs2020/2020117.pdf

McIntyre, D. J. (1980). Teacher evaluation and the observer effect. *National Association of Secondary School Principals, 64*(434), 36–40. https://journals.sagepub.com/doi/pdf/10.1177/019263658006443408

McLanahan, S. (2004). Diverging destinies: How children are faring under the second demographic transition. *Demography, 41*(4), 607–627.

McLanahan, S., & Jacobsen, W. (2015). Diverging destinies revisited. In P. R. Amato, A. Booth, S. M. McHale, & J. Van Hook (Eds.), *Families in an era of increasing inequality: Diverging destinies* (pp. 3–23). New York: Springer.

McLanahan, S., & Sawhill, I. (2015). Marriage and child wellbeing revisited: Introducing the issue. *Future of Children, 25*(3), 3–9.

McLanahan, S., Tach, L., & Schneider, D. (2013). The causal effects of father absence. *Annual Review of Sociology, 39*(1), 399–427.

McMahon, W. (2018). The total return to higher education: Is there underinvestment for economic growth and development? *Quarterly Review of Economics and Finance, 70*, 90–111.

Meissner, C. A., & Brigham, J. C. (2001). Thirty years of investigating the own-race bias in memory for faces: A meta-analytic review. *Psychology, Public Policy, and Law, 7*(1), 3–35. https://doi.org/10.1037/1076-8971.7.1.3

Mendez, I., & Zamarro, G. (2018). The intergenerational transmission of noncognitive skills and their effect on education and employment outcomes. *Journal of Population Economics, 31*(2), 521–560.

Merrill, D. C., Reiser, B. J., Ranney, M., & Trafton, J. G. (1992). Effective tutoring techniques: A comparison of human tutors and intelligent tutoring systems. *Journal of the Learning Sciences, 2*(3), 277–305.

Michalec, P., & Wilson, J. L. (2021). Truth hidden in plain sight: How social-emotional learning empowers novice teachers' culturally responsive pedagogy in Title I schools. *Journal of Education.* https://doi.org/10.1177/0022057421991866

Middleton, K. E., & Petitt, E. A. (2013). *Who cares? Improving public schools through relationships and customer service.* Tucson, AZ: Wheatmark.

Mikeska, J. N., Holtzman, S., McCaffrey, D. F., Liu, S., & Shattuck, T. (2019). Using classroom observations to evaluate science teaching: Implications of lesson sampling for measuring science teaching effectiveness across lesson types. *Science Education, 103*(1), 123–144. https://doi.org/10.1002/sce.21482

Miles, F. M. (September 2013). Teacher Excellence Initiative: Strategic Compensation.

Miles, F. M. (Revised June 2021). Third Future Schools Concept Paper.

Minney, D., Garcia, J., Altobelli, J., Perez-Brena, N. J., & Blunk, E. (2019). Social-emotional learning and evaluation in after-school care: A working model. *Journal of Youth Development, 14*(3). https://jyd.pitt.edu/ojs/jyd/article/view/19-14-03-PA-02

Mishkind, A. (2014). Definitions of college and career readiness: An analysis by state. Washington, DC: American Institutes for Research.

Mitchell, L. L., Zmora, R., Finlay, J. M., Jutkowitz, E., & Gaugler, J. E. (2021). Do big five personality traits moderate the effects of stressful life events on health trajectories? Evidence from the health and retirement study. *Journals of Gerontology, Series B, 76*(1), 44–55. https://doi.org/10.1093/geronb/gbaa075

Mitrovic, A., & Ohlsson, S. (2016). Implementing CBM: SQL-Tutor after fifteen years. *International Journal of Artificial Intelligence in Education, 26*(1), 150–159.

Mohanty, M. S., & Ullah, A. (2012). Why does growing up in an intact family during childhood lead to higher earnings during adulthood in the United States? *American Journal of Economics and Sociology, 71*(3), 662–695.

Mojarad, S., Baker, R. S., Essa, A., & Stalzer, S. (2021). Replicating studying adaptive learning efficacy using propensity score matching and inverse probability of treatment weighting. *Journal of Interactive Learning Research, 32*(3), 169–203.

Monrad, M. (2007, September). High school dropout: A quick stats fact sheet (p. 4). National High School Center at the American Institutes for Research. https://files.eric.ed.gov/fulltext/ED501066.pdf

Moore, M., Boardman, A., & Vining, A. (2013). More appropriate discounting: The rate of social time preference and the value of the social discount rate. *Journal of Benefit–Cost Analysis 4*(1), 1–16.

Moore, M., Boardman, A., Vining, A., Weimer, D., & Greenberg, D. H. (2004). "Just give me a number!" Practical values for the social discount rate. *Journal of Policy Analysis and Management, 23*(4), 789–812.

Moretti, E. (2004). Estimating the social returns to higher education: Evidence from longitudinal and repeated cross-sectional data. *Journal of Econometrics, 121*, 175–212.

Morgan, S. L., & Todd, J. J. (2009). Intergenerational closure and academic achievement in high school: A new evaluation of Coleman's Conjecture. *Sociology of Education, 82*(3), 267–286.

Morissette, R., Chan, P. C. W., & Lu, Y. (2015). Wages, youth employment, and school enrollment: Recent evidence from increases in world oil prices. *Journal of Human Resources, 50*(1), 222–253.

Moynihan, D. P. (1965). *The Negro family: The case for national action.* Washington, DC: Office of Policy Planning and Research, US Department of Labor.

Murnane, R. (2013). US high school graduation rates: Patterns and explanations. *Journal of Economic Literature, 51*(2), 370–422.

Murray, B., Domina, T., Petts, A., Renzulli, L., & Boylan, R. (2020). "We're in this together": Bridging and bonding social capital in elementary school PTOs. *American Educational Research Journal, 57*(5), 2210–2244.

Murray, C. A. (2012). *Coming apart: The state of White America, 1960–2010.* New York: Crown.

Musaddiq, T., Stange, K. M., Bacher-Hicks, A., & Goodman, J. (2021). The pandemic's effect on demand for public schools, homeschooling, and private schools (Working Paper No. 29262). National Bureau of Economic Research.

National Assessment of Educational Progress (NAEP). (n.d.). National Center for Education Statistics. https://www.nagb.gov/naep/about-naep.html

National Association of Secondary School Principals (NASSP). (n.d.). *Student data privacy.* Retrieved December 20, 2021, from https://www.nassp.org/top-issues-in-education/position-statements/student-data-privacy/

National Center for Education Statistics (NCES). (2021). *High school graduation rates.* Department of Education. https://nces.ed.gov/fastfacts/display.asp?id=805

National Center on Education and the Economy. (2020, November 6). The widening achievement gap in the U.S. https://ncee.org

National Institute of Out-of-School-Time. NOIST.org

NCES. (2020). Estimated average annual salary of teachers in public elementary and secondary schools: Selected years, 1959–60 through 2019–20. *Digest of Education Statistics, 2020.* National Center for Education Statistics. https://nces.ed.gov/programs/digest/d20/tables/dt20_211.50.asp

NCES. (2022). "NCES Database." NCES. nces.ed.gov/nationsreportcard

NCES Annual Reports. (2021a). *Characteristics of public school teachers.* National Center for Education Statistics. https://nces.ed.gov/programs/coe/indicator/clr

NCES Annual Reports. (2021b). *Racial/ethnic enrollment in public schools.* National Center for Education Statistics. https://nces.ed.gov/programs/coe/indicator/cge

NCTQ. (2016). *The national picture: State teacher evaluation policies (2015)* (p. 102). National Council on Teacher Quality. https://www.nctq.org/dmsView/Evaluation_Timeline_Brief_AllStates

NCTQ. (2019). *State of the states 2019: Teacher and principal evaluation policy.* National Council on Teacher Quality. https://www.nctq.org/pages/State-of-the-States-2019:-Teacher-and-Principal-Evaluation-Policy

Neal, D. (1997). The effects of Catholic secondary schooling on educational attainment. *Journal of Labor Economics, 15*(1), 98–123.

Neild, R., Wilson, S., & McClanahan, W. (2019). *Afterschool programs: Review of evidence under the Every Student Succeeds Act.* United States Department of Education.

Nguyen, T. D., Pham, L. D., Crouch, M., & Springer, M. G. (2020). The correlates of teacher turnover: An updated and expanded meta-analysis of the literature. *Educational Research Review, 31*, 100355. https://doi.org/10.1016/j.edurev.2020.100355

Niskanen, W. A. (1968). Nonmarket decision making: The peculiar economics of bureaucracy. *American Economic Review, 58*(2), 293–305. JSTOR 1831817

Nixon, A., Packard, A., & Douvanis, G. (2010). Non-renewal of probationary teachers: Negative retention. *Education, 131*(1), 43–53.

Noonan, R. (2017). STEM Jobs: Update. Economics and Statistics Administration. US Department of Commerce, Washington, DC.

Nye, B., Konstantopoulos, S., & Hedges, L. V. (2004). How large are teacher effects? *Educational Evaluation and Policy Analysis, 26*(3), 237–257. https://doi.org/10.3102/01623737026003237

Nye, C., Turner, H., & Schwartz, J. (2006). Approaches to parent involvement for improving the academic performance of elementary school age children. *Campbell Systematic Reviews, 2*(1): 1–49. https://doi.org/10.4073/csr.2006.4

Oakes, J. (1983). Limiting opportunity: Student race and curricular differences in secondary vocational education. *American Journal of Education, 91*(3), 328–355.

Obama, B. (1995). *Dreams from my father: A story of race and inheritance.* Touchstone.

Ocumpaugh, J., Baker, R., Gowda, S., Heffernan, N., & Heffernan, C. (2014). Population validity for Educational Data Mining models: A case study in affect detection. *British Journal of Educational Technology, 45*(3), 487–501.

Okun, A. M. (1975). *Efficiency and equity: The big tradeoff.* Washington, DC: Brookings Institution.

O'Reilly-Shah, V. N., Gentry, K. R., Walters, A. M., Zivot, J., Anderson, C. T., & Tighe, P. J. (2020). Bias and ethical considerations in machine learning and the automation of perioperative risk assessment. *British Journal of Anaesthesia, 125*(6), 843–846.

Oreopoulos, P., Brown, R. S., & Lavecchia, A. M. (2017). Pathways to education: An integrated approach to helping at-risk high school students. *Journal of Political Economy, 125*(4), 947–984.

Oreopoulos, P., & Petronijevic, U. (2019). *The remarkable unresponsiveness of college students to nudging and what we can learn from it* (Working Paper No. 26059). National Bureau of Economic Research.

Organisation for Economic Co-Operation and Development (OECD). (2021). "OECD-Stat Database." Paris: OECD. https://stats.oecd.org/. Google Scholar.

Orr, L. L. (2015). 2014 Rossi award lecture: Beyond internal validity. *Evaluation Review, 39*(2), 167–178.

Oster, E. (2020). Schools are not spreading covid-19. This new data makes the case. *Washington Post.* https://www.washingtonpost.com/opinions/2020/11/20/covid-19-schoolsdata-reopening-safety/

Oster, E., Jack, R., Halloran, C., Schoof, J., & McLeod, D. (2021). *COVID-19 mitigation practices and COVID-19 rates in schools: Report on data from Florida, New York and Massachusetts.* medRxiv. doi: https://doi.org/10.1101/2021.05.19.21257467

Ouchi, W. G. (2009). *The secret of TSL: The revolutionary discovery that raises school performance.* New York: Simon & Schuster.

Pager, D., & Shepherd, H. (2008). The sociology of discrimination: Racial discrimination in employment, housing, credit, and consumer markets. *Annual Review of Sociology, 34*, 181–209.

Pandey, E. (2021, January 2). Private schools pull students away from public schools. *Axios.* https://www.axios.com/2021/01/02/private-schools-coronavirus-public-schools

Pane, J. F., Griffin, B. A., McCaffrey, D. F., & Karam, R. (2014). Effectiveness of cognitive tutor algebra I at scale. *Educational Evaluation and Policy Analysis, 36*(2), 127–144.

Pane, J. F., McCaffrey, D. F., Slaughter, M. E., Steele, J. L., & Ikemoto, G. S. (2010). An experiment to evaluate the efficacy of cognitive tutor geometry. *Journal of Research on Educational Effectiveness, 3*(3), 254–281.

Papay, J., Murnane, R., & Willett, J. (2015). Income-based inequality in educational outcomes: Learning from state longitudinal data systems. *Educational Evaluation and Policy Analysis, 37*(1), 29S–52S.

Paquette, L., Ocumpaugh, J., Li, Z., Andres, J. M. A. L., & Baker, R. S. (2020). Who's learning? Using demographics in EDM research. *Journal of Educational Data Mining, 12*(3), 1–30.

Park, S., Stone, S. I., & Holloway, S. D. (2017). School-based parental involvement as a predictor of achievement and school learning environment: An elementary school-level analysis. *Children and Youth Services Review, 82*, 195–206.

Patall, E. A., Cooper, H., & Wynn, S. R. (2010). The effectiveness and relative importance of choice in the classroom. *Journal of Educational Psychology, 102*(4), 896. https://doi.org/10.1037/a0019545

Payne, C. M. (2008). *So much reform, so little change.* Cambridge, MA: Harvard Education Press.

Pearlstein, M. (2011). *From family to collapse to America's decline.* Lanham, MD: Rowman & Littlefield.

Pham, L. D., Nguyen, T. D., & Springer, M. G. (2020). Teacher merit pay: A meta-analysis. *American Educational Research Journal, 58*(3), 527–566. https://doi.org/10.3102/0002831220905580

Phillips, A., Pane, J. F., Reumann-Moore, R., & Shenbanjo, O. (2020). Implementing an adaptive intelligent tutoring system as an instructional supplement. *Educational Technology Research and Development, 68*(3), 1409–1437.

Philp, K. D., & Gill, M. G. (2020). Reframing after-school programs as developing youth interest, identity, and social capital. *Policy Insights from the Behavioral and Brain Sciences 7*(1), 19–26.

Pianta, R. C., Hamre, B. K., & Allen, J. P. (2012). Teacher-student relationships and engagement: Conceptualizing, measuring, and improving the capacity of classroom interactions. In S. Christenson, A. Reschly, & C. Wylie (Eds.), *Handbook of research on student engagement* (pp. 365–386). Boston, MA: Springer. https://doi.org/10.1007/978-1-4614-2018-7_17

Plasman, J. S., & Gottfried, M. A. (2018). Applied STEM coursework, high school dropout rates, and students with learning disabilities. *Educational Policy, 32*(5), 664–696.

Plasman, J. S., Gottfried, M. A, & Klasik, D. J. (2021). Do career-engaging courses engage low-income students? *AERA Open, 7.*

Pluckrose, H., & Lindsay, J. (2020). *Cynical theories: How activist scholarship made everything about race, gender, and identity—and why this harms everybody.* Durham, NC: Pitchstone.

Podgursky, M., Monroe, R., & Watson, D. (2004). The academic quality of public school teachers: An analysis of entry and exit behavior. *Economics of Education Review, 23*(5), 507–518.

Podgursky, M. J., & Springer, M. G. (2007). Teacher performance pay: A review. *Journal of Policy Analysis and Management, 26*(4), 909–950. https://doi.org/10.1002/pam.20292

Podgursky, M., & Springer, M. (2011). Teacher compensation systems in the United States K-12 public school system. *National Tax Journal, 64*(1), 165–192. https://doi.org/10.17310/ntj.2011.1.07

Podolsky, A., Kini, T., & Darling-Hammond, L. (2019). Does teaching experience increase teacher effectiveness? A review of US research. *Journal of Professional Capital and Community, 4*(4), 286–308. https://doi.org/10.1108/JPCC-12-2018-0032

Pruett, M. K., Cowan, P. A., Cowan, C. P., Gillette, P., & Pruett, K. D. (2019). Supporting father involvement: An intervention with community and child welfare–referred couples. *Family Relations, 68*(1), 51–67.

Pugatch, T. (2014). Safety valve or sinkhole? Vocational schooling in South Africa. *IZA Journal of Labor & Development, 3*(1), 1–31.

Putnam, R. D. (2015). *Our kids: The American dream in crisis.* New York: Simon & Schuster.

Qin, X., Deutsch, J., & Hong, G. (2021). Unpacking complex mediation mechanisms and their heterogeneity between sites in a Job Corps evaluation. *Journal of Policy Analysis and Management, 40*(1), 158–190.

Quillian, L., Pager, D., Hexel, O., & Midtbøen, A. H. (2017). Meta-analysis of field experiments shows no change in racial discrimination in hiring over time. *Proceedings of the National Academy of Sciences, 114*(41), 10870–10875.

Quinn, D. M. (2021). How to reduce racial bias in grading: New research supports a simple, low-cost teaching tool. *Education Next, 21*(1), 72–78.

Radhakrishnan, L., Leeb, R. T., Bitsko, R. H., et al. (2022, February 25). Pediatric emergency department visits associated with mental health conditions before and during the COVID-19 pandemic—United States, January 2019–January 2022. *Morbidity and Mortal Weekly Report (MMWR), 71*(8), 319–324. https://www.cdc.gov/mmwr/volumes/71/wr/mm7108e2.htm

Rappolt-Schlichtmann, G., Cipriano, C., Robinson K., & Boucher, A. (In press). Universal design for social and emotional learning. In K. R. Harris & S. Robinson (Eds.), *Universal design for learning in the classroom: Practical Application* (2nd ed.). Guilford.

Reardon, S. F., Weathers, E. S., Fahle, E. M., Jang, H., & Kalogrides, D. (2021). Is separate still unequal? New evidence on school segregation and racial academic achievement gaps (CEPA Working Paper No. 19-06, p. 60). Stanford Center for Education Policy Analysis. https://vtechworks.lib.vt.edu/bitstream/handle/10919/97804/SeparateStillEqual.pdf?sequence=1&isAllowed=y

Redding, C., & Smith, T. M. (2016). Easy in, easy out: Are alternatively certified teachers turning over at increased rates? *American Educational Research Journal, 53*(4), 1086–1125. https://doi.org/10.3102/0002831216653206

Redstone, I., & Villasenor, J. (2020). *Unassailable ideas: How unwritten rules and social media shape discourse in American higher education.* New York: Oxford University Press.

Rhinesmith, E. (2017). A review of the research on parent satisfaction in private school choice programs. *Journal of School Choice, 11*(4), 585–603.

Riddell, W. C., & Song, X. (2017). The role of education in technology use and adoption: Evidence from the Canadian Workplace and Employee Survey. *International Labor Review, 70*(5), 1219–1253.

Rigby, J. G., Larbi-Cherif, A., Rosenquist, B. A., Sharpe, C. J., Cobb, P., & Smith, T. (2017). Administrator observation and feedback: Does it lead toward improvement in inquiry-oriented math instruction? *Educational Administration Quarterly, 53*(3), 475–516. https://doi.org/10.1177/0013161X16687006

Roderick, M., Kelley-Kemple, T., Johnson, D. W., & Ryan, S. (2021, September). *The preventable failure: Improvements in high school graduation rates when high schools focused on the ninth grade year* (Working paper). University of Chicago Consortium on School Research. https://consortium.uchicago.edu/publications/the-preventable-failure

Rodriguez, L. A. (2020). Understanding tenure reform: An examination of sense-making among school administrators and teachers. *Teachers College Record: The Voice of Scholarship in Education, 122*(11), 1–42. https://doi.org/10.1177/016146812012201112

Rodriguez, L. A., Nguyen, T. D., & Springer, M. G. (2020). Revisiting teacher quality gaps: Geographic disparities in access to highly effective teachers across Tennessee (Working paper). New York: New York University.

Rodriguez-Menes, J., & Donato, L. (2015). Social capital, social cohesion, and cognitive attainment. In Yaojun Li (Ed.), *The handbook of research methods and applications in social capital* (pp. 324–343). England: Edward Elgar.

Rosenbaum, J. E. (2001). *Beyond college for all: Career paths for the forgotten half.* New York: Russell Sage Foundation.

Rosenbaum, P. R., & Rubin, D. B. (1984). Reducing bias in observational studies using subclassification on the propensity score. *Journal of the American Statistical Association, 79*(387), 516–524.

Ross, E., & Walsh, K. (2019). *State of the states 2019: Teacher and principal evaluation policy* (p. 21). National Council on Teacher Quality. https://www.nctq.org/pages/State-of-the-States-2019:-Teacher-and-Principal-Evaluation-Policy

Ross, E., & Worth, C. (2018). *Databurst: Strategic teacher compensation* (p. 4). National Council on Teacher Quality. https://www.nctq.org/dmsView/Strategic_Compensation_Databurst

Roth, J. L., Malone, L. M., & Brooks-Gunn, J. (2010). Does amount of participation in afterschool programs relate to developmental outcomes? A review of literature. *American Journal of Community Psychology, 45*(3–4), 310–324.

Rothstein, J. (2009). Student sorting and bias in value-added estimation: Selection on observables and unobservables. *Education Finance and Policy, 4*(4), 537–571. https://doi.org/10.1162/edfp.2009.4.4.537

Rouse, C. E. (1998). Private school vouchers and student achievement: An evaluation of the Milwaukee Parental Choice Program. *Quarterly Journal of Economics, 113*(2), 553–602.

Rouse, C. E., Hannaway, J., Goldhaber, D., & Figlio, D. (2013). Feeling the Florida heat? How low-performing schools respond to voucher and accountability pressure. *American Economic Journal: Economic Policy, 5*(2), 251–281.

Roza, M. (2010). *Educational economics: Where do school funds go?* Washington, DC: Urban Institute.

Rubin, D. B. (2001). Using propensity scores to help design observational studies: Application to the Tobacco Litigation. *Health Services and Outcomes Research Methodology 2*, 169–188.

Saarni, C. (1999). *The development of emotional competence.* New York: Guilford.

Salary equity among the counties; state salary supplement, WV Code § 18A-4-5. (2018). https://law.justia.com/codes/west-virginia/2018/chapter-18a/article-4/section-18a-4-5/

Sales, A. C., & Pane, J. F. (2020). *The effect of teachers reassigning students to new cognitive tutor sections.* Proceedings of the 13th International Conference on Educational Data Mining.

Sales, A. C., Wilks, A., & Pane, J. F. (2016). *Student usage predicts treatment effect heterogeneity in the Cognitive Tutor Algebra I program.* Proceedings of the 9th International Conference on Educational Data Mining.

Salovey, P., & Mayer, J. D. (1990). Emotional intelligence. *Imagination, Cognition and Personality, 9*(3), 185–211.

Sanders, W. L., & Rivers, J. C. (1996). Cumulative and residual effects of teachers on future student academic achievement (p. 14). University of Tennessee Value-Added Research and Assessment Center. https://www.beteronderwijsnederland.nl/files/cumulative%20and%20residual%20effects%20of%20teachers.pdf

Sartain, L., & Steinberg, M. (2021). *Can personnel policy improve teacher quality? The role of evaluation and the impact of exiting low-performing teachers* (EdWorkingPaper No. 21-486). Annenberg Institute at Brown University. https://www.edworkingpapers.com/ai21-486

Sass, T. R. (2008). The stability of value-added measures of teacher quality and implications for teacher compensation policy (p. 8) [4]. CALDER (National Center for Analysis of Longitudinal Data in Education Research). https://files.eric.ed.gov/fulltext/ED508273.pdf

Scafidi, B., Tutterow, R., & Kavanagh, D. (2021). This time really is different: The effect of COVID-19 on independent K-12 school enrollments. *Journal of School Choice, 15*(3), 305–330.

Schoenfeld, A. H. (2006). What doesn't work: The challenge and failure of the What Works Clearinghouse to conduct meaningful reviews of studies of mathematics curricula. *Educational Researcher, 35* (2006), 13–21.

Schwalbach, J., & DeAngelis, C. A. (2020). School sector and school safety: A review of the evidence. *Educational Review, 74*(4), 882–898.

Sedlak, A. J., Mettenburg, J., Basena, M., Petta, I., McPherson, K., Greene, A., & Li, S. (2010). *Fourth national incidence study of child abuse and neglect (NIS–4): Report to Congress.* Washington, DC: US Department of Health and Human Services, Administration for Children and Families.

Self, J. (1999). The defining characteristics of intelligent tutoring systems research: ITSs care, precisely. *International Journal of Artificial Intelligence in Education, 10*(3–4), 350–364.

Shadish, W. R., Clark, M. H., & Steiner, P. M. (2008). Can nonrandomized experiments yield accurate answers? A randomized experiment comparing random and nonrandom assignments. *Journal of the American Statistical Association, 103*(484), 1334–1344.

Shakeel, M. D., Anderson, K. P., & Wolf, P. J. (2021). The participant effects of private school vouchers around the globe: A meta-analytic and systematic review. *School Effectiveness and School Improvement, 32*(4), 509–542. https://www.tandfonline.com/doi/abs/10.1080/0924 3453.2021.1906283

Shakeel, M. D., & Peterson, P. E. (2021). *A half century of progress in U.S. student achievement: Agency and Flynn effects; ethnic and SES differences.* Cambridge, MA: Program on Education Policy and Governance, Harvard University.

Shute, V. J., & Psotka, J. (1994). *Intelligent tutoring systems: Past, present, and future.* Technical Report, Armstrong Lab, Brooks Air Force Base. US Air Force.

Shute, V. J., Ventura, M., & Kim, Y. J. (2013). Assessment and learning of qualitative physics in Newton's Playground. *Journal of Educational Research, 106*(6), 423–430.

Siew, N. M., Geofrey, J., & Lee, B. N. (2016). Students' algebraic thinking and attitudes towards algebra: The effects of game-based learning using Dragonbox 12+ app. *Electronic Journal of Mathematics and Technology, 10*(2), 66–79.

Simonsmeier, B. A., Flaig, M., Deiglmayr, A., Schalk, L., & Schneider, M. (2022). Domain-specific prior knowledge and learning: A meta-analysis. *Educational Psychologist, 57*(1), 31–54. https://doi.org/10.1080/00461520.2021.1939700

Singla, A., Rafferty, A. N., Radanovic, G., & Heffernan, N. T. (2021). *Reinforcement learning for education: Opportunities and challenges.* Proceedings of the International Conference on Educational Data Mining.

Slade, S., & Prinsloo, P. (2013). Learning analytics: Ethical issues and dilemmas. *American Behavioral Scientist, 57*(10), 1510–1529.

Smith, T. E., Sheridan, S. M., Kim, E. M., Park, S., & Beretvas, S. N. (2020). The effects of family-school partnership interventions on academic and social-emotional functioning:

A meta-analysis exploring what works for whom. *Educational Psychology Review, 32*(2), 511–544.

Sowell, T. (1978). Three Black histories. In T. Sowell (Ed.), *American ethnic groups*. Washington, DC: Urban Institute.

Sparr, M., Frazier, S., Morrison, C., Miller, K., & Bartko, W. T. (2020). *Afterschool programs to improve social-emotional, behavioral, and physical health in middle childhood: A targeted review of the literature*. Washington, DC: Office of the Assistant Secretary for Planning and Evaluation & Office on Women's Health, Office of the Assistant Secretary for Health, U.S. Department of Health and Human Services.

Springer, M. G., Bastian, K. C., & Brooks, C. (2021). *The unpacking is underway: Current and future directions for teacher preparation data systems* (p. 10). National Institute for Excellence in Teaching. https://www.niet.org/assets/ResearchAndPolicyResources/9afb58ea2d/unpacking-underway-current-future-directions-teacher-preparation-data-systems-springer-bastian-brooks.pdf

Springer, M. G., Halpin, P. F., Springer, J. A., Stuit, D. A., Cohen-Vogel, L., & Brooks, C. D. (2023). Disproportional assignment: The need for strategic student-teacher rostering practices. In T. Downes & K. Killeen (Eds.), *Recent advancements in education finance and policy*. Charlotte, NC: Information Age Publishing.

Springer, M. G., Pane, J. F., Le, V.-N., McCaffrey, D. F., Burns, S. F., Hamilton, L. S., & Stecher, B. (2012). Team pay for performance: Experimental evidence from the Round Rock pilot project on team incentives. *Educational Evaluation and Policy Analysis, 34*(4), 367–390. https://doi.org/10.3102/0162373712439094

Springer, M. G., Swain, W. A., & Rodriguez, L. A. (2016). Effective teacher retention bonuses: Evidence from Tennessee. *Educational Evaluation and Policy Analysis, 38*(2), 199–221. https://doi.org/10.3102/0162373715609687

Springer, M. G., & Taylor, L. L. (2021). Compensation and composition: Does strategic compensation affect workforce composition? *Journal of Education Human Resources, 39*(2), 101–164. https://doi.org/10.3138/jehr-2020-0029

Springer, M. G., & Winters, M. A. (2009, April). *The NYC teacher pay-for-performance program: Early evidence from a randomized trial* (p. 48). Center for Civic Innovation at the Manhattan Institute. https://files.eric.ed.gov/fulltext/ED505911.pdf

Startz, D. (2017, May 11). Education programs and (un)selective colleges. *Brown Center Chalkboard* (blog). Washington, DC: Brookings Institution. https://www.brookings.edu/blog/brown-center-chalkboard/2017/05/11/education-programs-and-unselective-colleges/

St. Clair, L., & Stone, T. (2016). Who gets the better educators in afterschool? An analysis of teaching and learning interactions and student economic status. *School Community Journal, 26*(2), 71–81.

Steenbergen-Hu, S., & Cooper, H. (2013). A meta-analysis of the effectiveness of intelligent tutoring systems on K–12 students' mathematical learning. *Journal of Educational Psychology, 105*(4), 970–987.

Steinberg, M. P., & Garrett, R. (2016). Classroom composition and measured teacher performance: What do teacher observation scores really measure? *Educational Evaluation and Policy Analysis, 38*(2), 293–317. https://doi.org/10.3102/0162373715616249

Steinberg, M. P., & Sartain, L. (2015). Does teacher evaluation improve school performance? Experimental evidence from Chicago's Excellence in Teaching project. *Education Finance and Policy, 10*(4), 535–572. https://doi.org/10.1162/EDFP_a_00173

Stephenson, N. (2003). *The diamond age: Or, a young lady's illustrated primer*. Spectra.

Stevens, A. H., Kurlaender, M., & Grosz, M. (2019). Career technical education and labor market outcomes evidence from California community colleges. *Journal of Human Resources, 54*(4), 986–1036.

Stone, J. R., III, & Aliaga, O. A. (2005). Career and technical education and school-to-work at the end of the 20th century: Participation and outcomes. *Career and Technical Education Research, 30*(2), 123–142.

Student Data Privacy Consortium. (2021). Standard Student Data Privacy Agreement (NDPA Standard Version 1.0) Version 1r7. https://cdn.ymaws.com/www.a4l.org/resource /resmgr/files/sdpc-publicdocs/final_sdpc_ndpa_v1-7.pdf

Student Privacy Compass. (2021, October 5). Student Privacy Primer. https://studentprivacy compass.org/resource/student-privacy-primer/

Sublett, C., Ecton, W., Klein, S., Atwell, A., & D'Amico, M. M. (2021). Community college alignment of workforce education and local labor markets. *Journal of Applied Research in the Community College, 28*(1), 13–29.

Sum, A., Khatiwada, I., McLaughlin, J., & Palma, S. (2009). *The consequences of dropping out of high school.* Boston: Northeastern University. https://www.prisonpolicy.org/scans /The_Consequences_of_Dropping_Out_of_High_School.pdf

Swain, W. A., Rodriguez, L. A., & Springer, M. G. (2019). Selective retention bonuses for highly effective teachers in high poverty schools: Evidence from Tennessee. *Economics of Education Review, 68*, 148–160. https://doi.org/10.1016/j.econedurev.2018.12.008

Sweeney, M. M. (2011). Family-structure instability and adolescent educational outcomes: A focus on families with stepfathers. In G. J. Duncan & R. J. Murnane (Eds.), *Whither opportunity? Rising inequality, schools, and children's life chances* (pp. 229–254). New York: Russell Sage Foundation.

Tan, C. Y., Lyu, M., & Peng, B. (2020). Academic benefits from parental involvement are stratified by parental socioeconomic status: A meta-analysis. *Parenting: Science and Practice, 20*(4), 241–287.

Taylor, E. S., & Tyler, J. H. (2012). The effect of evaluation on teacher performance. *American Economic Review, 102*(7), 3628–3651. https://doi.org/10.1257/aer.102.7.3628

Taylor, R. D., Oberle, E., Durlak, J. A., & Weissberg, R. P. (2017). Promoting positive youth development through school-based social and emotional learning interventions: A meta-analysis of follow-up effects. *Child Development, 88*(4), 1156–1171. https://doi .org/10.1111/cdev.12864

Tenenbaum, H. R., & Ruck, M. D. (2007). Are teachers' expectations different for racial minority than for European White students? A meta-analysis. *Journal of Educational Psychology, 99*(2), 253–273. https://doi.org/10.1037/0022-0663.99.2.253

TenEyck, M. F., Knox, K. N., & El Sayed, S. A. (2021). Absent father timing and its impact on adolescent and adult criminal behavior. *American Journal of Criminal Justice.*

Theobald, R. J., Goldhaber, D. D., Gratz, T. M., & Holden, K. L. (2019). Career and technical education, inclusion, and postsecondary outcomes for students with learning disabilities. *Journal of Learning Disabilities, 52*(2), 109–119.

Therborn, G. (2004). *Between sex and power: Family in the world 1900–2000.* London: Routledge.

Thernstrom, A., & Thernstrom, S. (2003). *No excuses: Closing the racial gap in learning.* New York: Simon & Schuster.

Tipton, E., & Olsen, R. B. (2018). A review of statistical methods for generalizing from evaluations of educational interventions. *Educational Researcher, 47*(8), 516–524.

Turney, K., & Goodsell, R. (2018). Parental incarceration and children's wellbeing. *Future of Children, 28*(1), 147–164.

Tyack, D. (1974). *The one best system: A history of American urban education.* Cambridge, MA: Harvard University Press.

UNICEF. (2020, November). *Averting a lost COVID generation.* https://www.unicef.org /reports/averting-lost-generation-covid19-world-childrens-day-2020-brief

Unterhalter, E. (2009). What is equity in education? Reflections from the capability approach. *Studies in Philosophy and Education, 28,* 415–424. https://doi.org/10.1007/s11217-009 -9125-7

US Bureau of Labor Statistics. (2017, March 17). *Employer costs for employee compensation— December 2016.* News Release USDL-17-0321, table A, p. 2.

US Bureau of Labor Statistics. (2021). *Education pays.* https://www.bls.gov/emp/chart-unem ployment-earnings-education.htm

US Census Bureau. (2019). *2019 public elementary-secondary education finance data.* https://www.census.gov/data/tables/2019/econ/school-finances/secondary-education -finance.html

US Census Bureau. (2021, March 22). *Homeschooling on the rise during COVID-19 pandemic.* https://www.census.gov/library/stories/2021/03/homeschooling-on-the-rise-during-covid -19-pandemic.html

US Department of Commerce. (2019). https://www.commerce.gov/data-and-reports/reports

US Department of Commerce, Census Bureau. (2000, 2010, & 2018, October Supplement). *Current Population Survey (CPS): Digest of Education Statistics 2019,* table 302.60.

US Department of Education. (2015).Every Student Succeeds Act (ESSA). https://www .ed.gov/essa?src=rn

US Department of Education. (2015). *High school longitudinal study of 2009: 2013 update.* Institute of Education Sciences. National Center for Education Statistics. https://nces .ed.gov/surveys/hsls09/index.asp

US Department of Education. (2019a). *Young adult educational and employment outcomes by family socioeconomic status.* National Center for Education Statistics. https://nces.ed.gov /programs/coe/indicator/tbe

US Department of Education. (2019b). *Integrated Postsecondary Education Data System (IPEDS), winter 2016–17, graduation rates component: Digest of Education Statistics 2017, 2019b,* table 326.10. National Center for Education Statistics. https://nces.ed.gov/pro grams/raceindicators/indicator_red.asp#info

U.S. Department of Education (2021). *Digest of Education Statistics.* Table 326.10. 2021 Tables and Figures. https://nces.ed.gov/programs/digest/d21/tables/dt21_326.10.asp. (Accessed November 19, 2022).

US Department of Justice. (2000). *Annual report to Congress.* National Institute of Justice. https://www.ojp.gov/pdffiles1/nij/189105.pdf

US Office of Management and Budget. (2003, September 17). *Circular A-4: Regulatory analysis.* https://obamawhitehouse.archives.gov/omb/circulars_a004_a-4/

*USA Today.* (2013). "Obama speaks on importance of fatherhood," February 17, 2013. https://www.usatoday.com/story/theoval/2013/02/17/obama-chicago-fatherhood-econ omy-gun-control/1925727/

Valant, J. (2020, July 29). School reopening plans linked to politics rather than public health. *Brown Center Chalkboard* (blog). https://www.brookings.edu/blog/brown-centerchalk board/2020/07/29/school-reopening-plans-linked-to-politics-rather-than-public-health/

Vance, J. D. (2016). *Hillbilly elegy*. New York: HarperCollins.

Vandell, D. L., Reisner, E. R., & Pierce, K. M. (2007, October). Outcomes linked to high-quality afterschool programs: Longitudinal findings from the study of promising afterschool programs. Policy Studies Associates, with Charles Stewart Mott Foundation.

VanLehn, K. (2011). The relative effectiveness of human tutoring, intelligent tutoring systems, and other tutoring systems. *Educational Psychologist, 46*(4), 197–221.

Veney, D., & Jacobs, D. (2021). Voting with their feet: A state-level analysis of public charter school and district public school enrollment trends. https://www.publiccharters.org/our-work/publications/voting-their-feet-state-level-analysis-public-charter-school-and-district

Vidourek, R. A., & King, K. A. (2019). Socio cultural influences on teenage pregnancy and contemporary prevention measures.

Vining, A., & Weimer, D. (2010). An assessment of important issues concerning the application of benefit-cost analysis to social policy. *Journal of Benefit–Cost Analysis, 1*(1), 1–38.

Vining, A., & Weimer, D. (2019). The value of high school graduation in the United States: Per-person shadow price estimates for use in cost–benefit analysis. *Administrative Sciences, 9*(4), 81–96.

von Hippel, P. T., & Bellows, L. (2018, May 8). Rating teacher-preparation programs. *Education Next, 18*(3), 34–41. https://www.educationnext.org/rating-teacher-preparation-programs-value-added-make-useful-distinctions/

Walker, T. (2022, February 1). Survey: Alarming number of educators may soon leave the profession. *NEA News*. https://www.nea.org/advocating-for-change/new-from-nea/survey-alarming-number-educators-may-soon-leave-profession

Wallace, A., & Palmer, J. (2018, June). *Building social and emotional skills in afterschool programs: A literature review*. In National Conference of State Legislatures. https://www.ncsl.org/Portals/1/Documents/educ/Social_Emotional_32470.pdf

Wallerstein, J., Lewis, J., & Rosenthal, S. P. (2013). Mothers and their children after divorce: Report from a 25-year longitudinal study. *Psychoanalytic Psychology, 30*(2), 167–184.

Washington State Institute for Public Policy. *Benefit–cost technical documentation.* (2019, December). https://www.wsipp.wa.gov/TechnicalDocumentation/WsippBenefitCostTechnicalDocumentation.pdf

Weimer, D. (2017). *Behavioral economics for cost–benefit analysis: Benefit validity when sovereign consumers seem to make mistakes*. New York: Cambridge University Press.

Weimer, D. L., Moberg, D. P., French, F., Tanner-Smith, E. E., & Finch, A. J. (2019). Net benefits of recovery high schools: Higher cost but increased sobriety and increased probability of high school graduation. *Journal of Mental Health Policy and Economics, 22*(3), 109–120.

Weimer, D., & Vining, A. (Eds.). (2009). *Investing in the disadvantaged: Assessing the benefits and costs of social policies*. Washington, DC: Georgetown University Press.

Weisberg, D., Sexton, S., Mulhern, J., & Keeling, D. (2009). *The widget effect: Our national failure to acknowledge and act on differences in teacher effectiveness* (p. 48). The New Teacher Project. https://tntp.org/assets/documents/TheWidgetEffect_2nd_ed.pdf

Weisman, S. A., & Gottfredson, D. C. (2001). Attrition from after school programs: Characteristics of students who drop out. *Prevention Science, 2*(3), 201–205.

Werner, K., Blagg, K., Acs, G., Martin, S., McClay, A., Moore, K. A., Pina, G., & Sacks, V. (2021). *Social genome model 2.0 technical documentation and user guide*. Urban Institute.

West, K. L., & Mykerezi, E. (2011). Teachers' unions and compensation: The impact of collective bargaining on salary schedules and performance pay schemes. *Economics of Education Review, 30*(1), 99–108. https://doi.org/10.1016/j.econedurev.2010.07.007

West, M. R., & Peterson, P. E. (2006). The efficacy of choice threats within school account-ability systems: Results from legislatively induced experiments. *Economic Journal, 116*(510), C46–C62.

White House, The. (2011, March 14). *President Obama calls on Congress to fix No Child Left Behind before the start of the next school year* [Press release]. https://obamawhitehouse. archives.gov/realitycheck/the-press-office/2011/03/14/president-obama-calls-congress-fix -no-child-left-behind-start-next-schoo

Wilcox, W. B. (2018, March 22). For black boys, family structure still matters. *Institute for Family Studies* (blog). https://ifstudies.org/blog/for-black-boys-family-structure-still-matters

Wilcox, W. B., & Stokes, C. E. (2015). The family foundation: What do class and family structure have to do with the transition to adulthood? In P. R. Amato, A. Booth, S. M. McHale, and J. Van Hook (Eds.), *Families in an era of increasing inequality: Diverging destinies* (pp. 147–157). Cham: Springer International.

Will, M. (2018, September 28). From "rotten apples" to martyrs: America has changed its tune on teachers. *Education Week.* https://www.edweek.org/teaching-learning/from-rotten -apples-to-martyrs-america-has-changed-its-tune-on-teachers/2018/09

Williams, J. C. (2017). *White working class: Overcoming class cluelessness in America.* Cambridge, MA: Harvard Business Review.

Wilson, W. J. (1987). *The truly disadvantaged: The inner city, the underclass, and public policy.* Chicago: University of Chicago Press.

Winn, M. T., & Winn, L. T. (2021). *Restorative justice in education: Transforming teaching and learning through the disciplines.* Cambridge, MA: Harvard Education Press.

Winters, M. A., & Greene, J. P. (2011). Public school response to special education vouchers: The impact of Florida's McKay Scholarship Program on disability diagnosis and student achievement in public schools. *Educational Evaluation and Policy Analysis, 33*(2), 138–158.

Winters, M. A., Haight, R. C., Swaim, T. T., & Pickering, K. A. (2013). The effect of same-gender teacher assignment on student achievement in the elementary and secondary grades: Evidence from panel data. *Economics of Education Review, 34*(C), 69–75.

Wolf, P. J. (2007). Civics exam: Schools of choice boost civic values. *Education Next, 7*(3), 66–72.

Wolf, P. J., Kisida, B., Gutmann, B., Puma, M., Eissa, N., & Rizzo, L. (2013). School vouch-ers and student outcomes: Experimental evidence from Washington, DC. *Journal of Policy Analysis and Management, 32*(2), 246–270.

Wolf, P., & McShane, M. (2013). Is the juice worth the squeeze? A benefit/cost analysis of the District of Columbia Opportunity Scholarship program. *Education Finance and Policy, 8*(1), 74–99.

Wolfe, B., & Haveman, R. (2001). Accounting for the social and non-market benefits of education. In J. F. Helliwell (Ed.), *The contribution of human and social capital to sustained economic growth and well-being* (pp. 221–250). Vancouver: University of British Columbia Press.

Woods, J. R. (2016, May). *Mitigating teacher shortages: Alternative teacher certification* (p. 7). Education Commission of the States. https://www.ecs.org/wp-content/uploads/Mitigating -Teacher-Shortages-Alternative-Certification.pdf

Xia, M., Asano, Y., Williams, J. J., Qu, H., & Ma, X. (2020, August). *Using information visu-alization to promote students' reflection on "gaming the system" in online learning.* Proceedings of the Seventh ACM Conference on Learning@Scale, pp. 37–49.

Xu, Z., Wijekumar, K., Ramirez, G., Hu, X., & Irey, R. (2019). The effectiveness of intelligent tutoring systems on K-12 students' reading comprehension: A meta-analysis. *British Journal of Educational Technology, 50*(6), 3119–3137.

Yacobson, E., Fuhrman, O., Hershkovitz, S., & Alexandron, G. (2021). De-identification is insufficient to protect student privacy, or—What can a field trip reveal? *Journal of Learning Analytics, 8*(2), 83–92.

Yeager, D. S., Purdie-Vaughns, V., Hooper, S. Y., & Cohen, G. L. (2017). Loss of institutional trust among racial and ethnic minority adolescents: A consequence of procedural injustice and a cause of life-span outcomes. *Child Development, 88*(2), 658–676.

Yettick, H., Cline, F., & Young, J. (2012). Dual goals: The academic achievement of college prep students with career majors. *Journal of Career and Technical Education, 27*(2), 120–142.

Yeung, R. (2020). The effect of the Medicaid expansion on dropout rates. *Journal of School Health, 90*(10), 745–753.

Young, S., Range, B. G., Hvidston, D. J., & Mette, I. M. (2015). Teacher evaluation reform: Principals' beliefs about newly adopted teacher evaluation systems. *Planning and Changing, 46*(1/2), 158–174.

Zamarro, G., Camp, A., Fuchsman, D., & McGee, J. (2021). *Understanding how COVID-19 has changed teachers' chances of remaining in the classroom* (EDRE Research Brief No. 2021–01). University of Arkansas. https://edre.uark.edu/_resources/pdf/teacher_turnover_covid.pdf

Zeide, E. (2017). The structural consequences of big data-driven education. *Big Data, 5*(2), 164–172.

Zenou, Y., & Boccard, N. (2000). Racial discrimination and redlining in cities. *Journal of Urban Economics, 48*(2), 260–285.

Zerbe, R. O., Plotnick, R. D., Kessler, R. C., Pecora, P. J., Hiripi, E., O'Brien, K., Williams, J., English, D., & White, J. (2009). Benefits and costs of intensive foster care services: The Casey Family programs compared to state services. *Contemporary Economic Policy, 27*(3), 308–320.

Zief, S. G., Lauver, S., & Maynard, R. A. (2006). Impacts of after-school programs on student outcomes. *Campbell Systematic Reviews, 2*(1), 1–51.

Zilic, I. (2018). General versus vocational education: Lessons from a quasi-experiment in Croatia. *Economics of Education Review, 62*, 1–11.

Zill, N. (2015, February 3). More than 60% of U.S. kids live with two biological parents. *Institute for Family Studies* (blog). https://ifstudies.org/blog/more-than-60-of-u-s-kids-live-with-two-biological-parents

Zimmerman, K. O., Akinboyo, I. C., Brookhart, M. A., Boutzoukas, A. E., McGann, K. A., Smith, M. J., Panayotti, G. M., Armstrong, S. C., Bristow, H., Parker, D., Zadrozny, S., Weber, D. J., & Benjamin, D. K., Jr.; ABC Science Collaborative. (2021). Incidence and secondary transmission of SARS-CoV-2 infections in schools. *Pediatrics, 147*(4).

Zins, J. E., Bloodworth, M. R., Weissberg, R. P., & Walberg, H. J. (2007). The scientific base linking social and emotional learning to school success. *Journal of Educational and Psychological Consultation, 17*(2–3), 191–210. https://doi.org/10.1080/10474410701413145

# Index

Abecedarian Program, 4
accountability: in school reform, 9; student
    funding and, 42; in systems, 205, *209,*
    *210*; for teachers, 158–60
ACGR. *See* adjusted cohort graduation rates
achievement gap, 17; parental involvement
    in, 27; socioeconomic status (SES) and,
    161–62; in systems, 196, 200, 208
Adamson, F., 161
adjusted cohort graduation rates (ACGR),
    97, 97n1; for minorities, 98–99, *99*
adolescence: after-school programs for, *59;*
    student outcomes in, 4, *5*
adolescents, of single-parent homes, 18
adulthood, student outcomes in, *5*
Advanced level, of System Review Rubric,
    213–14
Affordable Care Act, 113
after-school programs, 7, 55–64; behavioral
    problems and, 58, 62–63; CEA for,
    61–62, *62;* future research on, 63–64;
    government funding for, 55–56,
    60–61; implementation of, 58–61, *59;*
    personnel and attendance for, 59–60;
    programming recommendations for, 58,
    *59;* quality in, 56, 58; recreation in, 57;

    SEL in, 56–57, 61, *63;* STEM in, 57,
    *59;* student outcomes from, 56
Agostinelli, F., 45
AI. *See* artificial intelligence
alcohol abuse, 7; after-school programs and,
    58; of parents, 4
ALEKS, 123, 125
algorithmic bias, 8, 123–24, 126–29, 131
Aliaga, O. A., 71–72
American Academy of Child and Adolescent
    Psychiatry, 178
American Academy of Pediatrics, 178
American Education Research Association,
    18–19
American Federation of Teachers, 38
American Indians/Native Americans: in
    college, 109; graduation rates of, 99;
    teachers of, 161
*American Journal of Sociology,* 20
American Political Science Association,
    18–19
American Pulse Survey, 48
American Rescue Plan (ARP), 41, 190
Anderson, K. P., 42
anger bias, 179
apprenticeships, with CTE, 73, 89, 92

ARP. *See* American Rescue Plan
artificial intelligence (AI), 2, 8, 123–24;
    privacy with, 128; promise of, 124–26
Asians: in college, 109; in CTE, 78; family
    involvement of, 27; graduation rates of,
    99, *99*
Association for Career and Technical
    Education, 80
attachment theory, 14–15, 21, 27–28
attendance, 7; in CTE, 91; single-parent
    homes and, 21; teachers and, 143, 145
Atwell, A., 73
Australia, 181
automation, 2; graduation rates and, 107

Bacher-Hicks, A., 40
Baker, R. S., 126–27
Bartanen, B., 156
Bartik, T., 112
Batalden, Paul, 197n5
Becker, Gary, 15, 16, 21
Bedrick, J., 48
behavioral problems/negative behavior, 7;
    after-school programs and, 58, 62–63;
    CEA for, 61; two-parent homes and, 21
Bellows, L., 147n9
Betts, J. R., 42
Biden, Joe, 60
Blacks: achievement gap of, 17; anger bias
    of, 179; in college, 109; COVID-19
    school closures and, 45; in CTE, 78,
    80, 87, 91; family involvement of, 18;
    graduation rates of, 99, *99*, 108; racism
    toward, 178–79; SEL for, 183; teachers
    for Black students, 113–14; teachers of,
    145, 161; two-parent homes of, 25
blended families, 13
Bloom, H. S., 114
Blueprint, of RULER, 181
Blunt, Roy, 41
Boardman, A., 102, 103
Bonilla, S., 71
Boys and Girls Clubs, 56
Brink, H. M., van den, 112
Brooks, C. D., 151n11
Brooks-Gunn, J., 56
Brunner, E., 71

Cabus, S., 112
California, 38; class-size reduction policy
    in, 19
Campbell Collaborate, 26
Canada, 181
Cantrell, S., 142, 155–56
Career and Technical Education (CTE), 7,
    69–93; access to, 90–91; apprenticeships
    with, 73, 89, 92; attrition from, 75;
    counseling for, 89; data on, 74–76;
    descriptive findings on, 76–80, *77–79*;
    equity in, 91–93; government funding
    for, 71; in international context, 73–74;
    marginalized and, 71; partnerships
    for, 89–90; policy and practice
    recommendations for, 88–93; quality
    of, 90, 92; relevance of, 90; student
    outcomes of, 70–73, 88–89; study
    methods for, 80–84, *81–83*; study results
    and discussion on, 85–88, *86, 87*
caregivers: instability of, 27–29; looping
    of, 6; SEL with, 187–88; single-parent
    homes and, 6
Carruthers, C. K., 73
Carver-Thomas, D., 157
CASEL. *See* Collaborative for Academic,
    Social, and Emotional Learning
CBA. *See* cost-benefit analysis
CCDBG. *See* Child Care and Development
    Block Grant
CCLC. *See* 21st Century Community
    Learning Centers
CDC. *See* Centers for Disease Control and
    Prevention
CEA. *See* cost-effectiveness analysis
Cellini, S., 71–72
Census Bureau, U.S., 45, 48
Centers for Disease Control and Prevention
    (CDC), 38
charter schools, 27, 48; in COVID-19
    pandemic, 39; home visits with, 29;
    systems of, 201
Chetty, R., 25, 142, 143, 145, 151n11, 164
child abuse, 21
Child Care and Development Block Grant
    (CCDBG), 60, 61
Children's Hospital Association, 178

Chile, 181
China, 181
Chow, J., 56, 63
Civil Rights Act of 1964, 17
Classroom Assessment Scoring System
     (CLASS), 153
class-size reduction policy, in California, 19
Cline, F., 71–72
Clinton, Bill, 18
Cognitive Tutor (Mathia), 123, 125
Coleman, James, 15, 17, 20, 27
Coleman Report *(Equality of Educational
     Opportunity)*, 17–18, 19, 20
Collaborative for Academic, Social, and
     Emotional Learning (CASEL), 187
college: CTE and, 7, 70–71, 72–73, 85;
     enrollment rates for, 109; graduation
     rates and, 104–5, 112; teachers and,
     143, 145; two-parent homes and, 14, 21
Colombia, 73
Colorado, 204
community involvement, 13–29;
     educational research on, 25–26; SEL
     with, 187–88; social capital and, 25; in
     systems, 203
compensation: in school reform, 9; in
     systems, 206, *211–12*; of teachers, 8, 9,
     144, 146–49, 146nn7–8, 147n9, *148,*
     164–65, 202
cost-benefit analysis (CBA), 7, 100–101,
     106, 107, 110–12
cost-effectiveness analysis (CEA), 7, 61–62,
     *62,* 100–101, 107, 110–12
counseling, 7, 111; for CTE, 89; graduation
     rates and, 113; in public schools, 14
COVID-19 pandemic, 2, 14, 195–96;
     politicization of, 39–40; private schools
     in, 37–38, 40, 41; public schools in,
     37–40, 41; remote schooling in, 48;
     school closures in, 6, 45–46; SEL in,
     178; STEM in, 197; student funding in,
     37–41; teachers and, 157n16; teachers
     unions in, 37–40, 41
crime. *See* juvenile crime/delinquency
Croatia, 74
Cronbach's alpha, 22
Crouch, M., 18, 157

CTE. *See* Career and Technical Education
Cunha, F., 16

Dallas, Texas, 204
D'Amico, M. M., 73
Danielson, Charlotte, 153
Darling-Hammond, L., 157, 161
day care: private schools as, 38; for teenage
     pregnancy, 111–12
DeAngelis, C. A., 43
Dee, T., 40
defunding, of public schools, 44–45
Democratic Socialists of America, 39
demographic data: algorithmic bias and, 8;
     privacy and, 131
Department of Education, U.S., 69, 74
depression: two-parent homes and, 21, 24;
     UAS on, 22
De Ridder, K. A. A., 145n6
Desai, V., 128
DeSantis, Ron, 40
Deutsch, N., 56–57
De Witte, K., 112–13
*Diamond Age* (Stephenson), 124
disabled students: in CTE, 70, 72, 74,
     75n1, 76, 87, 88, 91; SEL of, 186
discipline, in schools, 19, 29
discount rate, for graduation rates, 105–7,
     *106*
divorce, 14; rate increase in, 20
Doepke, M., 45
Dominican Republic, 73
Dougherty, S., 71, 72, 73
Dragonbox, 123
drop outs. *See* graduation rates
drug abuse, 7; after-school programs and,
     58
Ducey, Doug, 40
Durlak, J. A., 56, 57
dynamic complementarity, 16

early childhood education, 3–6; after-school
     programs for, *59*; RULER for, 181
ecological systems theory, 180
Ecton, W. G., 72, 73
educational technology: algorithmic bias
     in, 8, 123–24, 126–27, 128–29, 131;

equity and privacy with, 8, 123–32; marginalized and, 127. *See also* artificial intelligence

education production function, family involvement and, 16–17

education savings account program, 6; increased number of states with, 48; parental involvement in, 47–48

Egalite, A. J., 42, 157

Emotional Intelligence Charter, of RULER, 180

emotional intelligence theory, 180

employment: CTE for, 7, 69–93; distribution polarization, 1; graduation rates and, 108, 109; single-parent homes and, 22–23, *23*; two-parent homes and, 21–23, *23*

England, 181

*Equality of Educational Opportunity* (Coleman Report), 17–18, 19, 20

Equitable Rostering Solution (ERS), 163, 167

equity: in CTE, 91–93; educational technology and, 8; education and, *3*; privacy and, 8, 123–32; SEL for, 179, 181–89; systems for, 194–208, *209–14*; with teachers, 160–63

ERS. *See* Equitable Rostering Solution

Every Student Succeeds Act (ESSA), 60–61, 190

eXchange, 128

family involvement, 13–29; of Blacks, 18; Coleman Report and, 17–18; education production function and, 16–17; evaluation of interventions in, 26–27; in graduation rates, 109, 113; human capital and, 16–17; policy, practice, and future research on, 27–29; in private schools, 41–43; in public schools, 41–43; RULER for, 181; schools and, 28–29; student funding and, 42; student outcomes and, 15, 17–18, 20–26, *23, 24,* 41–43; in systems, 203; UAS and, 22–25; waning attention to, 18–19. *See also* parental involvement

fertility rate, 20

Figlio, D. N., 42

Finch, Andrew J., 111

Finger, L. K., 40

Flanders, 40

Florida, 111–12

food stamps, 43

foster care: costs of, 61; graduation rates and, 101

4-H, 56

Framework for Teaching, 153

French, F., 111

Freudenberg, N., 145n6

Garcia, J. L., 4

Gates Foundation, 153

Gehringer, E., 128

gender identity, SEL for, 177

Gershenson, S., 113–14

GI Bill, 43

gig work, 107

Gilmour, A., 153

Glazerman, S., 162

globalization, 107

Goldhaber, D. D., 161

Goodman, J., 40

Gottfried, M., 72

governance: of private schools, 41; of public schools, 41; in school reform, 9; student funding and, 37, 41; of systems, 201, 204

GPA: in CTE, 91; in Social Genome Model, 4; teachers and, 145

grade retention: graduation rates and, 113; teacher value-added score and, 143

graduation rates: after-school programs and, 58, 61, *63*; benefits in, 105–7, *106*; CBA for, 7, 100–101, 106, 107, 110–12; CEA for, 7, 100–101, 107, 110–12; CTE and, 71, 72, 76, 87–88; discount rate for, 105–7, *106*; employment and, 108, 109; equity in, 97–115; incarceration and, 145n6; income and, 98–109, *103, 106*; of minorities, 98–100, *99,* 108–14; policy implications for, 114–15; productivity and, 100–101, 103–4; requirements for, 197; shadow price and, 101–9, *103, 106*; single-

parent homes and, 18; social value of, 100–101; teachers and, 145, 145n6; two-parent homes and, 18, 21
Granger, R., 56
Grannis, K. S., 62
Greenberg, D., 102
Grissom, J. A., 156, 157
Groot, W., 112
Grosz, M., 73
growth mind-set, in SEL, 183, 188

Hanselman, P., 161, 163
Hanushek, E. A., 142, 143
Harris, D. N., 156
Hart, C. M. D., 113–14
Hartney, M. T., 40
Haveman, R., 108
Hawn, M. A., 126–27
Hawrilenko, M., 45
Head Start, 43
Heckman, J. J., 4, 16, 103
Hemelt, S., 71
Henderson, M. B., 37
Hendren, N., 25
Herschbein, B., 112
Hess, F. M., 29
Hidi, S., 57
high-risk sexual behavior: after-school programs and, 56, 61. *See also* teenage pregnancy
high school: after-school programs for, *59*; RULER for, 181; two-parent homes and, 14. *See also* Career and Technical Education; graduation rates
*High School and Beyond,* 20
High School Longitudinal Study of 2009 (HSLS), 74, 76, 84
*Hillbilly Elegy* (Vance), 13, 28
Hippel, P. T von, 147n9
Hispanics: in college, 109; COVID-19 school closures and, 45; in CTE, 78, 80, 87, 91; family involvement of, 27; graduation rates of, 99, *99*; teachers for Hispanics students, 113–14; teachers of, 145, 161
Hollands, F., 110–11
homeschooling, 48

home visits, 29
Honein, M. A., 39
HSLS. *See* High School Longitudinal Study of 2009
Huffaker, E., 40
human capital: after-school programs and, 63; Coleman Report and, 17–18; family involvement and, 16–17; social capital and, 20
*Human Capital* (Becker), 16
Hurd, N., 56–57
Hyman, J., 113–14

IEP. *See* Individual Education Plan
Improving America's Schools Act, 55
incarceration, 4; costs of, 61; graduation rates and, 145n6; numbers in, 62; teachers and, 145n6
income: graduation rates and, 98–109, *103, 106*; polarization, 1; single-parent homes and, *23,* 23–24; teachers and, 143, 145; two-parent homes and, *23,* 23–24
India, 73
Individual Education Plan (IEP), 75n1
Inq-ITS, 125
intact homes. *See* two-parent homes
intelligent tutoring systems, 124–25
intentionality, in after-school programs, 6–7, 55–64
Italy, 181

Jackson, C. K., 143, 144, 144n5, 145, 165
Jacobs, D., 48
Jarmolowski, H., 150
Jepsen, C., 73
Job Corps, 7, 110
Jobs for the Future, 80
JOBSTART, 7, 110
Jones, M. R., 25
Justice Policy Institute, 62
juvenile crime/delinquency, 7; after-school programs and, 55, 58, 61, 62–63, *63*; graduation rates and, 101; in public and private schools, 43

"Kalamazoo Promise" Universal Scholarships, 112

Kane, T., 142, 153, 155–56
Karumbaiah, S., 127
Kavanagh, D., 40
Kearney, M. S., 21
Kemple, J., 71
King, K. A., 61
King, Martin Luther, 18, 61
KIPP. *See* Knowledge Is Power Program
Kizilcec, R. F., 127
Klein, S., 73
Klose, M., 128
Knowledge Is Power Program (KIPP), 27
Koedel, C., 151n11
Kolderie, Ted, 204
Kraft, M., 153
Kreisman, D., 72
Kremer, K. P., 56
Kurlaender, M., 73

Lachowska, M., 112
language: CTE and, 74; early childhood
    education and, 4; in SEL, 185, 186
Leaf, D. E., 4
Lee, H., 127
Lenard, M. A., 71
Lester, A., 56, 63
Levin, H. M., 61
Levine, P. B., 21
Lindsay, C. A., 113–14, 157
Loeb, S., 161
looping, of caregivers, 6

Macchia, S. E., 111
Machin, S., 105
machine learning, 126
Malone, L. M., 56
Maranto, R., 18, 28–29
marginalized: CTE and, 71; educational
    technology and, 127; SEL and, 185
Marie, O., 105
marriage rate, 20
Massive Online Open Courses, 130
Mathia (Cognitive Tutor), 123, 125
Mayer, S. E., 14
Maynard, B. R., 56
McAuliffe, Terry, 49
McCaffrey, D. F., 153

McClanahan, W., 56
McEwan, P. J., 61
McShane, M. Q., 28–29
Measures of Effective Teaching (MET), 153,
    155, 155n13
Medicaid, 43, 44
Medicare for All, 39
Melton, T., 56, 63
MET. *See* Measures of Effective Teaching
Meta-Moment, of RULER, 181, 184
Mexico, 181
Mihaly, K., 151n11
Miles, Mike, 205n7
Miller, T., 153
mini-systems, 198
minorities: graduation rates of, 98–100, *99,*
    108–14; teachers for minority students,
    113–14. *See also specific racial groups*
*Missouri v. Jenkins,* 28
Moberg, D. P., 111
Monte Carlo simulation, for graduation
    rates, 102, 103, 105, 106
Mood Meter, of RULER, 180, 187
Moynihan Report, 18
Musaddiq, T., 40
Myung, J., 161

Nascent level, of System Review Rubric,
    *209*
National Center for Education Statistics
    (NCES), 74, 75–76, 77
National Council on Teacher Quality, 150
National Education Association, 38
National Guard Young Challenge (NGYC),
    7, 110
National Longitudinal Study of Adolescent
    Health, 21
National School and Child Nutrition
    Program, 99
National School Boards Association
    (NSBA), 48–49, 48n23
Native Americans. *See* American Indians
Navarré Point, 198–99, 204
NCES. *See* National Center for Education
    Statistics
negative behavior. *See* behavioral problems
Neild, R., 56

net present value (NPV), for graduation
rates, 103, 107
New Chance, 7, 110
New York City, 114, 166
Next Generation Science Standards, 125
Nguyen, T. D., 150, 157
NGYC. *See* National Guard Young
Challenge
No Child Left Behind, 200
Noonan, R., 56
normal birth weight, 4
North Carolina, 114
Norway, 74
NPV. *See* net present value
NSBA. *See* National School Boards
Association
nuclear families, 13

Obama, Barack, 13, 14, 18, 26, 152–53
OECD. *See* Organisation for Economic Co-
operation and Development
Office of Juvenile Justice and Delinquency
Prevention Organization, 62
Office of Management and Budget, U.S.
(OMB), 106–7
OLS. *See* ordinary least squares
OMB. *See* Office of Management and
Budget, U.S.
ordinary least squares (OLS), for CTE, 80,
*81, 85, 86*
Organisation for Economic Co-operation
and Development (OECD), 1
Ouchi, W. G., 29

Pachan, M., 57
Paeplow, C. G., 71
Panamá, 181
Pandey, E., 37
Papageorge, N. W., 113–14
Paquette, L., 127
parental involvement, 13–29; in
achievement gap, 27; educational
research on, 25–26; in education savings
account program, 47–48; in graduation
rates, 109; SEL with, 187–88; student
outcomes and, 25; in systems, 202
Payne, C. M., 29

Pell Grants, 43
Perkins Act, 71
per-pupil expenditure: in school reform, 9;
since 1960, *2*
Peterson, P. E., 37
Pham, L. D., 150, 157
Phillips, C., 40
Physics Playground, 123
Pittsburgh Science of Learning Center
DataShop, 128
Plasman, J., 72
Polanin, J. R., 56
Porter, S. R., 25
Prados, M. J., 4
privacy: algorithmic bias and, 128–29, 131;
alternative protections for, 129–30;
equity and, 8, 123–32; prioritization of,
127–29; recommendations for, 130–31
private schools: in COVID-19 pandemic,
37–38, 40, 41; as day care, 38; family
involvement in, 41–43; governance of,
41; student funding of, 37–49; vouchers
for, 6, 47
probation, for teachers, 8
productivity, graduation rates and, 100–
101, 103–4
Proficient level, of System Review Rubric,
*211–12*
Progressing level, of System Review Rubric,
*210*
Project STAR, 19
"proof point" strategy, 204
propensity scores, for CTE, *83,* 84, 84n2,
85, *85*
public schools: counseling in, 14; in
COVID-19 pandemic, 37–40, 41; CTE
in, 69; defunding of, 44–45; family
involvement in, 41–43; governance of,
41; student funding of, 37–49; student
outcomes in, 41–43
pupil-teacher ratio, *2*

quality: in after-school programs, 6–7,
55–64; of CTE, 90, 92

Race to the Top (RTTP), 152–53, 154,
158, 200

racism, 18, 40; SEL for, 177, 178–79
Recognize, Understand, Label, Express, and Regulate (RULER), 9, 179–81, 183, 184, 185, 187, 188–89
Recovery High School (RHS), 111
recreation, in after-school programs, 57
Regulatory Impact Analysis, 107
reinforcement learning, 126
remote schooling, in COVID-19 pandemic, 48
Renninger, K. A., 57
Rhinesmith, E., 43
RHS. *See* Recovery High School
Rivkin, S. G., 142
Rockoff, J. E., 151n11
Rodriguez, L. A., 163
Rosenbaum, J. E., 84n2
Ross, E., 155
Roth, J. L., 56
Rothstein, J., 151n11
RTTP. *See* Race to the Top
Rubin, D. B., 84n2
Ruglis, J., 145n6
RULER. *See* Recognize, Understand, Label, Express, and Regulate

Sagara, E., 40
Sanford, T., 73
SAT, 145
Sawhill, I. V., 62
Scafidi, B., 40
SCED. *See* School Course for the Exchange of Data
scholarships, 6; graduation rates and, 112
school closures, in COVID-19 pandemic, 6, 45–46
School Course for the Exchange of Data (SCED), 76
school reform, 9
schools: Coleman Report and, 17–18; discipline in, 19, 29; family involvement and, 28–29; graduation rates and, 113. *See also specific topics*
Schwalbach, J., 43
Second Demographic Transition, 20
SEL. *See* social and emotional learning
self-efficacy, AI for, 126

self-esteem, two-parent homes and, 21
self-incapacitation effect, 105
*Serrano v. Priest,* 19
SES. *See* socioeconomic status
sexism, 40
shadow price, graduation rates and, 101–9, *103, 106*
Shakeel, M. D., 42
single-parent homes, 13; adolescents of, 18; caregivers and, 6; childhood development and, 1; employment and, 22–23, *23*; graduation rates and, 18; income and, *23,* 23–24; positive and negative affect and, 24, *24*; school attendance and, 21; school discipline and, 19; student outcomes and, 1, 22–23, *23,* 25; time and affection of, 15
smoking, 19; by parents, 4
social and emotional learning (SEL), 9, 177–90; accessibility of, 186–87; in after-school programs, 56–57, 61, *63*; best practices in, 181–89; continuous improvement of, 189; curricula and, 9, *63*; for equity, 179, 181–89; ethnocentrism in, 184–85; feedback in, 188; growth mind-set in, 188; language in, 185, 186; marginalized and, 185; as prevention, 188; as priority, 182; relevance of, 183–84; RULER and, 9, 179–81, 183, 184, 185, 187, 188–89; staff for, 182–83; two-parent homes and, 21
social capital, 20; community involvement and, 25; parental involvement and, 25
Social Genome Model 2.0, 4, *5*
socioeconomic status (SES): achievement gap and, 161–62; CTE and, 75, 78, 80–81; graduation rates and, 145n6; SEL for, 177; teachers and, 162, 163
Song, Y., 128
Sorrenti, G., 45
Spain, 181
Sparr, M., 58
special education, 75n1
"split screen" strategy, 204
Springer, M. G., 150, 151n11, 157, 162, 167

SQL-Tutor, 125
staff-to-student ratios, 14
Staiger, D., 153
standardized tests, 21; teachers and, 143, 144
Stange, K. M., 40, 72
State Longitudinal Data Systems, 92
STEM: in after-school programs, 57, *59*; in COVID-19 pandemic, 197; CTE for, 71, 73, 87, 91; teachers of, 156n15, 157
Stephenson, N., 124
Stevens, A. H., 73
Stone, J. R., 71–72
Student Data Privacy Consortium, 128
student funding, 37–49; accountability and, 42; in COVID-19 pandemic, 37–41; family involvement and, 42; governance and, 37, 41; incentives for, 43–46, *46*; state policy recommendations for, 47; teachers unions and, 37–41, 44
student outcomes: from after-school programs, 56; Coleman Report and, 17–18; of CTE, 70–73, 88–89; family involvement and, 15, 17–18, 20–26, *23, 24,* 41–43; KIPP and, 27; parental involvement and, 25; in public schools, 41–43; SEL and, 9; single-parent homes and, 1, 22–23, *23,* 25; in Social Genome Model 2.0, 4, *5*; teachers and, 8, 141–42, 151; from two-parent homes, 20–21, 22–23, *23*
students. *See specific topics*
student surveys, 144n4
Sublett, C., 73
substance abuse: after-school programs and, 56, 63; graduation rates and, 101. *See also* alcohol abuse; drug abuse
Supporting Father Involvement, 26
suspensions, 143, 144, 145
Sweden, 74
System Review Rubric, 208, *209–14*
systems: accountability in, 205, *209, 210*; achievement gap in, 196, 200, 208; adaptability of, 207, *214*; budget priorities in, 206, *211*; capacity of, 206, *212*; change to, 200–202; community involvement in, 203; compensation in, 206, *211–12*; for equity, 194–208,

*209–14*; failure to assess future of, 200; family involvement in, 203; governance of, 201, 204; innovation in, 203–4, *214*; interconnection of, 199; leadership density in, 206, *212*; monitoring progress in, 206, *210*; obstacles to, 198–201; operational level of, 205–7; pace of change in, 207–8, *213*; parental involvement in, 202; principles for, 202–4, 206, *213*; for reimagined schools, 208; risk aversion in, 200; self-destruct ending point for, 204; status quo bias toward, 199; support for, 206, *209, 210*; teacher compensation in, 202

Talent Search, 7, 110
Tang, Y. E., 42
Tanner-Smith, E. E., 111
Tarnowski, E., 48
tax credits, for education savings accounts and scholarships, 6
teachers: accountability for, 158–60; compensation of, 8, 9, 144, 146–49, 146nn7–8, 147n9, *148,* 164–65, 202; COVID-19 pandemic and, 157n16; distribution of, 166; economic value of, 139–66; economic value quantified for, *140,* 140–45; equity with, 160–63; evaluation of, 152–60, 152n12, 156nn14–15, 158n17, 165; observations of, 144n4; performance incentives for, 149–51; policy reforms for, 146–51; probation for, 8; retention of, 152–60, 165–66; of same ethnicity as students, 113–14; in school reform, 9; of STEM, 156n15, 157; student outcomes and, 141–42; tenure of, 8, 158–60; value-added scores for, 19, 141–45, 141n1, 142n2, 143n3, 144nn4–5, 151n11, 154–56
teachers unions: in COVID-19 pandemic, 37–41; student funding and, 37–41, 44
technology. *See* Career and Technical Education; educational technology
teenage pregnancy, 6; after-school programs and, 58, 61, 63, *63*; graduation rates and, 111–12; teachers and, 143

Tennessee, 114, 162–63; Project STAR in, 19
tenure, of teachers, 8, 158–60
Texas, 204
TFS. *See* Third Future Schools
Therriault, D. J., 111
Third Future Schools (TFS), 204
Thyssen, G., 112
*A Treatise on the Family* (Becker), 16
Tutterow, R., 40
21st Century Community Learning Centers (CCLC), 55, 61
two-parent homes/intact homes, 14, 15; of Blacks, 25; employment and, 21–23, *23*; graduation rates and, 18; income and, *23*, 23–24; positive and negative affect and, 24, *24*; student outcomes from, 20–21, 22–23, *23*
TYRO Dads, 26

UAS. *See* Understanding America Study
Uganda, 73
Understanding America Study (UAS), 22–24
Unterman, R., 114

value-added scores, for teachers, 19, 141–45, 141n1, 142n2, 143n3, 144nn4–5, 151n11, 154–56
Vance, J. D., 13, 28
Veney, D., 48
Vidourek, R. A., 61
Vining, A., 100, 101, 102, 107
Virginia, 49
vocabulary gap, 4
vocational education. *See* Career and Technical Education
Vujić, S., 105

Walsh, K., 155
Washington State Institute for Public Policy (WSIPP), 100–101, 102, 103–4, 106
Weimer, D., 100, 101, 102, 107, 111
Weisberg, D., 152
Weissberg, R. P., 57
West, M. R., 37
West Virginia, 48
What Works Clearinghouse (WWC), 110–11
Whites: achievement gap of, 17; in college, 109; in CTE, 91; racism of, 179; SEL for, 185
Widget Effect Report, 152, 153, 154
Wilcox, W. B., 25–26
Wildox, 27
Wilner, C., 71
Wilson, S., 56
Wilson, W. J., 27
Wolf, P. J., 42
Wolfe, B., 108
Wood, R. C., 111
WSIPP. *See* Washington State Institute for Public Policy
WWC. *See* What Works Clearinghouse

Year of School Choice, 48
Yettick, H., 71–72
Yeung, R., 113
YMCA, 56
Young, J., 71–72
Youngkin, Glenn, 49

Zilibotti, F., 45
Zimmerman, K. O., 39
Zombinis, 123

# About the Editors and Contributors

## EDITORS

**Goldy Brown III** is director of Whitworth University's Educational Administration Program and assistant professor in Whitworth's Graduate School of Education, in Spokane, Washington. He has more than 20 years of educational experience as a teacher, administrator, professor, and researcher. He holds a doctorate in educational leadership and policy analysis from the University of Wisconsin-Madison. Schools that Goldy Brown led received four state recognition awards for closing the achievement gap between low-income students and affluent students. His research focuses on school leadership, an effective educational policy, programs, and systems for traditionally underserved students.

**Christos A. Makridis** holds academic appointments out of Columbia Business School, Stanford University, University of Nicosia, Arizona State University, and Baylor University. He is also an adjunct scholar at the Manhattan Institute and a senior adviser at Gallup. Christos has published more than 70 peer-reviewed research articles and earned dual master's and PhDs in economics and management science & engineering at Stanford University.

## CONTRIBUTORS

**Ryan Baker** is a tenured associate professor in the Graduate School of Education at the University of Pennsylvania. His primary appointment is in the teaching, learning, and leadership division. He is also affiliated with the higher education division and the Department of Computer and Information Science. He directs the Penn Center for Learning Analytics. Ryan also has an affiliate appointment at Worcester Polytechnic Institute in the Department of Social Science and Policy Studies and has courtesy appointments in the Department of Human Development at Teachers College Columbia University, at the University of Edinburgh Moray House School of Education and Sport, and at the University of Texas at Arlington LINK Research Lab.

**Marc A. Brackett** is the founder and director of the Yale Center for Emotional Intelligence and a professor in the Child Study Center of Yale University. He is the lead developer of RULER and author of *Permission to Feel* (2018). He also serves on the board of directors for the Collaborative for Academic, Social, and Emotional Learning (CASEL). As a researcher for more than 20 years, Brackett has focused on the role of emotions and emotional intelligence in learning, decision making, creativity, relationships, health, and performance. He has published 150 scholarly articles and received numerous awards and accolades for his work in this area. He also consults regularly with corporations, such as Facebook, Microsoft, and Google, on integrating the principles of emotional intelligence into employee training and product design.

**Christopher Brooks** is a PhD student in the School of Education at the University of North Carolina–Chapel Hill. His research focuses on teacher labor markets, educator policies, and the impacts of social policy on student outcomes. He can be reached at chbrooks@ad.unc.edu.

**Albert A. Cheng** is an assistant professor at the Department of Education Reform in the College of Education and Health Professions at the University of Arkansas, where he teaches courses in education policy and philosophy. His research focuses on character formation, virtue, faith-based schools, and school choice. He is a senior fellow at Cardus and an affiliated research fellow at the Program on Education Policy and Governance at Harvard University.

**Corey DeAngelis** is the national director of research at the American Federation for Children, the executive director at Educational Freedom Institute, an adjunct scholar at the Cato Institute, and a senior fellow at Reason Foundation. DeAngelis's research primarily focuses on the effects of school choice programs on nonacademic outcomes such as criminal activity, character skills, mental health, and political participation.

**Walter G. Ecton** is an assistant professor of educational leadership and policy studies at Florida State University. Dr. Ecton's research lies at the intersections between high school, higher education, and the workforce. His work focuses on students who take nontraditional pathways through education, with particular focuses on high school students in career and technical education, students who attend community college, and students who return to education later in life.

**Nicole A. Elbertson** is director of content and communications at the Yale Center for Emotional Intelligence in the Child Study Center of Yale University's School of Medicine and codeveloper of RULER, an evidence-based approach to social and emotional learning that has been adopted by more than 3,500 pre-K to high schools across the United States and globe. For more than 20 years, she has contributed to the design, development, implementation, and evaluation of SEL programming from early childhood through high school and has trained and coached thousands of school and district leaders and educators. She has coauthored numerous scholarly papers, book chapters, and popular articles on the topics of SEL and emotional intelligence. She also serves on the steering committee for the Social and Emotional Learning Provider Association (SELPA).

**Tangular A. Irby** is the program manager of content at the Yale Center for Emotional Intelligence. In this role, she serves as a RULER trainer and coach to school leaders and educators as well as develops social and emotional learning content for pre-K-12 schools. She has worked as an educator and administrator, serving students of all ages (early childhood through adults). She also is the author of four children's books.

**Robert Maranto** is the 21st century chair in leadership at the Department of Education Reform at the University of Arkansas and has served on his local school board. He currently serves on the board of the American Academy for Liberal Accreditation and on the Arkansas Advisory Committee to the U.S. Commission on Civil Rights. He does extensive work on school choice, school reform, and higher education reform. He edits the *Journal of School Choice*. With others, Bob has produced more than 90 peer-reviewed articles and 15 scholarly books including *Educating Believers: Religion and School Choice* (2020), *Homeschooling in the 21st Century* (2018), and *President Obama and Education Reform* (2012). He coedited the forthcoming National Association of Scholars report *Social Justice Versus Social Science: White Fragility, Implicit Bias, and Diversity Training*. Bob has written numerous commentaries for outlets including the *Wall Street Journal*, *National Review*, and *The Hill*.

**F. Mike Miles** has dedicated his career to serving his fellow citizens, beginning his career as an officer in the US Army and a foreign service officer with the US Department of State. He then became a teacher and rose through the ranks to become superintendent of Harrison School District Two and Dallas Independent School District, where he put a premium on developing principals as strong instructional leaders and consistently raised expectations for what is possible when schools are organized to support the success of low-income students and students of color. He is founder of Third Future Schools and the Academy of Advanced Learning, a K-6 public charter school focused on providing low-income students with a personalized, advanced education so that they are ready for the colleges and workplaces of the year 2025.

**Krista L. Smith** is a postgraduate associate at the Yale Center for Emotional Intelligence. Krista is a Hall of Fame inductee at the University of Florida and former Newman Civic Fellow selected for her demonstrated commitment and contributions to equitable practices in local communities. Her previous research experience has supported analysis of life story narratives and death education initiatives. She has served as a high school special education instructor in South Side Chicago with Teach For America where she simultaneously received her master of arts in teaching.

**Matthew G. Springer** is the Robena and Walter E. Hussman Jr. Distinguished Professor of Education in the School of Education at the University of North Carolina–Chapel Hill. His research focuses on compensation, accountability, and labor markets.

**Aidan Vining** Aidan retired in 2018 as the CNABS (Centre for North American Business Studies) Professor of Business and Government Relations in the Beedie School of Business, Simon Fraser University. He obtained his PhD from the Goldman School of Public Policy at the University of California, Berkeley. He also holds an LLB (King's College, London), an MBA (UC, Riverside), and an MPP (UC, Berkeley). He actively researches in the areas of public policy, cost-benefit analysis, public management, Indigenous peoples' management issues, and institutional analysis. Aidan has authored well over 100 articles in peer-reviewed journals.

**David Weimer** is the Edwin E. Witte Professor of Political Economy at the LaFollette School of Public Affairs, University of Wisconsin–Madison. His research focuses broadly on policy craft and institutional design. Although most of his recent research has addressed issues in health policy, he has done policy-relevant research in the areas of energy security, natural resource policy, education, criminal justice, and research methods.